Certified Information Systems Security Professional (CISSP)®

Third Edition

Certified Information Systems Security Professional (CISSP)®: Third Edition

Part Number: 085199
Course Edition: 1.0

NOTICES

Logical Operations Inc. wishes to acknowledge the contributions to the CISSP courseware revision by the Benchmark Learning Technical Writing Team of Kent Huelman, Shannon McColloch, and Jill Mittes.

HELP US IMPROVE OUR COURSEWARE

Your comments are important to us. Please contact us at Element K Press LLC, 1-800-478-7788, 500 Canal View Boulevard, Rochester, NY 14623, Attention: Product Planning, or through our Web site at **http://support.elementkcourseware.com**.

Certified Information Systems Security Professional (CISSP)®: Third Edition

Lesson 12: Legal, Regulations, Compliance, and Investigations

Appendix A: Mapping CISSP® Course Content to the (ISC)² CISSP Exam Objectives

About This Course

Welcome to Certified Information Systems Security Professional (CISSP)®: Third Edition. With your completion of the prerequisites and necessary years of experience, you are firmly grounded in the knowledge requirements of today's security professional. This course will expand upon your knowledge by addressing the essential elements of the 10 domains that comprise a Common Body of Knowledge (CBK)® for information systems security professionals. The course offers a job-related approach to the security process, while providing a framework to prepare for CISSP certification.

CISSP is the premiere certification for today's information systems security professional. It remains the premier certification because the sponsoring organization, the International Information Systems Security Certification Consortium, Inc., (ISC)²®, regularly updates the test by using subject matter experts (SMEs) to make sure the material and the questions are relevant in today's security environment. By defining 10 security domains that comprise a CBK, industry standards for the information systems security professional have been established. The skills and knowledge you gain in this course will help you master the 10 CISSP domains and ensure your credibility and success within the information systems security field.

Course Description

Target Student

This course is intended for experienced IT security-related practitioners, auditors, consultants, investigators, or instructors, including network or security analysts and engineers, network administrators, information security specialists, and risk management professionals, who are pursuing CISSP training and certification to acquire the credibility and mobility to advance within their current computer security careers or to migrate to a related career. Through the study of all 10 CISSP CBK domains, students will validate their knowledge by meeting the necessary preparation requirements to qualify to sit for the CISSP certification exam. The CISSP exam is intentionally difficult and should not be taken lightly. Even students with years of security experience should assume that they will have additional study time after class. Because the domains are so varied, it is unlikely that any one student will have experience in all 10 domains. Additional CISSP certification requirements include a minimum of five years of direct professional work experience in one or more fields related to the 10 CBK security domains, or a college degree and four years of experience.

Course Prerequisites

It is highly recommended that students have certifications in Network+ or Security+, or possess equivalent professional experience upon entering CISSP training. It will be beneficial if students have one or more of the following security-related or technology-related certifications or equivalent industry experience: MCSE, MCTS, MCITP, SCNP, CCNP, RHCE, LCE, CNE, SSCP®, GIAC, CISA™, or CISM®.

Course Objectives

In this course, you will analyze a wide range of information systems security subjects that are organized into 10 domains for CISSP exam certification.

You will:

● Analyze information systems access control.

● Analyze security architecture and design.

● Analyze network security systems and telecommunications.

● Analyze information security management goals.

● Analyze information security classification and program development.

● Analyze risk management criteria and ethical codes of conduct.

● Analyze software development security.

● Analyze cryptography characteristics and elements.

● Analyze physical security.

● Analyze operations security.

● Apply Business Continuity and Disaster Recovery Plans.

● Identify legal issues, regulations, compliance standards, and investigation practices relating to information systems security.

How to Use This Book

As a Learning Guide

This book is divided into lessons and topics, covering a subject or a set of related subjects. In most cases, lessons are arranged in order of increasing proficiency.

The results-oriented topics include relevant and supporting information you need to master the content. Each topic has various types of activities designed to enable you to practice the guidelines and procedures as well as to solidify your understanding of the informational material presented in the course.

At the back of the book, you will find a glossary of the definitions of the terms and concepts used throughout the course. You will also find an index to assist in locating information within the instructional components of the book.

In the Classroom

This book is intended to enhance and support the in-class experience. Procedures and guidelines are presented in a concise fashion along with activities and discussions. Information is provided for reference and reflection in such a way as to facilitate understanding and practice.

Each lesson may also include a Lesson Lab or various types of simulated activities. You will find the files for the simulated activities along with the other course files on the enclosed CD-ROM. If your course manual did not come with a CD-ROM, go to **http:// logicaloperations.com/file-downloads** to download the files. If included, these interactive activities enable you to practice your skills in an immersive business environment, or to use hardware and software resources not available in the classroom. The course files that are available on the CD-ROM or by download may also contain sample files, support files, and additional reference materials for use both during and after the course.

As a Teaching Guide

Effective presentation of the information and skills contained in this book requires adequate preparation. As such, as an instructor, you should familiarize yourself with the content of the entire course, including its organization and approaches. You should review each of the student activities and exercises so you can facilitate them in the classroom.

Throughout the book, you may see Instructor Notes that provide suggestions, answers to problems, and supplemental information for you, the instructor. You may also see references to "Additional Instructor Notes" that contain expanded instructional information; these notes appear in a separate section at the back of the book. Microsoft® PowerPoint® slides may be provided on the included course files, which are available on the enclosed CD-ROM or by download from **http://logicaloperations.com/file-downloads**. The slides are also referred to in the text. If you plan to use the slides, it is recommended to display them during the corresponding content as indicated in the instructor notes in the margin.

The course files may also include assessments for the course, which can be administered diagnostically before the class, or as a review after the course is completed. These exam-type questions can be used to gauge the students' understanding and assimilation of course content.

As a Review Tool

Any method of instruction is only as effective as the time and effort you, the student, are willing to invest in it. In addition, some of the information that you learn in class may not be important to you immediately, but it may become important later. For this reason, we encourage you to spend some time reviewing the content of the course after your time in the classroom.

As a Reference

The organization and layout of this book make it an easy-to-use resource for future reference. Taking advantage of the glossary, index, and table of contents, you can use this book as a first source of definitions, background information, and summaries.

Course Icons

Icon	Description
	A **Caution Note** makes students aware of potential negative consequences of an action, setting, or decision that are not easily known.
	Display Slide provides a prompt to the instructor to display a specific slide. Display Slides are included in the Instructor Guide only.
	An **Instructor Note** is a comment to the instructor regarding delivery, classroom strategy, classroom tools, exceptions, and other special considerations. Instructor Notes are included in the Instructor Guide only.
	Notes Page indicates a page that has been left intentionally blank for students to write on.
	A **Student Note** provides additional information, guidance, or hints about a topic or task.
	A **Version Note** indicates information necessary for a specific version of software.

Course Requirements

Hardware

- A CD-ROM drive.

- A 1024 x 768 resolution monitor.

- A projection system to display the instructor's Microsoft® PowerPoint® slides.

- An available Internet connection is recommended if you want to view security-related websites or examples.

Software

- A PowerPoint viewer application to display slide content.

Class Setup

There are no particular setup requirements for this course.

1 | Information Systems Access Control

Lesson Time: 4 hour(s)

Lesson Objectives:

In this lesson, you will analyze information systems access control.

You will:

● Identify security principles in data access design.

● Analyze system access and authentication.

● Identify common attacks and penetration tests.

Introduction

In this course, you will explore a broad range of security concepts and best practices designed to meet the demands of increasingly specialized information systems security. Before security policies are defined or network issues are addressed, it is important to ensure that your information system resources are secure. In this lesson, you will analyze information systems access control.

Most businesses use data systems to store sensitive company information. To secure an information system today, you should be able to balance authorized access needs with system and data protection. Because too much security prevents access, while too little leaves the system vulnerable to data theft or attack, controlling access to information systems will help you ensure a proper balance of security and access.

This lesson supports content found in the Access Control and Security Architecture and Design domains of the CISSP® certification.

TOPIC A
Data Access Principles

Protecting your organization's data is a legitimate corporate defense against internal and external risks and attacks. Before you can control access to your company's data, you need to determine the required method of control. To do this, you will analyze your access control requirements and determine the best means to control data access. In this topic, you will identify security principles in data access design.

In a dynamic business climate, you need multiple ways to control access to an information system. In some cases, a system may require access controls based upon organizational policies. Other situations may require access control based upon a business process, work function, or government/institutional regulation. By effectively evaluating data security requirements, you ensure that you select an appropriate access control model to protect your company's data.

The Information Security Triad

Information security seeks to protect three specific elements, or principles: confidentiality, integrity, and availability. This is called the *CIA triad* or *triple*. If one of the principles is compromised, the security of the organization is threatened. The CIA triad permeates everything the security professional does from system security to building security and it must be kept in mind at all times.

 A three-legged stool is much like the CIA triad. If a leg on a three-legged stool fails, the stool falls over.

Principles of the Information Security Triad

The CIA triad includes three fundamental principles that are essential to a robust security program. There are also the opposing forces of Disclosure, Alteration, and Destruction, (DAD).

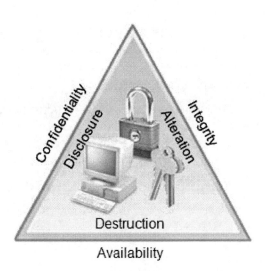

Figure 1-1: *The CIA triad and DAD.*

Principle	Description
Confidentiality	*Confidentiality* is the fundamental principle of keeping information and communications private and protecting them from unauthorized access.
	Confidential information includes trade secrets, personnel records, health records, tax records, and military secrets.
Integrity	*Integrity* is the property of keeping organization information accurate, without error, and without unauthorized modification. Integrity also protects important systems and help to maintain those systems against unintentional changes.
	For example, in the movie WarGames, Matthew Broderick's character is seen modifying his grades early in the movie. This means that the integrity of his grade information was compromised by unauthorized modification.
Availability	*Availability* is the fundamental principle of ensuring that systems operate continuously and that authorized persons can access data that they need. It also includes the need to access the data from anywhere and any device.
	Information available on a computer system is useless unless the users can get to it. Consider what would happen if the Federal Aviation Administration's air traffic controls system failed. Radar images would be captured but not distributed to those who need the information.

Access Control

Definition:

Access control is defined by the Official (ISC)²® Guide to the CISSP® CBK® as the process of allowing only authorized users, programs, or other computer systems such as networks to observe, modify, or otherwise take possession of the resources of a computer system. It is also a mechanism for limiting the use of some resources to authorized users.

In access control, the term *subject* is given to the entity requesting access and the term *object* is given to the entity being accessed. The access control process limits the subject's access to objects using pre-defined rules, roles, or labels. It is possible for a program or process to be both a subject and an object. Whether it is acting as a subject or object will depend on whether it is requesting access to objects or providing access to subjects.

Example:

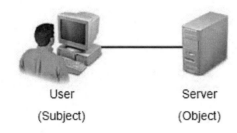

User
(Subject)

Server
(Object)

Figure 1-2: Access control.

Entities

The term *entity* is used to identify multiple things. A user is an entity when requesting access to a computer program, and the computer program is an entity when it requests access to a computer database, file, printer, or communication process.

Reference Monitors

Definition:

A *reference monitor (RM)* is a component of some types of access control systems that determines if the subject can access the object. RMs are found in operating systems and network access control systems. The *security kernel* implements the RM in an operating system. This RM implementation depends on the access control methods used, and it must possess specific characteristics.

- It must be tamper proof.
- It must always be invoked.
- It must fail "closed," which means that all processing tasks are stopped and all packets are denied.
- It must be compact and verifiable.

To ensure proper access control, the RM must not be manipulated and cannot be bypassed. It has to be small so the code inside can be analyzed for weaknesses. In all RM implementations, assume that subjects are not allowed access by default. Subjects may be allowed access if the rules have been configured to allow it.

Example:

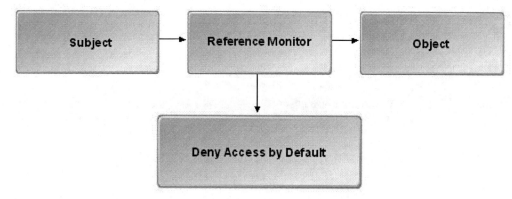

Figure 1-3: An RM.

Access Control Policies and Procedures

There are several well-known and commonly implemented access control principles that will form part of most organization's access control policies and procedures. They include:

● Least privilege.

● Need to know.

● Separation of duties.

● Job role rotation.

● Compartmentalization.

Least Privilege

Definition:

The principle of *least privilege* is a security principle that limits the need to know certain information. This principle ensures that employees and other system users have only the minimum set of rights, permissions, and privileges that they need to accomplish their jobs, without excessive privileges that can provide them with unauthorized access to systems. The individual is limited to that data or information within a certain area of interest and with the minimum exposure possible. The administrator needs to be careful to watch for "privilege creep," which can happen when elevated rights and permissions are assigned for temporary use and then are left in place.

Example:

A data entry clerk can perform his or her job with fewer privileges than a financial controller.

Data entry clerk

Low privileges

Financial controller

High privileges

Figure 1-4: *Least privilege.*

Need to Know

Definition:

Need to know is a security principle based on an individual's need to access classified data resources to perform a given task or job function. If an individual needs to access information to perform a job function, that individual may access a portion of information.

Access control rules are implemented by the security administrators once senior management and the data owner determine who should have access to what. It may seem impractical for senior management to determine who has access to systems and data, but they hold full responsibility for security within the organization.

The data owner is closer to the data and is responsible for guiding senior management as they make access limitations. Once the access determination has been made, the security administrators are responsible for implementing the restrictions in the access control system.

Example:

Top Secret

Congressional page

No need to know

U.S. Senator

Need to know

Figure 1-5: *Need to know.*

Example: Need to Know

The government classifies data to protect it from unauthorized access and disclosure. Even if someone has a need to know classified data, without the proper security clearance, the individual is denied access.

Separation of Duties

Definition:

Separation of duties (SoD) is a division of tasks between different people to complete a business process or work function. From a security standpoint, if a user seeks access to a system, then the security administrator provides access control limits, and the data owner and senior management define those limitations.

Example: Separation of Duties

SoD applies to many functions in the information technology world. In an accounts payable process, a clerk receives an invoice and enters it into the accounts payable system. Then, the supervisor reviews the invoice and approves it for payment. Finally, the manager or other senior executive reviews the payment ledger and signs the checks before they are mailed. The SoD concept provides checks and balances, which safeguard the system from fraud, collusion, and mistakes.

Job Role Rotation

Job rotation requires that multiple users rotate through the same job. The rotation can happen on a regular schedule or randomly. It serves the function of having users audit each other's activity. It can also help to prevent collusion where multiple users are needed to circumvent the system. It might have the additional benefit of keeping users interested and providing coverage for key positions.

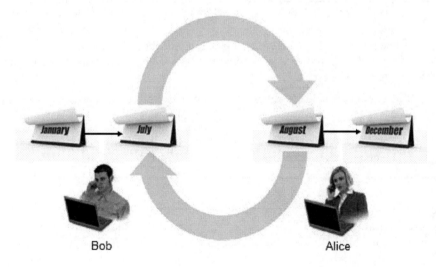

Figure 1-6: *Job role rotation example.*

Compartmentalization

Definition:

Compartmentalization complements least privilege and need to know by separating and isolating subjects that work on different projects. Companies might even need to physically isolate different components of the organization for regulatory purposes. Compartmentalization can help prevent information from flowing to the outside.

Example: Compartmentalization at a Company

A company has a highly specialized and highly secret research and development team. The company knows that their competitors would love to find out what they are up to; in fact, even their own sales people would like to know so they can get a jump on promoting the potential products coming out of research. To maintain security, the company has relocated the department to an unmarked building several miles away from the headquarters.

Access Control Service Types

There are several categories, or types, of access control services that support the phases of access control implementation.

Access Control Services	Description
I&A	Identification and authentication (I&A) provides a unique identifier for each authorized subject (user) attempting to access the object (system) followed by a method or methods to ensure the identity of the subject (authentication). I&A is typically administered with some type of Identity Management System and the support of a directory.
Authorization	Determines the capabilities or rights of the subject when accessing the object.
Audit	Creates a log or record of activities on the system.
Accountability	Reports and reviews the contents of the log files. Each subject identifier must be unique to relate activities to one subject.

The importance of uniqueness is hard to overstate as all auditing will rely on unique subject identifiers. It is also important in the identification mechanism that the systems that support access control services are reliable, scalable, and capable of the highest levels of confidentiality and integrity.

Access Control Services Implementation

Access control services implementation is required for all systems, regardless of the access control system type. Once the access control rules are provided and implemented, the system must then limit access based on those rules.

Implementing access control services involves:

1. Identifying the individual or entity attempting to access an object.
2. Verifying or authenticating the individual's identity.
3. Evaluating the rules and/or roles to see what the individual is permitted to do.
4. Creating an audit trail by writing each access attempt and function performed to a log file.

5. Reviewing the log to see what was completed when and by whom. This review is performed by managers and supervisors and helps to create accountability in the system access process.

Access Control Types

Access controls fall into different types or categories depending on their functions. Access control types break out as administrative, physical, and technical.

Access Control Type	Description
Administrative	*Administrative access controls* cover a broad area of security. Beginning with security policies and procedures, the administrative control types cover personnel security, monitoring, user and password management, and permissions management.
	For example, security guards may use a printed access list to determine whether individuals attempting access without having their name on the list should be held for further evaluation. Security awareness training is another good example of an administrative control.
Physical	*Physical access controls* are used to limit an individual's physical access to protected information or facilities. Locks, doors, fences, and perimeter defenses are all examples of physical access controls. Visible ID cards can also be used to identify people who are found in an unauthorized area.
	For example, an infrared monitoring system can detect the presence of an intruder and can signal a guard to respond when needed.
Technical	*Technical access controls* are implemented in the computing environment. They are often found in operating systems, application programs, database frameworks, firewalls, routers, switches, and wireless access points.
	For example, a user sign-in process on a computer utilizes a user ID and password to verify identification. In the case of three incorrect login attempts, the system logs the incorrect attempts and locks the user account for five minutes.

Access Control Categories

Each access control category has its own unique function and performance capability.

Access Control Categories	Description
Preventative	*Preventative access control* stops a subject's unauthorized access to an object. I&A in conjunction with authorization are preventative access control methods. The others are locks, doors, and other physical barriers.
Detective	*Detective access control* processes identify attempts to access an entity without proper authorization. The purpose of the detective control is to alert the administrators to the attempted security violation.

Access Control Categories	Description
Corrective	The *corrective access control* mechanism responds to the security violation to reduce or completely eliminate the impact. An intrusion prevention system (IPS) is a technical corrective process that stops unauthorized access over a computer network.
Directive	*Directive access control* provides direction to employees and can often take the form of policies and guidelines. For example, a company may have an acceptable use policy. There may be separate policies for contractors or temporary employees.
Deterrent	A *deterrent access control* discourages individuals from violating security policies. A policy against using protocol analyzers or sniffers in a network could be considered a deterrent, especially if the penalty is the loss of employment.
Recovery	*Recovery access control* is used to return the system to an operational state after a failure to protect the CIA triad. Recovery controls include backup tapes and offsite journaling.
Compensating	A *compensating access control* is often used when the system cannot provide protection required by the policy. For example, a corporate policy might require using a smart card ID system for entry into and exit out of secure areas. At a remote site, a smart card system has not been installed. Instead, a compensating control is used where experienced security guards validate the identity of each individual using a printed roster and personal evaluation. A written log of entry and exit times is also maintained.

In most cases, preventative, detective, corrective, and directive access controls are sufficient to maintain the CIA triad. However, deterrent, recovery, and compensating access controls are additional tools used to protect systems and facilities.

Access Control Functions

The access control functions are implemented in the three different access control types in the security environment.

	Administrative	Physical	Technical
Directive	X		
Preventative	X	X	X
Detective		X	X
Corrective			X
Deterrent		X	X
Recovery	X		X
Compensating	X		X

Figure 1-7: Access control functions are implemented as different access control types.

The Evolution of Control Types

In the earliest days of computer security, physical controls were the most important controls. If you could not access the computer facility, you could not access the information stored there. Eventually, when multiple users could access computer systems, the security requirements changed. Direct access terminals were the first connections used. Shortly thereafter, the users' rights to the data on computers needed to be limited. The first instance of technical controls came with the advent of the access control matrix. As you continue to change how and where you do computing, the need to reevaluate how and where you will apply security will be ongoing.

The Access Control Matrix

Definition:

The *access control matrix* is a technical access control consisting of a tabular display of access rights. It uses the concepts of need to know, least privilege, and SoD to assign rights to users. It shows the users who can access the system, the resources to access in the system, and the rights assigned.

Permissions indicate the subject's access capabilities to the object. The lack of assigned permissions in the access control matrix dictates that a user has no access to the file and is an implicit deny. Many systems also allow for an explicit deny that trumps all other permissions.

Permission Codes in an Access Control Matrix

Depending on the system implementation, the permissions are indicated by a capability to read, write, execute, or have owner status of the file, as shown here:

- r = read
- w = write
- x = execute
- o = owner

Other rights such as modify (m) are used in different operating systems.

Example: A Simple Access Control Matrix

In this very simple example of an access control matrix, the subjects, or users, are seen in the left-hand column of the matrix. The names of the files to be accessed are seen in the first row of the table. Bob and Alice work together and need to access the file parts used for manufacturing operation. The access limits for these two users are different. Alice can query the file, but Bob can update and change the access rights to the file since he is the file owner.

	Pay1	*People1*	*Part1*	*Control1*
Bob		r	rwo	r
Alice		r	r	rwo
Boris	rw	rw		
Natasha	rwo	rwo		r

Natasha is the manager of the personnel and payroll departments. She is the data owner and has allowed Boris to edit the payroll and people files. She has also allowed Alice and Bob to view the personnel file, so they can view which staff is available for manufacturing from time to time. However, the control file can be viewed by Bob and Natasha but can only be updated by Alice.

Consider the challenge of using an access control matrix in a large system with 3,000 users and 30,000 files. For each user, the matrix row is established and permissions are configured. In most cases, users have very limited access to files. Although the matrix is very large, the areas it uses are small. In the end, this option can take a lot of administration work for very little benefit.

Access Control Models

The three primary access control models are discretionary access control, mandatory access control, and non-discretionary access control. Each model has a place in security planning just as each model has benefits and drawbacks.

Discretionary Access Control

Definition:

Discretionary access control (DAC) is a means of restricting access to objects based on the identity of the subjects and/or groups to which they belong. Assigning a user ID and password to an individual user is an exemplary case of DAC. The controls are discretionary in the sense that a subject with certain access permissions is capable of passing those permissions (perhaps indirectly) on to any other subject (unless restrained by another access control method).

Example: Limited Access Control

In the access control matrix, Natasha is the data owner of the People1 file and can grant or delegate read/write access to Bob.

	Pay1	*People1*	*Part1*	*Control1*
Bob		rw	rwo	r
Alice		r	r	rwo
Boris	rw	rw		
Natasha	rwo	rwo		r

Access Control Lists

Definition:

In a DAC model, an *access control list (ACL)* is a list of permissions that is associated with each object, which specifies the subjects that can access the object and the subjects' levels of access. In modern security systems, an ACL is employed as a solution or variation of the access control matrix.

 The term "ACL" as it is used here is a little different than Cisco's use of the term. Cisco routers and switch administrators can use an ACL as a filter for traffic moving through the networking device.

Example: ACL Illustration

In this illustration of an ACL, the subjects that have access to the objects are listed. The third column displays the permissions assigned. The ACL only includes subjects that have access to the objects listed.

Object	Subject	Access
Pay1	Boris	rw
	Natasha	rwo
People1	Bob	rw
	Alice	r
	Boris	rw
	Natasha	rwo
Part1	Bob	rwo
	Alice	r
Control1	Bob	r
	Alice	rwo
	Natasha	r

Capability Lists

A second variation of access control is the capability list. In this list, the objects are assigned to the subjects with the result being that each subject will have certain capabilities.

Subject	Object	Access
Boris	Pay1	rw
	People1	rw
Bob	People1	rw
	Part1	rwo
	Control1	r
Natasha	Pay1	rwo
	People1	rwo
	Control1	r
Alice	People1	rw
	Part1	r
	Control1	rwo

Mandatory Access Control

Definition:

Mandatory access control (MAC) is a means of restricting access to objects based on the sensitivity (as represented by a label) of the information contained in the objects and the formal authorization (for example, clearance) of subjects to access information of such sensitivity. MAC is employed in cases where high levels of security are required and information needs to be protected based on its sensitivity, and is the most restrictive access control model.

Top Secret government information requires a high level of protection and is classified accordingly. Only users with a Top Secret clearance may access Top Secret information. The formal authorization to access Top Secret information for an individual is determined by the system based on labels and categories. Within classifications, categories can be used to group information within a specific topic or project area.

Example: Classification Table

This table depicts three different classification levels of information with associated categories assigned to different projects.

Classification	Categories		
Top Secret	Gold		
Secret		Silver	
Confidential		Silver	Red

Only individuals with a Top Secret clearance and authorization for Gold can access Top Secret/Silver information.

Only individuals with Secret clearances can access Secret/Silver information, but they may also access Confidential/Silver information because they hold a higher classification level.

Individuals with Confidential clearances and authorization for Silver cannot access Secret/Silver because their level of clearance is not high enough.

Red information may only be accessed by those with a Confidential clearance and authorization for Red.

The security clearance and classification levels are the enforcing principles. A subject with a given clearance level may only access an object with an equal or lower classification level. Most MAC systems primarily deal with the confidentiality of high-security documents but you will see later that they can also be used to promote integrity of information,

Labeled Access and Categories

Labeled access provides protection for the information under MAC. Labels include two components: a security level and a security category. Labels are applied to objects. A data custodian or security administrator will determine the appropriate level and apply these labels according to strict rules. Information protected by the U.S. government is classified using a hierarchical level. Each level in that system depicts the impact suffered when the protected data is lost or disclosed.

The second part of the security label is the category. The compartment provides for additional protection of the object based on a need to know. During WWII, the highly classified atomic bomb creation project had the code name Manhattan. Information about the project was classified Top Secret, but only those cleared for the Manhattan project were able to access that information. Though an individual had a clearance for Top Secret, that individual may not have been cleared for Manhattan and would therefore be denied access.

Levels

Department of Defense (DoD) publication 5200.1-R provides the following information about classified information levels.

Level	Description/Function
Top Secret	Information at this level is protected with the highest level of security and any unauthorized disclosure could cause grave damage to the national security in which the original classification authority is able to identify or describe.
Secret	Information disclosed at this level could be expected to cause serious damage to the national security that the original classification authority is able to identify or describe.
Confidential	Information disclosed at this level could be expected to cause damage to the national security that the original classification authority is able to identify or describe.
For Official Use Only (FOUO)	A designation that is applied to unclassified information that may be exempt from mandatory release to the public under the Freedom of Information Act (FOIA).
Sensitive but Unclassified (SBU)	Information originated within the Department of State that warrants a degree of protection and administrative control and meets the criteria for exemption from mandatory public disclosure under the FOIA.
Unclassified	Information that is not classified.

Subjects are assigned a security clearance (or privilege) level. Higher levels will require more thorough background checks and screenings. This is an expensive process but justified given the security required.

Non-Discretionary Access Control Techniques

To implement non-DAC and non-MAC practices, non-discretionary access control techniques are often required to provide a restraining influence on the subject's access of an object.

Non-Discretionary Access Control Technique	Description
RBAC	*Role-based access control (RBAC)* is implemented when the subject's access to objects is based on the job performed by the subject. In RBAC, administrators create groups that provide access controls and then assign users to the groups. Rather than working with each individual user's permissions, the group permission and group membership simplifies administrative overhead.
	Sometimes RBAC is used when a limited duration assignment to a job exists. For example, a hospital uses nurses from a pool of available staff. When a nurse comes in for a shift, that individual is assigned to a group with visiting nurse capabilities, and then when the shift ends, that individual is removed from the group.
Rule-based	*Rule-based access control* is based on a set of operational rules or restrictions. For example, a set of firewall restrictions based on port restriction rules is a type of rule-based access control.
	Rule sets are always examined before a subject is given access to objects.
Context dependant	*Context dependent access control* will determine the context of the request before processing the request.
	For example, a stateful inspection firewall can determine if the packet request came from the inside or outside the network and use that context information to determine whether to route it or drop it.
Content dependent	*Content dependent access control* limits the subject's access to objects by examining object data to see if the subject has access rights.
	An attempt to access the CEO's payroll information by a payroll clerk may be denied when the system checks the clerk's access rights against the CEO's salary level. This is because not all clerks can see the CEO's payroll information; only those with special access capabilities are permitted.
	Content dependent access controls put extra overhead on the process because object information must be accessed to determine if the subject can see the information.
Constrained interfaces	*Constrained interfaces access control* limits access to information by constraining the interface.
	An ATM machine is a perfect example because there are a limited number of keys, a limited screen display, and limited functions that can be performed on an ATM.
Time-based	*Time-based access control* limits when an individual can access the system.
	In some organizations, users are allowed access to their workstations between 8:00 a.m. and 5:00 p.m., and access outside of those hours is denied. Individuals who do not have authorized access through those workstations will also be denied.

 The term *non-discretionary access control* is not as commonly used in the information systems industry as is *RBAC*. However, as indicated in the table, RBAC is a technique, or method, of non-discretionary access control.

ACTIVITY 1-1
Discussing Data Access

Scenario:

In this activity, you will discuss the principles, characteristics, and types of data access.

1. **Which of the access control models is generally considered the most restrictive?**

   a) DAC

   b) MAC

   c) RBAC

   d) Constrained Interface

2. **Another name for the information security triad is:**

   a) The FBI triad.

   b) The ISS triad.

   c) The CIA triad.

   d) The IST triad.

3. **Which one of these represents the property of keeping an organization information accurate, without error, and without unauthorized modification?**

   a) Availability

   b) Integrity

   c) Confidentiality

   d) Accountability

4. **What is the appropriate description for each data access process?**

___ Least privilege	a.	The limitation of access based on rules provided through the identification of the entity attempting to access an object.
___ Access control services	b.	The process of determining and assigning privileges to various resources, objects, and data.
___ SoD	c.	A division of tasks between different people to complete a business process or work function.
___ Access control	d.	The security principle that limits the access of information to the minimum necessary.

5. **Which one or more access control categories are sufficient to maintain the CIA triad?**

   a) Detective

   b) Preventative

   c) Compensating

   d) Corrective

6. **Which one of the following access control services determines the capabilities of a subject when accessing the object?**

   a) Accountability

   b) Authorization

   c) Audit

   d) I&A

7. **Which one of the following access control types covers personnel security, monitoring, user and password management, and permissions management?**

   a) Corrective

   b) Physical

   c) Administrative

   d) Technical

8. **What is the appropriate description for each security term?**

   ___ Confidential   a. Information that is not classified.

   ___ Secret   b. Disclosure could cause serious damage.

   ___ FOUO   c. Information protected with the highest level of security.

   ___ Top Secret   d. Unclassified information that may be exempt from mandatory release.

   ___ Unclassified   e. Disclosure could cause damage.

   ___ SBU   f. Warrants a degree of protection and administrative control.

9. **True or False? A separation of duties policy would require a division of tasks between different people to complete a business process.**

   ___ True

   ___ False

10. **Restricting access to objects based on the sensitivity of the information contained in the objects is an example of:**

    a) MAC.

    b) DAC.

    c) RBAC.

    d) ACL.

11. **Which one of the following non-discretionary access control techniques limits a subject's access to objects by examining object data so that the subject's access rights can be determined?**

    a) Rule-based

    b) Role-based

    c) Time-based

    d) Content dependent

TOPIC B
System Access and Authentication

Controlling access to data is only one part of achieving comprehensive access control to protect your organization's information systems and assets. The second part of access control is defining the privileges and accountability of those who enter the system. In this topic, you will analyze system access and authentication.

You know that information systems security requires both denial and access to data. To ensure that only authorized users are granted access to the system, it is important to validate their identities and determine if access should be granted. A comprehensive system of identification and authentication is an effective tool to fulfill user access requirements, while efficiently controlling access to select parts of your information systems.

Identification Types

For identifications to be useful, each identity must be unique. Using "guest" as an identification is not appropriate because it is impossible to identify which guest performed which operation in the auditing and accountability processes. In addition to the identities being unique, it is necessary to have a way to prove the identity of the user.

ID Cards and User IDs

An identification is often claimed by entering a user ID during a system login function or by presenting an identity card at an access portal.

Identification Type	Description
ID cards	An ID card is a physical device that often contains a picture of the subject, the subject's name, and other identifying characteristics. Matching the picture on the ID card to the carrier is one way of providing identification. ID cards might also include a mechanism to provide electronic access to systems or facilities.
User IDs	A user ID is a string of characters, unique to one individual, used to provide identification of the user to the system being accessed. Traditionally, user IDs have not been kept secret from others, but the disclosure of a user ID may lead to attempts to access a system without permission. If user IDs are standardized based on employee names, they may be easy to guess. An account number might also be used to provide uniqueness and thereby serve as a user ID.

Identification Type Weaknesses

Along with the different identification types comes some weaknesses. An ID card can be copied or re-created easily using modern computer printing techniques. Security can be added to the card by using smart card technology with embedded logic or applying a corporate logo image with a hologram.

The user ID is also subject to attacks such as social engineering techniques and shoulder surfing.

Authentication Types

Once an identity has been claimed, the subject is then required to prove the identity through authentication. This is an extremely important step. The information used for authentication is typically protected because the identification component might be commonly known. The methods used to authenticate identity have been broken down into three distinct areas: something you know, something you have, and something you are.

Something You Know

Something you know as an authentication factor includes the use of passwords and password variants such as passphrases and personal identification numbers (PINs). An individual assigned a user ID establishes a password in the system as part of the authentication process. Passwords are not the best authentication solution because of their inherent problems. They can be communicated to coworkers or disclosed through bad practices such as writing them down where they can easily be found.

 Something you know is sometimes referred to as authentication by knowledge.

Passwords, properly protected, also need to be modified periodically so that techniques such as password guessing cannot be used over a period of time to gain unauthorized access.

Types of Passwords

There are several types of passwords used in something you know authentication.

Password Type	Description
Password	A password is a string of numbers, letters, and/or special characters used to authenticate an identity. Longer passwords are more secure than shorter passwords due to the number of different character combinations available.
Passphrase	A passphrase is sometimes termed a *virtual password*. A long phrase is known to the individual and is entered into the password administration system.
	It is easier for most people to remember a passphrase than a password. On the other hand, the passphrase is longer and takes more time to enter. It is helpful if the password system allows spaces so users can use favorites lines from songs, movies, or books. If the passphrase "It was the best of times, it was the worst of times," is used, it is a very long 51 character password.
PIN	PINs are short passwords, typically numeric, used with certain systems such as ATMs and voicemail. Using a four-digit numeric PIN, there are only 10,000 unique combinations, which makes PINs the most vulnerable of the password types. Most systems allow for longer PINs; however, users are slow to change them.

Password Type	Description
Graphical password	In high security areas, where there is a concern that a keystroke logger might be able to capture a user typing in their password, an organization may present an onscreen keyboard. This allows users to click on letters with a mouse rather than type them. Keystroke loggers typically do not capture the coordinates of mouse clicks so password capture is avoided.
	This can also be useful in a situation where the repeated entry of a PIN could show wear on the device and reveal helpful information to an attacker. In this case, a small screen can be used to scramble the numbers so even though the same PIN is entered, variable wear patterns will be created.

Password Administration and Password Management

Passwords should be changed frequently. In some organizations, passwords are changed weekly, and in others, passwords are changed every six months. There should be an administrative policy dictating how often passwords should be changed. It might also include password length, the reuse of older passwords, and the need for special characters. The administrative policy is then followed up with a technical policy. The more frequently passwords are changed, the more likely they are written down. The less frequently passwords are changed, the more likely that password-cracking techniques can be employed to gain access. In the end, it is up to the users to protect their passwords. Security administrators should have no knowledge of any user password, other than for the initial setting when a new account is created or a password is lost.

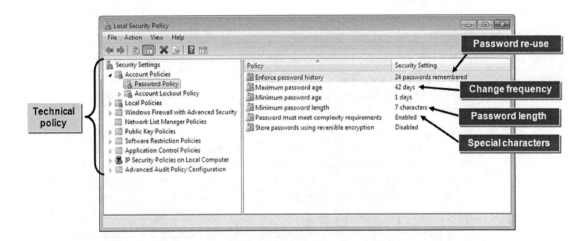

Figure 1-8: A Microsoft® Windows® security policy showing password settings.

Something You Have

In a something you have method, the individual possesses a physical device of some type that provides authentication capabilities. Devices in this category include magnetic strip cards, proximity cards, smart cards, Radio Frequency Identification (RFID) cards, or token devices.

 Something you have is sometimes referred to as authentication by possession.

In each case, the individual possesses the device and uses it for access when necessary. One potential downside is that theft of the devices prohibits access by the authorized user and may, in some cases, allow access by an unauthorized user. Most of these devices also require the use of secondary authentication, such as a PIN. The theft of a device must be combined with the theft of the associated PIN to complete an unauthorized authentication. This is an important consideration and all users should be trained in the proper use and protection of their device or devices.

Smart Cards

Smart cards provide an increasingly popular way to support something you have authentication. Smart cards are typically credit card-sized devices that contain a chip that can provide storage and intelligence to the authentication process. The chip can store data such as certificates and it can read and write a small amount of data to provide basic authentication functions.

Smart cards come in two basic types: contact and contactless. *Contact cards* have small metal contacts and must be used with its corresponding reader. These provide an electric pathway for power and data exchange. *Contactless cards* do not require the user to place the card into the reader, but communicate with the reader using radio waves and must be used in close proximity to the reader.

From a security standpoint, smart cards also present the opportunity to perform authentication at the end point as opposed to at a central server. This can help prevent the attack of authentication information in transit. Because smart cards are flexible and yet have chips embedded on them, they can be subject to high failure rates. If a card is unable to function, it can prevent a legitimate user from gaining access.

Figure 1-9: *A smart card.*

Token Devices

Token devices can be synchronous or asynchronous.

An *asynchronous token system* establishes a challenge response scenario. After an initial connection is made, the system will generate a challenge which the user will enter into a token device. The token will generate an appropriate response. If the user does not possess the token device, they will be unable to generate an appropriate response.

A *synchronous token* also presents information to the authentication server. This information may be based on time or a counter mechanism. The information that is presented will typically include a PIN that the user knows. This information will be checked against the information the authentication device is expecting and is thus considered synchronous. With synchronous tokens, all information is included with the initial authentication request, whereas in asynchronous tokens, there is a need to establish communication before the challenge is delivered.

Synchronous tokens typically display a number that changes frequently—usually every 60 seconds—and the number is only good during that window of time. There is usually an indication to the user on how soon the next number will be displayed. Counter-based systems will proceed through tokens in such a way that the authentication server will expect the user to present a particular token. Once a token is used, it will increment to the next token.

A good example of a token device is the RSA securID® product set. This device continually displays a number that is used with a PIN provided by the user. When challenged by the authentication system, the user keys in the number on the securID device and then keys in his or her PIN. When the numbers are not keyed in time, the authentication attempt fails and another attempt must be made.

Figure 1-10: *An RSA token device.*

Challenge and Response

A computer sends another computer a question, or "the challenge," and the receiving computer provides a valid answer, or "the response" in order to be authenticated. In the Challenge Handshake Authentication Protocol (CHAP), the authentication server issues the challenge, the client uses the challenge to encrypt the password, and then returns the response. The server can then decrypt the response and see if the challenge is the same as originally sent, and if so, will grant authentication.

Something You Are

The something you are method uses biometric measurements or personal attributes for authentication. These attributes are unique to the individual seeking to authenticate identification. Examples include fingerprints, hand geometry, retina scans, iris scans, facial recognition, and behavioral characteristics such as voiceprints. To make authentication comparisons, individuals must be registered or enrolled in the biometric system. This enrollment should take no more than two to three minutes per person. The subsequent authentication should take no more than five to 10 seconds. Of all the authentication types mentioned so far, biometrics incurs the most user reluctance. There are concerns ranging from ideals of civil liberties to the practicalities of sanitation that need to be considered with any implementation.

 Something you are is sometimes referred to as authentication by characteristic.

Types of Biometric Devices

There are several types of biometric devices used in something you are authentication. They can be divided into those measuring physiological traits or behavioral traits.

Physiological Biometric Device Type	Description
Fingerprint	Capturing and comparing fingerprints of the individual with previously captured fingerprints to determine a match.
Hand geometry	Comparing the hand structure of an individual to a previously captured hand structure to determine a match.
Iris scan	Comparing the patterns of the colored part of the eye to previously captured iris images to determine a match.
Retina scan	Comparing the blood vessel patterns in the back of the eye to previously captured patterns. This method can be affected by pregnancy, diabetes, and diseases of the eye.
Facial recognition	Comparing the facial structure to a previously captured facial structure to determine a match. Facial recognition can be applied individually and it has also been applied to crowds. Casinos have used this technology for years and it has become more popular at large events to protect against terrorism.

Traditional biometrics have been based on a physical attribute of a person; a fingerprint or hand geometry, for example. Behavioral biometrics is based on a unique way that each individual would perform a function; walking or typing, for example. These are newer and not as well-tested, but they will likely be included in future biometric systems.

Behavioral Biometric Device Type	Description
Keystroke recording	Capturing the unique way individual users would type a common phrase can be used to uniquely identify a user.
Voiceprint	Comparing a spoken phrase to a registered phrase previously spoken by the individual.
Signatures	Capturing the speed, acceleration, and pressure applied while signing a pressure sensitive interface and comparing it to previously captured information.

Biometric Acceptance

Some biometric measurements are readily accepted by the user community. For example, fingerprints, voice analysis, and facial recognition are often associated with law enforcement and personal privacy. Retina scans and iris scans are not well-accepted because of health concerns.

Regardless of the methods employed, not all users will be satisfied with the results, and the risks associated with unauthorized access should be weighed against the users' concerns. Therefore, implementing a more balanced approach is ideal.

Biometrics products continue to mature and new ones will be developed. While biometrics provide very robust authentication, they have also been known to fail. All systems should be tested periodically.

Somewhere That You Are

Somewhere that you are is a recent form of authentication and security experts have not agreed on whether it should be a new type or be included with biometrics. It involves verifying where you are as part of the authentication process. The latest portable devices frequently have a GPS embedded in them and can be used to verify the location of a user as part of the authentication process. Credit card companies have used a variation of this for fraud protection for years. For example, if your credit card suddenly starts getting used in odd locations or simultaneously in geographically disparate areas, it will trigger fraud protection.

Biometric Errors

Any measurement process will suffer from some type of error. Biometrics are not immune to errors. Two types of errors occur when biometrics are used for authentication.

In one case, individuals are excluded when they should be allowed access because the biometric measure says they are not allowed access. The other type of error occurs when the biometric measure allows individuals access when they are not authorized.

In the first case, the individual who is denied access is delayed, and in the second case, the system or facility is under threat from the unauthorized individual given access.

Type I errors, also known as *false rejection rates (FRRs),* exist when an authorized individual is denied access. Systems with high sensitivity levels often result in Type I errors because they tend to reject authorized individuals more often.

Type II errors, also known as *false acceptance rates (FARs),* exist when an unauthorized individual is given access. Systems with low sensitivity levels often result in Type II errors because they allow more unauthorized access because they lack sufficient detection capabilities.

Most organizations will consider Type II errors more serious. However, it is important to remember that Type I errors can keep legitimate users from getting their work done.

Most systems will allow for a certain amount of sensitivity tuning.

The point at which the two errors intersect on a graph is called the *crossover error rate (CER)* and this affects both error types. The biometric measurements with the lowest CERs provide the best protection.

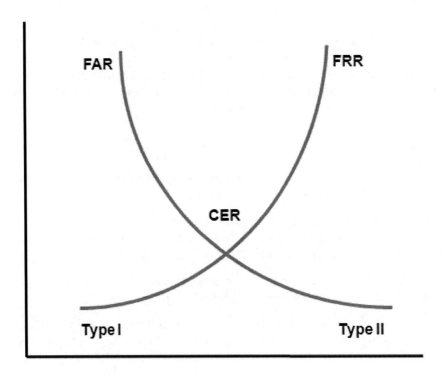

Figure 1-11: *A CER graphic example.*

Multifactor Authentication

Definition:

Multifactor authentication is a system wherein more than one type of authentication is used in accessing a system or facility. Using a fingerprint scanner device with a PIN is a simple example of two-factor authentication. In this case, something you are is matched with something you know to gain access. There is also three-factor authentication where you might also have to present an ID badge. All of these are sometimes called strong authentication, but that term is considered ambiguous and is falling out of favor.

It is important to make the distinction that using the same type of authentication twice is not multifactor authentication. For example, being prompted for your password to log in and then prompted for another password to access an application uses the same type of authentication twice. You need to use two different authentication types for it to be multifactor.

Example:

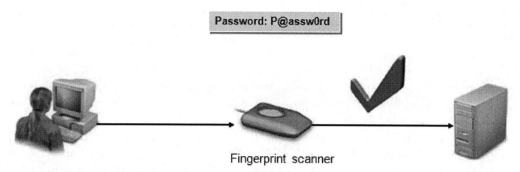

Figure 1-12: *Multifactor authentication.*

 Multifactor authentication is necessary to safeguard systems and facilities where using simple passwords is not sufficient.

Single Sign-On

Single sign-on (SSO) is a method of access control wherein a single user ID and password will allow a user to access all of his or her applications. Because users are often challenged to remember different user IDs and passwords to gain access to systems, SSO plays an essential role in today's computer environment. It eliminates this challenge entirely by recognizing the authentication and automatically connecting users to other systems. Therefore, one successful authentication attempt allows access to resources of multiple software systems.

Although SSO reduces the number of user IDs and passwords that an individual has to remember, it also presents problems. Primarily, when a user ID and password is exposed to an unauthorized user, it can result in a threat to all systems the authorized user can access.

In a simple SSO system, there may be a single repository of user credential information. With a single login, a user will have access to files, printers, and other shared resources and not be prompted for additional logins. In large systems that have multiple directories of different types, the situation becomes more complex and there is a need to share or synchronize information between systems. When organizations create partnerships and want to share information between them without the burden of multiple sign-ins, they might develop a federated trust relationship.

SSO Methods

There are three methods employed for SSO.

SSO Method	Description
Kerberos	The implementation of *Kerberos* is specified in Internet Request for Comments (RFC) 4120. Kerberos was initially developed at MIT. The name comes from Greek mythology. Kerberos was the three-headed dog that guarded the gates to Hades. The name was chosen because Kerberos addresses three security concerns; authentication, authorization, and accounting.
	In the Kerberos process, there are three primary systems. The user enters access credentials that are then passed to a Key Distribution Server, which also acts as an Authentication Server (AS), which contains the allowed access credentials. The AS verifies the credentials and passes a Ticket Granting Ticket (TGT) back to the requesting user. When a user requires the resources of another object, they use their TGT. That ticket contains a verification of the user's credentials, and is then passed to another element of the system called the Ticket Granting Server (TGS). The TGS then verifies the request to access a given system or application and provides access rights.
	A Service Ticket (ST) is then returned to the user. The ST is sent to the application server or network resource, and verifies that the user is allowed access to the system and that the user is authorized to use the system.
	Kerberos can suffer from denial of service (DoS) attacks if there is only a single server. Overwhelming the AS or TGS restricts the number of users who can authenticate or get authorization. An AS or TGS failure also presents a single point of failure. No access will be given if the AS or TGS fails.
SESAME	*Secure European System for Applications in a Multi-vendor Environment (SESAME)* is an SSO created in Europe. SESAME tries to overcome a couple limitations of Kerberos by using distributed servers that do not require replication and by using symmetric and asymmetric keys. In SESAME, the client receives a Privileged Attribute Certificate (PAC) from a Privileged Attribute Server (PAS).
Federations	When organizations want the ability to access information in their partners' systems but do not want to create accounts on those systems, it would be beneficial if they could take advantage of their own account stores for authentication. With federation trust, you create a resource domain and an account domain that trust each other. As an account is making request for resources, the authentication request is processed by the account partner. This implies a series of trusts to be in place. It also typically involves certificates and public key infrastructure (PKI).

The RFC Series

For more information on the RFC series and to access RFC publications that pertain to specific Internet-related knowledge areas, visit **www.rfc-editor.org/**.

Access Control Administration Methods

There are three significant access control administration methods.

Access Control Administration Method	Description
Centralized	Centralized access control involves administering access controls at a centralized site. All requests for access are handled by a single group of administrators.
	When administered centrally, requests are handled uniformly by the staff. Centralized access control is often administered using protocols specifically designed for this type of process, such as Remote Authentication Dial-in User Service (RADIUS), Terminal Access Controller Access Control System (TACACS), and Diameter.
Decentralized	In decentralized access control, the administration of the access control elements are in distributed locations throughout the enterprise. By moving this administrative process to localized parts of the enterprise, it is placed closer to the individuals requesting access. This often eliminates the bottlenecks found in centralized administration, where requests may be delayed due to workload. Local administrators are often more aware of critical situations and can react quickly when necessary.
	Nevertheless, decentralized administration does have a few disadvantages. Occasionally, the local administrator can be coaxed into doing something that does not comply with policy. Also, if the local administrator is sick or on vacation, work can be delayed unless others are trained in the processes.
Hybrid	It may be possible to implement access control using a centralized function with local administration. For example, a local administrator has access to the centralized RADIUS system to establish new accounts and manage existing accounts.
	The benefits of both types of access control administration are found in the hybrid system. A disadvantage is the lack of a control mechanism to specify which administrators are allowed to update which accounts. Changes made by a local administrator may be modified by a centralized administrator, or vice versa.

ACTIVITY 1-2
Discussing System Access and Authentication

Scenario:

In this activity, you will discuss the principles, characteristics, and types of system access and authentication.

1. **True or False? For identification to be useful, it is sufficient for each identity to be recognizable to the system.**

   ___ True

   ___ False

2. **What one or more methods are used to authenticate an identity?**

   a) Something you have

   b) Somewhere you have been

   c) Something you are

   d) Something you know

3. **What is the appropriate description for each authentication method?**

___ Something you know	a. An authentication factor that uses passwords and password variants.
___ Something you have	b. An authentication factor that uses a personal attribute such as fingerprints.
___ Something you are	c. An authentication factor that uses a physical device such as a magnetic strip.

4. **Which one of the following authentication methods is necessary to safeguard systems and facilities in high-security environments?**

   a) A token

   b) A PIN

   c) Biometrics

   d) Multifactor authentication

5. **Though single sign-on can be convenient, what is a potential security problem?**

   a) It can allow an unauthorized user access to all systems.

   b) It can allow hackers through the firewall.

   c) It can allow an unauthenticated user access to secure facilities.

   d) If you forget your user ID and password, you will not have access to any systems.

6. **Which one of the following access control administration methods involves distributing the process to localized parts of the enterprise?**

    a) Centralized

    b) Hybrid

    c) Decentralized

    d) RADIUS

TOPIC C
Attacks and Penetration Tests

Implementing an effective access control strategy is not enough to ensure the security of your information systems. You need to determine if the controls that you implement function as designed, and also identify areas of system vulnerability. In this topic, you will identify common attacks and penetration tests.

Ensuring the security of your information systems involves constant improvement. This means knowing that authorized users have access, identifying vulnerabilities in your system, and addressing system intrusion issues. One way to obtain this knowledge is to stage attacks on your system in what is commonly referred to as penetration testing. An effective information security professional will perform penetration tests to assess the security of the system.

Access Control Attack Methods

There are many different methods you can use to attack an access control system. There are two basic approaches: attacking the software components and attacking the human elements. The easiest method might be to simply capture a user ID and steal a password. An unauthorized user might also attempt to guess the password or employ a brute force process. If two-factor authentication is used, then the attacker will have to defeat both methods to gain access.

Assessing Security and Access Controls

In a defense-in-depth approach, multiple control types are used to protect systems. While this is very valuable, it is also necessary to constantly monitor for effectiveness. It is important for users to upgrade skills and protection mechanisms, but it is also important to periodically audit protection mechanisms to maintain security. There is a wealth of information in the audit logs and you need to ensure that they are being reviewed. Vulnerability testing and security assessments can also be performed.

Software-Based Access Control Attacks

Some access control attacks are software based.

Software-Based Attack Method	Description
DoS	A *denial of service (DoS)* attack focuses on the availability aspect of the CIA triad. DoS can target network devices, bandwidth availability, servers, applications, and workstations. This type of attack attempts to limit or eliminate the user's ability to access the network and/or data.
	A simple example of a DoS attack involves parking a car in the drive-through lane of a bank so cars cannot get through.
DDoS	*Distributed denial of service (DDoS)* uses multiple source machines to perpetrate a logical DoS against a chosen victim. This is sometimes done using previously compromised PCs that have been organized into a *botnet*.

Software-Based Attack Method	Description
Buffer overflow	A *buffer overflow* is an attack against the buffers that are written into applications and hardware devices. These buffers are meant for temporary storage of information and are usually fairly small in size. The attacker will intentionally send more information than allowed in the hopes of pushing through the buffer, possibly causing system failure or compromise. Buffer overflows can typically be addressed by boundary checking and can normally be fixed when discovered.
Malicious software	*Malicious software* is a type of attack that causes system failures or malfunctions. Malware, viruses, and worms are all examples of software gone bad. *Spyware* is another form of malicious software that is secretly installed on a user's computer to gather data about the user and relay it to a third party. All of these programs can cause serious system failures or malfunctions that compromise information integrity and confidentiality.
Mobile code	Mobile code is software that is transmitted from one device to another and then executed on the new host. It is different from traditional software in that it does not need to be installed but can execute nonetheless. JScript and ActiveX are common examples. Not all mobile code is malicious. It is dangerous because it can circumvent normal software restrictions and checks.
Brute force	*Brute force* is a type of password attack where an attacker uses an application to exhaustively try every possible alphanumeric combination to try to crack encrypted passwords and circumvent the authentication system. Creating complex passwords can increase the amount of time it takes for a brute force attack to succeed. Using brute force to crack a wireless network may result in access capabilities to many corporate resources.
Dictionary attack	A *dictionary attack* uses a set of predefined words from a dictionary to crack a password. Creating a dictionary of pre-hashed passwords can provide a Rainbow Table to speed up the password attack.
Sniffing	*Sniffing* involves using special monitoring software to gain access to private communications on the network wire or across a wireless network. This type of attack is used either to steal the content of the communications itself or to gain information that will help the attacker later gain access to your network and resources. This type of attack is also known as eavesdropping. Encryption of data in transit can help prevent sniffing.
Emanation	*Emanation* is an attack where protected information is leaked through the natural process of electrons passing through a wire or over the radio. These electrons can be detected by sophisticated monitoring devices, and then be captured and turned into information that can be used by an attacker. Keyboards, cathode ray tube (CRT) monitors, cabling, and computers are all subject to emanations. Wireless is practically emanation by design. Encryption can help here as well. Another emanation example is the vibration of window glass caused by the human voice. With the use of a monitoring device, the vibrations can be captured and the speech recorded from a distant location.

Software-Based Attack Method	Description
Object reuse	As a software attack, *object reuse* is the act of reclaiming classified or sensitive information from media once erroneously thought to have been erased or overwritten. Hard drives and other forms of read/write devices may end up with data left on them unintentionally. For example, ribbons from impact printers have been used to recover information. Print queues hold a copy of a file for a short time and an unscrupulous administrator might have the ability to read those files before they are cleaned up.
Data remanence	Occasionally, deleted information remains available due to an electronic property known as *data remanence,* where faulty information is left on media during the file erasure and deletion process. Applications will store information in memory where it may be left for another process to find. Sophisticated means are necessary to actually erase information during this process.
Trapdoor, backdoor, and maintenance hook	A *trapdoor attack* is where a hidden entry point into a program or operating system bypasses the normal identification and authentication processes.
	A *backdoor attack* is a type of software attack where an attacker creates a software mechanism called a *backdoor* to gain access to a computer. The backdoor can be a software utility or an illegitimate user account. Typically, a backdoor is delivered through use of a Trojan horse or other malware. Backdoor software typically listens for commands from the attacker on an open port. The backdoor mechanism often survives even after the initial intrusion has been discovered and resolved.
	The terms trapdoor and backdoor are frequently used interchangeably. *Maintenance hooks,* on the other hand, are frequently created by the developer of the application or hardware device. They are intended for use by technicians during development and should always be removed before the product is shipped so that they cannot be exploited.
	Trapdoor and backdoor activities are not included in the audit trail so there is no accounting for what happens.
Spoofing	*Spoofing,* or masquerading, comes in many forms wherein the attacker assumes an electronic identity to conceal his or her true person.
	Internet Protocol (IP) address spoofing:
	• Creates IP packets with a forged source IP address to mask the sender's identity. The attempt is to make it appear as if the packet came from a legitimate and trusted source.
	Media Access Control (MAC) address spoofing:
	• Intercepts frames by sending false Address Resolution Protocol (ARP) packets to a router or a switch.
	• ARP frames containing the MAC address of an attacker's machine replace the correct entries in the router and switch with the attacker's incorrect addresses.
	• The router and server send the frame to the attacker's MAC address where the information in the packets can be intercepted and modified.
	Domain Name System (DNS) spoofing:
	• Substitutes a different IP address for a domain name or host name within the DNS system.
	• Corrupts the DNS database of a user's DNS server to match human-legible computer names to physical IP addresses.

Although emanations are listed here as a software-based attack method, they are more precisely a phenomenon of electrons and electronic systems.

Human-Based Access Control Attacks

Some access control attacks are directed against people.

Human-Based Attack Method	Description
Guessing	*Guessing* is an attack where the goal is to guess a password or PIN through brute force means or by using deduction. For example, PINs are often the last four digits of a person's Social Security number or the four digits of his or her birth month and day.
Shoulder surfing	*Shoulder surfing* is an attack where the goal is to look over the shoulder of an individual as he or she enters password information or a PIN number. This is much easier to do today with camera-equipped mobile phones.
Dumpster diving	*Dumpster diving* is an attack where the goal is to reclaim important information by inspecting the contents of trash containers. This is especially effective in the first few weeks of the year as users discard old calendars with passwords written in them.
Theft	*Theft* is an attack where the goal is to blatantly steal information and resources. This usually requires unauthorized access or collusion with a disgruntled employee.
Social engineering	*Social engineering* is a type of attack that uses deception and trickery to convince unsuspecting users to provide sensitive data or to violate security guidelines. It exploits weaknesses in human judgment and may employ spoofing techniques to acquire access to another human being.

Social engineering is often a precursor to another type of attack. Because these attacks depend on human factors rather than on technology, their symptoms can be vague and hard to identify. Social engineering attacks can occur through a variety of methods: in person, through email, or over the phone.

For example, placing a phony help desk call to ask a user to provide his or her user ID and password so that the help desk member can check the account. On the Internet, this is often seen in the form of *phishing*, or false emails asking for account information. |
| Spoofing | Spoofing can occur in human-based form if employed in email, where various email message headers are changed to conceal the originator's identity. |

Intrusion Detection Systems

Definition:

An *intrusion detection system (IDS)* is a hardware or software solution that identifies and addresses potential attacks on a computer (or host) or a network. IDSs can be pattern based, where the IDS searches for certain data sequences that can identify a potential attack. Pattern-based systems use a signature file provided by the software vendor. The signature file contains profiles of known threats that are compared to data sequences seen by the IDS. The signature file, like a virus scanner file, must be updated frequently to keep up with current threats.

Another type of IDS is behavior based or anomaly driven. These systems detect changes in normal operating data sequences and identify abnormal sequences. When behavior-based systems are installed, they have no baseline or acceptable traffic pattern defined. Initially, these systems will report all traffic as a threat. Over time, however, they learn which traffic is allowed and which is not with the assistance of an administrator. These systems can identify new threats before the pattern-based systems do, but they tend to require more support.

Example:

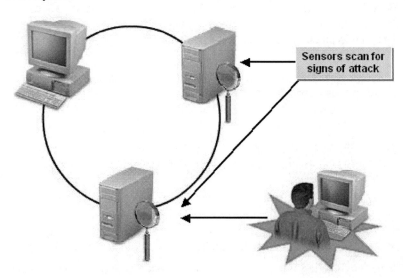

Figure 1-13: *An IDS.*

IDS Modes

IDS systems can be used into two modes. The first mode is monitoring, where the IDS system analyzes traffic as it passes by and provides alerts to the administrators if unacceptable traffic patterns arrive. This is truly an intrusion detection implementation.

The second mode is prevention. An *intrusion prevention system (IPS)* is a similar device to IDS, but instead of just monitoring, it will attempt to prevent intrusions. All traffic flows through the IPS. Traffic that violates the restrictions found in the signature file or anomaly database is blocked, thereby preventing damage to the system or network.

An IDS is considered a technical, detective control while an IPS is considered a technical, preventive control.

Access Monitoring or Prevention

The decision to monitor or prevent attacks or unacceptable traffic is based on risk. If there is a high risk of damage to the network or organization due to a DoS attack, an IPS that blocks the attack is most appropriate. Monitoring is best employed when experience shows that little or no threat exists to network security, and a warning of possible problems is sufficient.

IDS Categories

There are eight IDS categories.

IDS Category	Description
Network	IPS or IDS systems or appliances that monitor network traffic and restrict (IPS) or alert (IDS) when unacceptable traffic is seen.
Host-based	An IDS or IPS capability installed on a workstation or server to protect that single device.
Signature-based	An IDS or IPS solution that uses a predefined set of rules provided by a software vendor to identify traffic that is unacceptable.
Anomaly-based	An IDS or IPS solution that uses a database of unacceptable traffic patterns identified by analyzing traffic flows. Anomaly-based systems are dynamic and create a baseline of acceptable traffic flows during their implementation process.
Protocol-based	These IDS implementations focus on a limited number of protocols rather than the traffic on the entire network. Placing a protocol-based IDS that monitors HTTP traffic in front of a web server would be an example of this type of implementation.
Application protocol-based	Similar to protocol-based IDS systems, application protocol-based IDS could analyze specific application traffic, such as SQL requests and responses between an application server and a database server.
Hybrid	Hybrid systems implement two or more IDS approaches.
Passive or reactive system	Passive systems provide alerts when violations occur. Reactive systems block traffic when violations occur.

These types are not exclusive, so you could have a host-based system that is signature-based, for example.

Information System Auditing and Monitoring

It is necessary to monitor the access activities of information systems. Auditing is the principal function for monitoring access. Information systems maintain records of access attempts, access failures, application access attempts, application activities and functions, and other similar actions of users and other individuals in the system. These records are maintained in an *audit log* or *audit file*.

From a security perspective, the audit log is an important viewpoint into past system activity. The audit log allows administrators and auditors to evaluate who did what, and when. The audit log requires periodic evaluation and must be used to back up security policies. Access violations and application violations found in the log analysis process can lead to the disclosures of unauthorized access and activities.

 National Institute of Standards and Technology (NIST) 800-92 provides guidance on the types of audits and logs an organization should collect.

Penetration Testing

Definition:

Penetration testing is the controlled use of attack methods to test the security of a system or facility. It is used to verify that access control methods work, or to expose weaknesses that can be corrected.

Penetration tests can be performed by internal security personnel or an external organization. Penetration testers may be given no information about the system being tested, creating a black box testing situation. Another approach is to provide the testers with as much information as they request, giving them a white box view of the process.

 Penetration testing is sometimes referred to as ethical hacking.

Example:

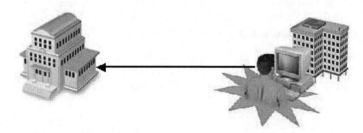

Figure 1-14: *Penetration testing.*

Example: Dummy Attacks

For example, a financial firm hires an outside company to perform a dummy attack on the firm's information systems to confirm whether they are adequately protected.

The Penetration Test Process

Penetration testing requires a multiphase approach.

1. Planning. It is important to include what is in scope for the test and out of scope and how or if users will be notified.

2. Reconnaissance involves collecting as much information about the target system as possible. For example, it is used to locate a web server within the organization.

3. Enumeration is the process of gaining more detailed information about the target system. For example, it is used to find all application services running on the web server.

4. A vulnerability analysis examines the available applications through the port numbers to check for any known vulnerabilities.

5. Vulnerabilities are exploited and system penetration occurs.

6. Reporting. It should be decided ahead of time who will receive the reports.

Penetration Test Types

There are seven different types of penetration tests.

Penetration Test Type	Description
Network scanning	*Network scanning* uses a port scanner to identify devices attached to the target network and to enumerate the applications hosted on the devices. This function is known as fingerprinting.
Social engineering	Attempts to get information from users to gain access to a system. This tests for adequate user training.
War dialing	*War dialing* uses a modem and software to dial a range of phone numbers to locate computer systems, Private Branch eXchange (PBX) devices, and heating, ventilating, and air conditioning (HVAC) systems.
War driving	*War driving* locates and then attempts to penetrate wireless systems.
Vulnerability scanning	*Vulnerability scanning* exploits known weaknesses in operating systems and applications that were identified through reconnaissance and enumeration.
Blind testing	*Blind testing* occurs when the target organization is not aware of penetration testing activities. Security administrators may respond to penetration testing as if an actual attack is underway.
Targeted testing	*Targeted testing* occurs when the target organization is informed of the test. There is less disruption to the organization due to the event response seen.

 NIST Special Publication 800-42 provides documentation on different types of penetration testing.

ACTIVITY 1-3
Discussing Penetration Tests

Scenario:
In this activity, you will discuss features, methods, and types of penetration tests.

1. **What is the simplest way to attack an access control system?**

   a) Break into a building.

   b) Social engineering.

   c) Capture a user ID and steal a password.

   d) Guess a password through a brute force process.

2. **What is the appropriate description for each software-based attack method?**

   ___ DoS

   ___ Malicious software

   ___ Sniffer

   ___ Data remanence

   a. Programs such as malware, spyware, viruses, and worms may cause system failures or malfunctions.

   b. Information left on media after erasures or deletions.

   c. A protocol analyzer is used to capture user IDs and passwords.

   d. Limits or eliminates the user's ability to access the network and/or data.

3. **What is the appropriate description for each additional software-based attack method?**

   ___ Dictionary attack

   ___ Trapdoor

   ___ Brute force

   ___ Emanation

   ___ Object reuse

   a. Passing electrons through a wire or over the radio to leak protected information.

   b. Attempting to access a system by trying every possible combination of a password or PIN number.

   c. Reclaiming information from media thought to be erased.

   d. A set of predefined words from a dictionary to crack a password.

   e. Accessing a program or operating system through a hidden entry point.

4. **An attack where an attacker pretends to be someone else to hide his or her actual identity is known as:**

    a) Spoofing.

    b) Shoulder surfing.

    c) Theft.

    d) Guessing.

5. **True or False? The audit function is the principal function for monitoring access.**

    ___ True

    ___ False

6. **The controlled use of attack methods to test the security of a system or facility is known as _____ _____ .**

7. **Which one of the following penetration test process phases includes gaining more detailed information about the selected or potential target?**

    a) Vulnerability

    b) Network scanning

    c) Enumeration

    d) Reconnaissance

8. **True or False? War dialing locates and then attempts to penetrate wireless systems.**

    ___ True

    ___ False

Lesson 1 Follow-up

In this lesson, you analyzed the basic principles, services, tools, and techniques involved in information systems access control. This information will help you effectively select and implement the best access control methods to secure your information system resources, as well as balance authorized access needs with system and data protection.

1. **With which types of access control systems are you most familiar? How would you compare their effectiveness to their convenience?**

2. **Have you ever experienced an access control attack on your information systems? How did you or your organization respond to the known attacks? What methods or techniques were implemented to prevent attacks?**

2 | Security Architecture and Design

Lesson Time: 2 hour(s), 45 minutes

Lesson Objectives:

In this lesson, you will analyze security architecture and design.

You will:

- Evaluate security models.
- Select security modes.
- Evaluate system assurance.

Introduction

You can use security models to control access to your organization's information systems, as well as secure system architecture for optimal protection of data that has varying degrees of sensitivity. Here, you will identify overall system architecture and design from a security perspective. You will select security models, modes, and information evaluation methods to enforce various levels of confidentiality, integrity, and availability within your organization. In this lesson, you will analyze security architecture and design.

Your system architecture directly affects the ease with which you are able to implement security within your organization. Poor system architecture security can seriously impact the confidentiality, integrity, and availability of your systems. Using tools, such as security and information evaluation models, will allow you to efficiently design security to meet the demands of your current and future systems.

This lesson supports content found in the Telecommunications and Network Security and Security Architecture and Design domains of the CISSP® certification.

TOPIC A
Security Architecture Frameworks and Security Models

Security architecture frameworks and security models specify how to build and control access to system resources. The security architecture of the organization will define the framework of the organizations security programs, projects, policies, and processes. The security programs will be ongoing efforts encompassing any number of security projects. Understanding a network's security architecture is critical to ensuring that security functionality is acceptable and that security mechanisms are implemented effectively. In this topic, you will evaluate security models.

You know that models allow you to adapt a proven process or structure to a set of unique requirements. Models exist for information systems security as well. Your understanding of the available security models is key to selecting the security approach best suited to the security requirements of your organization.

Common Security Architecture Frameworks

There are many security frameworks and models to choose from, but one of the largest considerations in choosing one is to make sure it will work with your organization's business objectives and that it has the support of upper management. It is important not to look at these tools as confining or constraining your efforts, but rather as a method that can be used to consistently address security. Rather than create piecemeal, reactive security policies or products, a better approach would be to have a consistent framework that supports your business and your security.

Some of these frameworks and models are not unique to security but are used in risk analysis and project management as well.

Framework	Description
Zachman	Named for John Zachman, the *Zachman* framework is designed to get the different groups working on a project to communicate with each other. It also helps to define what the different groups expect the project to deliver. The Zachman framework was not originally designed for security but it has been widely adopted to help build secure systems. The Zachman framework is commonly associated with the who, what, when, how, where, and why of information security. These objectives are matched with the roles of planner, owner, designer, builder, programmer, and user. There is also a concern with mapping technology projects to business objectives.
ISO/IEC 27001	*ISO/IEC 27001* is concerned with the standardization of a company's Information Security Management System (ISMS). Because it is a formal standard, the company can elect to be audited to assure its compliance. ISO/IEC 27001 frequently uses the security controls put forth in ISO/IEC 27002 though it is not a requirement. ISO/IEC 27001 came from ISO 1799, which came from BS 7799.

Framework	Description
COBIT	*Control Objectives for Information and related Technologies (COBIT)* is a framework for security governance best practices. There are 34 high level objectives that are divided into the four domains, Plan and Organize, Acquire and Implement, Deliver and Support, and Monitor and Evaluate. COBIT works to help companies realize value from IT initiatives. COBIT was developed by the Information Systems Audit and Control Association (ISACA).
ITIL	IT Infrastructure Library (ITIL) was developed by the Central Computer and Telecommunications Agency (CCTA) as a collection of best practices for IT governance. The five key areas of focus for ITIL are Service Strategy, Service Design, Service Transition, Service Operations and Continual Service Improvements.
TOGAF	*The Open Group Architecture Framework (TOGAF)* is an open framework seeking to provide common terms and methods that can be followed to create a secure organization. TOGAF was developed in the mid 1990s. It is based on earlier work done by the U.S. Department of Defense. TOGAF has evolved to version 9, which was released in February 2009. It provides design, planning, implementation, and governance modeled at four levels or domains. The levels are Business, Application, Data, and Technology. The inclusion of an Architecture Development Method (ADM) is important as it gives guidance on how to develop an enterprise architecture that meets the business and IT needs of a company.

Framework Illustration

The following table is an example of the Zachman framework.

	Who	What	Why	When	Where	How
Planner						
Owner						
Designer						
Builder						
Programmer						
User						

Trusted Computing Base

Definition:

The *Trusted Computing Base (TCB)* is a hardware, firmware, and software components of a computer system that is responsible for ensuring that the security policy is implemented and the system is secure. This means that the security properties of an entire system could be jeopardized should defects occur inside the TCB. The TCB is implemented in the hardware through processor rings or privileges, in the firmware through driver and resource protection, and in software through using the operating system's isolation of resources from applications.

The operating system will also frequently use a ring approach, with the most trusted components operating at ring zero and then moving outward to ring three, which might provide the shell to the users. The TCB will account for the enforcement of the reference monitor (RM) as well as the implementation of identity and authentication (I&A) It is the totality of the system's security.

Example:

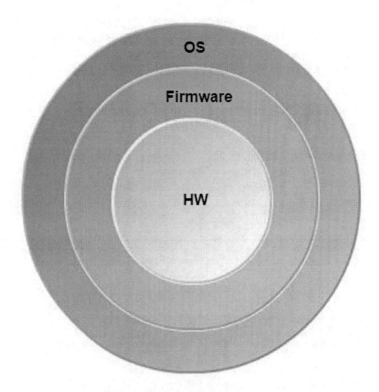

Figure 2-1: Components of the TCB.

The Security Perimeter

The *security perimeter* is an imaginary line that surrounds the TCB and separates the trusted and untrusted parts of a computer system. The trusted part of the system is the interior processes controlled by the TCB. If an application needs to be inside the security perimeter, it will need to be thoroughly tested and possibly certified and accredited. The security perimeter is a logical function rather than a physical barrier. Strong software interfaces control the communications between the trusted and untrusted parts of the system.

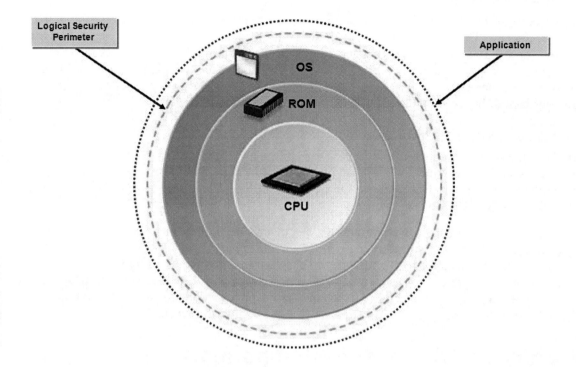

Figure 2-2: *A logical security perimeter.*

Computer Architecture Security Design

In the design, development, and implementation of a computer system, security elements are the highest priority and are included at many levels. Access control to the computer system is implemented in the RM. The RM is almost always loaded when the operating system is loaded. As the operating system loads, the RM should be one of the very first components called. In high security environments, the RM can be additionally invoked by hardware.

When building the TCB:

1. Hardware design initiates system protection.

2. Firmware or software development is implemented, which controls elementary hardware elements.

3. Software protection is designed.

If the TCB is not adequately designed, developed, and implemented, the RM will be unable to control access.

Figure 2-3: *Computer architecture security design.*

Layered Protection

The process of building security into the various components is called *layered protection* or *layered defense*. Those attempting to penetrate the protections must go through many layers to do so. These layers also mask the complexity of the system from the end user. As they are moving between applications and possibly even between networks, the higher layers will not be disturbed, thereby hiding the work that is being done by the lower layers. Encapsulation and abstraction between the layers further protects the systems.

Component Security Protection

In the earliest computer systems designs, the mainframe was the area of security concern. Physical security was important since access to the mainframe was through a physical door into the computer room. Once access was extended to remote or online access, the importance of protecting the TCB became evident.

Today, many different devices are protected. The mainframe still exists but the architecture of modern systems requires protecting many different components. Networked systems support using servers and clients. The client/server architecture is supported by different operating systems and network protocols. Desktop, laptop, personal data assistants (PDAs), smartphones, video games, and many other types of systems are integrated into the network environment. Security protection must be provided to each of these component types.

Hardware Architecture Components

There are several different components that form the hardware architecture of a computer system.

Hardware Component	Description
CPU	The *Central Processing Unit (CPU)* is at the core of the implementation of security in a modern system. The CPU executes instructions that allow the system to operate successfully. The failure of CPU design can lead to system failure, which then affects the availability of applications that the users need.
	CPU design often includes a layered protection process. Based on the principle of least privilege, some instructions in the CPU are limited to using the operating system, while other instructions are available to the operating system and to the user programs.
	When a CPU is in *supervisor state,* also known as *kernel mode,* it can execute any instructions that are available. When in *user* or *application state*, a CPU can execute only non-privileged instructions. This protects the system from unauthorized activities by user programs. These protection schemes are often implemented in rings with the most secure ring in the center, progressing to the least secure ring at the outer edge of the design.

Hardware Component	Description
Primary storage	Information that must be immediately available to the system is stored in either long-term memory or short-term memory depending on the need. *Random Access Memory (RAM)* is a type of computer data storage that uses short-term memory to store program instructions and data for immediate use. *Read Only Memory (ROM)* is a type of computer data storage that uses long-term memory to store program information and configuration information used during the initiation, or boot, process of a computer. RAM will usually lose its ability to store information once power is removed from the system. ROM, on the other hand, maintains the information indefinitely. Because memory is an information storage location that is immediately available, it is often called *primary storage*. A special category of RAM is *cache memory*. The CPU uses cache memory to expedite access to instructions that require processing.
Secondary storage	Other storage means include disk drives, magnetic tapes, non-volatile memory disk replacements, CD-ROMs, and DVDs. These *secondary storage* elements store information for long periods of time and in great volumes. The type of secondary storage used affects the performance of the system. Retrieving information from modern disk drives is fast and efficient. Retrieving and storing information on magnetic tape is slow and requires sequential access. All of the information on magnetic tape must be read to get to the information at the end of the tape. Disk drives, memory disk replacements, CD-ROMs, and DVDs are all random access devices. They eliminate the need to read a lot of information to get the small quantity that a user may need.
Virtual memory	A special category of storage is *virtual memory*. Virtual memory uses random access disks to temporarily store information needed by the operating system and application programs. If an area of RAM is not actively required by the operating system, it can be written to disk and then recalled at a later time as desired. It is called virtual memory because it is not actually in memory but can be found and reloaded when needed. Virtual memory can allow a system to appear to have a large amount of RAM when, in fact, it has limited RAM and uses disks to store swapped information temporarily. This swapping, or paging, of programs and data can seriously impact performance if the system has to wait for the disk's input/output to complete.
I/O devices	Input to the computer system and output from the computer system is provided by *input/output (I/O)* devices. Secondary storage is a form of an I/O device. Keyboards, monitors, mice, sound cards, scanners, printers, and network interfaces are all I/O devices. I/O devices are attached to computer systems via cabling or are directly connected to the computer bus.
Computer bus	In computer architecture, a *computer bus* is the set of physical connections between devices that are attached to the computer's motherboard, or primary circuit board. Buses can be serial or parallel with multiple communication pathways. Parallel buses include three different physical pathways to transfer information between a CPU and an I/O device. One pathway is the *data path*. Another pathway is the *instruction path*, and the last pathway is the *addressing path*. The CPU sends a request via the instruction path to a device identified by an address sent on the addressing path. In return, the I/O device returns the information to the CPU via the data path.

Hardware Component	Description
Drivers	The orderly exchange of information between the I/O devices and the CPU is controlled by the operating system that supports the application programs. *Drivers* are special software modules that interface between the operating system and the I/O devices. Some drivers are generic and others are device specific. Device-specific drivers are associated with communications activity.

Hardware TCB Protection

With so many different hardware aspects to consider, secure information systems designers must understand the strengths and weaknesses of the hardware architecture. They need to determine if the hardware presents ways to circumvent protection schemes and to allow unauthorized access.

Firmware

Definition:

Firmware is small chips designed to hold a small set of instructions to assist devices. Motherboards, network interface cards (NIC), printers, smartphones, and many other devices rely on these special chips to perform a variety of tasks. These are frequently referred to as Read Only Memory (ROM) chips, but in fact, many of them are not technically read only. So, a more technically accurate term that should be used is Electronically Erasable Programmable ROM (EEPROM).

Through a process known as flashing, the code can be updated.

The Basic Input Output System (BIOS) is a common use for firmware. When the PC is turned on, the BIOS will perform a power-on self-test (POST). Once the POST is complete, it will locate the boot sector, which contains instructions on loading the operating system. The BIOS may also provide an option for authentication and require the user to provide a password, thus providing another layer of security, one that is enforced even before the loading of the operating system.

One of the newest uses for firmware is the Trusted Platform Module (TPM). It has a Rivest, Shamir, Adleman (RSA) key burned into it and can be used for storing and creating other cryptographic keys, for pseudo random number generation, and for binding and sealing of data.

Example:

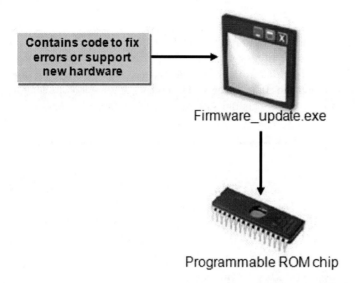

Figure 2-4: Firmware.

Software Architecture Categories

From a security perspective, software architecture is composed of two main categories: operating systems and application programs.

Software Architecture Category	Description
Operating system	Operating systems control the activity of the application programs and I/O devices. Implementing access controls as one of its functions, the operating system is the first line of defense in a system. The protection provided by the operating system is found in the system or security kernel.
	Application programs attempting to access system resources or data send requests to the operating system. The operating system then determines if the request is authorized.
	No application programs may access any resource without going through the operating system kernel. The security kernel is the implementation of the TCB, and therefore, the RM.
	The operating system works with the CPU to control system activity. When the operating system is in control, the CPU is in supervisor or privileged state. When the operating system allows applications to execute, the CPU is switched to problem or user state. Only non-privileged instructions are allowed to execute. This feature implements separation of duties (SoD) within the system environment.
	The operating system controls the program execution sequence and controls which programs are executing and which programs are waiting.

Software Architecture Category	Description
Application programs	Application programs are all programs that are not associated with the operating system. The computing environment is protected from application programs by requiring that all access to the resources go through the protected operating system. Putting the CPU into user state when applications are utilizing the CPU protects the system from unauthorized access to resources.

Software TCB Protection

A serious breach of security occurs when access capabilities that circumvent the security kernel are placed in the operating system. Allowing application programs to enter supervisory mode is another area of concern. As security professionals evaluate operating systems and applications for security issues, assuring TCB protection is one of the most important items.

Multitasking and Multithreading

In a computer system with a single processor, the operating system divides time among the programs using a technique called *multitasking*. By giving each program a bit of time to execute, multitasking allows more than one program to run at one time.

Threading is a computing technique that enables a program to split itself into two or more concurrently running tasks. If a program needs to perform more than one function at a time, it may ask the operating system to help by implementing *multithreading*. This technique allows the parallel execution of multiple threads on a computer system.

Multiprogramming is an older term that may still be seen. Multiprogramming allows for the simultaneous execution of more than one program. This is very common in desktops and laptops, but is not always available in low power or low processor devices.

Multistate is the ability to run in different execution modes. Operating systems have a similar ability to run in "normal" mode or "safe" mode.

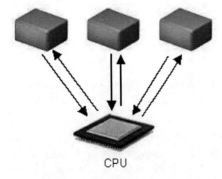

CPU

Figure 2-5: Multitasking and multithreading.

Word Processing

You may need a word processing program to simultaneously spell check a document as you enter the text. When the word processor indicates to the operating system that it needs resources for spell checking, the operating system creates a new thread. Although the thread may appear as another program to the operating system, it is actually related to the word processor. The thread gets a time slice like any other program, but only when the word processor gives it something to do.

Multiprocessing

In computer systems with multiple processors, the operating system may be capable of *multiprocessing*, controlling all of the processors in such a way that the system's optimum performance is reached. Several programs can be run in a multiprocessing environment, which enables the operating system to multitask across multiple processors. A particular version of an operating system may dictate how many processors are supported.

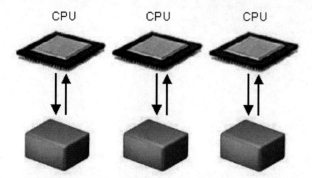

Figure 2-6: Multiprocessing.

Distributed System Architecture

Distributed system architecture is a term used for systems in which a number of computers are networked together and share application processes and data. The TCB is extended from individual machines to the entire distributed environment. Attempting to access data on a server requires the RM on the client device to authorize network access and the use of the RM on the server. Finally, the RM authorizes access to the data.

Verifying the correct TCB functionality for the client, server, and networking devices helps to ensure the security of the distributed architecture.

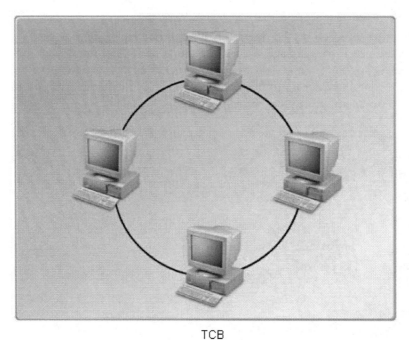

TCB

Figure 2-7: *A distributed system architecture.*

Security Models

Security models provide guidelines and frameworks for implementing security policies to protect the confidentiality, integrity, and availability of information on devices or networks. Many of these models will support the concepts of either discretionary, non-discretionary, or mandatory access control (MAC).

Types of Security Models	Description
Lattice	The *Lattice Model* is used to implement MACs where data (objects) is classified or labeled and users (subjects) are cleared for access. Lattice Models provide strict rules on what is allowed or not allowed between subjects and objects.
Non-Interference	The *Non-Interference Model* limits the interference between elements at different security levels. Non-Interference Models create barriers between levels so that information cannot inadvertently leak between them.
Information Flow	The *Information Flow Model* controls the direction of data flow among the various security levels when allowed. This model is also useful for detecting unauthorized data flows, or communications paths, called *covert channels*.
	Information Flow Models are not a category unto themselves but are a collection of other models that control information flow. By analyzing sources and information destinations controlled by Information Flow Models, it is possible to discover covert channels that may leak information between different levels of security.

Types of Security Models	Description
State Machine	The "state" of a system is a single point in time. The *State Machine Model* monitors the system as it moves from one state to another. More specifically, it looks at what operations are allowed or not allowed as the system moves from one state to the next. A security policy will provide the rules for the system.
BLP	The *Bell-LaPadula (BLP) Model* was developed by the U.S. Department of Defense. It limits the access to classified objects to those subjects with equal or higher clearance. This model is primarily used for maintaining confidentiality. The intent is to prohibit classified information from being moved to a lower classification level. Access modes described in the BLP Model include the Simple Security Property, which is equivalent to the read property; the * Security Property, which is generally referred to as the star (*) or write property; and the Strong * Property, where read and write are at your level.
	In BLP, subjects cannot read up to objects with a higher classification and information cannot be written down, or moved down, to a lower classification level. Simply stated, BLP implements no read up or no write down policies. It is important to remember that BLP is primarily concerned with the confidentiality of documents.
Biba	The *Biba Model* is an integrity model that uses integrity levels to depict the information trust level. Information with high trust needs to be protected from the insertion of information with a low trust level. Like BLP, access modes described in Biba include the Simple Integrity Axiom (read property) and the * Integrity Axiom (write property).
	In Biba, subjects cannot read down to objects with a lower integrity level and information cannot be written up, or moved up, to a higher integrity level. Simply stated, Biba implements no read down or no write up policies. Biba reverses BLP and is sometimes referred to as upside down BLP. It is important to remember that Biba is primarily concerned with the integrity of documents.
Clark-Wilson	It is said that the *Clark-Wilson Model* extends Biba. It is an integrity model that relates trust to the integrity of the processes surrounding the data. Clark-Wilson features three essential tenets:
	1. No changes are made by an unauthorized subject.
	2. No unauthorized changes are made by an authorized subject.
	3. No mistakes are made in making any changes.
	Changes are made by well-formed transactions or programs, rather than by directly manipulating the data in a file.
Graham-Denning	The *Graham-Denning Model* deals with creating and deleting objects and subjects, as well as the reading, granting, deleting, and transferring of access rights.
Harrison-Ruzzo-Ullman	The *Harrison-Ruzzo-Ullman Model* is a variation of the Graham-Denning model and deals with changing access rights and creating and deleting subjects or objects. It also addresses situations where you do not want a subject to gain permissions.
Brewer-Nash	The *Brewer-Nash Model* relates to the control of the conflict of interest. If a user is accessing Client A data, then the user cannot access any other client information until Client A's access is discontinued. Brewer-Nash can be implemented at the system level and extend into the process level. Brewer-Nash is sometimes called the Chinese Wall model.

The Impact of Biba

The concepts surrounding the Biba Model are often difficult to understand because most governmental systems deal with confidentiality, not integrity. In Biba, an integrity label is used. For example, a policy is built indicating that data is labeled based on trust using L1 through L4, with L1 being no trust and L4 being the highest level of trust.

A military scenario works well to illustrate this model. Rumors of enemy activity heard on the street are trusted at L0 because there is little or no supporting information. Rather, intelligence gathered about enemy activity by trained intelligence officers who actually viewed the movements are trusted at L4. For example, an intelligence officer with an L3 rating cannot read down to L1 or L2 information and bring it into an L3 storage area because the information with lower trust levels would pollute the L3 information. The same officer cannot write up information from L3 to L4 because it would give the L3 information more credibility than it deserves.

ACTIVITY 2-1
Discussing Security Models

Scenario:

In this activity, you will discuss components and characteristics of security models.

---

1. **True or False? Because the TCB ensures system security through the implementation of security policies, protection against system-wide deficiencies is guaranteed.**

    ___ True

    ___ False

---

2. **Which of the following descriptions best explains the function of the security perimeter?**

    a) It acts as a physical barrier to the TCB.

    b) It determines access to objects by subjects.

    c) It separates the trusted and untrusted parts of a computer system.

    d) It implements the RM in an operating system.

---

3. **What is the order of the process steps for designing, developing, and implementing a computer system?**

    Firmware or software development

    Software protection design

    Hardware design

---

4. **Which of the following statements best describes the primary objective for implementing layered protection?**

    a) It eliminates the risk of security infringements.

    b) It manages the security of computer components.

    c) It creates a series of layers that impede penetration attempts.

---

5. **What is the appropriate description for each hardware component?**

___	CPU	a.	Devices that provide input to and output from a computer system.
___	Primary storage	b.	Software modules that interface between an operating system and I/O devices.
___	Secondary storage	c.	Executes security instructions that allow a computer system to successfully operate.
___	Virtual memory	d.	A category of storage that uses random access disks to temporarily store information needed by the operating system and application programs.
___	I/O	e.	A common term used for memory based on its immediate availability as an information storage location.
___	Computer bus	f.	The set of physical connections between devices that are attached to a computer's motherboard.
___	Drivers	g.	A means of storage that keeps information for long periods of time and at great volumes.

6. **Which one or more categories form the software architecture of a computer system?**

   a) Operating systems

   b) Firmware

   c) Appliances

   d) Application programs

7. **Which software category is the first line of defense in a computer system?**

   a) Operating system

   b) Application program

8. **Which of the following techniques allows several programs to appear to operate simultaneously in a single-processor computing system?**

   a) Threading

   b) Multitasking

   c) Multithreading

9. **True or False? Multiprocessing facilitates an operating system's capacity to support more than one processor and allocate tasks between processors.**

   ___ True

   ___ False

10. **Which one of the following items is software that is used on hardware devices to control their elementary functions?**

    a) Microcontroller

    b) CPU

    c) Spyware

    d) Firmware

11. **What is the order of the phases that occur when access rights are evaluated in a distributed system architecture?**

    RM authorization of data access

    RM authorization on the client device to access the network and use the RM on the server

    Extension of the TCB from separate machines to the distributed environment

12. **Which one or more of the following security models are integrity models?**

    a) BLP

    b) Lattice

    c) Biba

    d) Clark-Wilson

13. **There are times when a user is prevented from accessing specific data on a computer because of competing system information. A user's access to additional information may be dependent upon the discontinuation of active data access. Which security model does this represent?**

    a) Harrison-Ruzzo-Ullman

    b) Graham-Denning

    c) Non-Interference

    d) Information Flow

    e) Brewer-Nash

TOPIC B
Security Modes

Designing an effective security system architecture ensures that you build security features and functionalities into your system. You also need to consider the levels of security for your information systems. In this topic, you will select a security mode that is appropriate to your system architecture, security considerations, and data recovery needs.

As you have identified the importance of distinguishing between users, you now need to revisit this principle in the system architecture domain. When operational requirements vary, you have to offer different levels of system access. Your ability to choose appropriate security modes is vital to the confidentiality of information within your system.

TCB Vulnerabilities

The Trusted Computing Base (TCB) is vulnerable to many different problems ranging from poor hardware protection to inferior hardware design.

TCB Vulnerability	Description
Backdoors and trapdoors	These are shortcuts and codes added to a system, usually surreptitiously. Then they provide access to unauthorized users and typically go around the RM. They will also attempt to avoid showing up in the audit logs.
Maintenance hooks	These hooks are intentionally added to software and sometimes hardware during the development phase. They are useful to the developers for easy access to the system; however, if they are not removed before the product ships they can provide unintended access to the product.
TOC/TOU	*Time of check/time of use (TOC/TOU)* uses a weakness in the TCB where access is granted at one point in time and used much later on. Often, an attacker will modify information between the two authorized accesses.
Race condition	A *race condition* occurs when two processes try to access and modify information at the same time. Process A must perform its update before Process B. If Process B can manipulate the sequence and execute first, then the result is incorrect.
Buffer overflow	*Buffer overflow* moves too much information into a program memory area. For example, the system may have a username field set to 15 characters, but the user enters 35 characters. If the system is not doing boundary checking, those extra 20 characters are going to go to the buffer. This can cause a program failure because unexpected information will leak into other program data or instruction areas.
Covert channel	A covert channel provides access to information in an unintentional way. There are two types: *covert storage* and *covert timing*. In covert storage, a file saved by one process should be unavailable to another, but the second process may be able to learn information just by seeing that a file exists. In covert timing, the watching process is able to monitor the traffic or CPU utilization, and even though it cannot read the information, it can make determinations based on the amount or type of traffic it sees.

Firmware and Driver Errors

Firmware errors and driver errors can cause system failures, and operating system inefficiencies and errors may cause availability problems and system failures. The popularly called "blue or black screens of death" are illustrations of the problems that appear when the operating system fails to protect the TCB.

TCB Compromise

Some systems with established and verified TCB protection may also be compromised by replacing a trusted component with an untrusted component. For example, you compile a Linux operating system with a replacement identification and authentication (I&A) component and the resultant code is installed on many different computers, compromising the TCB. Without a clear change control process, the operating system modification will go unnoticed.

Data Recovery Levels

When a system fails, data recovery attempts can be made at two levels.

Data Recovery Level	Description
Trusted recovery	*Trusted recovery* is a protection mechanism used in data recovery that ensures the security of a computer system that crashes or fails by recovering security-relevant elements in a trusted or secure state. A system must restart without compromising its protection settings.
	Trusted recovery requires the use of standardized and secure procedures and practices. These include:
	1. Rebooting the system into a single user mode with security protections enabled.
	2. Recovering all system files active at the crash point.
	3. Restoring damaged or missing files from recent backups and databases.
	4. Recovering security parameters.
	5. Checking critical files such as the system password file.
	When trusted recovery is complete, the system can be made available for multiuser or network access.
Untrusted recovery	An *untrusted recovery* is a data recovery process that does not result in secure and trusted environments. In certain cases, it may be impossible to perform a trusted recovery. Some documents, like the Director of Central Intelligence Document (DCID) 6/3, specify that exclusive documentation be provided for critical situations and that mitigation efforts be implemented.

Trusted Recovery Methods

There are essentially four different methods for performing a trusted recovery.

Trusted Recovery Method	Description
Manual	The system operator manually performs the recovery process. The system is then rebooted and, if necessary, the operating system and data files are reloaded. Software can be used to verify the proper system security environment before normal operation continues.
Automatic	The system restarts using an automatic process that identifies security issues and then prompts the operator or administrator to perform specific functions to return the system to a secure state.
Recovery without errors	The best security environment for a trusted recovery is when the recovery is completed without any errors. The recovery may be manual or automatic, but the targeted objective is a fully recovered system.
Recovery with limited errors	In some cases, a trusted recovery can be accomplished, but with a limited number of errors. After analyzing the system state, a decision can be made to begin operations with the existing errors in place under the condition that a target be set for removing all errors within a given time period.

Security Mode Types

A system is often rated based on its security mode, which depicts an individual's required access limits or credentials when attempting to access the system.

Security Mode	Description
Dedicated	In dedicated systems, all objects have the same classification labels. This, in turn, requires that all users have this same classification. All users must have proper security clearance, formal access approval, a signed non-disclosure agreement (NDA), and a valid need to know for *all* information on the system. In a dedicated security mode system, all users can access *all* data.
System-high	In system-high implementations, there will be objects with varying classification labels. Users are required to have a proper security clearance, formal access approval, a signed NDA, and a valid need to know for *some* information on the system. In a system-high security mode, all users can access *some* data based on their need to know.
Compartmented	All users must have a proper clearance for the *highest* level of data classification on the system, formal access approval for *all* information they will access on the system, a signed NDA for *all* information they will access on the system, and a valid need to know for *some* of the information on the system. Access is granted to *some* information based on a need to know and formal access approval. Objects will be placed in the appropriate compartments.

Security Mode	Description
Multilevel	All users must have proper security clearance for information they will access on the system, formal access approval, a signed NDA, and a valid need to know for *some* information on the system. In a multilevel security mode system, all users can access *some* data based on clearance, formal access approval, and their need to know. The reference monitor will provide security between subjects and objects.

Requirements for User Access

Each security mode has specific requirements for user access.

- A = Applies to *All* information on the system
- S = Applies to *Some* information on the system

Security Mode	Signed NDA	Proper Clearance	Formal Access Approval	Need to Know
Dedicated	A	A	A	A
System-high	A	A	A	S
Compartmented	A	A	S	S
Multilevel	A	S	S	S

ACTIVITY 2-2
Discussing Security Modes

Scenario:
In this activity, you will discuss the characteristics and vulnerabilities of security modes.

1. **What is the appropriate description for each TCB vulnerability?**

    ____ Maintenance hooks

    ____ TOC/TOU exploits

    ____ Race conditions

    ____ Buffer overflows

    a. Vulnerabilities in which two processes try to access and modify information at the same time.

    b. Make use of a weakness in the TCB where access is granted at one point in time and used much later on.

    c. Move too much information into a program memory area.

    d. Methods that are placed in operating systems and applications used for maintenance during development that can be used for unauthorized access.

2. **What is the order of the process steps when performing a trusted recovery?**

    Verify that all security-relevant items are correct

    Operate and run the system in single user mode to ensure file recovery

    Provide system availability for multiuser or network access

    Restore missing or corrupt files to obtain the most recent backups

3. **Which data recovery process potentially produces an insecure system environment?**

    a) Trusted recovery

    b) Untrusted recovery

4. **What is the appropriate description for each type of security mode?**

____ Dedicated

a. All users must have a proper clearance for the highest level of data classification on the system, formal access approval for all information they will access on the system, a signed NDA for all information they will access on the system, and a valid need to know for some of the information on the system.

____ System-high

b. Users are required to have a proper security clearance, formal access approval, a signed NDA, and a valid need to know for some information on the system.

____ Compartmented

c. All users must have proper security clearance for information they will access on the system, formal access approval, a signed NDA, and a valid need to know for some information on the system.

____ Multilevel

d. All users must have proper security clearance, formal access approval, a signed NDA, and a valid need to know for all information on the system.

TOPIC C
System Assurance

Addressing ways to ensure that your system architecture provides the anticipated security levels is paramount for an effective information systems security specialist. Knowing how to ensure that the appropriate safeguards remain in place is equally important. In this topic, you will evaluate system assurance components, standards, and processes.

Taking advantage of predefined models can save you time and take less effort. Using defined models to evaluate the system and assign levels of trust provides you with proven, accepted benchmarks. Thoroughly analyzing these system information evaluation models can increase your ability to ensure the trustworthiness of your system. Most organizations would not have the skills or resources to effectively test systems, especially systems, hardware, and software that they have purchased. In this case, it is often helpful to rely on work that is done by testing organizations. A vendor will submit their product, and have it independently evaluated against a system assurance model, and then be able to provide a rating to potential customers.

Trusted Computer System Evaluation Criteria

An organization's policy sets the security requirements for its systems. Once the systems are selected, the organization must evaluate them to determine whether they fulfill policy objectives. If each selecting organization separately evaluated each system, it would have overwhelming effects and produce a staggering workload.

The U.S. Department of Defense (DoD) realized this problem early on and decided to implement an evaluation process that was universal throughout the DoD. The first attempt of a system security evaluation was the *Trusted Computer System Evaluation Criteria (TCSEC)*.

The evaluation criteria were published in a book as part of a set called the *Rainbow Series*. Each book in the set had a different colored cover. The TCSEC specification was published with an orange cover and is often called the *Orange Book*. Due to its age and the fact that it is no longer actively used, some have wondered if it is still valid. Since it was so significant for so long and because it is the one that others are built from, it is still important to understand.

Trusted Network Interpretation

The DoD's Trusted Network Interpretation (TNI) extended TCSEC to include secure participation in computer networks. The TNI evaluates the TCB as it applies to networking, and determines the level of protection or risk when a network is used. This is called the *Red Book* in the *Rainbow Series*.

Trusted Data Interpretation

The DoD's Trusted Data Interpretation (TDI) is the extension of evaluation criteria to database implementations. Rather than looking at the database as a part of the host system's TCB, the database is evaluated as a standalone system with its own security environment and TCB. The TDI represents the first attempt to evaluate a system in parts. For example, the evaluation of an Oracle database can extend to any system using that database system. This is the *Purple Book*.

TCSEC Objectives

TCSEC designates different evaluation levels based on the implementation of certain objectives.

TCSEC Objective	Description
Policy	• Mandatory security policy—Implementing mandatory access control (MAC) • Discretionary security policy—Implementing discretionary access control (DAC)
Accountability	• Identification—Requiring a unique identification • Authentication—Requiring an authentication process • Auditing—Logging of access attempts and activities
Assurance	• Assurance mechanisms—Architecture, system integrity, security testing, design specification and verification, covert channel analysis, trusted facility management, trusted recovery, configuration management, and trusted distribution • Continuous protection assurance—Continual verification of the TCB
Documentation	• The *Security Features User's Guide* • The *Trusted Facility Manual*—Includes trusted recovery documentation • Test documentation and design documentation

TCSEC Divisions and Classes

TCSEC includes a specific series of divisions and classes.

Division	Classes
A—Verified protection	A1—Verified design • Employs formal methods of design verification
B—Mandatory protection	B3—Labeled security • Defines the security administrator • Trusted recovery • Monitoring and automatic notification B2—Structured protection • Device labels and subject sensitivity labels • Trusted path • Separation of duties (SoD) • Covert channel analysis B1—Labeled security • Labels and MAC • Process isolation and protection • Design specification and verification

Division	Classes
C—Discretionary protection	C2—Discretionary protection • Audit trail protection • Object reuse control C1—Controlled access • I&A • Discretionary resource protection
D—Minimal security	Not applicable

Information Systems Security Standards

Following the creation of the *Rainbow Series,* a number of other evaluation systems evolved, starting with a European-developed process and then a combination of views from Europe and the United States.

Security Standard	Description
ITSEC	Developed in Europe, the *Information Technology Security Evaluation Criteria (ITSEC)* security standard evaluates systems based on Security Targets (ST), provided by the customer, against the vendors, called Targets of Evaluation (TOE). The evaluations include functionality, how well the system works, and assurance—which rates the ability to evaluate the security of the system. Ratings are classified with Fn and En numbers, with the lowest numbers being the lowest evaluation scores. Functional levels are F1-F10, and assurance ratings are E0-E6. For example, a TOE may be evaluated as an F3+E3 system, which is equivalent to a TCSEC rating of B1. The functional levels are usually written to match TCSEC so "F3" is written as "F-B1." One significant difference between TCSEC and ITSEC is that ITSEC did not have specific security requirements mapped to particular levels. The security targets would specify what the requirements were and the evaluation was based on meeting those requirements. ITSEC vs. TCSEC: • E1, F-C1 = C1 • E2, F-C2 = C2 • E3, F-B1 = B1 • E4, F-B2 = B2 • E5, F-B3 = B3 • E6, F-B3 = A1

Security Standard	Description
Common Criteria	Developed in Europe, the United States, and Canada as a replacement for TCSEC and ITSEC. *Common Criteria* was published as ISO/IEC 15408. Similar to ITSEC, security targets can be submitted by consumers and describe system protection expectations. It can be difficult to compare competing products if each customer uses their own ST, so protection profiles (PP), which are a universal set of functional and assurance requirements for a category of products, are also included. The vendors will submit their Target of Evaluation (TOE) similar to ITSEC. Common Criteria labs perform system evaluations and produce ratings called *Evaluation Assurance Levels*. There are seven levels, EAL1 through EAL7, with EAL7 being the highest. Common Criteria levels: ● EAL1: Functionally Tested ● EAL2: Structurally Tested ● EAL3: Methodically Tested and Checked ● EAL4: Methodically Designed, Tested, and Reviewed ● EAL5: Semi-formally Designed and Tested ● EAL6: Semi-formally Verified, Designed, and Tested ● EAL7: Formally Verified, Designed, and Tested Common Criteria is groundbreaking because it offers consumers evaluated systems that match their needs. Participants in many different countries can share a single evaluation.
CMMI	The Software Engineering Institute created the *Capability Maturity Model Integration (CMMI)* to rate the quality of software coding practices. The evaluation looks at the processes involved in producing the software. By comparing different software organizations' CMMI ratings, associations can be made.
ISO 27002	Starting as British Standard (BS) 7799, then BS 17799, and renamed *International Organization for Standardization (ISO) International Electrotechnical Commission (IEC) 27002,* this document is the current international standard for information systems security. It provides guidance and best practices in the following areas: ● Security policy ● Organization and information security ● Asset management ● Human resources security ● Physical and environmental security ● Communications and operations management ● Access control ● Information systems acquisition, development, and maintenance ● Information security incident management ● Business continuity management ● Compliance

Certification and Accreditation

The last step in implementing system security is the certification and accreditation (C&A) process. *Certification* is essentially a risk evaluation and *accreditation* is an acceptance of the risk by the Designated Approving Authority (DAA).

Any system used by the U.S. federal government must have a C&A process performed successfully before it receives approval to operate. The NIST Special Publication 800-37 "Guide for Applying the Risk Management Framework to Federal Information Systems" provides instruction and guidance on certification and accreditation.

The phases of the security C&A process include:

1. Establishing a preferred level of security.
2. Defining a specific environment for system use.
3. Evaluating individual system security.
4. Evaluating network system security.
5. Evaluating physical security.
6. Comparing evaluations to security requirements.
7. Approving the system for a specific time period if the system meets requirements.
8. Evaluating and approving operation if substantial system changes occur before expiration.

ACTIVITY 2-3
Discussing System Assurance

Scenario:

In this activity, you will discuss the criteria, standards, and practices for implementing system assurance.

---

1. **Which of the following acronyms applies to the first national standard for system security evaluations?**

   a) DoD

   b) TCSEC

   c) TDI

   d) TNI

---

2. **What is the appropriate description for each TCSEC objective?**

   ___ Policy

   ___ Accountability

   ___ Assurance

   ___ Documentation

   a. This objective requires access to specific types of reference materials, such as the Security Features User's Guide, the Trusted Facility Manual, and test and design records.

   b. There are two types of this security objective: mechanisms and continuous protection.

   c. This objective includes three requirements: identification, authentication, and auditing.

   d. There are two types of this security objective: mandatory and discretionary.

---

3. **What is the appropriate description for each information systems security standard?**

____ ITSEC	a. This security standard was developed in Europe, the United States, and Canada as a replacement for TCSEC and ITSEC. Protection profiles are produced by systems consumers and describe system protection expectations.
____ Common Criteria	b. This security standard began as a British Standard. It is now the current international standard for information systems security.
____ CMMI	c. This security standard was created to rate the quality of software. The evaluation process reviews the methods involved in producing the software.
____ ISO 27002	d. This security standard evaluates TOE systems. Evaluations include functionality and assurance.

4. **What is the order of the first six phases of the security C&A process?**

Establishing a preferred level of security

Defining a specific environment for system use

Evaluating network system security

Comparing evaluations to security requirements

Evaluating physical security

Evaluating individual system security

Lesson 2 Follow-up

In this lesson, you analyzed security models and modes as well as system assurance requirements, and identified their relationships to security architecture and design. Using tools such as
security and information evaluation models will enable you to efficiently design a security
scheme that meets the demands of your current and future information systems.

1. **What unique system architecture security concerns would you have if your organization uses a distributed network?**

2. **What best practices would you consider for choosing the appropriate security mode
for your organization to ensure that the system functions within the appropriate
parameters?**

3 | Network and Telecommunications Security

Lesson Time: 3 hour(s)

Lesson Objectives:

In this lesson, you will analyze network security systems and telecommunications.

You will:

- Identify data network models and design.
- Identify remote data access to network systems.
- Analyze data network security.
- Apply data network management.

Introduction

Controlling user access to information is just one aspect of working in the information systems security industry. With those controls in place, you can focus on building network systems that provide a secure environment to share and distribute information. In this lesson, you will analyze network systems and telecommunications.

Access control provides security through established points of entry in a system. However, the nature of computer networks offers its own set of security concerns. Because network systems distribute users across broad geographic areas, other points of system penetration are created. By securing your network, you can ensure the reliability of stored and transmitted data.

This lesson supports content found in the Telecommunications and Network Security, Cryptography, Operations Security, and Physical (Environmental) Security domains of the CISSP® certification.

TOPIC A
Data Network Design

The assurance of network system security is dependent upon the design of an effective and well-rounded data network. The application of specialized models, topologies, protocols, and services is instrumental in building a secure data network from the ground up and employing secure data exchange as well as distributing confidential information among network resources. In this topic, you will identify data network design principles, topologies, protocols, and services.

Good network design will also influence the integrity and availability of the network. The layout of your data network can either be an asset to security or can increase the system's vulnerability for unauthorized access. In addition to improving system security, your design can enhance the manageability of the data network. Effective data network design can also have significant effects on data transmission time, improving user productivity. Utilizing proper data network design techniques can increase your ability to efficiently provide security and convenience to your network users.

Data Networks

Definition:

A *data network* is a collection of hardware and software that allows the exchange of information between sending and receiving application processes. Networking components include network media, such as a cable, to carry network data; network adapter hardware to translate the data between the computer and the network media; a network operating system to enable the computer to recognize the network; and perhaps most importantly, a network protocol to control the network communications.

Example:

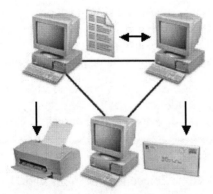

Figure 3-1: *A data network.*

The OSI Model

The evolution of data networks began in the early 1970s. At that time, each vendor created its own unique communications protocols with little or no interoperability. Beginning work in 1977 and publishing in early 1980, the International Organization for Standardization (ISO) implemented the *Open Systems Interconnection (OSI) model* for data communications. The intent was to provide a framework for all communications systems. The ISO committees were well aware of the various networking efforts. The goal was to create interoperability in networking products, as well as a way to reference networking topics. As part of this effort, they promoted encapsulation at the layers to allow for a certain amount of independence. The headers established for the layers allow for layer identification and communication. Abstraction is also part of this process. Abstraction attempts to hide header information from all but the immediately adjacent layers,

Today, the OSI model is used to describe the various functions provided in an information network without regard for any specific implementation. Consisting of multiple layers, it is a reference model for how data is exchanged between any two points in a network. Though the OSI model may seem a bit dated, the layers are still referenced frequently in documentation and by product vendors to indicate the function of devices; a Layer 3 switch, for example.

Figure 3-2: The OSI model.

OSI Model Layers

The OSI model encompasses seven different layers or functional differences.

OSI Model Layer	Function
Layer 7: Application	The *Application layer* is where applications send information into the communications network. Application interfaces built into the operating systems provide a portal for sending and receiving information.
	Examples of Layer 7 protocols include Simple Mail Transport Protocol (SMTP), Post Office Protocol version 3 (POP3), File Transfer Protocol (FTP), and the Hypertext Transfer Protocol (HTTP), amongst others. Many of the layers include a *Protocol Data Unit (PDU),* which is a unit of data as it appears at each later of the OSI model. The PDU at Layer 7 is the "data."
Layer 6: Presentation	The *Presentation layer* ensures that the receiver can properly interpret the transmitted information. Early issues included the translation from the Extended Binary Coded Decimal Information Code (EBCDIC) used on mainframe systems and the American Standard Code for Information Interchange (ASCII). Today, data representations such as MPEG, GIF, JPEG, and others are tagged when included in web pages, emails, or other documents to ensure the correct display of information. The Presentation layer can provide compression and encryption services as well.
Layer 5: Session	A *network session* is a persistent, logical connection between two hosts or nodes. When an application requires the creation of a session for any reason, the *Session layer* is used. Session startup, session continuation, and session termination are all functions of this layer.
	The Session layer allows for the transmission of information in three different modes:
	● *Full-duplex*—Simultaneous two-way data communication. A phone call is a full duplex conversation with both parties able to talk at the same time.
	● *Half-duplex*—Two-way data communication over a single channel; conversations with walkie-talkies are half-duplex with only one person being able to talk at a time.
	● *Simplex*—One-way data communication only; a radio station provides simplex communication.
	The network file system (NFS) and remote procedure calls (RPCs) use the Session layer.
Layer 4: Transport	As application information is delivered to the *Transport layer*, an application identifier is added to the data so that the receiving device knows which application is to receive the information. This application identifier is commonly implemented as a port number. The Transport layer accepts information and then creates smaller units called *segments* to control information flow, making sure it is more acceptable to the Layer 3 and 2 networks. The Transport layer may also implement some type of flow control so that information is not lost due to buffer overflow or other network problems. The Transport layer builds on the work done by the Session layer to create end-to-end connections between hosts.
	Examples of protocols that function at Layer 4 include Transmission Control Protocol (TCP) and the User Datagram Protocol (UDP). The protocols are functionally equivalent, but TCP is connection-oriented while UDP is connectionless. The decision regarding which of those two protocols to use is usually determined by the application, with a possible override by the user or an administrator. The PDU at the Transport layer is a "segment."
	Firewalls, gateways, and Layer 4 switches are all Transport layer devices.

OSI Model Layer	Function
Layer 3: Network	The *Network layer* is where the concept of logical networking is introduced. Layer 3 networks use a component of the logical addresses to represent networks. The logical address will be an IP address in most modern networks. In the past, it might have included Novell® IPX™ or Apple® AppleTalk®. In allowing the forwarding of packets and datagrams, Layer 3 can connect different physical networks by augmenting the Data Link layer information. The ability to move information between different physical networking structures gives data networks flexibility.
	At Layer 3, devices are grouped together in networks by a common network address. Each device must have a unique device within a network. A Layer 3 function called *routing* allows the devices in one network to send information to and receive information from other logical network devices. This requires the use of a *routable* protocol such as Internet Protocol (IP). Not all early protocols were routable because they had no way to distinguish unique networks.
	An example of a Layer 3 address is the IP address used in networks, such as the Internet, that are based on the Transmission Control Protocol/Internet Protocol (TCP/IP). An IP address, along with its subnet mask, can uniquely identify the network and the node of any device on the network.
	Routers and gateway devices support Layer 3. Routers can use dynamic routing protocols like Routing Information Protocol (RIP) and Open Shortest Path First (OSPF) to help discover available networks. The PDU at the Network layer is either packet or datagram, with packet being the most common term.
Layer 2: Data Link	The *Data Link layer* is where bits are organized into frames. Most Data Link layer protocols define the structure of a frame and introduce the use of Media Access Control (MAC) addresses. The MAC address is a 48-bit hexadecimal number that identifies the Organizationally Unique ID (OUI) and the serial number of the device. When transmitting a frame on the media, most protocols include a MAC address to indicate the sending and receiving devices.
	Transmission error detection is often included in a Data Link layer protocol. Ethernet uses a *Cyclical Redundancy Check (CRC)* function to discover errors. The CRC is included in a trailer or footer of each frame and is checked by the receiver. If the receiver's CRC calculation does not match the sender's, the receiver knows the frame no longer has integrity. At Layer 2, all network devices are considered to be on the same physical network. The Data Link layer was later split into two sub-layers, the Logical Link Control (LLC) and the MAC layers. LLC interfaces with the network layer above and the MAC with the Physical layer below.
	Bridges and switches support Layer 2.
	The PDU at Data Link layer is a "frame."
Layer 1: Physical	The *Physical layer* is where bits are transmitted across a physical medium. This layer describes the type of wire, fiber, or wireless communication medium and the transmission of bits. Connectors and physical network termination are also part of the Physical layer.
	Examples of Layer 1 items include Ethernet signaling, cabling, RJ45 connectors and jacks, and wireless access point frequencies.
	Repeaters, network interface cards (NICs), and hubs support Layer 1.
	The PDU at the Physical layer is a "bit."

Mnemonics and the OSI Model

Remembering the OSI layers is an essential task required of every CISSP® candidate. People often use the following mnemonics as a memory tool to help recall the order of layers.

- Please Do Not Throw Sausage Pizza Away (PDNTSPA) identifies the order of Layer 1 through Layer 7.

- Please Don't Nudge The Sleeping Porpoises Again (PDNTSPA) identifies the order of Layer 1 through Layer 7.

- All People Seem To Need Data Processing (APSTNDP) identifies the order of Layer 7 through Layer 1.

The TCP/IP Model

The *TCP/IP model* represents a collection of communications protocols used to govern data exchange on the Internet. It was developed in the late 1960s from a project sponsored by the Defense Advanced Research Projects Agency (DARPA) to design the Internet's protocols. Not only is TCP/IP the de facto protocol suite for the Internet, many vendors have adapted it for their default protocol as well. For example, Microsoft and Novell both now use TCP/IP as their networking protocol. Nearly all the work done on TCP/IP is documented in request for comments (RFCs).

TCP/IP Model Layers

The TCP/IP model is simple and specifies four different layers in the communication function.

TCP/IP Model Layer	Function
Application	The *Application layer* is similar in function to the Session, Presentation, and Application layers of the OSI model. At the Application layer, application programs begin the process of sending information, and end the process at the destination device or application.
Host-to-Host	The *Host-to-Host layer* is similar in function to the Transport layer of the OSI model. At the Host-to-Host layer, the TCP and UDP protocols support application-to-application information transfer using port numbers to identify the applications. These port numbers become very important for firewalls and other network devices to identify traffic on the network.
Networking	The *Networking layer* creates logical networks using IP network addresses. It is similar in function to the Network layer of the OSI model.
	IP is the networking protocol used in this model.
Network Access	The *Network Access layer* covers the physical networking requirements of generating frames on a cable, fiber, or wireless network. It is often compared to the Physical and Data Link layers of the OSI model.
	Ethernet is an example of a Network Access layer protocol that is used on the local area network (LAN). Frame Relay, X.25, and Asynchronous Transfer Mode (ATM) are examples of Network Access layer protocols used on the Wide Area Network (WAN).

The OSI model and the TCP/IP model are not related but their functions are often compared.

TCP/IP Protocols

There are several primary communications protocols that constitute the TCP/IP protocol suite.

TCP/IP Protocol	Description
ARP	The *Address Resolution Protocol (ARP)* is used in the TCP/IP model to resolve known IP addresses to unknown MAC addresses. By resolving the IP address of a device to an address that can be used to send information over the local LAN, IP devices are able to communicate over the Ethernet network.
RARP	The *Reverse Address Resolution Protocol (RARP)* is used when a device knows its MAC address but needs to request an IP address from a server. It can be used by diskless workstations in high-security environments.
IP	*IP* is used to move information between nodes on an IP network. It supports logical addressing in the form of an IP address and subnet mask combination. The IP protocol establishes encapsulation and support for the data delivered from the upper layers. IP is a connectionless protocol but it does check for header integrity with a checksum. IPv4 provides 32 bits for addressing. IPv6 provides 128 bits for addressing.
TCP	*TCP* is a connection-oriented protocol used in the TCP/IP model.
	TCP features a session establishment process, process identification using port numbers, a data accounting feature, data segmentation to meet network frame size limitations, error detection, retransmission of lost segments, flow control, and a session termination process.
UDP	*UDP* is a connectionless protocol that supports process identification using port numbers and error detection.
DHCP	The *Dynamic Host Configuration Protocol (DHCP)* is used to assign IP addresses to devices in an IP network. This occurs in the following four-step process using a DHCP server:
	1. Clients request the services of a DHCP server. This request will be sent as a broadcast to the entire network, as the client does not have a server's IP address to which it could send a unicast.
	2. When a client request is received, the server will send an offer. This offer will go out as a broadcast, as the client does not have an IP address at this time.
	3. When the client receives the offer, it will return a request for an address. The DHCP server manages a group of addresses known as a pool for each network. Addresses are assigned on a first come, first served basis.
	4. The server returns the address assigned. Addresses are provided for a given period of time using a lease process.
DNS	*Domain Name Service (DNS)* is a protocol that is used to resolve or translate device and domain names into IP addresses using a central repository of device names and IP addresses in each organization, and a locator function in the Internet to locate the organizational repositories.

TCP/IP Protocol	Description
IGMP	The *Internet Group Management Protocol (IGMP)* is used with IP multicasting to indicate when a device is joining a multicast-enabled application data stream.
ICMP	The *Internet Control Message Protocol (ICMP)* is used by operating systems and network devices to send error messages or relay messages back to devices that a device is unavailable. Ping and Traceroute use ICMP to help system administrators discover network congestion.
SMTP	The *Simple Message Transport Protocol (SMTP)* is a standard for email delivery. SMTP is used for outbound mail and for mail between messaging servers. Much of its earliest success was attributed to the "store and forward" method it used for delivering mail between systems.
POP and IMAP	Both the *Post Office Protocol (POP)* and *Internet Message Access Protocol (IMAP)* are considered mail retrieval protocols. IMAP generally leaves the messages on the server, allowing the user to check mail from several different hosts. POP generally pulls the mail down to the host the user is using. If the user checks email from multiple hosts, there is the potential for mail to be located on multiple machines.

 For a complete listing and description of protocols, visit **www.protocols.com/pbook/tcpip1.htm**.

Network Architecture Components

There are various components that make up the network architecture of a computer system.

Network Architecture Component	Description
Router	A *router* is a networking device used to connect multiple networks that employ the same protocol. Routers send data between networks by examining the network addresses contained in the packets they process. Routers can work only with routable protocols, which are network protocols that provide separate network and node addresses. Routers in turn use special routing protocols like RIP, Border Gateway Protocol (BGP), and OSPF to exchange information about routes between themselves. They then use this information to build routing tables. Routing protocols help establish the distance and/or cost to get from one network to another. They will also recalculate the routing tables if the network topology changes.
	A router can be a dedicated device, or it can be implemented as software running on a node, typically with two network interface cards. Routers can also be used as security devices because they can be configured to limit traffic entering or leaving different networks.
	Routers help to optimize network traffic by segmenting it into broadcast domains to reduce the number of stations competing for access to a particular network segment. Routers are Layer 3 devices.

Network Architecture Component	Description
Switch	A *switch* is an interconnecting network device that forwards frames to the correct port based on Media Access Control (MAC) addresses. A *MAC address* is a unique, hardware-level address assigned to network access devices, such as Ethernet cards, by its manufacturer.
	Switches work with pairs of ports, connecting two segments as needed. Most switches can work with multiple pairs of ports simultaneously to improve performance.
	Switches can be used as security devices by shutting down unused ports, by restricting port use to authorized devices, and by building virtual local area networks (VLANs) to isolate workgroup traffic on the same switch.
	Switches can optimize network traffic by segmenting into collision domains to reduce the number of stations competing for access to a particular network segment.
	Unless otherwise indicated, switches are Layer 2 devices. Modern switches may be capable of working at Layer 3 and even Layer 4, but they will be identified as such.
Gateway	A *gateway* is a device, software, or a system that converts data between incompatible systems. Gateways can translate data between different operating systems, between different email formats, or between totally different networks.
	Gateways can work at many different layers, from Layer 2 all the way to Layer 7.
Firewall	A *firewall* is a software program or hardware device that protects networks from unauthorized data by blocking unsolicited traffic. Firewalls allow incoming or outgoing traffic that has been specifically permitted by a system administrator, and enable incoming traffic that is sent in response to requests from internal hosts. Firewalls use complex filtering algorithms that analyze incoming packets based on destination and source addresses, port numbers, and data types.
	Firewalls can be found from Layer 3 through Layer 7.
Appliance	An *appliance* is a specialized device that supports one of many different network function types. An appliance is usually a single-purpose device with functionality that is limited to providing support for a single task.
	One example of an appliance is a bandwidth-limiting device. To better serve many different traffic types, it may be necessary to limit the amount of bandwidth used by one traffic type to allow other traffic to flow more readily. A *traffic shaper*, or *bandwidth limiter*, may restrict the amount of instant messaging traffic so that Voice over Internet Protocol (VoIP) traffic may use more bandwidth.
	Another example of an appliance might be a storage area-networking data repository.
	Appliances are available for every OSI layer.

It is important not to confuse a gateway with the default gateway in TCP/IP, which just forwards IP data packets. In the earliest days, routers were called gateways and they were the default route from one network to the next.

Data Network Types

Many types of data networks are commonly employed to allow users to share resources such as files, printers, and email.

Data Network Type	Description
LAN	A *local area network (LAN)* is a network established within a limited scope. Depending on the LAN protocol used, LANs are often implemented within workgroups, or a single building, floor, or room. In most cases, LANs are implemented using copper-based wiring systems or wireless components.
	An Ethernet LAN is an example of a data network. Ethernet network interface cards (NICs), wiring, switches, router interfaces, and driver software all make up the Ethernet network.
CAN	A *campus area network (CAN)* is used to connect buildings within a campus setting, such as a university or enterprise campus. Due to the extended distance between the network elements, CANs are often implemented using fiber optic media.
MAN	A *metropolitan area network (MAN)* is used within a metropolitan area, such as a provider-supplied network encircling a major metropolitan network. MANs are often implemented as Synchronous Optical Networking (SONET) rings. Metro Ethernet is becoming much more common.
WAN	A *wide area network (WAN)* is used to connect physically distributed networks over long, geographical distances. A WAN may use a provider service or may be a dedicated service created by the enterprise. WAN protocols are usually not the same as the protocols used in LAN, CAN, or MAN networks.
	A WAN includes technologies such as X.25, frame relay, High-Level Data Link Control (HDLC), and so on.
PAN	*Personal area networks (PANs)* are very small and might include small office home office (SOHO) networks, or just a mobile phone and a headset. Bluetooth is often used in a PAN. Bluetooth is a wireless technology operating in the 2.4 GHz spectrum.
	There are three classes of Bluetooth. Class one devices can work up to 100 meters, Class two is 10 meters, and Class three is less than 10 meters. Bluetooth security has been shown to be vulnerable and should be disabled if not needed.
Switched networks	Switched networks forward traffic between segments using a single type of network protocol, such as Ethernet. Switched networks provide traffic isolation services and forward frames at the Data Link layer of the OSI model.
Routed networks	Routed networks connect similar or dissimilar physical networks based on the existence of logical networks at Layer 3 of the OSI model. Routers may be used to connect various LANs or to connect LANs to CANs. A router is required when connecting a LAN to a WAN.

WAN Technologies

Here are some resources for future study on WAN technologies: **www.networkdictionary.com/ networking/WideAreaNetwork.php** and **http://en.wikipedia.org/wiki/HDLC**.

Data Network Topologies

Definition:

A *data network topology* is the physical and logical arrangement of nodes in a network. The physical arrangement describes the physical connections of cables and nodes. The logical arrangement describes the logical patterns of data flow. The most common types of data network topologies are star, bus, ring, and mesh. Networks can be cabled or wireless.

It is important to remember that the physical and the logical topology do not need to match. For example, a network could be a physical star and a logical bus. Every combination has been tried at some point and they all have conceptual advantages and disadvantages.

Example:

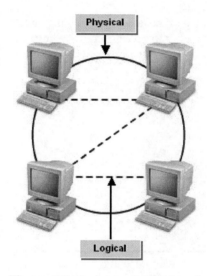

Figure 3-3: A data network topology.

Data Network Topology Types

The various topology types implemented have various advantages in terms of speed, efficiency, reliability, redundancy, and cost.

Data Network Topology Type	Description
Star	A *star topology* is a network topology in which all devices are connected to a central device that performs a traffic distribution function.
	In this topology, problems with cabling are usually isolated to a single device. But, you will need to run cable for each device back to the central collection point, resulting in a much larger amount of cable than in a bus, for example.

Data Network Topology Type	Description
Bus	A *bus topology* is a network topology in which all devices are connected to a single, linear communication path that is shared by all.
	The amount of cable is small, but a single break in that cable can result in the entire network being unavailable.
Ring	A *ring topology* is a network topology in which all devices are connected to a single, circular communication path with a structure that requires each node to connect directly to two other nodes.
	The amount of cable is only slightly more than a bus, but it can still suffer an outage if the ring is broken. Some implementations saw the use of dual rings to help provide resiliency, but this requires more cabling. Rings might also suffer from the delay of waiting for a token to make its way around the ring in order for you to communicate.
Mesh	A *mesh topology* is a network topology in which all devices, such as nodes, are directly connected to all other devices.
	This provides great resiliency, but can require an enormous amount of cabling and interfaces. It is usually only found on critical devices in the data center. The formula for determining the number of cables is (N * (N - 2)) / 2, where N is the number of devices.

Data Network Media Types

There are two main types of data network media.

Data Network Media Type	Description
Cabled	If your network is connected with physical cabling, then depending on the topology in use, the cabling of the network may be simple or complex. A star network is wired similarly to an enterprise telephone system, with all wiring going from a wall jack to a central location on a floor in a building. A mesh network is most complex because all devices must be connected.
	The type of cable you choose will also affect the security of the network. Copper cables will typically be more susceptible to interference and potential eavesdropping. Twisted pair cabling uses four pairs of wires twisted around each other. It can be either shielded twisted pair (STP) or unshielded twisted pair (UTP). The twist helps to prevent signals from one wire interfering with another, a phenomenon known as crosstalk.
	A cabled network is also referred to as a "bound" network.

Data Network Media Type	Description
Wireless	Wireless networking reduces the cabling burden for any topology. Most wireless devices today work as if they were wired in a star configuration with a central access point for the wireless network.
	Wireless networks can greatly increase the chance for eavesdropping as the signal is being propagated through the air. Wireless networks will typically use some sort of frequency hopping as a way to prevent eavesdropping or enhance quality. However, because these signals are being freely propagated through the air, some type of encryption is nearly mandatory.
	A wireless network is also referred to as an "unbound" network.

Cabled Network Media Types

There are multiple cabled network types.

Cabled Network Media	Description
Twisted pair wires	Twisted pair wires are categorized by type or category, with different types supporting faster transmissions. Category 3 cable is the minimum to support 10 MB Ethernet, with Category 5 supporting 100 MB and Category 5e and 6 supporting 1,000 MB.
Coax cable	Coax cable is a copper cable with a single core surrounded by an insulator, which in turn is covered with a metallic shield and then a plastic cover. It is used in older networks.
Fiber optic cable	Fiber optic cable is more expensive and physically more fragile than copper cables, but is nearly immune to eavesdropping. Fiber optic cable uses light waves instead of electrons to carry data and is capable of long distances and very high bandwidths. Fiber optics can use wave division multiplexing (WDM) by employing lasers of different frequencies to send multiple signals on the same piece of fiber optic cable. Fiber optic cable generally comes in multi-mode and single-mode. Multi-mode is a slightly larger cable (50-100 microns) and the light will reflect in slightly different paths down the cable. It is suitable for shorter distances, as the light is gradually dispersed. Single-mode is a smaller cable (10 microns) where the light is sent down the center of the cable and is capable of greater distances.

Network Transmission Methodologies

Some data network protocols are used on the physical network, OSI layers 1 through 3, while others provide support for connection and connectionless communications between applications, OSI layers 4 through 7.

Network Trans- mission Methodology	Description
Ethernet	*Ethernet* is a LAN and CAN protocol that supports communication between devices at the Physical and Data Link layers of the OSI model.
	Ethernet is supported by addresses assigned to each Ethernet interface. The MAC address uniquely identifies each Ethernet interface.
Cable modem	A *cable modem* is a specialized interface device used in a cable television infrastructure to provide high-speed Internet access to homes and small businesses.
DSL	*Digital Subscriber Line (DSL)* is an Internet access protocol that uses telephone lines and connections, such as Public Switched Telephone Networks (PSTNs), and digital signaling at high frequencies to attach users to the telephone company-supplied Internet Service Providers (ISPs).
T1s and T3s	There are several circuit standards that involve the bonding of multiple carrier channels to provide high-speed connections. A T1 carries 24 channels via time division multiplexing (TDM) and provides 1.544 Mb of throughput. A T3 is 28 T1s combined to give a throughput of 44.73 Mb.
Frame relay	Frame relay is a Layer 2 WAN protocol that uses permanent virtual circuits (PVC). Frame relay is a packet switched network with customers paying for data transferred. It uses a Data Link Connection Identifier (DLCI) as a Layer 2 address.
ATM	*Asynchronous Transfer Mode (ATM)* is a protocol used to move all types of data at high speeds in a fiber-based network.
	ATM creates a consistent 53-byte cell for all data entering the network so that traffic can be controlled without regard to the original size of the data packet.
MPLS	*Multiprotocol Label Switching (MPLS)* is a way to aggregate different types of traffic onto a MPLS cloud. MPLS uses labels to identify different types of traffic and can support voice and data on the same network. It is supported by the Internet Engineering Task Force (IETF) and is standardized in RFC 3031.
SONET	*Synchronous Optical Networking (SONET)* is a fiber optic-based network that is used to move data at higher speeds than a traditional WAN.
	SONET is often provided by common carriers like the local telephone companies. It is the foundation of many MAN implementations.
VPN	A *Virtual Private Network (VPN)* is not a technology or protocol as much as it is an idea. The idea is to create a protected pathway secured with various means and used to move enterprise information between corporate locations using the Internet instead of private corporate resources.
	The VPN allows connections between routers or concentrators when two locations are connected, or from a PC to a router when a single user connects to a corporate network.

Data Services

Definition:

Data services are the functions provided and the applications that are accessible when connecting devices to a network. They are combinations of hardware and software dedicated to managing network functions and resources. Typically, a data service is defined by its function. This goes back to the idea of subjects and objects.

Example: PC-to-LAN Connection

When you connect a PC to the LAN in an organization, the data service represented by the corporate email function is available to you.

Email client   Email server

Figure 3-4: *Email is a data service.*

Types of Data Services

There are many different types of network data services, including file, mail, and print services.

Data Service Type	Description
RPC	A *remote procedure call (RPC)* is a process used to cause the execution of a module, subroutine, or procedure at a remote location.
	Because accessing a file across a network system may involve using disparate systems that are not compatible, a broker agent may be invoked to make access available. RPC is associated with Layer 5 of the OSI model.
Directory services	A *directory service (DS)* is a data technology used to provide information about users and resources in a computer network.
	Many directory services contain access control mechanisms such as user identifications and authentication methods.
Data access services	A *data access service* is a function that mediates the access of data over a network.
	For example, Microsoft® uses the Common Internet File System (CIFS) to move data between machines in a network. Unix and Unix-like operating systems traditionally use a Network File System (NFS) for the same purpose.

Data Service Type	Description
Messaging services	Messaging services can be asynchronous or synchronous.
	Asynchronous messaging is a function where the sender and receiver are not directly and simultaneously interacting, and where some delay is included in the communication process.
	● Email is an example of an asynchronous messaging protocol. Email messages are composed and then transmitted over the network to an email server. At a later time, the email recipient retrieves the email from the server.
	● Email protocols include SMTP, POP3, and IMAP4.
	● The Network News Transfer Protocol is also asynchronous. Information is published on a news server and service consumers can go to the common repository to retrieve the posted information.
	Synchronous messaging is real-time communication between two or more people.
	● Instant messaging (IM) is a synchronous messaging protocol.
	● In IM, both participants in the communication process are online and send and receive messages to and from each other at the same time.
Data exchange services	A *data exchange service* is a protocol that allows individuals to access information on a central server and, in some cases, transfer that information to the individuals' local computers.
	The World Wide Web (WWW) uses Hypertext Transfer Protocol (HTTP) to make information available in a formatted structure to a computer with a web browser application. The format of the information is predetermined by the web designer. Other than small amounts of form data sent from the browser to the server, the majority of web traffic is from the server to the client.
	The File Transfer Protocol (FTP) is used to transfer raw data, pictures, and other information, without regard to the format, between a server and a client device. The FTP protocol does not restrict the direction of traffic between the client and server unless security restrictions are in place.
Peer-to-peer services	A *peer-to-peer service* is an application that does not use the typical client/server model for implementation. In peer-to-peer applications, all participants in the application are considered equals.
	A common example of peer-to-peer applications is a file-sharing application, like Napster, where all users are equal and no central server stores the information being shared.
Administrative services	*Secure Shell (SSH)* is an administrative services protocol that replaces Telnet and provides a secure, encrypted environment for command line access to devices, such as routers and switches, for configuration purposes.
	SSH can also be used to access some legacy applications that use a non-graphical user interface.
RAS	*Remote Access Service (RAS)* provides access to a computer system or network from a separate location, often for administrative reasons.
	In this context, applications such as Telnet, Remote Login (rlogin), Remote Copy (rcp), and Remote Shell (rsh) provide access to a second computer to control functions on that computer. The protocols listed here have no built-in security mechanisms other than the identification and authentication (I&A) afforded by the operating system of the machine being accessed.

Data Service Type	Description
Information services	An example of a network-based information service is the *Network Time Protocol (NTP)*. Using NTP, computers, routers, switches, firewalls, and other network components can synchronize their clocks with a central clock source. Many recent authentication protocols require a synchronized clock to prevent a replay attack, where a transmitted packet or message is captured and then sent at a later time for the purpose of breaking security.
VoIP	*Voice over IP (VoIP)* is a protocol that implements the transmission of voice using TCP/IP or UDP/IP.

ACTIVITY 3-1
Discussing Data Network Design

Scenario:

In this activity, you will discuss the principles, topologies, protocols, and services of data network design.

1. **Which one or more of the following items must be included in a data network?**

   a) Network protocol

   b) Network adapter hardware and drivers

   c) Network application

   d) Network media

2. **Which of the following reference models is a theoretical framework for the exchange of data between any two points on a telecommunications network?**

   a) Data service model

   b) TCP/IP model

   c) OSI model

   d) Data network model

3. **Which one of the following OSI model layers is not correct?**

   a) Layer 7: Application

   b) Layer 3: Physical

   c) Layer 6: Presentation

   d) Layer 2: Data Link

   e) Layer 5: Session

4. **Which model was developed in the late 1960s from a project sponsored by DARPA to design the Internet's protocols?**

   a) TCP/IP model

   b) OSI model

   c) ISO model

   d) IPX/SPX

5. **What is the appropriate description for each TCP/IP model layer?**

___ Network Access	a. Supports application-to-application information transfers using port numbers to identify the applications.
___ Networking	b. Handles the physical networking requirements of generating frames on a cable, fiber, or wireless network.
___ Host-to-Host	c. Creates logical networks using IP network addresses.
___ Application	d. Begins the process of sending information using application programs, then ends the process at the destination device or application.

6. **A multinational company with offices all over the world needs to communicate. What type of network will this be?**

   a) CAN

   b) WAN

   c) MAN

   d) LAN

7. **What is the appropriate description for each network component?**

___ Router	a. A networking device that connects various network segments based on hardware addresses.
___ Switch	b. A networking device used to connect multiple networks that employ the same protocol.
___ Firewall	c. A networking device that supports many different types of network functions.
___ Appliance	d. A software program or hardware device that protects networks from unauthorized data by blocking unsolicited traffic.

8. **What is a type of data network topology in which all devices are connected to a central device that performs a traffic distribution function?**

9. **What is a type of data network topology in which all devices are connected to all other devices?**

10. **Which one of the following is a connection-oriented protocol used in the TCP/IP model?**

    a) UDP

    b) TCP

    c) IP

    d) DNS

11. **True or False? Data services are combinations of hardware and software dedicated to managing network functions and resources.**

    ___ True

    ___ False

TOPIC B
Remote Data Access

As a security professional, understanding network security helps ensure you eliminate the risk of exposing network resources to unauthorized users. Added security measures for remote access users are critical because their identities cannot be verified by simple passwords alone. In this topic, you will identify remote data access to network systems.

Initially, data networks were designed to provide access to shared resources among users connected directly to the information system. Today, businesses and personnel are distributed around the globe. Remote users still require the same secure access to system resources and information, but added security measures are critical to ensure that your network is not compromised by unauthorized users. To create availability and integrity for remote users, you need to provide effective remote access to a data network. As users expect to be able to work farther from the office, using their own devices as well as devices supplied by the organization, companies will need to continually examine their remote access technologies.

Remote Access Technologies

Remote access is enabled through the use of dial-up telephone services, virtual private networking, and wireless services.

Remote Access Technology	Description
Dial-up	Using dial-up can be slow, but the technology is ubiquitous. While this is less applicable than it was a few years ago, this is still widely regarded as a plus when comparing dial-up to other technologies. Dial-up requires the use of a modulator-demodulator (modem) to translate digital information from a computer into a form that will be accepted by the analog telephone system.
	Dial-up services are limited to a 53 kilobit per second (kbps) transfer rate due to the nature of the telephone systems supporting the data transfer.
VPN	Implementing a VPN allows remote access to another network by transferring information from the remote client over the Internet. Because of the open nature of the Internet, it is important that a virtual "tunnel" is created to protect the data. Using secure transport protocols like Layer 2 Tunneling Protocol (L2TP) and Internet Protocol security (IPsec) helps accomplish this.
Wireless	The use of wireless networking as a remote access capability can be seen in two distinct ways.
	• A direct connection to a local network using 802.11 wireless capabilities.
	• A high-speed wireless interface connection to the mobile phone network.
	The mobile access capability is truly a remote access technology. The Wireless Access Protocol (WAP) provides security for handheld devices and is designed to use Wireless Transport Security (WTLS).

The IEEE 802.11 Standard

The 802.11 standard is a family of specifications developed by the Institute of Electrical and Electronics Engineers (IEEE) for wireless LAN technology. 802.11 specifies an over-the-air interface between a wireless client and a base station or between two wireless clients.

802.11 defines the access method as Carrier Sense Multiple Access With Collision Avoidance (CSMA/CA). For reliability, it specifies spread spectrum radio devices in the 2.4 gigahertz (GHz) band. It was amended to add the 5 GHz spectrum. It provides for both frequency-hopping spread spectrum (FHSS), direct-sequence spread spectrum (DSSS), and orthogonal frequency division multiplexing (OFDM). The 802.11b standard also defines a multichannel roaming mode and automatic data rate selection. It is important to remember that the 802.11 committees did not specify encryption or authentication. These were addressed with WEP, WPA, and WPA2.

Remote Access Protocols

Some remote access protocols deal with the Physical and Data Link layers while others focus on I&A.

Remote Access Protocol	Description
SLIP	The *Serial Line Internet Protocol (SLIP)* is a simple communications protocol that encapsulates IP datagrams carried over dial-up networks.
	The protocol is capable of identifying the beginning and end of an IP datagram. It does not employ error detection or correction. It also does not provide for authentication or encryption.
PPP	The *Point-to-Point Protocol (PPP)* is currently used to support dial-up services. It supports automatic configuration using the associated Link Control Protocol (LCP).
	For authentication, early PPP used a two-step authentication process known as the *Password Authentication Protocol (PAP)*. PAP should be abandoned because it sends passwords in cleartext. Current implementations use a three-step authentication processes known as the *Challenge-Handshake Authentication Protocol (CHAP)*. CHAP is a more sophisticated authentication process, relying on a three-way handshake. When a connection is requested, the server sends a challenge to the client. The client will use the challenge to create a hash of the password, which is returned to the server. The server can use the challenge it sent to hash the stored password and compare the hashes to see if the user is valid.
PPTP	The *Point-to-Point Tunneling Protocol (PPTP)* represents one of the earliest protocols used to implement VPNs. PPTP encapsulated PPP packets for remote delivery with IP over the Internet to the target network.
L2TP	*Layer 2 Tunneling Protocol (L2TP)* is a combination of PPTP and Layer 2 forwarding (L2F). It provides for authentication but not for confidentiality. For this reason, it is often implemented with IPsec, which can provide confidentiality and integrity.
IPsec	IP security (IPsec) is a framework of protocols and processes working together to provide security. IPsec can be deployed host-to-gateway, gateway-to-gateway, and host-to-host. IPsec can involve many different types of encryption to provide confidentiality, integrity, and authentication and non-repudiation.

Extensible Authentication Protocol

Extensible Authentication Protocol (EAP) is an authentication protocol that enables systems to use hardware-based identifiers, such as fingerprint scanners or smart card readers, for authentication. It also supports authentication at Layer 2. EAP categorizes the devices into different EAP types depending on each device's authentication scheme. The EAP method associated with each type enables the device to interact with a system's account database. The EAP client is referred to as the supplicant and it provides credentials to the authenticator. The authenticator can in turn request the services of an Authentication Server (AS). EAP was a part of 802.1x.

Wireless Security Protocols

Wireless security protocols need to evolve in order to adequately safeguard and protect network data. Due to the unbound nature of wireless, it is a tempting target.

Wireless Security Protocol	Description
WEP	*Wired Equivalent Privacy (WEP)* was the first attempt at securing wireless transmissions over the 802.11 networks. As the name implies, the level of security provided by WEP was equivalent to a wired network. WEP, however, has been shown to be vulnerable to attacks and can now be compromised in minutes.
WPA	*Wi-Fi Protected Access (WPA)* is a security standard that provides additional encryption capabilities for wireless transmissions. WPA introduced the *Temporal Key Integrity Protocol (TKIP)* as an improvement to the number of keys and usage of keys.
802.11i or WPA2	*802.11i,* also known as *WPA2,* is the latest advancement in the wireless protection protocols. It includes stronger encryption types than were available when WPA was introduced.

ACTIVITY 3-2
Discussing Remote Data Access

Scenario:

In this activity, you will discuss remote data access to network systems.

1. **Which one of the following remote access technologies uses secure transport protocols like IPsec to transfer information from a remote client over the Internet?**

    a) Dial-up

    b) Ethernet

    c) Wireless

    d) VPN

2. **Which one of the following actions is a capability of the PPTP remote access protocol?**

    a) Supporting automatic configuration using the associated LCP

    b) Encapsulating PPP packets for remote delivery over the Internet to the target network

    c) Identifying the beginning and end of an IP datagram

    d) Securing wireless transmissions over the 802.11 networks

3. **True or False? Wi-Fi Protected Access (WPA) is the latest advancement of the wireless protection protocols.**

    __ True

    __ False

TOPIC C
Data Network Security

With data access allocated to both local and remote users, and data networks designed to provide for data integrity, ensuring confidentiality is the next phase in networking systems and telecommunications. Enforcing rigorous security protocols and mechanisms is essential for preventing unauthorized intrusions and guarding against network attacks. In this topic, you will analyze data network security.

In a perfect world, the availability and integrity of the data network would be your only concern. Unfortunately, the world is not perfect and network administrators have numerous concerns for network security. Network vulnerabilities can be exploited and result in compromised system resources. Therefore, you need to take necessary measures to secure your data network.

Network Attacks

Networks are subject to a number of different attacks that jeopardize their ability to support confidentiality, integrity, and availability.

Network Attack	Description
DoS	Denial of service (DoS) attacks can be used to target the availability of the network or network services. DoS attacks may cause excessive use of network resources. They may also attempt to exclude user access to resources by causing a server overload or failure.
	Some examples of DoS attacks include the ping of death, smurf attacks, Fraggle attacks, and the TCP SYN flood.
	In a *SYN flood attack*, an attacker sends multiple SYN messages initializing Transmission Control Protocol (TCP) connections with a target host.
DDoS	A distributed denial of service (DDoS) is built on the idea of a DoS being propagated by thousands of hosts simultaneously. This is accomplished by compromising machines surreptitiously and then using those machines as a botnet.
Man-in-the-middle	A *man-in-the-middle attack* occurs when an attacker interposes a device between two legitimate hosts to gain access to their data transmissions. The attacker captures and reads each packet, responds to it, and forwards it to the intended host, so that both the sender and receiver believe that they are communicating directly with each other. This deception allows attackers to manipulate the communication rather than just observe it passively.
Spam	While *spam,* sometimes referred to as unsolicited commercial email (UCE), it usually does not cause a failure, but it can cause network over-utilization by filling networks with unwanted email messages. It also has the ability to fill email server storage systems to capacity and block needed emails in lieu of the spam content.
	As a network attack, spam is a general nuisance to users, help desk personnel, staff, and administrators.

Network Attack	Description
Virus	A *virus* is a malware or malicious program that attaches itself to another program. When the target program executes, the virus takes over and circumvents the security features of the system.
	Viruses can be used to steal data or cause a system failure.
Worm	A *worm* is a malware program that does not require the support of a target program like a virus. A worm is independent but is capable of duplicating itself to other devices in the network.
Trojan horse	A *Trojan horse* or *Trojan program* is unauthorized software that masquerades as legitimate software.
	Downloading a shareware program to clean a disk drive may look harmless, but if the program cleans the drive by reformatting it, the harm is obvious.
Malicious code	A *malicious code attack* is a type of attack where an attacker inserts some type of malicious software, or *malware*, into a user's system to disrupt or disable the operating system or an application. A malicious code attack can also force the target system to disrupt or disable other systems on the same network or on a remote network.

Security Protocols

Most security protocols today have been upgraded from their initial versions to provide increased protection, or have used other protocols to encapsulate their data in a secure envelope.

Security Protocol	Description
SSL	*Secure Sockets Layer (SSL)* is a protocol used to provide confidentiality services to an IP protocol suite for information transfer. While SSL is often associated with HTTP, it can be used by a much wider set of protocols.
	The identity of the server is authenticated so that server spoofing cannot occur. Server authentication is often enabled by using a digital certificate.
TLS	*Transport Layer Security (TLS)* is an updated version of SSL. Added services include mutual authentication.
HTTPS	HTTP was not initially secure. *Hypertext Transfer Protocol Secure (HTTPS)* is a secure version of HTTP that supports web commerce by providing a secure connection between the web browser and server. To gain security, SSL or TLS is used to protect information carried in an HTTPS message.

S-HTTP

The *Secure Hypertext Transfer Protocol (S-HTTP)* is an alternate form of protection for HTTP data. It was an attempt to provide encryption at Layer 7, and encrypt the page data but leave the rest of the packet unchanged. Because it was not adopted by Netscape® or Microsoft®, it fell from favor with those companies accepting the HTTPS solution.

Network Security Mechanisms

Networks can be protected from attacks by using different mechanisms to prevent or identify the attacks as they occur.

Network Security Mechanism	Description
ACL	An access control list (ACL) on a router can protect traffic with rules that either permit or deny traffic through the router. With a consistent *deny all* philosophy, rules can be written to permit access by IP address, protocol type, application type, and session status. When implemented in a router, the ACL is taking time away from the routing function, so limiting the number of rules is a best practice. ACLs attempt to prevent attacks.
Firewall	Many administrators place hardware-based firewalls between the external and internal network components to protect the systems. Firewalls are rule-based devices like routers, but unlike routers, they are dedicated to protection. Firewalls may come with a predefined set of rules that can be implemented quickly.
IDS	An implemented intrusion detection system (IDS) can detect unwanted network attacks and alert an administrator to such events. IDS devices use a signature file that contains patterns of activity known to represent an attack. Signature-based IDS systems require frequent updates of signature files to remain current on known attacks. In some cases, the IDS uses behavioral analysis to detect attacks. Behavioral IDS systems develop a baseline of allowed network activity through experience and take time to build effectiveness. An IDS relies on the administrator to react to the intrusion events. It is a passive device. There are *network intrusion detection systems (NIDS)* and *host-based intrusion detection systems (HIDS)*.
IPS	Using an intrusion prevention system (IPS) can be helpful in network security. The IPS is placed inline: once in place, it can monitor and react when intrusions are identified and block the event. IPS devices are active and can be subject to a DoS attack when the IPS itself is attacked. There are *network intrusion prevention systems (NIPS)* and *host-based intrusion prevention systems (HIPS)*.
SEM	*Security event management (SEM)* is the collection and analysis of security event logs from a wide variety of devices. It could include servers, routers, IDS, and IPS. It involves using system logic to reduce the tens of thousands of log entries into a manageable number.

Types of Firewalls

Firewall configuration and deployment comes in many different forms, depending on the purpose of the firewall. It pays to think about the layers of the OSI model that different types of firewalls operate at. Packet filtering and stateful inspection firewalls look at the information in Layer 3 and Layer 4 headers. Proxy and application layer firewalls look at Layers 5 through 7.

Firewall Type	Description
Packet filtering firewalls	These firewalls make decisions on packets as they move through the firewall. Each packet is treated individually and oftentimes the firewall is simply making decisions on the Layer 4 port number. The firewall generally starts by blocking all ports and then, as business needs dictate, certain ones are opened up. For example, the company may decide that it needs SMTP (25) and HTTPS (443) to be allowed through.
Stateful inspection firewalls	These firewalls are a bit more sophisticated than packet filtering firewalls and will actually be able to determine the "state" of the packet. These firewalls can determine if the packet being evaluated is related to an earlier packet and if the conversation was initiated inside or outside.
Proxy firewalls	Devices that act as intermediary servers or gateways. They will terminate the connection and then re-initiate it if the traffic is warranted. A proxy firewall also has the added benefit of hiding the identity of the original sender, as it now appears that the conversation is coming from the proxy firewall.

Additional Firewall Terms

Additional firewall terms include:

- A hardened server may present itself as a *bastion host.* By removing all unnecessary services from the bastion host, the device becomes less vulnerable to attacks and protects itself. Servers presented to the Internet should be configured as bastion hosts for the greatest level of protection.

- *Dual-homed firewalls* have two network ports. One port faces the Internet, or the untrusted part of the network, and the other port faces the trusted part of the network. These often form the inner and outer perimeters of networks.

- A *screening host* is a firewall with limited capabilities, such as a router that protects the trusted part of the network with ACLs.

- A *screened subnet* is often called a *demilitarized zone (DMZ).* The DMZ is an area in a network where resources are made available to Internet users. The devices in the screened subnet are often bastion host devices with specific applications used by external users and internal users alike. Some screened subnets are termed *extranets* because they provide corporate information systems access to external customers and partners.

- *Network Address Translation (NAT)* is frequently the firewall's job. A NAT device translates a private IP address used inside networks, as defined by RFC 1918, to a public IP address that is routable on the Internet. *Port Address Translation (PAT)* is a type of NAT that uses port numbers, as a means of providing uniqueness, to allow hundreds of internal users to be serviced by a single, exterior IP address.

Remote Access Security Mechanisms

You can use centralized authentication protocols, such as RADIUS, TACACS, and Diameter, to secure remote access connections to your system.

Remote Access Security Mechanism	Description
RADIUS	The *Remote Access Dial-In User Service (RADIUS)* is an authentication protocol that verifies the identification of authorized users and then performs authentication. Once RADIUS has authenticated the remote user, predetermined user attributes stored in the RADIUS database are provided to the access hardware and/or software. Upgrades have also provided an auditing component which allows it to complete the "AAA" functions for authentication, authorization, and accounting.
	RFC 2865 describes RADIUS as a client/server protocol. As users attempt to gain access to the networks through the Network Access Server (NAS), credentials are sent to the RADIUS server. The RADIUS server is responsible for receiving connection requests, authenticating the user, and passing access capabilities and configuration information back to the access server.
	User profiles are maintained in a centralized database accessed by the RADIUS processes. Even though RADIUS was initially designed to support dial-in services, RADIUS servers can provide controlled access to wireless networks and, through the support of 802.1X, provide authenticated access at Layer 2 for Ethernet switches.
	RADIUS is not a single sign-on (SSO) solution, but an authentication capability.
TACACS, TACACS+, XTACACS	The *Terminal Access Controller Access Control System (TACACS)* is a RADIUS-like system with improvements.
	RFC 1492 describes the inner workings of TACACS. TACACS accepts login requests and authenticates the access credentials of the user. Extensions to the TACACS protocols exist, such as Cisco's TACACS+ and XTACACS. XTACACS was created to extend the original TACACS protocol.
	TACACS includes process-wide encryption for authentication while RADIUS only encrypts passwords.
Diameter	*Diameter* is an authentication protocol that improves upon RADIUS by strengthening some of its weaknesses. Diameter is backward-compatible with RADIUS.
	RFC 3588 describes Diameter as follows: "The Diameter base protocol is intended to provide an AAA framework for applications such as network access or IP mobility. Diameter is also intended to work in both local AAA and roaming situations."
	The name Diameter comes from the claim that Diameter is twice as good as RADIUS. Diameter is a stronger protocol in many ways but is not as widespread in its implementation due to the lack of products using it.

ACTIVITY 3-3
Discussing Data Network Security

Scenario:

In this activity, you will discuss data network security.

1. **What is the appropriate description for each network attack method?**

   ___ DoS
   a. Causes network over-utilization by filling networks with unwanted email messages.

   ___ Spam
   b. A malware or malicious program that attaches itself to another program.

   ___ Virus
   c. Unauthorized software that masquerades as legitimate software.

   ___ Worm
   d. An independent malware program capable of duplicating itself to other devices in the network.

   ___ Trojan horse
   e. Causes excessive use of network resources and excludes user access to resources by causing a server overload or failure.

2. **A user calls the help desk complaining that there is a strange application on his computer. Upon further investigation, you discover that he had downloaded what he thought was a music application, but was actually some type of unauthorized software. Which of the following attacks could this be?**

   a) Spam

   b) DoS

   c) Worm

   d) Trojan horse

3. **Your users cannot access a server and you notice almost 100% network saturation. Which of the following attacks might be underway?**

   a) Spam

   b) DoS

   c) Worm

   d) Trojan horse

4. **Which one of the following security protocols is an upgraded version of SSL?**

   a) TLS

   b) S-SSL

   c) HTTPS

   d) S-HTTP

5. **Which of the following network security mechanisms detects unwanted network attacks and alerts an administrator to the event?**

   a) Firewall

   b) ACL

   c) IPS

   d) IDS

6. **Your company uses an IP mobility application and you want your roaming wireless remote users to be able to access the company network securely. Which one of the following remote access mechanisms will you check?**

   a) TACACS

   b) RADIUS

   c) Diameter

   d) Circumference

7. **Your network has been attacked and you want to check the inline device that should have identified the intrusion and blocked it. Which of the following network security mechanisms will you check?**

   a) Firewall

   b) ACL

   c) IPS

   d) IDS

TOPIC D

Data Network Management

A thorough and complete network design provides for convenient access to system resources by both local and remote users. If implemented successfully, the shared data is valid and the system is secure. The next step is to incorporate the controls needed to keep the network operating at peak efficiency. In this topic, you will apply data network management.

A data network should be designed for performance, usability, and security. But what happens when the data network goes down? Users are unable to access system resources, productivity decreases, and the business suffers. Or worse, data could be irrevocably damaged or lost. To ensure reliability and avert a data-related catastrophe, you need to effectively manage the data network.

RAID

Redundant Array of Independent Disks (RAID), or *Redundant Array of Inexpensive Disks*, is used to provide better disk performance or data redundancy depending on the implemented RAID type. RAID systems can incorporate striping, mirroring, and parity to provide high availability.

- RAID can be used to increase performance if striping is implemented. *Striping* is a disk-performance-enhancement feature in which data is spread across multiple drives to improve read and write access speeds. By distributing data among drives, the disk-platter rotation and disk-actuator movement that controls the read/write head can be optimized. Striping offers no protection to data if a drive is lost.

- To improve data redundancy, RAID may be used to automatically *mirror* information written on one drive to a second drive. If the first drive fails, the second drive is automatically put in service.

- *Duplexing* is the additional protection of having multiple hard drive controllers.

- *Parity* is another method that can improve redundancy. With a parity system, data is written as if it were being striped, but one of the volumes contains information that will allow the re-creation of lost data if a drive fails.

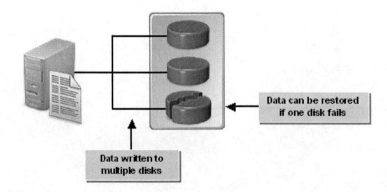

Data can be restored if one disk fails

Data written to multiple disks

Figure 3-5: RAID.

RAID Levels

Many types of RAID have been tried over the years. Some like RAID 0, 1, and 5 have become industry standards. RAID 2, 3, and 4 were not widely adopted but still helped to define techniques used today. The CISSP candidate should be familiar with all of the following RAID levels.

RAID Level	Description
Level 0	Striping of data on multiple disk drives for better performance. Provides no redundancy.
Level 1	Mirroring or duplexing of data on drives for redundancy. In *mirroring*, the two disks share a drive controller. In *duplexing*, each disk has its own drive controller, so the controller card does not impose a failure. Data is written to both halves of the mirror simultaneously. Disk write performance may be negatively impacted but disk reads may be slightly improved. This increases hardware costs because you will need to purchase two drives for every single device equivalent.
Level 2	Striping of data with an error correction code (ECC) for redundancy. It is not commercially viable.
Level 3	Striping of data at the byte level with parity information on a single drive for redundancy. It does not improve performance. The dedicated parity disk can be a bottleneck when implementing RAID 3. The single parity disk is also a risk to redundancy if the drive fails.
Level 4	Striping of data at the block level with the parity information on a single drive for redundancy. It does not improve performance. As with RAID 3, the dedicated parity disk can be a bottleneck when implementing RAID 4. The single parity disk is also a risk to redundancy if it is the drive that fails.
Level 5	Striping of the data and the parity information spread across all drives for redundancy. RAID 5 tolerates a single drive failure without forcing a recovery. Distributing parity in RAID 5 removes the bottlenecks seen in RAID 3 and 4. It requires a minimum of three drives. It has a higher hardware cost than RAID 0 but less than RAID 1.
Level 6	Striping of data with two levels of parity calculation and parity information spread across drives for redundancy. RAID 6 tolerates two drives failing without forcing a recovery.
Level 10	A combination of RAID level 1 and RAID level 0. Data is first mirrored onto the RAID drives for redundancy. Each mirrored set is then striped for performance. This is sometimes referred to as nested RAID. You might also see it as RAID 1 + 0 or RAID 5 + 0.

SAN, NAS, and RAIT

Storage Area Networks (SANs) and *Network Attached Storage (NAS)* devices will include many different options to allow for redundancy. Many of these are built on the concepts of RAID. The concepts of RAID can also be extended to tape drives, in which case it is referred to as *Redundant Array of Independent Tapes (RAIT)*.

 The idea of presenting multiple disks to the operating system as a single disk or volume, as in RAID, is also referred to as concatenation.

Data Backup

Definition:

A *data backup* is a second copy of data captured at a point in time and stored in a secure area as a precautionary safeguard in case of a disaster. Backups can use a variety of media copy mechanisms and different methods for selecting the data to back up. These variables affect the amount of data stored and the amount of time and media required for the backup.

Example:

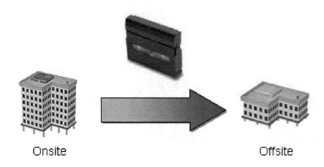

Onsite   Offsite

Figure 3-6: Data backup.

Example: Magnetic Tape Database Backup

Organizations often back up databases to magnetic tape on a regular basis and then transport the tapes to an offsite, secure storage facility for protection. This affords protection in case of catastrophic losses at the original location. Even though the industry has relied on tapes for years, many organizations are moving to disk-to-disk and online backups.

Data Backup Methods

There are several standardized data backup methods.

Data Backup Method	Description
Full backup	A *full backup* is a method that backs up all selected files. It is used as a starting point for all backup activities. As the name suggests, all information is copied to the backup media.
	Microsoft® operating systems use the archive bit to identify modified files. Other backup software keeps track of modifications internally. When a file is modified, the archive bit is turned on. The full backup then clears the archive bit, making it easier to identify files needing backup and those that have not been modified.
Incremental backup	An *incremental backup* clears the archive bit and reduces backup time and media. An incremental backup copies files and databases that have been modified since the last full backup.
	Restoring an incremental backup requires the copying of the last full backup plus all incremental backups in the sequence in which they were created.

Data Backup Method	Description
Differential backup	A *differential backup* copies all modifications since the last full backup to the backup media. It does not turn off the archive bit; over a period between full backups, the amount of media required for a differential backup continues to grow.
	Restoring the differential backup requires copying the last full and last differential backups.
Remote journaling	*Remote journaling* is a method wherein real-time copies of database transactions are stored in journals at a remote location. Journals can be replayed to transfer a database back to normal conditions.
	Should a disaster occur, the latest copy of the database is restored and the database then reprocesses the remote journal up to the last successfully completed transaction.
Electronic vaulting	*Electronic vaulting* is used to copy modified files to an offsite location. It is not done in real time like remote journaling.
	To restore an electronic vault after failure recovery, the files are copied back to the failed site over the network.

Single Points of Failure

A *single point of failure* is any device, circuit, or process that causes the unavailability of data upon failure, thus requiring consistent maintenance and redundancy.

Failure Point	Description
Disks	All RAID forms except for RAID 0 reduce the threat of loss due to disk failures and provide protection.
Circuits	To reduce the damage caused by the loss of a communications circuit in a data network, a backup circuit should be made available and installed. The backup circuit may be used on either an on-demand basis or all the time. If the primary circuit is interrupted, the network continues to operate on the second, or backup, circuit on a limited performance basis.
Servers	Server clustering allows servers to work together to provide access, ensuring minimal data loss from a server failure. Should one of the servers in the cluster fail, the remaining servers, or server, will assume the responsibilities, but with the possibility of decreased performance. When the failed server is restored, it will integrate back into the cluster and reinstate full performance.
Routers	*Router redundancy* is the technique of deploying multiple routers in teams to limit the risk of routing failure should a router malfunction. The routers in a redundant environment share common configurations and act as one to route and control information. They communicate with each other to determine if everything is functioning well. If one of the redundant routers fails, the remaining routers assume the load and sustain the routing process.

ACTIVITY 3-4
Discussing Data Network Management

Scenario:

In this activity, you will discuss the application of data network management.

1. **What may be used to improve data redundancy by automatically mirroring information written on one drive to a second drive?**

2. **Which data backup method is used to copy modified files to an offsite location?**
    a) Remote journaling
    b) Electronic vaulting
    c) Incremental backup
    d) Differential backup

3. **Which of these are single points of failure?**
    a) Disks
    b) A local LAN
    c) Servers
    d) Circuits

4. **As a starting point for all backup activities, what backup method should be used?**
    a) Electronic vaulting
    b) Incremental backup
    c) Differential backup
    d) Full backup

5. **A single drive has failed but recovery is not forced due to distributing parity information on all striped drives. What RAID level is in use?**
    a) Level 4
    b) Level 5
    c) Level 0
    d) Level 1

Lesson 3 Follow-up

In this lesson, you analyzed the models and topologies, services and technologies, and protocols and attack methodologies that apply to network systems and telecommunications. This information will help you effectively build networks that provide a secure environment to share and distribute information. Securing your network systems properly will limit system attacks, ultimately ensuring the reliability of stored and transmitted data.

1. **Which backup methods have you used in your organization?**

2. **What OSI models have you implemented on the job? How do you apply the OSI model to your data network environment?**

4 | Information Security Management Goals

Lesson Time: 2 hour(s), 15 minutes

Lesson Objectives:

In this lesson, you will analyze information security management goals.

You will:

● Identify organizational security.

● Identify the application of security concepts.

Introduction

With access controls and network security addressed, it is important for management to assess its organizational goals to ensure that security issues are aligned with business objectives. In this lesson, you will analyze information security management goals.

Security is a collective responsibility within any organization. However, without the backing of management, little can be done to enforce a comprehensive security program. By aligning your security management goals with business goals, you can guarantee the support you will need to initiate and manage a successful security program.

This lesson supports content found in the Information Security Governance & Risk Management and Legal, Regulations, Investigations, and Compliance domains of the CISSP® certification.

TOPIC A
Organizational Security

Implementing active security practices allows you to effectively negate threats, vulnerabilities, and risks to your information systems. Organizing security helps to manage identified setbacks by providing preventive and protective measures to ensure the confidentiality, integrity, and availability of data and resources. In this topic, you will identify organizational security goals, concepts, practices, and processes.

Because security management is the foundation for a dependable and protected business environment, organizational security needs to be well established. Even though senior management is ultimately responsible for security, it is important for everyone in your organization to understand and be responsible for his or her own role in maintaining security. Employing the applicable organizational goals and concepts set forth by security management will help you implement security policies and protection mechanisms in your organization.

The Importance of Information Security

Information security provides protection for important business resources. Often, information security focuses on safeguarding data to enforce protection based on the confidentiality, integrity, and availability of that data in a logical sense. This protects the network so that hackers cannot gain access to specific resources. It is also important to protect information through good physical security practices. Unauthorized access to computer facilities, telecommunications closets, and wired network resources can drastically compromise security and damage your information systems.

Another reason that information security is important is that corporations and other business entities have an obligation under law to provide protection. Government laws and regulations place the burden of providing adequate data protection on organizational management.

Security Goal Categories

There are three security goal categories designed to address the short-, medium-, and long-term security goals of an organization.

Security Goal Category	Description
Operational	Short-term security goals. These deal with the daily and weekly operations of the organization, including how tasks are performed.
Tactical	Medium-term goals. These deal with security issues that require weeks to months of effort to accomplish.
Strategic	Long-term security goals. Timelines of months to years are involved. These deal with the overall integration of security into the foundation of the organization.

Security Goal Considerations

Regardless of the type of security model employed, security goals are necessary in an organization to support the maintenance of the confidentiality, integrity, and availability (CIA) triad of information. Examples of security goals can include:

● Implementing strong network logon authentication with single sign-on (SSO) capabilities.

● Increasing security by preventing users from downloading or using non-trusted content.

● Using certificates to provide integrity and *non-repudiation*, or proof that a given sender did send a message, for general business email messages sent within the organization.

● Providing integrity, non-repudiation, and confidentiality for all business email messages between executive management and trusted executive staff members.

● Enforcing authentication, integrity, and confidentiality for all accounting transactions.

● Enforcing security programs that limit the opportunity for fraud and collusion within the organization.

 Some of these goals are stronger than others. General email may need integrity and non-repudiation, but email between corporate officers is afforded confidentiality protection as well. Security goals will vary among different organizations. There is no one right set of goals. Goals are established based on protection requirements.

The Risk Assessment Process

Determining what to do first in information security is influenced by the amount of risk involved in each environmental security threat. Prioritization of your security efforts, along with identifying whether the tasks are operational, tactical, or strategic is fundamentally important. For example, the absence of a security guard at the front door of a building may lead to unauthorized access to the facility. To properly identify what might happen in this scenario:

1. Conduct a vulnerability assessment to pinpoint the areas where an unauthorized individual might access or damage resources or data.

2. Ascertain the risk of someone actually accessing or damaging information.

3. Employ the appropriate countermeasure to help reduce the risk.

4. Periodically review the countermeasure to make sure it continues to be appropriate and effective.

The Evolution of Information Security Threats

The quick and constant changes in technical environments substantially impact the treatment and management of information security. As technologies, protocols, and business processes change, the security risks should be reassessed constantly.

Technical Environment Change	Security Impact
Computer systems	• Mainframe systems were physically isolated entities, and as such required strong physical security. • Users rarely came in direct contact with the mainframe, so the doors to the room or the building that housed the mainframe defined the security perimeter. • As online transaction processing began, users had virtual access to the system and were required to log in and be authenticated. • The way the user saw the computer changed. • Security became an individual's responsibility.
Computing processes	• Little or no logical security was initially used when computer terminals were replaced with personal computers. • The application's security was imbedded in the application. • Personal computer protection reverted to physical protection.
Personal computing and LANs	• As personal computers were attached to local area networks (LANs), systems changed and logical protection became necessary. • The login was used again.
Internet conception and evolution	• Before the Internet, information was controlled by organizations. • Outside information was introduced into the internal systems through well-controlled processes. • The Internet allowed any of its available source information to be introduced into organizations. • Risks rose to a very high level. • Safeguards such as virus scans, firewalls, intrusion detection systems (IDSs), and others raised the cost of information security in an effort to protect organizational resources.
Laptops and portable computing	• When business networks became open to portable computing and a mobile workforce, it increased asset vulnerability. • Greater protection was required to secure computer data from external threats such as physical laptop damage and theft. • Portable devices are becoming increasingly popular and powerful and are capable of holding significant amounts of company data. This will require securing the devices with passwords and encryption.
Virtualization	• As applications and server devices no longer have a one-to-one relationship with hardware, it will become increasingly important to track the use of virtual applications, virtual servers, and virtual storage.
Cloud computing	• In many cases, the cloud introduces additional virtualization of an organization's data with it being completely removed from the organizations.

Defense in Depth

Definition:

Defense in depth is a risk concept that is used to mitigate security threats at multiple levels within the networks and systems. Defense in depth employs a layered approach to keep hackers and malware out of a network. The firewall or router implements access rules; the stateful inspection firewall limits hacker access that is not caught by the first line of defense; virus detection software protects individual devices in the network; the IDS alerts managers to possible incursions; and the intrusion prevention system (IPS) eliminates the threats by blocking traffic.

Example:

Figure 4-1: Defense in depth.

A Physical Security Perspective

From a physical security perspective, defense in depth is implemented in the prison system to safeguard against risk and protect the surrounding community. Prisons use defense in depth to fortify the environment and keep inmates within the designated confines. Reinforced doors and small windows help to secure cells and deter inmates from escaping. Gates and bars keep prisoners in their respective areas. High walls help to reinforce perimeter security. Finally, high fencing, multiple fences, and razor wire act as protective countermeasures to defend society against prisoners.

Secure Outsourcing and Offshoring

Outsourcing is using a chosen partner organization for business processes that were previously completed internally. *Offshoring* is outsourcing in another country. The current trend in outsourcing security services and processes to external companies presents a myriad of security concerns. Outsourcing does not reduce security risks. Instead, security functions are transferred to the outsourcing provider or organization. This does not change the fact that the sponsoring organization is still ultimately responsible for its own security. The organization's management needs to manage the outsourcing partner as the organization would be managed. It is also important to make sure that, if work is offshored, the vendor will follow all of the relevant laws that apply to the originating organization. During the process of locating and contracting with outsourcing providers, an enterprise should perform several essential action items to negate adverse risks and maintain security. These action items are:

1. Evaluate the security environment and practices of each organization.

2. Enforce the same security requirements in the outsourcing provider that are found within the enterprise.

3. Audit and review security activities after the contract has been signed.

Internal and External Security Considerations

Before outsourcing to a particular organization, an enterprise should weigh the outsourcing provider's security practices against its own internal standards and criteria. A series of specific questions should be addressed to help the enterprise in its decision-making process. These include:

- What risks and threats are found at the location?
- What hiring procedures are in place?
- Are background checks used, and are they adequate?
- What security training practices are used?
- Is remote access to logs available?
- Does the outsourcing location allow unannounced, periodic audits?

Service Level Agreements

Definition:

A *service level agreement (SLA)* is a business document that is used to define a pre-agreed level of performance for an activity or contracted service. If the service is contracted and not delivered with the agreed-upon level of performance, the SLA has been violated and a penalty will be enforced. The internal use of an SLA in an organization will assist management in determining the level of performance for each business unit.

Example: Network Resource Uptime

For example, the IT department has developed and agreed to an internal SLA that requires 99.99% uptime for all network resources. The failure to meet the uptime requirement may point to many different issues that need remediation. Without the SLA, low performance levels are often difficult to determine. With the SLA, the accepted level of performance is agreed to in advance and under-performance is easily identified.

CISSP Risk Reduction Measures

CISSP® is a change agent in an organization. The 10 domains of the Common Body of Knowledge (CBK) represent the security practice areas that CISSP must understand to provide service to an employer or a client. CISSP can help reduce risk by:

● Evaluating the security posture of the organization to identify risks.

● Assisting in the creation of security policies that help identify risk and require appropriate risk-reduction measures.

● Providing training to all levels of the organization on present security risks and protection methods.

Specific Threats and Countermeasures

Specific security threats can be targeted through several countermeasures that provide proper risk protection against information disclosure or damage.

Security Threat	Description/Countermeasure
Social engineering	**Description:** Social engineering crimes like phishing are perpetrated to gain access to personal information. They use the trust of the targeted individual to overcome information safeguards. **Countermeasure:** You can help eliminate the risk of phishing by educating users, and by educating yourself about how criminals use advanced network analysis tools and techniques to bypass the protections that are in place.
Network attacks	**Description:** Network attacks, such as a man-in-the-middle attack, intercept messages between the sender and receiver. By retrieving and modifying information as it passes through the network, these attacks have a great impact on data integrity. **Countermeasure:** Encryption is typically used to reduce the risk of man-in-the-middle attacks.
Intellectual property exposure	**Description:** Intellectual property, like pending patent information and trade secrets, are subject to unauthorized release to the general public if they are not properly protected. **Countermeasure:** Songs, books, movies, and research material are afforded copyright protection, and proper safeguards ensure that copies of these materials can be appropriately downloaded.
Privacy and ano-nymity breaches	**Description:** The risk of exposing personal information in the areas of finances and healthcare has been the focus of federal laws in the United States. **Countermeasure:** Laws have been passed that require holders of this type of information to provide risk-reducing safeguards.

Security Threat	Description/Countermeasure
User computer vulnerabilities	**Description:** User computers in the workplace are particularly vulnerable and present a special risk situation. Installing unauthorized software may expose computers to viruses, worms, or Trojan programs. When a signed-on computer is left alone, it is that much more susceptible to unauthorized access. Physical computer theft also introduces significant data access risks. **Countermeasure:** Physical and logical safeguards, along with ample user security training, can help reduce computer security risks.

Organizational Information Security Factors

The structure and management style of an organization can reinforce or limit the use of risk-reducing measures, thus affecting information security.

An organization's corporate culture—the acceptable activities and relationships within an organization—often affects how the organization addresses security. If the organization has a laissez-faire management approach, it may be difficult to enforce a strict security policy because of management's lack of interest. On the other hand, a strict management approach might limit security effectiveness because of varying employee reactions to management. To better understand an organization's management approach, it is necessary to recognize its vision and mission.

Organizational Goals

Many organizations summarize their organizational goals and objectives in vision and mission statements.

Statement	Description/Example
Vision statement	**Description:** Communicates the organization's purpose to its employees, customers, and suppliers. In high-level terms, management uses vision statements to describe its organizational aspirations. Vision statements help personalize the organization. **Example:** Everything for Coffee is a retail company that sells multiple coffee-related products. Their company vision communicates "Everything fair trade. Everything organic. All the time." This statement conveys Everything for Coffee's desire to be a principal fair-trade importer in the organic coffee industry. It also assures coffee consumers that the coffee products they procure and drink were purchased under fair conditions. Vision statements are not expressions of *how* something is achieved, but *what* will be achieved.

Statement	Description/Example
Mission statement	**Description:** Communicates how something will be achieved. It may include specific steps, milestones, or activities that the organization will implement to achieve its vision. **Example:** Everything for Coffee's mission statement communicates that the company is striving "To become the leading fair-trade-certified coffee supplier in Western New York by continually paying regulated fair-trade prices and by financially and technically assisting small, international coffee farmers in a transition to organic farming, improving their community development, education, health, and environmental stewardship." The mission is to become the number one merchant in Western New York that provides certified fair-trade coffee. The *how* is through paying standardized trade fees on a continual basis and supporting the economic well-being of international coffee farmers.

How Vision and Mission Affect Security

If an organization focuses only on the goals of the vision statement or the achievements of the mission statement, security may fail. Information security is expensive, so it can have a negative, short-term effect on the bottom line. Saving money increases the return to stockholders; however, if threats take advantage of vulnerabilities, information disclosure is costly. Senior management has to balance security with return to successfully meet the organization's vision and mission.

Organizational Structures

The way that organizations are structured can have a direct impact on security. As organizations change the way they do business and realign their strategies, it is important to identify who is responsible for the various security functions and whom these people will report to. It is also important that security enhances and protects the business, and that the business will be able to react in a way that makes it competitive.

Organizational Security Reporting Structures

Security is an extremely important organizational component, though it can be difficult to determine where the information technology (IT) security department fits into an organizational structure. Whether the top security position is a Chief Information Security Officer (CISO), an Information Security Officer (ISO), or a Chief Security Officer (CSO), the position includes the responsibility to safeguard the corporation's IT assets. Some parts of the security office are charged with day-to-day security operations. Other parts are responsible for providing advice for tactical and strategic requirements to maintain future organizational security.

Security Reporting Options

An information security department's reporting structure can have a significant influence on how it operates. The following are examples of reporting structures and the possible pros and cons. There is no one right answer for all organizations.

Security Reporting Option	*Pros and Cons*
Chief Executive Officer (CEO)	**Pros:** • Top-level visibility • Accessibility to resources **Cons:** • Lack of independence
Internal audit department	**Pros:** • Develops strong relationship • Provides good feedback **Cons:** • Audit should be independent of other departments and activities • Violates separation of duties (SoD)
IT department	**Pros:** • Most security issues are IT-related • A strong working relationship is important **Cons:** • Lack of independence • Violates SoD
Administrative services department	**Pros:** • Independent of most other departments **Cons:** • Department management may not understand security requirements and needs
Insurance and risk management department	**Pros:** • In tune with security needs • Understands risk **Cons:** • May not understand computer security risks
Legal department	**Pros:** • Knows security-related legal requirements **Cons:** • Not usually technically driven • May focus on the legal requirements, not on the risk-reduction aspects in other areas

Security Reporting Option	Pros and Cons
Corporate security	**Pros:** ● Security oriented **Cons:** ● Focus may be physical security only ● May not understand information security issues

Governance

Governance in an organization refers to the organization's methods of exercising authority or control as well as its system of management.

In IT security, governance starts at the top with the CEO and Board of Directors, who are tasked with exercising authority and control over the entire corporation. Authority of the IT security practices flows downward through the organization to the security department and to individuals who are responsible for conducting a security program based on policy.

The Chief Information Officer (CIO) and Board of Directors are responsible for ensuring that the corporation is using well-established security policies and that the security of information is protected. The essence of good security is a security policy that makes the wishes of top management known to the security organization. The policy is not a technical document, but is a high-level statement that clearly dictates expectations. Policies that support the governance activities of the board should be developed.

Figure 4-2: Organizational governance structure.

Audit Committee Responsibilities

The *audit committee* is part of the organizational structure related to law and regulation compliance oversights. Ideally, the audit committee is composed of corporate board members who are not part of the governing process of the corporation, but who have audit responsibility only. With smaller boards, some members may end up with multiple roles. The audit committee is responsible for ensuring accuracy of corporate records, tax reporting, Sarbanes-Oxley (SOX) Act compliance, and other issues.

Security Committee

The security committee is often a missing link in the corporate structure. It should maintain a function similar to the audit committee in overseeing an organization's information security systems. Just as the audit committee is charged with accuracy and best practices compliance, the security committee is responsible for ensuring the secure posture of an organization.

Governance Requirements

The IT Governance Institute (ITGI), a research group established in the late 1990s, provides the global business community and enterprise leaders with valuable references, tools, and support for governing their IT-enabled business systems. ITGI suggests several expected governance activities:

- Strategic alignment of information security with business strategies to support organizational objectives.

- Risk management by executing appropriate measures to manage and mitigate risks, and reducing potential impacts on information resources to an acceptable level.

- Resource management by efficiently and effectively using information security knowledge and infrastructures.

- Performance measurement by evaluating, monitoring, and reporting information security governance metrics to ensure that organizational objectives are achieved.

- Value delivery by optimizing information security investments that support organizational objectives.

 For more information on ITGI, such as its products and services, visit **www.itgi.org**.

ISO Responsibilities

The Information Security Officer (ISO) is charged with providing support for expected governance activities. By reviewing the activities as stated, the ISO develops a program that reviews organizational security assets from an operational, tactical, and strategic viewpoint.

The ISO must be able to balance security needs with business objectives. For example, it may not be possible to implement all of the required security safeguards because of limitations in resources, time, and staff. Safeguard prioritization is then necessary. Prioritization decisions are not determined by the ISO; their implementation is the responsibility of the board and CEO.

The ISO's Role

To support the governance responsibilities of the board, the ISO is required to perform many different functions and assume numerous roles in the organization.

ISO Role	Description
Understand the business	<ul><li>Become knowledgeable about the business operation and goals.</li><li>Understand the vision and mission, and how IT security helps to meet goals.</li><li>Be a member of the management team.</li><li>Provide insightful security guidance as it applies to the entire organization.</li></ul>
Budget	<ul><li>Develop the budget for the organization and justify expenses.</li><li>Communicate budget needs to senior management to increase the likelihood of approval.</li><li>Ask for needs rather than wants.</li></ul>
Develop	<ul><li>Develop security awareness programs in the corporation.</li><li>Develop security management skills within the security organization.</li></ul>
Train	<ul><li>Ensure user and management training in information security protection.</li><li>Train security staff in new threats, new safeguards, and current operations.</li></ul>
Ensure compliance	<ul><li>Ensure compliance to laws, regulations, and policies within areas controlled by information security.</li><li>Coordinate with the legal department as necessary.</li></ul>
Promote awareness	<ul><li>Promote a climate of security awareness in all parts of the company.</li><li>Communicate the importance of business continuity and disaster recovery planning.</li></ul>
Inform	<ul><li>Be the conduit for security information in the organization.</li><li>Provide frequent updates on the status of the organization's security environment.</li><li>Provide information about pending changes in advance so that adequate training can be planned.</li></ul>
Measure	<ul><li>Measure security effectiveness by conducting penetration testing and other similar activities.</li><li>Work with internal and external auditors to determine any weaknesses in safeguards.</li></ul>
Assist	<ul><li>Assist senior management in understanding the requirements for information security.</li><li>Assist application designers and developers in understanding how to provide security in new and existing systems.</li></ul>
Report	<ul><li>Report security accomplishments and limitations to senior management.</li><li>Provide details regarding security violations.</li></ul>

The Organizational Security Model

Definition:

The *organizational security model* is the totality of information security implementations in an organization. The model varies from one organization to the next depending on governance structure, security goals, regulatory environment, and risk level. It separates the various security-requiring aspects of the organization into layers. The bottom layer represents the total desired security. All other layers are dependent upon the needs of the organization. Each lower layer must support those layers on top of it.

Example:

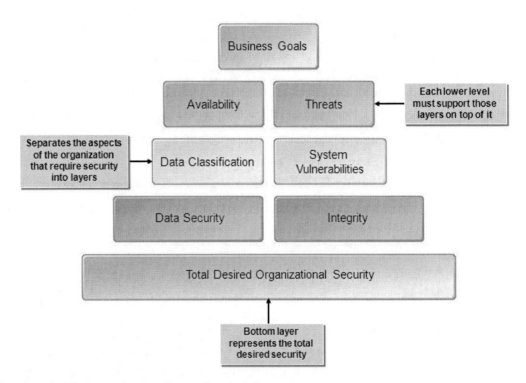

Figure 4-3: The organizational security model.

An Organizational Security Model

The following example represents a model style of organizational security.

Our Global Company has chosen an organizational security model that features a distributed security environment with security departments at each operating location responsible for local security. Their policies will be governed by local requirements with oversight from the corporate security department.

Security Audit Frameworks and Methodologies

Many ideas have been put forth to support a structured approach to security auditing and risk assessment. Some of the following were created specifically for security and others have been adopted from other fields.

Audit Framework	Description
ISO 27000 Series (ISO 17799/BS 7799)	Includes ISO 27001 and 27002. ISO 27001 describes a process for creating, maintaining, and auditing a security management system and is based on BS 7799. ISO 27002 is based on ISO 17799 and describes security best practices. It provides 134 security controls based on the 11 areas mentioned in Lesson 2.
ITIL	The IT Infrastructure Library (ITIL) is a set of books based on work done by the British government. It contains best practices for IT in areas like change management, incident management, and service management.
COBIT	Control Objectives for Information and related Technology (COBIT) is a framework for employing security governance best practices. It is published by the IT Governance Institute. COBIT has four domains: Plan and Organize, Acquire and Implement, Deliver and Support, and Monitor and Evaluate.

ACTIVITY 4-1
Discussing Organizational Security

Scenario:
In this activity, you will discuss organizational security goals, concepts, practices, and processes.

1. What benefits does information security provide?

2. Which one of the following should be conducted to determine areas where an unauthorized person could access or damage resources or data?
   a) Vulnerability assessment
   b) Risk assessment
   c) SLA
   d) Defense in depth

3. How would you characterize the approach that defense in depth uses to keep hackers and malware out of a network?

4. In a typical defense in depth approach, what does the stateful inspection firewall protect networks from?
   a) Excessive traffic
   b) Inappropriate access levels
   c) Viruses
   d) Hackers not caught by the edge router

5. Which one or more of the following essential action items should an enterprise perform prior to engaging an outsourcing provider?
   a) Evaluate the provider's security.
   b) Audit the provider's current security activities.
   c) Create a layered security system.
   d) Enforce security requirements for the outsourcing provider.

6. **A contract that requires 95% uptime for all network resources is an example of which of the following?**

   a) Corporate culture

   b) CBK

   c) Risk-reduction measures

   d) SLA

7. **True or False? One way in which the CISSP helps to reduce risk is by providing training to everyone in the organization on present security risks and protection methods.**

   ___ True

   ___ False

8. **As an information security consultant, knowing a corporation's vision and mission statements would help you determine which of the following?**

   a) Corporate morale

   b) Corporate culture

   c) Corporate structure

   d) Corporate divisions

9. **What is the corresponding security impact of each technical environment change?**

___ Personal computers were attached to LANs	a. Strong physical security was provided for large, centralized systems.
___ Mainframe computers began to use online transaction processing	b. The use of virus scans, firewalls, and IDSs raised the cost of information security to protect organizational resources.
___ Computer terminals were replaced with PCs	c. Computer security was decentralized to individual desktop systems.
___ Conception and evolution of the Internet	d. Administrators became increasingly concerned with both desktop security and network security.

10. **Which organizational position includes the responsibility to safeguard the corporation's IT assets?**

11. **True or False? The audit committee is responsible for SOX Act compliance.**

    ___ True

    ___ False

12. **Which one or more of the following are recommended security governance-level activities, according to the ITGI?**

    a) Strategically align information security with business strategies.

    b) Maintain day-to-day oversight of the security infrastructure.

    c) Execute appropriate measures to manage and mitigate risks.

    d) Evaluate, monitor, and report information security governance metrics.

    e) Optimize information security investments.

13. **What is the appropriate description for each ISO role action item?**

    ___ Inform

    ___ Budget

    ___ Develop

    ___ Train

    ___ Ensure compliance

    a. Ensure that certain laws, regulations, and policies are adhered to.

    b. Develop a plan and justify the expenditures for the organization.

    c. Ensure the user and management are prepared for information security procedures.

    d. Transmit security information in the organization.

    e. Create security awareness in the corporation.

14. **What role does the organizational security model provide?**

15. **What is the appropriate description for each security goal?**

    ___ Operational

    ___ Strategic

    ___ Tactical

    a. Long-term security goals

    b. Short-term security goals

    c. Medium-term security goals

16. **What types of information can be included in security goals?**

TOPIC B
The Application of Security Concepts

Although the implementation of security goals does decrease risk potential and help guard against system attacks, overriding intrusions and security infringements are still a concern. Proactive efforts should always be sought when protecting your information systems. In this topic, you will identify the application of security concepts to sustain effective management goals and fortify the security infrastructure of your organization.

Once security goals are in place, there are a number of concepts that can be applied to reinforce security within your organization. Techniques such as personnel management are critical components to strengthening organizational security. Employing these techniques will help you increase security levels and protect your information systems from intrusive, unauthorized access.

Job Rotation

Definition:

Job rotation is a security principle that encourages organizations to build a highly qualified staff by exposing employees to different job areas. By implementing a policy of job rotation, individuals within an organization can benefit from an enhanced understanding of the business and the tasks others perform. The availability of trained staff is improved by having an increased number of people qualified to perform specific job functions.

Example:

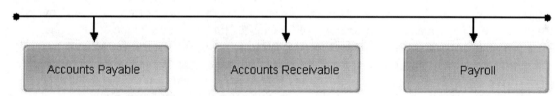

Figure 4-4: Job rotation.

Example: Internal Department Rotation

An organization may choose to rotate people within the accounting department from accounts payable, accounts receivable, and payroll. At the end of the rotation, each individual will be trained in the job functions performed in the three areas.

Job Rotation Security Applications

In a security department, staff may be rotated among security administration, encryption and key management, and penetration testing. The trained individual can be used in any of the three sectors as the need arises. In general, job rotation limits the amount of time it takes an individual to perform a single job. This provides an incentive to build new and better skills while limiting the individual's ability to negatively affect the security environment.

Job rotation also adds value by aiding in the discovery of improper activities performed by staff members. When an individual rotates to a new job, additional audits of their activities may uncover fraudulent or criminal activities. As a deterrent, employees will be made aware that their work will be subject to review at a later date as they rotate positions. This will reduce the risk of individual criminal acts.

Separation of Duties Security Applications

Fraud and collusion often occur when a control mechanism fails to detect or correct improper activities. One way that computer crimes occur is when one individual completes all phases of a transaction process. Separation of duties (SoD) can be applied as a security concept to distribute this type of transaction control among different individuals. For instance, an accounts payable system may ensure its checks and balances through implementing a four-step process performed by four separate people: an accounts payable clerk, an accounts payable supervisor, an accounts payable manager, and a Chief Financial Officer (CFO).

Least Privilege Security Applications

Least privilege can be applied as an organizational security concept because users are granted the minimum permissions required for completing their designated tasks. Users should not be allowed to perform administrator functions, because that would exceed the privileges that the users need. Administrators are given increased permissions because they must perform more technically advanced functions. Their level of least privilege is higher than a normal user.

Applying the least privilege concept to programs or applications is not obvious, but it is necessary. Application programs should not have access to the operating system or supervisor-level instructions of the central processing unit (CPU). While SoD is used to control and limit fraud and collusion, least privilege is used as a way to prevent mistakes by disallowing unauthorized user modifications, which are attacks on integrity.

Mandatory Vacation Security Applications

Mandating employee vacations is a personnel management issue that has security implications. From a security standpoint, mandatory vacations provide an opportunity to review employees' activities. The typical mandatory vacation policy requires that employees take at least one vacation a year in a full-week increment, so that they are away from work for at least five days in a row. During that time, the corporate audit and security staffs have time to investigate and discover any discrepancies in employee activity. When employees understand the security focus of the mandatory vacation policy, the chance of fraudulent activities decreases.

Security Awareness Programs

It is important for all organizations have methods to promote security topics amongst all their employees. The level of training will vary by job role, but all employees must have at least a basic understanding of their roles. Some managers may require training that is more specific. IT employees frequently require even higher levels of training. This training needs to be meaningful and easily understood by the audience. The program should include multiple methods to increase awareness. Some methods may include newsletter articles, online training, and security posters in highly visible locations. Periodically testing the effectiveness of the training is also important for the employees and for those developing the programs.

Evaluate Security Incidents

Companies can form a *computer incident response team (CIRT)* trained to respond appropriately to security events. These teams may include individuals from IT, HR, legal, and others, and should be provided with adequate training to ensure the best possible information is obtained during any type of security event. They should also develop processes and procedures to be followed when an event occurs. The teams should conduct regular exercises to measure their effectiveness. After significant events, they should meet to discuss successes and failures and look for opportunities to improve. The team will also work closely with management to report events.

Job Position Sensitivity Profiling

Job position sensitivity profiling is the security practice of determining an individual's need-to-know information as it relates to the individual's specific job function. The individual's required access rights to specific system information needs to be carefully assessed before authorization is granted. First, data owners must determine the need-to-know information for each organizational job function, and work with the security department to document it in a *sensitivity profile* for each job. The profiles are created based on the tasks performed, not on the individuals performing the tasks. Then, during the position-assignment process, the sensitivity profiles help administrators assign authorization permissions to individuals.

Need to Know vs. No Need to Know

A payroll clerk must have access to a limited amount of general, personal employee information. The payroll clerk needs to know employee names, addresses, telephone numbers, and numbers of dependents. The payroll clerk does not need to know employees' previous job performance ratings, security clearance levels, or educational degrees.

Job Position Sensitivity Profiling Considerations

There are several key considerations that must be addressed when performing sensitivity profiling for job positions.

Sensitivity Profile Consideration	Description
Change authentication methods frequently	Due to the high risk potential for losing sensitive information, passwords and other authentication methods need to be changed frequently for users who have authorized access. While all business information is important to protect, some information is more sensitive than others.
	For example, if an individual has access to the encryption keys for a cryptosystem, the password used to access the keys requires frequent updating. If the password remains the same for too long, it is subject to password guessing and to lazy practices, such as password sharing, on the part of the password holder. Changing the password regularly reduces the risk of password guessing and sharing.

Sensitivity Profile Consideration	Description
Frequent reviews of privileged users	Frequent reviews of account access capabilities are required to ensure that the privileges granted to a user are still required. While normal users may be required to change their passwords and be subject to access right reviews every 180 days, privileged users may be reviewed every 90 days or less.
	Privileged users are subject to more frequent reviews because they may have rights to information that they should not be accessing in their current job role.
	For example, two months ago, users were accessing a database with the appropriate need-to-know privileges. Today, they still have access to the sensitive database, but they are in a different job role with no need to know. If the information owner offered frequent, periodic reviews, it would eliminate this type of access problem by identifying users with excessive privileges or no need to know, and then removing those users' access rights.
	These practices may vary with organizational requirements, but in most cases, privileged users are under more scrutiny than those without privileges.

Hiring Practice Applications

When hiring a new employee, it is important to match the appropriate employee with the applicable job and security responsibilities.

Hiring Practice	Description
Baseline hiring procedures	General hiring practices for all positions should include:
• A personal interview to evaluate the potential employee's personality.
• Work history verifications.
• Criminal history checks.
• Drug use checks.
• Reference checks to verify the information provided on the application. If the potential employee is misstating facts on the application, there is a strong potential that the individual will be unreliable and untrustworthy.

Be sure to conduct all history and background checks in accordance with the relevant federal, state, or other governmental fair hiring regulations that pertain to your locality. Some organizations opt to hire third-party firms that have specialized expertise in conducting these types of checks and investigations. |

Hiring Practice	*Description*
Position sensitivity screening	Hiring for security-sensitive positions should include: ● Financial and/or credit history reviews. ● Personality screenings. ● Lie detector testing. ● Extended background investigations. ● Security clearances. Especially when you conduct more detailed and intensive security checks, be sure to comply with the relevant federal, state, or other governmental regulations that pertain to your locality.

ACTIVITY 4-2
Discussing the Application of Security Concepts

Scenario:

In this activity, you will discuss the application of security concepts to sustain effective management goals and fortify the security infrastructure of your organization.

1. **What benefits does the security principle known as job rotation provide?**

2. **True or False? SoD combat threats of fraud and collusion that otherwise might occur.**

    ___ True

    ___ False

3. **True or False? Least privilege can be applied as an organizational security concept because users are granted the minimum permissions required for completing their designated tasks.**

    ___ True

    ___ False

4. **From a security standpoint, what security benefit do mandatory vacations provide?**

5. **How is a sensitivity profile developed and what is the benefit?**

6. **How can you address the major considerations of sensitivity profiling for job positions?**

_____

7. **Which one or more of the following should be included in general hiring practices for all positions?**

    a) Financial and/or credit history reviews

    b) Lie detector testing

    c) Criminal history checks

    d) Reference checks

    e) Work history verifications

8. **Which one or more of the following should be included in hiring practices for security-sensitive positions?**

    a) Lie detector testing

    b) Security clearances

    c) Financial and/or credit history reviews

    d) Extended background investigations

    e) Racial profiling

Lesson 4 Follow-up

In this lesson, you analyzed information security concepts and practices and identified security management goals. Evaluating organizational goals is essential for management to ensure that security issues are aligned with business objectives. Aligning security management goals with business goals helps to support the initiation and development of a successful security program.

1. **In your own words, describe the security benefits of understanding the organizational factors of your enterprise.**

2. **Have you had personal experience or exposure to any of the security applications?**

5 Information Security Classification and Program Development

Lesson Time: 2 hour(s)

Lesson Objectives:

In this lesson, you will analyze information security classification and program development.

You will:

● Identify information classification.

● Identify security program development.

Introduction

You have a clear set of security management goals. The next task is to transform these goals into a workable security program by classifying the security level of information. In this lesson, you will analyze the security classification of information and security program development.

Classifying your information security is key to developing effective organizational security programs. Recognizing different classification schemes and roles and identifying how to adequately distribute information throughout your organization will help you employ rigorous, company-wide security policies. With these policies in place, you can appropriately prepare security planning efforts and implement valuable security training to provide immediate and ongoing awareness.

This lesson supports content found in the Information Security Governance & Risk Management domain of the CISSP® certification.

TOPIC A

Information Classification

As you begin the process of security program development, you should first address the application of appropriate security measures to specific information. Classifying organizational data helps quantify access restrictions by assigning parameters to information based on varying degrees of sensitivity. In this topic, you will identify the schemes, roles, and distribution regulations for classifying information.

It is extremely important to be able to place different levels of security on data. Some data requires tight security; others, less. Without a system to determine the type and degree of security, all data would either be universally available or not available at all. Your awareness of how to classify information will ensure the appropriate level of security for all the different types of information within your organization.

Classification Schemes

To adequately protect information from disclosure and other threats, you need to understand the risks associated with the release or modification of the information. Determining the risk of loss or modification is often measured by labeling the information. Labeling schemes are often known as *classifications*.

Classification processes come in two forms: military and commercial. Military classification is implemented by the U.S. federal government, while commercial classification is employed by commercial organizations. Military classification is a strictly defined and very rigid and part of the mandatory access control system. Commercial schemes need to be developed to support the particular needs of the business. Developing an information classification system is a difficult but important task and it will need the buy-in of senior management. As the systems are being built, it is important to consider the different types and locations of data. Most organizations have files stored digitally on servers, backed up to tape, and possibly even hard copy. This data is also stored locally and offsite, and perhaps even housed by an outsource partner. The system will need to be able to track all of that. Once developed, employees will need to be trained on the processes and procedures involved in classification and distribution of documents. While commercial classifications are voluntary and more varied than the military schemes, they are no less important.

Military Classification Schemes

Military classification schemes are composed of four classification levels.

Military Classification Scheme Level	Description
Top Secret	Information that, if disclosed to unauthorized individuals, will present the risk of grave damage to national security.
Secret	Information that, if disclosed to unauthorized individuals, will present the risk of serious damage to national security.

**Military Classifi-
cation Scheme**

Level	Description
Confidential	Information that, if disclosed to unauthorized individuals, will present the risk of damage to national security.
Unclassified	Information that, if disclosed to unauthorized individuals, will present no risk of damage to national security.

 For the CISSP® exam, it is important to know the varying levels of risk for each military classification level.

Commercial Classification Schemes

Commercial classification schemes do not use standard naming conventions, but implement levels based on the severity of loss.

**Commercial Classifi-
cation Scheme**

Level	Description
Corporate Confidential	Information that should not be provided to individuals outside of the enterprise.
Personal and Confidential	Information of a personal nature that should be protected.
Private	Correspondence of a private nature between two or more people that should be safeguarded.
Trade Secret	Corporate intellectual property that, if released, will present serious damage to the company's ability to protect patents and processes.
Client Confidential	• Client personal information that, if released, may result in the identity theft of the individual. • Client corporate information or intelligent property. You may need to sign a non-disclosure agreement (NDA) to keep organization information about a client confidential.

 The schemes listed are only samples. For the CISSP exam, it is important to understand the concept of commercial classification schemes, but not these examples specifically.

Classification Roles

Two primary roles carry different responsibilities for classifying data.

Classification Role	Description
Classifier	The classifier is the data owner who determines the classification of data based on risk by executing the following tasks: 1. Being aware of the data and information that requires safeguarding 2. Evaluating the data's risk of disclosure 3. Providing a classification level based on the risk of disclosure 4. Following policies, standards, and guidelines that specify the classification process and procedure
Protector	The protector is the custodian who is charged with safeguarding previously classified information by employing the following tasks: 1. Being aware of the classification afforded to information under his or her control 2. Providing the labeling of media, as necessary 3. Implementing system safeguards to ensure the non-release of classified information 4. Keeping records of access to classified information 5. Maintaining records of responsibilities when information is transferred 6. Ensuring that the proper destruction procedures are followed 7. Following policies, standards, and guidelines that specify the required safeguarding of classified information 8. Informing management when classified information is accessed by unauthorized individuals

Information Distribution

Classified information can be made available to those individuals that have a clearance at the same level or higher than the information. This is even true in commercial organizations where rigid classification schemes are not used.

All information in an organization is subject to the policy of need to know. Limiting information to those with a need to know requires implementing access control policies and practices.

Physical and Logical Access Control

Access control may be implemented in physical or logical ways. Physical access control limits what an individual may access by restricting the individual to areas of the company where suitable controls are in place. For example, individuals without a Top Secret clearance will not be given access to a room where Top Secret information is stored or used.

Access controls may also be logical. Employees working in the accounts payable department will not be given access to the payroll database because they do not need to know that particular information. The system's access control mechanism will not authorize access even if the individual has the proper identification and authentication (I&A).

ACTIVITY 5-1
Discussing Information Classification

Scenario:
In this activity, you will discuss information classification.

1. **What are two primary forms of classification schemes?**

   a) Commercial

   b) Private

   c) Military

   d) Confidential

2. **What is the appropriate description for each military classification scheme level?**

   ___ Secret

   ___ Confidential

   ___ Top Secret

   ___ Unclassified

   a. Information that, if disclosed to unauthorized individuals, will present the risk of grave damage to national security.

   b. Information that, if disclosed to unauthorized individuals, will present the risk of damage to national security.

   c. Information that, if disclosed to unauthorized individuals, will present no risk of damage to national security.

   d. Information that, if disclosed to unauthorized individuals, will present the risk of serious damage to national security.

3. **What is the appropriate description for each commercial classification scheme level?**

   ___ Trade Secret

   ___ Private

   ___ Corporate Confidential

   ___ Personal and Confidential

   ___ Client Confidential

   a. Information of a personal nature that should be protected.

   b. Information that should not be provided to individuals outside of the enterprise.

   c. Correspondence of a private nature between two people that should be safeguarded.

   d. Client personal information that, if released, may result in the identity theft of the individual.

   e. Corporate intellectual property that, if released, will present serious damage to the company's ability to protect patents and processes.

4. **True or False? The classifier is the custodian who is charged with safeguarding previously classified information.**

   ___ True

   ___ False

5. **Which one or more of the following are protector-specific classification tasks?**

   a) Keeping records of access to classified information

   b) Ensuring that the proper destruction procedures are followed

   c) Providing the labeling of media, as necessary

   d) Evaluating the data's risk of disclosure

   e) Being aware of the data and information that requires safeguarding

TOPIC B
Security Program Development

After your data is fully classified, it is important to determine how users may access information and to acknowledge the business impact should the security of that data be compromised. As a next step, ensuring that everyone in your organization adheres to security goals and complies with security measures, standards, and practices is essential. In this topic, you will identify best practices, policy types and roles, planning efforts, and awareness training for developing and implementing an effective organizational security program.

Security programs are only as good as the people who employ them. Successful programs effectively communicate the security goals and requirements of the organization to those within the organization. Your ability to develop and disseminate security policies, procedures, standards, baselines, and guidelines is your best measure to ensure a successful security program.

Security Policy Best Practices

Developing an effective security policy requires clearly defining an organization's information protection needs. A rigorous security implementation plan can be launched and established using a series of best practices. Organizations like the National Institute of Standards (NIST) and SysAdmin, Audit, Network, Security (SANS) have documents that support security best practices.

Guidelines

To properly enforce a successful security policy:

* Generate a high-level security policy stating the source of authority and responsibilities.
* Create and implement a Disaster Recovery Plan (DRP) and a Business Continuity Plan (BCP).
* Encourage ethical behavior and the acceptable use of corporate information technology (IT) systems.
* Identify organizational data classification and valuation standards and practices.
* Protect data and manage appropriate data disposal.
* Assess information ownership and resource controls.
* Determine access control and authorization.
* Use and protect intellectual property.
* Allocate operations and systems responsibilities carefully.
* Promote security awareness and user responsibilities.
* Report and respond to security incidents methodically.
* Ensure legal and regulatory compliance.

Example: Top-Level Security Policies

For example, the top-level security policy does not address implementation. It addresses the need to create and apply standards, guidelines, and procedures to implement the issues included in the policy. For example, the policy might require using two-factor authentication. It does not state that RSA securID® tokens and biometric methods should be used. The security department proposes implementation parameters, while corporate management defines the requirements.

Security Policy Objectives

Security policies can fulfill multiple objectives for an organization and you are likely to have multiple policies. They can inform employees about their security-related duties and responsibilities. They can define an organization's security goals. They can outline a computer system's security requirements. The specific objective of a security policy depends on the requirements of the organization. However, all security policies have one objective in common: to disseminate standardized information to ensure that all personnel can fulfill their duties in accordance with the security requirements of the organization. Policies need to be long enough to explain but short enough to be understood. It is important that policies can be read and understood by all employees and that employees know where they can find a policy.

Security Policy Types

Senior management defines information security policies to communicate how information assets within the organization will be protected.

Security Policy Type	Description
Advisory	Advisory policies:
	• Indicate certain types of actions as being more appropriate or effective than others.
	• Include consequences and reprimands that may be experienced if actions taken are not as indicated.
	• Are commonly used for indicating how to handle private documentation and money.
Informative	Informative policies:
	• Provide data to employees on a specified subject.
	• Include no ramifications.
	• Are often used as instructional instruments.
Regulatory	Regulatory policies:
	• Address industry regulations regarding the conduct of organizations.
	• Are commonly used for health care and financial organizations.

Security Document Types

There are generally five different documents that help define the security environment of an organization.

Security Document Type	Description
Policies	A *policy* is a high-level statement of management intentions. Policies do not get into specifics but leave that for procedures, standards, and guidelines. A policy should contain the purpose, scope, and compliance expected of the employee.
	Example: Information security will ensure the protection of information by implementing security best practices.
Standards	A *standard* describes a required implementation or use of tools. Standards help to define the requirements of a policy and can be more technical in nature.
	Example: The corporation *must* implement 802.1x security for all wireless networks.
Guidelines	A *guideline* is a recommendation or suggested action, implementation, or use of tools that is considered a best practice for meeting the policy standard.
	Example: When travelling with laptops, users *should* use safety precautions to prevent laptop theft, damage, or data loss.
Procedures	A *procedure* is an implementation document that describes the steps taken to complete an activity. Procedures help maintain compliance of policies and standards.
	Example: To implement Secure Shell (SSH) on the router, enter the **enable** mode and then enter the appropriate commands for the router.
Baselines	A *baseline* is a security document that specifies the minimum security required in a system or process. Security may be stronger than what is required in the baseline, but deviations to reduce security levels below the baseline require management approval. Auditing can help ensure that baselines are being met.
	Example: Trivial File Transfer Protocol (TFTP) must be disabled in all servers except for those specifically used for the TFTP service.

 These document types are not restricted to security but are used throughout the organization to define the purpose and process of various company activities.

Guidelines vs. Standards

For a guideline to be practical, it often employs the word "should." The guideline provides non-specific guidance in a given area. The previous example relating to laptops states that users should employ preventative measures to acceptably safeguard their equipment and system data. This implementation may not actually mandate the use of the guideline specification. However, the guideline's strong suggestion provides input to those who may be unaware of proper laptop security maintenance.

Conversely, standards often use the word "must." For example, when traveling with laptops, users *must* use safety precautions to prevent laptop theft, damage, or data loss.

This statement clearly indicates that laptop security is a system-specific requirement that must be met by everyone while traveling.

The Security Policy Process

When applying policies, standards, baselines, procedures, and guidelines, the relationships between each of these elements must be considered.

1. The overall document environment is controlled by the policies.

2. As management creates policies, standards and guidelines are prepared to implement them.

3. To put policies and guidelines into action, procedures and baselines are created.

Organizational Policy Roles

Different people within an organization are required to perform certain roles with respect to the security policy and its components. The Chief Executive Officer (CEO) and the Board of Directors are responsible for documenting organizational security goals and objectives. The security department determines how to put the established goals into practice. And finally, all staff members and employees are responsible for adhering to the goals by implementing them in their day-to-day activities.

Security Planning

Security planning efforts ensure that an organization's advanced preparations comply with security policies.

Security Planning Effort	*Description*
Strategic planning	*Strategic planning* is a long-range (three- to five-year) planning process that looks at required security activities, focusing on major changes or improvements in the security posture of an organization. Strategic planning must stay aligned to the business objectives. These plans need to be reviewed annually at a minimum, or more frequently if there are major changes to an organization. Mergers and acquisitions, right-sizing, or significant outsourcing could trigger a review.
	A strategic planning item might include a planned movement to a facial recognition system for authentication in five years when the technology has improved.
Tactical planning	*Tactical planning* is a mid-term planning process that supports strategic planning. Tactical planning might encompass the next six to 18 months, depending on corporate policy.
	A tactical planning item might be a move to Remote Authentication Dial-In User Service (RADIUS) for all remote and local network access authentication. RADIUS implementation is a major step for any organization and must be well planned to succeed.
Operational and project planning	*Operational and project planning* is a planning process that deals with the near term. Operational planning supports the tactical plans and includes project plans with milestones and completion dates that are communicated regularly.
	An operational planning item might be to plan for a penetration test in three months.

Failing to plan for security may increase the risk to corporate information because appropriate methods, tools, and practices may not be implemented in response to potential industry and threat changes.

Security Awareness and Training

Improving security awareness within your organization and offering security training will help ensure that your staff is knowledgeable about the security policy and its benefits and is prepared to perform in accordance with its mandates.

 At a minimum, all staff should attend security awareness training at least once a year. This also includes management. More frequent training may be necessary in environments where security risk is high.

Guidelines

To promote security awareness and provide effective training:

- Plan professional career development and training efforts.
  - Offer the necessary training so staff members can improve their skill levels.
  - Consider training offered by vendors during product announcements and product updates.
  - Invest in organizational career development to help increase staff morale.
  - Encourage organizational security memberships at the national or local level.
- Develop security awareness training points.
  - Address password protection.
  - Discuss information protection.
  - List procedures to follow if unauthorized individuals are detected in the facility.
  - Identify tactics to defeat social engineering.
  - Characterize email threats.
  - Analyze virus and worm prevention.
  - Assess information disclosure prevention.
  - Review virtual private network (VPN) practices to protect data.
- Offer online or instructor-led training.
  - Contract with commercial vendors for product-specific or generic security training.
  - Arrange mandatory, instructor-led presentations and seminars.

Example: Organizational Security Programs

For example, while developing a security program for his organization, Sam prepares training objectives and facilitates an education initiative for management and staff. He concentrates on addressing specific security policies, threat concerns, system information protection mechanisms, and attack prevention strategies. He documents organizational security guidelines, methodologies, and best practices. He also arranges brown-bag lunch seminars, web-based training, classroom training, podcasts, email blasts, and other forums to provide effective awareness training and periodic security updates.

Awareness Program Objectives

Awareness programs can have many objectives. One of the most common objectives is preventing internal personnel from accessing information that they are not authorized to access. Often, people attempt to access data that requires authorization simply because they do not know it is not allowed. Another objective is increasing the efficacy of a security policy through actual implementation of the policy. Finally, awareness programs often attempt to reduce any misuse of company resources, such as data and hardware. To achieve these goals, programs use methods like presentations, incentives, posters, and newsletters. These allow management to circulate the policy message to those who need it, as well as get employees involved in security awareness and accountability.

ACTIVITY 5-2
Discussing Security Program Development

Scenario:

In this activity, you will discuss security program development.

1. **True or False? There is one objective that all security policies have in common: the dissemination of standardized information to ensure that all personnel receive information necessary to fulfill their duties.**

   ___ True

   ___ False

2. **A rigorous security implementation plan can be launched and established using a series of best practices. Which one or more of the following describe a best practice that should be used?**

   a) Promote security awareness and user responsibilities.

   b) Generate a high-level security policy stating the source of authority and responsibilities.

   c) Assess information ownership and resource controls.

   d) Determine access control and authorization.

   e) Establish dress codes.

3. **Security policies can fulfill multiple objectives for an organization. Which one or more of the following are objectives that the security policy can fulfill?**

   a) They can outline the computer system's security requirements.

   b) They can define an organization's security goals.

   c) They can inform employees about their duties and responsibilities.

   d) They can help to identify how many employees need to be hired.

4. **What is the appropriate example of each security document type?**

___	Policies	a.	Information security will ensure the protection of information by implementing security best practices.
___	Standards	b.	When travelling with laptops, users should use safety precautions to prevent laptop theft, damage, or data loss.
___	Guidelines	c.	The corporation must implement 802.1x security for all wireless networks.
___	Procedures	d.	To implement SSH on the router, enter the enable mode and then enter the appropriate commands for the router.
___	Baselines	e.	TFTP must be disabled in all servers except for those specifically used for the TFTP service.

5. **True or False? Standards are a security document type that describes a required implementation or use of tools.**

___ True

___ False

6. **True or False? In the security policy process, the overall document environment is controlled by policies.**

___ True

___ False

7. **What is the obligated security component responsibility of each role?**

___	CEO and Board of Directors	a.	Responsible for adhering to security goals by implementing them in their day-to-day activities
___	Security department	b.	Responsible for establishing organizational security goals and objectives
___	Employees	c.	Responsible for determining how to put the established goals into practice

8. **What is the appropriate example of each security planning effort?**

____ Strategic planning

a. At a mid-size company, the server space will be running out in approximately 35 weeks. The IT team purchases the necessary equipment and hardware and plans a data move to two new servers.

____ Tactical planning

b. The president of a large university is looking to hire top-quality professors, but the university currently has an inexpensive firewall in place to protect important research. To attract elite professors to the school, he decides that the university must invest more money into equipment to ensure that data is secure.

____ Operational and project planning

c. Inventory records at a large school district have indicated the need for new equipment. The school district budget, however, has indicted that only one-fourth of the equipment can be purchased in each of the next four years. The IT department creates a plan to replace the oldest equipment first and continue for the next four years.

9. **Which one or more of the following are considered effective training methods that can promote security awareness?**

a) Encourage organizational security memberships at the national or local level.

b) Address password protection in the training.

c) Characterize email threats for staff.

d) Review VPN practices to protect data.

e) Store the only copies of the security manuals in the locked server room for safe-keeping.

Lesson 5 Follow-up

In this lesson, you analyzed security classification schemes and roles as well as methods for distributing classified information. You also identified best practices for implementing security policies, listed the policy types and roles that help in security program development, and applied the value of proactive security planning, training, and awareness. Recognizing how to apply the appropriate measure of security to specific information will help you effectively classify your security data and ensure organizational compliance through security policy and training implementations.

1. **What classification scheme are you familiar with or think would work in your organization?**

2. **What types of security policies have you come across in your organization?**

6 | Risk Management and Ethics

Lesson Time: 2 hour(s), 15 minutes

Lesson Objectives:

In this lesson, you will analyze risk management criteria and ethical codes of conduct.

You will:

- Apply risk management techniques and strategies.
- Identify ethical codes of conduct.

Introduction

You have applied classification schemes to your security information systems and transformed them into a practical security program for your organization. Now that your program is in place, it is important to identify risk factors as well as distinguish between ethical and unethical behavior standards. In this lesson, you will analyze risk management criteria and ethical codes of conduct.

Analyzing security risks is essential to adequately protect your information systems from potential intrusion violations and threats. Furthermore, risk identification coupled with a thorough knowledge of company ethics codes can help improve security and be a counteractive measure that negates criminal attacks. Performing detailed risk analyses, applying knowledge of risk types and principles, considering probability and prioritization factors, implementing asset valuation methodology, and recognizing vulnerability areas as well as complying with ethical code standards and regulatory requirements will help you select the proper safeguards to effectively manage and secure your information systems.

This lesson supports content found in the Information Security Governance & Risk Management and the Legal, Regulations, Investigations, and Compliance domains of the CISSP® certification.

TOPIC A
Risk Management

As your security program takes shape, one of the final steps in successful security management is analyzing and mitigating risk. Because information security risks can adversely affect an organization's business goals and technical stability, it is essential to have a structured, proactive approach to alleviate system infractions and ensure protection. In this topic, you will apply risk management techniques and strategies to your organization.

All companies have information that, if released or compromised, could have serious ramifications and jeopardize organizational goals. Remember, in today's business climate, information is a business asset. To that end, it is your job to recognize the threat to those assets. Gaining a thorough understanding of how to identify risks will allow you to employ security measures that mitigate risk to acceptable levels.

What Is Risk?

Risk is the likelihood that a threat will exploit a vulnerability. It is often shown as the equation Risk = Threat * Vulnerability. A big part of risk analysis, then, is to understand the vulnerabilities and threats that lead to risk. *Vulnerability* is defined as any weakness in a system or process that could lead to harm. A *threat* is the agent that will expose the vulnerability and cause the harm. Another factor to consider is that different assets have different vulnerabilities and threats. For example, a warehouse will have significantly different vulnerabilities than an intellectual property (IP) application.

The Risk Analysis Process

When determining how to protect computer networks, computer installations, and information, *risk analysis* is the security management process for addressing any risk or economic damages that affect an organization and are ascertained in various phases. Risk analysis is an ongoing activity that involves periodic reviews along with special reviews around significantly changed processes. Special risk analysis efforts are needed before, during, and after the acquisition.

Risk Analysis Process Phase	Description
Asset identification	Identifying the assets that require protection and determining the value of the assets. Assets might include data, data systems, buildings, and employees. Determining what the assets are is generally easier than determining the value of the assets.
Vulnerability identification	Identifying vulnerabilities so the analyst can confirm where asset protection problems exist. Locating weaknesses exposes the critical areas that are most susceptible to vulnerabilities.
Threat assessment	Once vulnerabilities are understood, the threats that may take advantage of or exploit those vulnerabilities are determined.
Probability quantification	Quantifying the likelihood or probability that threats will exploit vulnerabilities.
Probability qualification	For assets that are difficult to quantify, an organization may use quality as a determining factor.

Risk Analysis Process Phase	Description
Financial impact evaluation	Once the probabilities are determined, the financial impact of these potential threats needs to be evaluated.
Countermeasures determination	Determining and developing countermeasures to eliminate or reduce risks. The countermeasures must be economically sound and provide the expected level of protection. In other words, the countermeasures must not cost more than the expected loss caused by threats that exploit vulnerabilities.

Risk Analysis Matrix Types

There are several types of risk analysis matrixes that can be used in risk analysis. The Australia/New Zealand (AS/NZS) 4360 Standard on Risk Management is one way to evaluate the likelihood and consequence impact during risk analysis.

Likelihood	Consequence				
	Insignificant	Minor	Moderate	Major	Catastrophic
5. Almost certain	H	H	E	E	E
4. Likely	M	H	H	E	E
3. Possible	L	M	H	E	E
2. Unlikely	L	L	M	H	E
1. Rare	L	L	M	H	H
	L = Low	M = Medium	H = High	E = Extreme	

Figure 6-1: An example of the Australia/New Zealand 4360 Standard on Risk Management.

Results of Improper Risk Management

In the information management world, risks come in many different forms. If a risk is not managed correctly, any of the following could result:

● Disclosure of a critical asset

● Modification of a critical asset

● Loss/destruction of a critical asset

● Interruption of a critical asset

Understanding and reducing risk will help to minimize the impact of these losses.

Risk Management Principles

The foundation of risk management is to recognize and understand the risk and then apply the appropriate principle to manage it.

Risk Management Principle	Description
Avoidance	An organization may take steps to eliminate threats through mitigation. By eliminating the threat, no risk is present. With no risk, avoidance is implemented.
	If an office contains a large amount of computer equipment that could be removed if a window is broken, a potential risk is present. Deciding to keep the computing equipment at an alternate location will reduce the risk.
Mitigation	An organization may use methods that help to curtail the severity of risk or lessen the probability of a loss occurring. Risk reduction is an effective management treatment for strengthening system protection and ensuring fewer security deficits.
	The organization may choose to leave the window in place but reduce the risk of equipment theft by putting bars in front of the window. The bars will reduce—but not remove—the threat of equipment theft. The risk of loss will be minimal.
Transfer	An organization may resort to reallocating risk acceptance to another party, such as an insurance company, by means of a contract. This transfer method helps to shift liability and maintain organizational profitability despite the potential exposure to unwanted security and business risks.
	The organization may choose to leave the window in place with no bars, but raise the insurance premiums to compensate for the loss should the window be broken and the equipment be stolen. The risk has been transferred to the insurance company for an increased premium.
Acceptance	An organization may analyze the risk and determine that the value of equipment, if stolen, is less than the cost of implementing protective countermeasures. Rather than respond to the risk, the organization may choose to accept it and employ no countermeasures.
	The organization may determine that intrusion barriers for the equipment storage room are firmly secured and that the window is high enough to prevent forced entry and theft. Therefore, no countermeasures are enforced and the organization retains the risk of damages incurred upon an unexpected loss.

Asset Valuation

Asset valuation is the practice of determining an asset's worth to an organization. It requires taking all costs into consideration. The specific costs associated with an asset depend on the asset's financial impact when it is affected by a threat. Asset valuation answers two essential questions:

1. What requires protection?

2. How much loss will be sustained if the asset is misplaced or damaged?

Asset Valuation Methods

Assets can be identified through different organizational systems and asset value can be determined in several different ways.

Asset Valuation Method	Description
Asset management system	A corporate or organizational system that contains a detailed record of corporate property and similar assets. Facilities, furniture, computers, and other real property are recorded in the asset management system. Purchase prices, depreciation, and other financial asset information may also be found in the system. The asset management system provides an asset value based on accounting principles.
Accounting system	Additional asset information may be present in a general accounting system. For example, the cost to develop software packages may be expensed in the accounting system. If it is, there is a software book value that can be used to quantify the risk of damage if the original software source is lost.
Insurance valuation	Often, insurers are a good source of asset valuation. They accept the risk of loss for the assets they insure and perform an analysis of the risk associated with the policies they issue.
Delphi method	The *Delphi method* is another way to value assets, especially those that do not have an accounting foundation. This method is a systematic and interactive communication technique that involves iteratively questioning a panel of independent experts to obtain asset value forecasts. A facilitator collects and summarizes these forecasts, evaluates individual judgment criteria, and encourages panel members to compare estimates and revise their opinions to reach a group consensus.
	This cyclical process uses a Subject Matter Expert (SME) to answer questions about risk. The SME remains anonymous and a facilitator distributes the results. The process is repeated in two or more rounds to narrow down estimation outcomes and ensure the stability of the resulting value for the asset in question. This value is determined by calculating the median score once the final rounds are completed. This method can be especially helpful with assets that have a hard-to-ascertain value, such as brand identity.
	In many cases, the Delphi method also helps determine risk.

Vulnerability

In computer security, *vulnerability* is a system weakness or safeguard deficiency that enables an attacker to violate a particular system's integrity. A vulnerability may exist only in theory, or it may actually have a proven instance of an exploit. If the risk of data loss by theft is identified, the assessed vulnerability might be either the absence of a security guard or the lack of door locks. Both are critical safety provisions that can help prevent unauthorized, physical intrusion disturbances and data security breaches.

Areas of Vulnerability

Once risks are discovered, it is essential to ascertain the specific areas of an organization that are especially vulnerable to known risks.

Vulnerability Area	Description
Physical structure	Window accessibility in a room where secure information is stored can expose vulnerabilities and create a venue for sudden intrusion threats.
Electrical	A single electrical feed that supports an entire building or enterprise can exploit an instance of vulnerability. Should that single feed fail, it will endanger the availability of system data.
Software	Worms, viruses, and Trojans are software that threaten systems. Routinely using computer virus scanners can help lessen or eliminate vulnerabilities.
Network	The failure to encrypt private information as it travels across a network can heighten system vulnerability. The information may be intercepted by an unauthorized user.
Personnel	If key personnel that are trained to handle situations in a critical event are not available, this can cause additional corporate-wide vulnerabilities.

Risk Types

System security risks come in many forms and are often categorized as natural or man-made.

Risk Type	Description
Natural disasters	Natural disasters are related to weather or other non-controllable events that are residual occurrences of the activities of nature. Different types of natural disasters include: ● Earthquakes. ● Wildfires. ● Flooding. ● Excessive snowfalls. ● Tsunamis. ● Hurricanes. ● Tornados. ● Landslides.

Risk Type	Description
Man-made disasters	Man-made disasters are residual occurrences of individual or collective human activity. Man-made events can be caused intentionally or unintentionally. Intentional man-made disasters include: ● Arson. ● Terrorist attacks. ● Political unrest. ● Break-ins. ● Theft of equipment and/or data. ● Equipment damage. ● File destruction. ● Information disclosure. Unintentional man-made disasters include: ● Employee mistakes. ● Power outages. ● Excessive employee illnesses or epidemics. ● Information disclosure.

Risk Probability and Prioritization

It is vital to appropriately identify the likelihood of risks and then evaluate the related potential severity of loss and probability of occurrence. In the earlier work that was done for risk analysis, it was quite likely that the impact of different risks are identified. This information will be helpful when prioritizing your risk management efforts. If impending risks are not appropriately discovered and accurately detected, your time and resource management will suffer from faulty prioritization and low profitability.

To properly assess the probability and prioritization of security risks, a series of strategic process phases should be practiced and applied to your organization's information systems.

Process Phase	Description
Phase 1	Perform risk analysis tasks on an individual basis.
Phase 2	List the various, ensuing risks discovered through analysis.
Phase 3	Determine risk probability.
Phase 4	Prioritize risks by probability levels and focus on high-probability risks when building a response process.

Quantitative vs. Qualitative Risk Analysis

When evaluating the impact of risks during an assessment, two methods are commonly used.

Risk Analysis Method	Description
Quantitative	*Quantitative risk analysis* is an estimate based on the historical occurrences of incidents and the likelihood of risk reoccurrence.
	Using various statistical and mathematical tools, it is a numerical analysis that produces concrete and tangible values for risks by attaching an actual figure to each risk and the loss experienced if the risk causes harm.
Qualitative	*Qualitative risk analysis* is not based on a numerical analysis or history. It is a *best-guess* estimate of risk occurrence. To complete a qualitative analysis, it is necessary to gain group acceptance of the probability of risk occurrence.
	Delphi technique: A team is evaluating various natural risks. Rather than determining a numeric risk value, they place a qualitative value on the risk, such as:
	1. Not at all likely to occur.
	2. Somewhat likely to occur.
	3. More likely than not to occur.
	4. Will occur.
	This qualitative value does not reflect experience or history, but it does indicate which risks are higher priorities and which are lower priorities based on the opinion of the analysts.

Risk and Vulnerability Determination Factors

Determining risks and vulnerabilities requires the evaluation of three factors.

Determination Factor	Description
Likelihood	The likelihood of an event occurring is stated as the *Annual* or *Annualized Rate of Occurrence (ARO)*. This is an equation percentage factor that estimates the number of times an identified event or threat will occur within a year. ARO = Event number / Years.
	If the electrical grid goes out four times a year, then the ARO will equal 4. If a flood occurs every 10 years and affects the availability of information, the ARO will be 1 in 10 years, or 1/10 or 0.1.

Determination Factor	Description
Impact	The impact of the event is known as the *Single Loss Expectancy (SLE)*. Risk analysts calculate impact by multiplying the *Exposure Factor (EF)* by the *Asset Value (AV)*. The EF is the estimated damage or loss caused by one event. The AV is the value of the asset prior to the damage-causing event. The formula for this is SLE = EF * AV.
	A team estimates that a facility damaged by flooding the will incur a 20% loss. The cost of the facility is $20 million. Using the formula EF * AV, the estimated SLE of the flood will cause a $4 million loss, as shown in the following equation:
	0.20 * $20,000,000 = $4,000,000
Risk	The *Annualized Loss Expectancy (ALE)* is the expected loss from each identified threat on an annual basis. It is equal to the likelihood times the impact: ALE = ARO * SLE.
	If flooding occurs once every 10 years and the damage caused by one flood is $4,000,000, the ALE equals $400,000, as shown in the following equation:
	0.10 * $4,000,000 = $400,000
	If the ALE in this example is $400,000, the organization can then spend up to $400,000 to provide safeguards for preventing flooding. Spending more than $400,000 on a yearly basis will result in higher costs to protect the asset than the estimated damage warrants. If the $400,000 will not eliminate but simply reduce the flooding, you will need to calculate a new ALE that takes into account the reduction in your SLE and/or ARO.

Safeguard Selection Criteria

Knowing or estimating possible losses helps you select and apply the proper safeguards based on both the probable impact of a disaster and the cost of implementing the safeguards.

Safeguard Selection Criterion	Description
Cost effectiveness	Selecting cost-effective safeguards eliminates wasted resources. If the ALE for a given risk is $400,000, spending $500,000 annually to eliminate the risk will be ineffective. Spending up to $400,000 a year will be cost effective if it eliminates or reduces the risk to a level where the remaining risk after safeguard selection is acceptable to the organization. It is important to account for any operational cost of the safeguard.
Risk reduction	Safeguards must be employed to reduce risk. Selecting a safeguard because it is new, interesting, expensive, or novel may not generate risk reduction. If the risk is related to unauthorized, individual access to a secure facility and the employed safeguard is an inexpensive motion detection system that fails 50% of the time, it is not a valid risk-reduction defense measure. Although it may have only cost $10,000, it is ineffective.

Safeguard Selection Criterion	Description
Practicality	Safeguards must be practical. To ward off building floods, a high concrete wall is erected around the facility. After spending the money to build the wall, an engineer evaluates the safeguard and finds that the wall will not protect against extensive flood-induced water pressure. As an alternative, a proposal suggests building a retention pond and diversion streams to help redistribute the flood water away from the building. While the wall had originally seemed like a reasonable solution to safeguard planners, it was not a practical solution.

ACTIVITY 6-1
Discussing Risk Management

Scenario:

In this activity, you will discuss risk management techniques and strategies for your organization.

---

1. **True or False? Risk analysis is the security management process for addressing any risks or economic damages that affect an organization.**

   ___ True

   ___ False

---

2. **What is the appropriate description for each risk analysis process phase?**

___	Asset identification	a.	This phase identifies threats and vulnerabilities so the analyst can confirm where asset protection problems exist.
___	Vulnerability identification	b.	This phase finds assets that require protection and determines the value of the assets.
___	Probability quantification	c.	This phase reduces or eliminates risk by developing countermeasures.
___	Countermeasures determination	d.	This phase determines the possibility that threats will exploit vulnerabilities.

---

3. **What is the appropriate description for each risk management principle?**

___	Avoidance	a.	Rather than respond to the risk, the organization may choose this principle and employ no countermeasures.
___	Reduction	b.	By eliminating the threat through mitigation, no risk is present. With no risk, this principle is implemented.
___	Transfer	c.	This principle helps to shift liability and maintain organizational profitability despite the potential exposure to unwanted security and business risks.
___	Acceptance	d.	This principle helps to curtail the severity of risk or lessen the probability of a loss occurring.

---

4. **True or False? Asset valuation is the practice of determining an asset's risk level to an organization.**

   ___ True

   ___ False

---

5. **What two essential questions does asset valuation answer?**

   a) How much did it cost to purchase the asset?

   b) What requires protection?

   c) How much loss will there be if the asset is misplaced or damaged?

   d) How will we maintain the asset?

6. **What is the appropriate description for each asset valuation method?**

___ Asset management system	a. This method includes additional asset information that may be present, such as the cost of developing software packages.
___ Accounting system	b. With this method, risk of loss for the assets is accepted and protected.
___ Insurance valuation	c. This method uses an organizational system that contains a detailed record of property and similar assets.
___ Delphi method	d. This method utilizes expert judgement to value assets, especially for those that do not have an accounting foundation.

7. **Which one or more of the following are considered natural disaster risk types?**

   a) Hurricane

   b) Flooding

   c) Theft

   d) Epidemics

   e) Wildfire

8. **To properly assess the probability and prioritization of security risks, a series of strategic process phases should be practiced and applied to your organization's information systems. In what order should the phases occur?**

   List the various, ensuing risks discovered through analysis.

   Perform risk analysis tasks on an individual basis.

   Prioritize risks by probability levels and focus on high-probability risks when building a response process.

   Determine risk probability.

9. **True or False? Qualitative risk analysis is based on numerical analysis and history.**

   ___ True

   ___ False

10. **What is an estimate based on the historical occurrences of incidents and the likelihood of risk reoccurrence?**

11. **In computer security, what is a system weakness or safeguard deficiency that enables an attacker to violate a particular system's integrity?**

12. **In what areas are organizations typically vulnerable?**

13. **Which one or more of the following are risk determination factors?**

    a) ARO

    b) SLE

    c) EF

    d) ALE

    e) SLA

14. **What criteria should be used in the selection of safeguards and why?**

TOPIC B

Ethics

While risk management helps identify vulnerabilities and quantify security gaps in your information systems, ethics establish a foundation for behavioral conduct that is conducive to protecting your organizational data, environment, and infrastructure. In this topic, you will analyze ethical issues that affect security implementations.

If your organization experiences a criminal attack, you need to be aware of the relevant regulatory requirements and ethical codes of conduct, as well as how to quickly and effectively counteract computer ethics fallacies. A thorough understanding of these principles and strategies will ensure that your organization successfully handles, from an ethical perspective, an attack from any source.

Ethics Issues in a Computing Environment

The conversation on ethics can become somewhat confused by the concept of "computer ethics." Remember that much of this revolves around people and processes, and the ethical concerns involved go beyond computers. The simple fact that so many of an organization's users are using computers all day, every day, and perform most of their work on computers, can raise certain ethical issues. For example, a company can effectively track an employee from the moment they arrive in the building until they leave at the end of the day. Systems can track usage, emails, telephone conversations, and more. It is important that employers and employees understand what is being monitored. Users that believed they could send an email anonymously because they could change the "From" address to a different user's account or perhaps even an account called "anonymous" might find out later that the employer can still trace the email back to their PC based on the IP address in the email header. In addition, the fact that a computer grants users access to a tremendous amount of information, but can seemingly also provide anonymity, can raise issues. These issues are not necessarily new. The concept of computer ethics tracks back as far as the 1940s.

Organizational Ethics

Ethics in an organization refers to the organization's principles of acceptable and proper conduct as well as its system of moral values.

When companies or governments adopt ethical codes, they often opt to document expectations for professional conduct and define responsibility standards. In doing so, determining and managing ethical behavior on an as-needed basis is less difficult. A company may also be bound to certain ethical standards by the regulatory requirements surrounding it, such as the Sarbanes-Oxley (SOX) or Payment Card Industry (PCI) standard.

Ethical code enforcement also helps regulate security by minimizing risk. Hiring and sustaining employees with high levels of ethical behavior are valuable safeguards for reducing or potentially eliminating man-made disasters and threats.

Additionally, organizations have a responsibility to their employees, customers, suppliers, and stakeholders to operate in an ethical manner. Therefore, organizational ethics are the foundation of honorable, accountable, and reliable performance.

Regulatory Requirements for Ethics Programs

Many different types of organizations implement ethics programs. Both the American Medical Association (AMA) and the U.S. federal government are institutions that commonly enforce codes of ethical conduct. If your organization is part of these institutions or does business with them, their ethics rules could apply. You need to be aware of the codes that pertain to your organization.

Federal laws and regulations such as the Sarbanes-Oxley (SOX) Act, the Health Insurance Portability and Accountability Act (HIPAA), and the Gramm-Leach-Bliley Act (GLBA) require the adoption of ethical standards within organizations and often require an annual briefing on ethical requirements.

CSEP Policies

The Center for the Study of Ethics in the Professions (CSEP) at the Illinois Institute of Technology maintains a compiled, online catalog of approximately 1,000 codes of ethics. CSEP has collected these codes from government agencies, businesses, professional organizations and foundations, and various other enterprises and establishments.

For more information on CSEP's ethical policies, visit **http://ethics.iit.edu/research/ codes-ethics-collection**.

Common Computer Ethics Fallacies

As a security professional, it may help you to defend against hackers and other information security criminals if you recognize that they often consider their motivations to be neither illicit nor unethical.

Ethics Fallacy	Motivation Factor
Free information	The criminal feels the information is yearning to be free and they want to help it escape.
Computer game	The criminal feels the computer is like a game; when the criminal plays the game, they can't attain the next level if they haven't achieved the objective of the preceding level. Therefore, if the computer lets them do something, it must be okay.
Taking candy from a baby	Because it is so easy to make a copy of a file and to leave the original intact, it must be okay, so the criminal questions why they should be worried about whether it is ethical.
Shatterproof	If the criminal did not break it, it must be okay to use it. Surely, the system would stop the criminal before they cause any damage. Since it has not stopped them, it must be okay.
The ends justify the means	If the criminal feels that he or she is learning from this to help him or herself and society, it is unlikely a wrongful act.

Internet Architecture Board Ethics

The Internet Architecture Board (IAB) views the Internet as a resource that is most valuable when its users are not performing certain actions to compromise its availability and accessibility. Therefore, IAB ethics primarily focus on unethical activities to avoid rather than ethical actions to encourage. Actions to avoid include:

- Seeking to gain unauthorized access to Internet resources.
- Disrupting intended Internet use.
- Wasting resources such as people, capacity, and computers through unprincipled actions.
- Destroying the integrity of computer-based information.
- Compromising user privacy.

 IAB ethics policies can be found in RFC 1087.

(ISC)² Code of Ethics

Before taking the CISSP® exam, the International Information Systems Security Certification Consortium (ISC)²® requires each candidate to subscribe to a mandatory Code of Ethics. Since it is a requirement, testing on this subject is likely. Compliance with the Preamble and Canons is mandatory. The order of Canons is also important. Any conflicts should be resolved in the order stated. Higher-level Canons take precedent over lower-level Canons.

Ethical Code	Goals
Preamble	The (ISC)² Code of Ethics preamble includes:
	• Ensuring the safety of the commonwealth and the responsibility and accountability to principals, (ISC)² committee members, and other CISSP professionals.
	• Requiring and acknowledging adherence to the utmost ethical values and standards of behavior.
	• Strictly observing this code to demonstrate compliance and fulfill the conditions of certification.
Canons	The (ISC)² Code of Ethics canons include:
	• Guarding the commonwealth, the infrastructure, and society.
	• Behaving responsibly, justly, honestly, honorably, and legally.
	• Providing adept, competent, and assiduous service to principals.
	• Improving, enhancing, and protecting the profession.

 A CISSP is expected to act in an ethical manner in support of employers, clients, and the computer community in general. Failure to act in an ethical manner can result in the revocation of CISSP certification.

Additional Canon Guidance

Additional guidelines are addressed and provided for each of the four canons. Although this guidance may seem mandatory, it is merely a collection of advisory principles for ethical conduct. These guidelines are designed to help professionals assertively identify and resolve inevitable ethical conflicts and dilemmas throughout their information security careers.

For more information on the (ISC)^2 Code of Ethics, visit **www.isc2.org/InnerPage.aspx?id= 558&=code+of+ethics**.

ACTIVITY 6-2
Discussing Ethics

Scenario:

In this activity, you will discuss ethics.

1. **True or False? Ethics establish a foundation for behavioral conduct that is conducive to protecting your organizational data, environment, and infrastructure.**

   ___ True

   ___ False

2. **When companies or governments adopt ethical codes, what benefits are generally created by doing so?**

3. **True or False? Typically, information security criminals recognize that their motivations are unethical.**

   ___ True

   ___ False

4. **Name some institutions that you have come in contact with that have commonly enforced codes of ethical standards.**

5. **What are some examples of typical ethics fallacies that information security criminals believe?**

6. **The IAB ethics primarily focuses on unethical activities to avoid. What are some of the actions to avoid?**

7. **As a prospective CISSP candidate, what are some examples of the ethics principles you will need to formally subscribe to as part of the (ISC)² Code of Ethics?**

Lesson 6 Follow-up

In this lesson, you analyzed risk management criteria and applied behavior standards to your organization's code of ethics. Employing the appropriate methodology and processes for performing risk assessments as well as supporting ethical code compliance will help you efficiently manage risk exposure, minimize security breaches, and defend against system vulnerabilities.

1. **What risks are prevalent in your field of expertise and how do you protect them?**

2. **What types of codes of ethics are you familiar with in your organization?**

7 | Software Development Security

Lesson Time: 3 hour(s)

Lesson Objectives:

In this lesson, you will analyze software development security.

You will:

- Analyze software configuration management.
- Analyze software control implementation.
- Identify secure database systems.

Introduction

Defining security management for your organization allows you to implement the policies and procedures from your security program. The first areas of application security you need to address are software development, operation, and maintenance. In this lesson, you will analyze application security and apply software configuration management strategies, software controls, and database system security mechanisms.

Having security awareness built into software applications is critical to your organization. Application development methods affect the integrity of processed data and immunize data from outside attacks. Your role as a security professional requires an understanding of the software development and change process to ensure the security of applications in your organization.

This lesson supports content found in the Software Development Security and Operations Security domains of the CISSP® certification.

TOPIC A
Software Configuration Management

You have created a security program and analyzed the risk within your organization. Now, you will apply security measures to your application development practices. Protecting your software ensures the integrity of data and applications. In large part, integrity means controlling changes in the development process. In this topic, you will analyze the processes, techniques, and models of software configuration management.

All software projects involve change. Applying the necessary controls to change ensures that everyone uses the correct versions of all system components. This includes code sets, design documents, and testing. Imagine how testing a new build of an application with the wrong test guidelines would impact business goals. Through software configuration management, you can efficiently develop a system to track and control changes within your organization and guarantee the integrity of your information systems.

Programming Basics

Although it is not an expectation of the CISSP® exam that candidates need to know how to program, having a basic understanding of programming terminology and practices will make you a better security professional. It may one day be your job to manage a development project and having a basic understanding of programming and software concepts will make the job easier and the organization more secure.

Machine Language, Assembly Language, and Source Code

Machine language or *machine code* is the lowest level of code, getting right down to the zeros and ones that a computer's central processing unit (CPU) will execute. *Assembly language* is a low-level programming language that needs to be processed by an assembler utility to be converted to machine code. *Source code* is a higher level programing language that is generally human readable; it has enough text-like qualities to start to recognize the intent of the program. Source code needs to be compiled in order for the CPU to recognize it as machine code. A compiler takes the source code and converts it to an executable file, usually displayed as an .exe file. There are also interpreted languages in which the source code is interpreted directly into machine code at program runtime. This interpretation happens with each execution, as compared to the compiled code that is permanently changed by the compile process.

Program Language Types

There are many ways to categorize programming languages. They can be categorized by compiled versus interpreted, or procedural versus object oriented. The following provides a high-level overview of some of the different types of languages used in application development.

Program Language Type	Description
Compiled languages	A *compiler* is a program that transforms the source of code of a higher-level language to object code that is understood by the device or operating system. It is often used to create an executable file. Once source code has been compiled into an executable, it can be run many times without the need to compile again. Common compiled languages include Fortran, COBOL, C, C++, and Java. Compiled code is generally considered faster than interpreted code.
Interpreted languages	Interpreted languages are not put through a compiler but rather use an interpreter that translates the code line by line into machine code each time the application is run. Common interpreted languages include Perl, Postscript, Python, and Ruby. Interpreted code has an advantage over compiled code because it can run on any machine that has an interpreter, thus providing write once, run many efficiencies.
Procedural languages	These languages use routines, subroutines, methods, and functions. Writing an application involves writing thousands of lines of code. It is considered linear programming.
Object Oriented Programming (OOP)	OOP creates reusable objects that combine methods and data. The reusable nature of OOP offers potential cost savings and also potential security enhancements. If an object has been deemed secure, it can be re-used with confidence.
Object Oriented Databases (OOD)	The object oriented programming approach has been extended into database design with OOD.
Distributed programming techniques	• *Object Request Brokers (ORBs)* can be used to locate objects and can act as middleware for connecting programs. • *Component Object Model (COM)* and *Distributed Component Object Model (DCOM)* are two Microsoft ORB tools. COM can discover objects on a local system and DCOM can discover objects on the network. • *Common Object Request Broker Architecture (CORBA)* is an open source ORB framework. CORBA seeks to separate the interface from the instance. This can provide flexibility in design but also provides encapsulation so the client is not able to see all the details of the object. • *Enterprise JavaBean (EJB)* is a tool from Sun Microsystems that allows for a distributed multi-tier application in Java.

Programming Language Generations

The historical progression of classes of programming languages is often referred to as the different "generations" of programming code. In general, each generation increases the degree to which the code is abstracted from the underlying computer hardware, making systems and software more and more portable and natural to both use and develop. Here is a list of the generally accepted taxonomy of language generations:

● First generation: Machine code

● Second generation: Assembly language

● Third generation (3GL): Compiled languages such as Fortran, COBOL, C, and Pascal

● Fourth generation (4GL): Complied languages that are used to reduce the cost and time of software projects, such as FoxPro, Cognos Powerhouse 4GL, and Oracle Reports

● Fifth generation (5GL): Natural language programs where a user simply asks questions and no program is required. They are used in expert systems and artificial intelligence applications.

 The first and second generation languages typically do not get the "GL" moniker, In fact, they were not even referred to as first and second generation until people started using the term "3GL" and then there was a need to define the ones that came before as first and second.

The term 5GL is controversial; some say there is no real distinction to qualify 5GL separately from 4GL.

The System Life Cycle

It is important to recognize the difference between the overall system life cycle (SLC) and the system development life cycle (SDLC). They sound very similar and are rather similar, but it is important to remember that the SLC is a more all-encompassing process that includes the important phases after system development, particularly operation, maintenance, and disposal. From a security standpoint, it is extremely important to account and plan for the disposal of the system even before it is built. Many systems are going to create tremendous amounts of data, and the proper protection and disposal of the data and the system is essential to maintaining confidentiality and integrity.

Software development activities use many different processes, but most will encompass certain prescribed phases. The following is a commonly referenced SLC implemented by the U.S. Department of Justice (DOJ).

Phase	Description
Project initiation	Research the general needs and feasibility of the project when a business need is identified and obtain management approval to continue software development.
System concept development	Once the business need and project are validated, the ideas for fulfilling the need are evaluated. Start to develop funding support. Begin scope documents.
Planning	Review concept integration into existing process. Look for existing or overlapping projects. Determine the functions to be performed during the project and prepare a project plan.

Phase	Description
Requirements analysis	Define functional requirements. Consider user requirements. Create a Functional Requirements Document.
System design	Proposed user inputs are reviewed by future end users of the system to see if they provide the desired functions.
Software development	Perform the actual programming activities to support the design. Acquire other hardware and software to support the application. This phase includes unit testing of specific modules as they are developed.
Integration and test	Components are brought together and tested. Quality assurance (QA) testing is performed. Possible certifications and accreditations are obtained.
Implementation	Prior to installation, evaluate the quality of the software using a separate QA group. Conduct user testing and acceptance, followed by user training. Software is installed following the change management group's approval.
Operational/maintenance	Conduct a post-implementation review. Continue the operation and maintenance of the software. Changes to the software must be coordinated through the change control function. In-process reviews are ongoing.
Disposal	Terminate the software usage and dispose of the system. Determine if the information in this soon-to-be disposed system needs to be brought forward or not. Ensure the security of the associated information in the system during and after the disposal phase.

SDLC and NIST Special Publication 800-14

NIST Special Publication 800-14 also identifies a SDLC and uses the words "secure" or "security" in each phase descriptor.

- Prepare a Security Plan: Ensure security through all phases

- Initiation: Conduct a security sensitivity assessment

- Development/Acquisition: Determine security requirements

- Implementation: Security testing

- Operation/Maintenance: Security operations and administration

- Disposal: Secure disposal

Security in the Software Development Processes

While software development processes may have different numbers of steps, different names, and in some cases, different step definitions, it is imperative to deal with security issues as early in the process as possible. Ideally, security personnel should assist in the process from project initiation through the disposal phase. Security that is implemented late in the development cycle will be less effective than security that is created early in the design phases, which is developed as part of the overall solution. Security that is introduced late in the project will also be disruptive and likely more expensive. Security professionals are also responsible for ensuring that information confidentiality exists during the disposal phase of any system.

Software Categories

There are two types of software categories that are used by organizations.

Software Category	Description
Proprietary software	*Proprietary software* is software that is developed by an organization that does not disclose the source code. From a security perspective, proprietary software is a "black box." The proprietary vendor's claims of security are validated by testing, but cannot be evaluated by code inspection. On some occasions this may be validated with a third party testing lab or the product may have achieved Common Criteria or other assurances already. This can still leave the software open to undisclosed or unexpected vulnerabilities. A well-known example of proprietary software is Microsoft® Windows®.
Open source software	*Open source software* is software that is provided to a buyer with a complete copy of the source code. Purchasers can evaluate the security of open source software by examining the code provided. While code inspection may not result in the discovery of all vulnerabilities, the purchaser has the opportunity to analyze the software rather than trust the vendor to supply vulnerability information. Since everyone in the open source community can look at the code, many believe that all errors will be discovered eventually. This is sometimes referred to as Linus' Law, which states, with sufficiently many eyeballs looking at the code, all bugs will become apparent. While this sounds good, it is also possible that a dishonest user will see the error and not report it until they know that customers are using the code. Then, when they reveal the bug, they will be compromising the company using the software. A well-known example of open source software is Linux. "Linus' Law" is a reference to the creator of Linux, Linus Torvalds.

Values of Proprietary vs. Open Source Software

Proprietary software, because of the closed nature of the system, presents an evaluation problem for security professionals. Open source software removes the evaluation limitations of proprietary software, yet hackers and other malware creators also have access to the open source and can create exploits based on their code analyses. Each type of software has its own benefits; however, security professionals continue to struggle with the limitations of each.

Disclosure

So what do you do when you have found a bug or security flaw in a piece of hardware or software?

Full disclosure involves releasing the information immediately and publicly. It is obviously controversial, but some feel that if they found it, others could have too, and everybody should know as quickly as possible. There are even publicly available websites dedicated to full disclosure. Most organizations would consider full disclosure unethical.

Partial disclosure, sometimes referred to as responsible disclosure, involves sharing the information with the hardware or software vendor first. This gives them a chance to fix the problem and release a patch. In some cases, if the reporting person feels the company is not taking them seriously or is taking too long to release a patch, the individual may resort to revealing the flaw publicly.

Software Escrow

When proprietary software is used, access to the source code is not available. If the vendor stops supporting the product with patches—or worse, goes out of business—risk increases. It is possible to work with the vendor to use a software escrow agent to hold onto a copy of the source code. There will be rules and restrictions around how and when access to the source code is granted, but it could protect the company, especially if the company plans to use the software for a long time.

Software Development Methods

Over the years, many different software development methods have been created to address the needs of large complex projects. Some of these have been adapted from other project management initiatives. Now, some of the tools developed for software development are now finding their way into project management. One of the more important components of the different methods is how they recognize and allow for security.

The Waterfall Software Development Model

The *waterfall software development model* creates software projects that flow from one defined phase to the next, as water flows from one level of a waterfall to another. The waterfall method was first used in manufacturing and was adapted for software development in the 1970s. The term is often used derisively to refer to a rigid, flawed model, but because so many other methods were derived from the waterfall method, it is important to understand. It is considered flawed because in the true waterfall, it is only possible to go down the falls. Once a step has been completed, it is nearly impossible to go back up the falls. In some development projects, this is thought to be an advantage because many checks exist before moving to the next stage, which could actually result in a more secure system or application. In actual implementation, it is typically okay to go back one step. This is sometimes referred to as the modified waterfall. Most waterfall diagrams fail to provide for disposal, which is another concern.

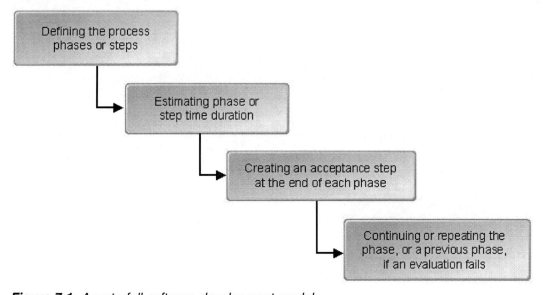

Figure 7-1: A waterfall software development model.

To help control software development, the waterfall model is implemented through a series of stages, which include:

1. Defining the process phases or steps.

2. Estimating the phase or step time duration to determine the project length.

3. Creating an acceptance step at the end of each phase; this is known as a milestone. The project status is evaluated during meetings held at the conclusion of each phase. Approval to proceed must be obtained before the project continues to the next step.

4. Continuing or repeating the phase, or a previous phase, if an evaluation fails.

The Sashimi Model

The *sashimi software development model* is a major modification of the waterfall model. There is intentional overlap between the phases, sometimes reaching as far as one or two stages back. It is named for the Japanese dish "sashimi" in which pieces of fish are overlapped.

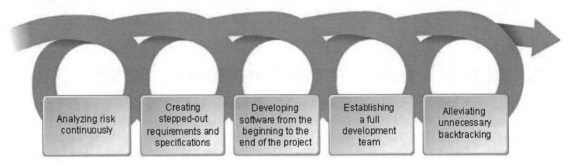

Figure 7-2: *The Sashimi model.*

The Spiral Software Development Model

In the *spiral model,* software development repeats an iterative process involving risk analysis, requirements specification, prototyping, and testing or implementation. As the project matures, the length of each step increases and the project focuses on the solution that meets requirements.

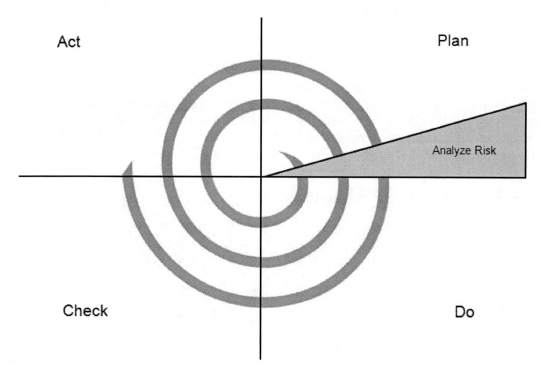

Figure 7-3: *A spiral software development model.*

The steps in the model include:

1. Continuously analyzing risk.

2. Creating stepped-out requirements and specifications.

3. Developing software from the beginning to the end of the project, starting with prototypes and completing with the finished product.

4. Establishing a full development team that includes users throughout the process.

5. Alleviating unnecessary backtracking if something is unacceptable; objectionable design or software elements are remedied in the next spiral cycle.

The Structured Development Model

The *structured development model* is based on structured programming concepts that require a careful combination of sequencing, selection, and iteration. It is possible to do structured programming in any language, though it is frequently used with a procedural programming language. By adhering strictly to the techniques of sequencing, selection, and iteration, and avoiding the GOTO technique, the code could be made very tight, making it easy to verify and test. It is usually deployed in a top-down model where developers map out the overall program and then break it into modules that can be independently tested. These modules can then be used by other programs and can possibly save costs and development time in future projects.

GOTO Statements

The GOTO statement is used to quickly jump around a program. You essentially "GOTO" another line or point in the program. If there are too many such commands, you are left with "spaghetti" code, a derisive term for a program that is hard to follow. "Hard to follow" also means "hard to evaluate" from a security standpoint.

The Cleanroom Model

The *cleanroom model* takes its name from the cleanroom that chip manufacturers use. It is based on the idea that it is easier and cheaper to keep dust out of the manufacturing process up front by building a cleanroom than it is to eliminate dust after the manufacturing. In software development, it is easier and cheaper to eliminate defects before code is written, rather than trying to remove them afterwards. When complex software projects have millions of lines of code, this approach makes a lot of sense. However, it also requires a great deal of upfront time in design, training, and testing, and this is when management is most anxious to see results. It can, however, save a lot of time in reduced quality testing effort and reworks.

The Prototyping Model

The *prototyping model* attempts to address the concerns of the waterfall method by providing early prototypes for users to see and test. The early feedback from these prototypes could be used to develop better products. The four basic steps of the prototype method are:

1. Identify basic requirements.
2. Develop an initial prototype.
3. Review the prototype.
4. Revise and enhance the prototype.

Agile Software Development

Agile software development was another response to the inflexibility of the waterfall method. Agile embraces flexibility, fast turnaround, frequent input from the customers, and constant improvement. It is very iterative with quick deliveries of prototypes that receive feedback from users to help improve the next iteration. Agile even has its own manifesto.

The Agile Manifesto

The "Agile Manifesto" was written in 2001 by a group of 17 software developers and is available on the Internet at **http://agilemanifesto.org/**. It states:

"We are uncovering better ways of developing software by doing it and helping others. Through this work, we have come to value:

● Individuals and interactions over processes and tools.

● Working software over comprehensive documentation.

● Customer collaboration over contract negotiation.

● Responding to change over following a plan.

That is, while there is value in the items on the right, we value the items on the left more."

SCRUM

SCRUM is a variation of Agile. The original authors referred to it in terms of a "holistic or rugby approach." They went on to describe the idea of a group that "tries to go the distance as a unit, passing the ball back and forth." Another author then used the rugby term "scrum" to describe this group and the term stuck. SCRUM uses "sprints to finish components of a project. Each sprint starts with a meeting and ends with a review."

 There are many more software development models and methods and there are sure to be more developed in the future. It is important for companies find a model to that will support their business and security objectives.

CASE

Computer-Aided Software Engineering (CASE) is not so much a model or a methodology but the adoption of tools and techniques to help with large-scale software projects. It can involve programming tools and computer utilities to help with projects that have many components and lots of people. As large projects are broken apart and assigned to different users scattered throughout an organization, the effort to put that all back together into a cohesive program is extremely challenging. CASE tools and training can help.

Function Points

A *function point* is a unit of measurement used to size software applications and convey the quantity of business functionality that an information system offers its users. Basic functional user requirements are identified and categorized into one of the following types:

- Outputs.
- Inquiries.
- Inputs.
- Internal files.
- External interfaces.

Creating a report is a function point and is categorized as an output. An input screen would be an input function point.

The software required to create a function point can be simple or complex. The scope of the software is not included in the function point; however, the result of the software is. A complex system with many function points takes substantially longer to develop than simple systems with fewer function points.

Because function points are software metrics that measure the functional size of an information system, they help estimate costs for application development and maintenance, project productivity, and software size. They can also be helpful in identifying the security concerns of the software. For example, if you are creating internal files, they need to be sufficiently protected.

One of the limitations of function points is that they are related to user-viewed functions. Internal functions are not part of the scope of function point definitions, and internal function size may not be included in the project scope. This results in understaffed and under-resourced projects.

The Capability Maturity Model®

The *Capability Maturity Model® (CMM®)* is a process capability model that evaluates the levels of sophistication or maturity found in an organization's software development process. The model was developed by the Software Engineering Institute (SEI) at Carnegie Mellon University (CMU) in the 1990s. CMM describes five levels of maturity, from lowest to highest, which include:

- Level 1: Initial. Processes are ad hoc and chaotic. It is a starting point.

- Level 2: Managed. Processes are established to track cost, schedule, and functionality. Processes can be repeated.

- Level 3: Defined. Processes are defined and part of standard procedure.

- Level 4: Quantitatively Managed. Process are quantitatively managed and understood. Metrics are in place.

- Level 5: Optimizing. Process optimization. Continual process improvement.

Each maturity level includes key practices that an organization must exhibit. The levels provide a path to improve development projects. Levels cannot be skipped; they must be achieved in order.

The target maturity level for most organizations is Level 3, where the organization exhibits well-defined processes, solid communications practices, and reviews of output by coworkers. CMM can be used to measure your internal development staff as well as to evaluate a potential outsource vendor.

Capability Maturity Model Integration®

Capability Maturity Model Integration® (CMMI®) is a process improvement project initiative that incorporates three popular CMMs into one cohesive collection of integrated models. It is the next evolution in the CMM process. In the early 1990s, the SEI at CMU created a new set of evaluations that merged many of the earlier models. This development effort has focused on creating models that help to integrate organizational activities, improve processes and communications, and set goals to improve organizations in disciplines that include systems engineering, software engineering, and integrated product and process development.

 For more information on the CMM and CMMI, such as maturity-level descriptions and key process areas, visit Carnegie Mellon's SEI website at **www.sei.cmu.edu/**.

The Change Control Process

Change control encompasses a series of process phases that are used to ensure that a system's confidentiality, integrity, and availability (CIA) triad is well maintained. Change management should be a structured, well-understood process like the organization's SDLC choice. People should know their roles and understand what to expect in change management.

Change Control Phase	Description
Requesting the change	The change request requires justification that supports the potential change and a full explanation of the change.
Approving the change	The Change Control Board (CCB) evaluates the change request and approves the change. No change can continue until it is approved.
Communicating the change	Communicate the change and its intended impact.
Documenting the change	The change is recorded and scheduled in the change log.
Testing and reporting results	The CCB should confirm that adequate testing has occurred before approving the change implementation. A backout or failure recovery plan must be in place.
Implementing the change	Changes are implemented within scheduled parameters including date, time, by whom, and so on.
Reporting the change	Successful or unsuccessful changes should always be reported to management so that progress is recognized.

Information Technology Infrastructure Library

The newest development in change control is the development and adoption of the Information Technology Infrastructure Library (ITIL®). The ITIL structure includes a definition and a procedure for change control. It provides concepts and techniques for conducting development, infrastructure, and operations management for information technology (IT).

ITIL is published and circulated in a book series that covers IT management. The name ITIL is a registered trademark of the United Kingdom's Office of Government Commerce (OGC). Other international governmental and commercial organizations are quickly embracing and implementing the ITIL structure.

The Configuration Management Process

Configuration management is the process used to track hardware and software components in an enterprise to ensure that existing configurations match implementation standards and should answer some key questions that are specific to each phase.

Configuration Management Phase	Key Question(s)
Configuration identification	What configurations are authorized and should be implemented in all current, in-use systems?
Configuration change control (or change management)	What changes are being made or have been made to the authorized configurations?
	Has the documentation on tests performed to support the new configuration been included?
Configuration status accounting	What modifications have been made to the authorized configurations and what changes are pending?

Configuration Management Phase	Key Question(s)
Configuration verification and auditing	Do the configurations in use today match the configurations found in the configuration management system?
	Have any unauthorized and untracked modifications been made?
	What are the security risks associated with the unauthorized changes?

 Large and small organizations alike practice configuration management.

Configuration Management Database

The *configuration management database (CMDB)* is a software tool that serves as a repository for configuration management information. Each hardware and software component is entered into the database and then modifications are tracked. Some items that might be found for each component include:

- The component name.
- The procurement date.
- The source.
- The model code, number, and/or component ID.
- The serial number.
- The location.
- The procurement cost.
- The asset accounting tag number.
- The administrator.

Changes that are entered into the CMDB for each component might also include:

- The change approval number.
- The change approval date.
- The change implementation date.
- The change implementer.

ACTIVITY 7-1
Discussing Software Configuration Management

Scenario:
In this activity, you will discuss the principles of software configuration management.

---

1. **What is the appropriate description for each phase of the software life cycle?**

   ___ Project initiation
   ___ Functional design analysis and planning
   ___ System design specifications
   ___ Software development
   ___ Installation/implementation
   ___ Operational/maintenance
   ___ Disposal

   a. Concludes software use and ensures continuation of secure data
   b. Prepares a detailed design of the software
   c. Supports software use and manages changes
   d. Determines the functions to execute during the project
   e. Coding activities to assist the design
   f. Assesses the quality of the software using a QA group
   g. Determines the needs for software development

---

2. **Which type of software is more likely to expose an organization to unexpected security vulnerabilities?**

   a) Open source software
   b) Proprietary software

---

3. **True or False? Security that is implemented late in the development cycle will be just as effective as security that is created early in the design phases.**

   ___ True
   ___ False

---

4. **Prioritize the stages in the waterfall model process.**

   Create an acceptance step at the end of each phase.

   Continue or repeat the phase, or a previous phase, if an evaluation fails.

   Estimate the phase or step time duration to determine the project length.

   Define the process phases or steps.

---

5. **True or False? The spiral model software development process is a repetitive process involving only risk analysis.**

   ___ True
   ___ False

---

6. **Which statement describes the CMM?**

    a) A capability model that includes a detection system to monitor an organization's software development process.

    b) A process capability model that evaluates the levels of sophistication or maturity found in an organization's software development process.

    c) A process capability model that evaluates the levels of sophistication in an organization's infrastructure.

    d) An evaluation tool used to measure the readiness of an organization's software development capabilities.

7. **True or False? The CMMI is a process improvement project initiative that incorporates the different CMMs into one cohesive collection of integrated models.**

    ___ True

    ___ False

8. **What is the appropriate description for each change control phase?**

___	Requesting the change	a.	Changes are put in place within scheduled parameters including date, time, by whom, and so on.
___	Approving the change	b.	Successful or unsuccessful changes should always be documented to management so that progress is recognized.
___	Documenting the change	c.	The change is recorded and scheduled in the change log.
___	Testing and reporting results	d.	The CCB evaluates the change request and approves the change. No change can continue until it is approved.
___	Implementing the change	e.	The CCB should confirm that an adequate evaluation has occurred before approving the change implementation. A backout or failure recovery plan must be in place.
___	Reporting the change	f.	This step requires justification that supports the potential change and a full explanation of the change.

9. **What are the appropriate key questions for each configuration management phase?**

___	Configuration identification	a. What modifications have been made to the authorized configurations and what changes are pending?
___	Configuration change control (or change management)	b. What configurations are authorized and should be implemented in all current, in-use systems?
___	Configuration status accounting	c. What changes are being made or have been made to the authorized configurations?
___	Configuration verification and auditing	d. Do the configurations in use today match the configurations found in the configuration management system? Have any unauthorized and untracked modifications been made? What are the security risks associated with the unauthorized changes?

10. **Explain the difference between compiled code and interpreted code.**

11. **Explain the difference between a SLC and a SDLC.**

TOPIC B
Software Controls

In the previous topic, you analyzed the processes, techniques, and models that are essential to manage software configurations. Software configuration management is only one way to protect the confidentiality, integrity, and availability of your organization's information systems. Using appropriate software controls is a prudent defense against attacks on your company's databases and the valuable data stored within them. In this topic, you will analyze software control implementation.

Applications are wide open for hackers to prey upon when there are no software controls. Performing configuration management is key to protecting your software from version control problems. But what about the threat of software attacks from outside sources, such as viruses? In today's world, these are real concerns that affect the integrity and availability of your software applications. To effectively guard against such attacks, you need to recognize the different methods, system structures, and prevention techniques that are essential to properly implement software controls.

Data Structures

Definition:

A *data structure* is a standardized format for storing information in a computer system so that this information can be efficiently accessed by applications. It becomes part of an outline or blueprint for how related data should be grouped together. Well-designed data structures typically enable the performance and completion of a wide range of critical operations and tasks while using as few resources as possible, such as execution time and memory space.

Example:

Figure 7-4: *A database is a data structure.*

Types of Data Structures

There are several types of data structures, from the most basic to the most complex, that consolidate and store information.

Data Structure	Description
Primitive	A *primitive* is a data element that is singular in nature and not broken down into small components when accessed. These include: ● Integers. ● Strings. ● Floating point numbers. ● Boolean true/false. ● Character.
Array	An *array* is a collection of primitives that are interrelated. A set of student grades might be stored in an array.
List	A *list* typically contains ordered arrays. Lists are usually considered one-dimensional arrays. When grades in an array are presented in a given sequence, they are displayed in a list format.
Matrix	A *matrix* is an array with more than one dimension. For example, a matrix could include the temperatures for each hour of the day, for each day of the month.

Flat Files

A *flat file* is the earliest mechanism used to store information in computer systems. Flat files were originally stored as unit records or on punch cards or magnetic tape, but were not very efficient. Each entry or record in the flat file represents a single transaction. Records are related to each other by controlling codes such as personal identification numbers (PINs) or part numbers.

Flat files include an additional shortcoming, however; modifications to flat file structures require detailed and complex modifications to the programs that access the flat files. The addition or deletion of a flat file field requires the recompilation of all programs that access the file. This is time consuming and can present security risks if all programs are not properly modified and recompiled.

Databases have largely replaced flat files. The database offers the ability to change the manner in which data is processed and organized. It can provide more efficient and more secure storage of data.

Artificial Intelligence Systems

Definition:

An *artificial intelligence (AI)* system is a mechanism that attempts to mimic or emulate the process of human intelligence by implementing algorithms that cause the system to learn about its environment and make decisions based on its learning. AI systems are implemented using neural networks that are meant to approximate the neural processes of the human brain.

For most of their existence, computers have been thought to be pretty stodgy devices. Input in, output out. Computers did not think, they just ran the numbers; they were glorified calculators. Pablo Picasso is quoted having said "But they [computers] are useless. They can only give you answers." That seems to be about to change. There are different terms and different levels but it is clear that they are becoming very sophisticated. For example, when IBM recently built a computer to play Jeopardy!, it was indeed quite good at giving answers. Much of the credit goes to the designers and programmers who are making this sort of artificial intelligence a reality.

Example: AI in Medicine and Stocks

AI systems have been used to assist in medical diagnosis processes and stock trading.

Knowledge-Based Systems

Definition:

A *knowledge-based system (KBS)* is a program that uses knowledge-based techniques to support human decision making, learning, and action. KBSs are capable of cooperating with human users. The quality of support and the information presentation are important implementation factors of these types of systems. A KBS performs decision-making and problem-solving functions through AI and access to a database of knowledge information.

Example: KBS in Information Storage

As corporate information becomes more diverse, companies are turning to KBSs to store their information. The KBS gives companies a centralized repository with search capabilities to make locating many different types of information related to a single subject possible.

Expert Systems

Definition:

An *expert system* is an extension of AI and KBS. Expert systems are built to provide problem-solving assistance. They are equipped with a knowledge base of information about a specific subject area such as a medical diagnosis. Included with the knowledge base is a set of rules that are used to link the information together. Expert systems often use inference to assist in the decision-making process.

Example: An Expert System

Dendral is a software program that originated at Stanford University in the mid-1960s to help organic chemists identify unknown organic molecules.

Security Considerations in Software Development

There are many different security considerations that must be taken into account during the software development process.

Software Vulnerability	*Best Practices*
Buffer overflow	Buffer overflows happen when more data is sent then the buffer is designed to accept and no boundary checking is in place. When the program writes the data that is beyond the buffer, it can result in existing information being overwritten, memory corruption, or in a worse-case scenario, the execution of unapproved code. To prevent buffer overflow exploitations, programmers should perform length checking or bounds checking on fields within a program.
Citizen programmers	These unskilled programmers create scripts and macros during their daily tasks and are often unaware of the risks triggered by their activities. Modern word processing applications and spreadsheets include scripting languages that give end users a lot of power. These activities can, subsequently, cause unnecessary problems with programming results. Be sure that you employ professional programmers and designers on your projects who have appropriate training and experience and follow commonly accepted best practices for application security design.
Covert channel	Unskilled programmers and designers often introduce and exploit covert channels in their designs and programs through unsound security practices. Be sure that the programmers and designers who work on your projects are well trained and adhere to the proper standards and specifications.
Malware	Programmers and designers must defend against malware when designing and writing systems. Internal program integrity checks can determine whether unwanted program additions have occurred through the emergence of the following types of malware: ● Viruses ● Worms ● Hoaxes ● Trojans ● Remote Access Trojans (RATS) ● Distributed denial of service (DDoS) zombies Furthermore, programming supervisory staff must review code prior to its release to confirm that none of the following malware has been introduced by programmers: ● Logic bombs ● Spyware ● Adware ● Easter eggs
Malformed input	Programmers have an obligation to ensure that information entered into fields is properly formatted; if not, it must be rejected. Allowing numeric input when alphabetic information is required is a form of malformed input. This may cause failures in programs accessing the defective data.

Software Vulnerability	Best Practices
Object reuse	Programmers should verify that previously recorded disk space is cleared as part of a cleanup process for temporary file storage areas.
Executable/mobile code	Web browsers suffer from failures such as the unexpected implementation of executable content or mobile codes on a server that has been injected into a Uniform Resource Locator (URL).
	Mobile code refers to executable software that is obtained from remote systems and installed on a local system without the recipient's knowledge, consent, or doing. Mobile code can include scripts, Adobe Flash® animations, Microsoft® ActiveX® controls, Java™ applets, Adobe® Shockwave® files, and macros.
	Programmers should be cognizant of these limitations and verify that system input does not contain unexpected information that may be executable and present a security risk.
Social engineering	To protect against social engineering attacks, such as shoulder surfing, programmers should employ simple programming techniques that circumvent echoing passwords or that mask password entries with characters such as asterisks (*).
Time of check/time of use	Programmers must be sensitive to the problems inherent in time of check/time of use (TOC/TOU) situations. TOC/TOU requires that certain things happen in a certain order. For example, it is important that the system check a user's credentials before using those credentials for access. Early data and data access edits and checks may lead to an insecure situation if the data is then accessed or applied at a later time. The check of data and the use of data must be performed within a minimal interval of time.
Trapdoors and backdoors	These common techniques for acquiring unauthorized program or system access during program development and testing are security risks at the system production phase. These must be removed before system implementation.

Software Control Types

An operating system environment contains various software control functions that help to secure systems during software development.

Software Control	Description
Security kernel	The part of the operating system that enforces the reference monitor (RM).
Processor privilege state	Ensures that only operating system functions are executed in the privileged or supervisory state of the CPU and that user programs do not access privileged instructions.
Buffer overflow security	Internal operating system controls on bounds that reduce the likelihood of buffer overflows.
Incomplete parameter	Incomplete parameter check and enforcement controls are imbedded controls in operating system modules that verify the usage of proper data types in system calls.

Software Control	Description
Memory protection	User programs must not be allowed to access operating system memory areas. The memory mapping function of the central processing unit (CPU) enforces this restriction.
Covert channel controls	Covert channel tools, such as the Information Flow Model, that perform a thorough system design analysis.
Cryptography	Encrypting information stored in online or offline media for data confidentiality and integrity protection. Encrypting data in transit with IP security (IPsec).
Password protection	Passwords must be protected through encryption techniques, such as hashing, when stored on computer systems.
Granularity of controls	Providing a sufficient level of access control limitations increases data protection. Applications can enforce their own access controls or integrate with single sign-on (SSO) options that may be available.
Environment separation	Just as separation of duties (SoD) provides additional security, controlling the software environment and separating information into views for different types of users also amplifies security.
Backups	Having backups available can protect the availability of data in the event of a disaster.
Training	Training developers and users of the application.
Scanning	Periodic scans and reviews of the applications to make sure there have been no modifications.

Cohesion and Coupling

Cohesion is the level of independence of software modules of the same application. A highly cohesive module is highly independent from other modules. It can perform its function with little interaction from other modules. The more a module can do on its own the better, because it makes it more independent in terms of modifications; in other words it would not affect other modules.

Coupling is the degree and complexity of interaction among modules in an application. When a module has to interact with other modules, which always happens in software, coupling can be low or high. Low coupling means a simple exchange of information in terms of amount and complexity. High coupling implies a higher level of dependencies between the modules. Higher levels of dependencies can create additional complexity, and in general, complexity is the enemy of security. Low coupling is better because it means more independence between modules and simpler software.

ACTIVITY 7-2
Discussing Software Controls

Scenario:
In this activity, you will discuss software control implementation.

---

1. **Which of the following statements describes a data structure?**

   a) A collection of databases that store mass amounts of data.

   b) An improvised or ad hoc information method for storing information.

   c) A standardized format for storing information in a computer system so that the information can be efficiently accessed by applications.

   d) A software application with the capability to read and store mass amounts of computerized information.

---

2. **What is the appropriate description for each data structure?**

___ Primitive	a. A collection of primitives that are inter-related.
___ Array	b. An array with more than one dimension.
___ List	c. A structure that contains ordered arrays.
___ Matrix	d. A data element that is singular in nature and not broken down into small components when accessed.

---

3. **True or False? AI systems are implemented using neural networks that are meant to approximate the neural processes of the human brain.**

   ___ True

   ___ False

---

4. **Which one of the following statements explains how a KBS operates?**

   a) Performs decision-making and problem solving functions through AI and access to a database of knowledge information

   b) Uses complex algorithms to mimic the human intelligence process and adapts and learns from the environment in order to make decisions

---

5. **What is the appropriate best practice for each software vulnerability?**

___	Buffer overflow	a.	Programmers have an obligation to ensure that information entered into fields is properly formatted; if not, it must be rejected.
___	Citizen programmers	b.	Programmers should perform length checking or bounds checking on fields within a program.
___	Covert channel	c.	Programmers and designers must defend against vulnerabilities from malicious code when designing and writing systems.
___	Malware	d.	Programmers on software development projects should be trained and experienced professionals who understand and follow acceptable procedures for application security design.
___	Malformed input	e.	Programmers and designers must avoid unsound security practices that can result in the introduction of these system exploitations into software designs.

6. **What is the appropriate best practice for each software vulnerability?**

___	Executable content and mobile code	a.	Programmers must ensure that data checks and data use occur within a minimal time interval.
___	Object reuse	b.	These development-phase access channels should be removed before system implementation.
___	Social engineering	c.	Programmers should verify that previously recorded disk space is cleared as part of a cleanup process for temporary file storage areas.
___	TOC/TOU	d.	Programmers should verify that system input does not contain unexpected information that may be executable and present a security risk.
___	Trapdoors and backdoors	e.	To protect against attacks that exploit human vulnerabilities, such as shoulder surfing, programmers should employ simple programming techniques that circumvent echoing passwords or mask password entries with characters such as asterisks (*).

7. **Which one of the following software controls is part of the operating system and enforces the RM?**

    a) Security kernel

    b) Buffer overflow security controls

    c) Cryptography

    d) Password protection

    e) Memory protection

TOPIC C
Database System Security

Database security extends beyond access controls, data reuse, and data sharing. It involves a proactive approach to protecting information resources contained in database systems from malicious attacks on distributed information systems. In this topic, you will identify database system security.

Organizational databases are commonly used to store sensitive business information. The same factors that make centralized databases efficient for data access and control also make them targets for attack. A compromised database can have severely adverse effects on business goals. Implementing rigorous database security will help you to ensure the integrity, availability, and confidentiality of your organization's data.

Database Systems

Definition:

A *database system* is a set of related information organized within a software framework for ease of access and reporting. The information can be added to, edited, or deleted. It uses a Database Management System (DBMS) to oversee data. The DBMS also provides the commands for performing functions to the data.

A modern database system provides many features, which include:

- A data definition language to create the structure of various tables.
- A query language to access the information in the database.
- Indexes or keys for efficient access to the information in the database.
- A security structure to limit access based on pre-defined criteria.
- Built-in bounds and limits checking.
- Enforcement of data content rules within the database. This backstops poor programming practices with database rule implementation.
- Internal integrity checks.

Example: Oracle and Microsoft® SQL Server

Oracle and Microsoft® SQL Server are both examples of a database system.

Database System Models

There are several database system models that each define how data is stored and accessed.

Database System Model	Description
Hierarchical Database Management Model	In this model, data is implemented in a tree-like structure. Relationships are created with a parent-child view. A single parent can have many children but each child can only have a single parent. These are largely legacy databases.

Database System Model	Description
Network Database Management Model	This model is a type of hierarchical database implemented using pointers to other database elements so that traversing information in the database requires the use of pointers to locate subsequent entries. Children can have many parents. It refers to networks of data relationships and is not related to communication networking.
Relational Database Management Model	This model allows a designer to create relationships among the various database components. Multiple tables are defined and the relationships between them are established through structured methods. This is the most common database model at this point.
Object-Oriented Database Model	The Object Oriented Database Model uses object-oriented programming (OOP) techniques with database technology. In object-oriented databases, the clients' access to the data is obtained by gaining entry to the database object in a closed environment. Programmers have limited control over the database. The object defines what may be accessed and how database access is accomplished.

Database Interface Languages

Just as a database system can be implemented using different models, a software program can use various database languages to access data.

Database Interface Language	Description
ODBC	*Open Database Connectivity (ODBC)* provides a standard application program interface (API) that allows programmers to access any database from any platform. ODBC was designed and developed by Microsoft and became part of the international SQL standard. The design of ODBC makes it independent of any specific programming language and any specific database system. It is also designed to be compatible with any operating system in which it is implemented.
JDBC	*Java Database Connectivity (JDBC)* is a mechanism that allows Java-based programs to access databases transparently. JDBC is specific to Java environments. Bridges have been developed to translate JDBC requests into ODBC requests for database access, when necessary.
XML	*eXtensible Markup Language (XML)* is a document description language that simplifies the presentation of database information in various formats.
OLE DB	The *Object Linking and Embedding Database (OLE DB)* allows the linking and embedding of documents, graphics, sound files, and other formatted information into a parent document. For example, a word-processing document might contain portions of an independent spreadsheet that is linked to or embedded in it using the OLE process. Updates to the spreadsheet are automatically viewable in the word-processing document when it is opened.

Database Access via the Internet

Databases can be accessed over the Internet using the web server environment. The web applications programmer can access any database in any location using ODBC and can format web pages using XML. Information security should be enforced within the ODBC framework.

Database Terminology

There is an assortment of significant terms that define the structure of database systems.

Database Term	Description
Table	A *table* is a set of rows and columns that contains related information.
Tuple	A *tuple* is a row, or record, in a database.
Attribute	An *attribute* is a column, or field, in a database.
Cell	A *cell* is the intersection, or value, of a row and column in a database.
Key	A *key* is an attribute that provides a unique value in a tuple or row that uniquely identifies that row. A key attribute cannot be null nor duplicated.
Foreign key	A *foreign key* is a cell value in one table that refers to a unique key in a different table. This enables the creation of relations between tables.
Cardinality	*Cardinality* involves the types of relationships available: one-to-one, one-to-many, and many-to-many.

Relational Database Management Systems

Definition:

A *Relational Database Management System (RDBMS)* is a collection of multiple tables that are related to one another through the use of foreign keys. Relational databases conform to the Relational Database Management Model.

An RDBMS employs *normalization* techniques to reduce redundant information and duplication between tables. This ensures that each table contains only the minimal number of rows and columns required to store information and retrieve it meaningfully.

Example: Key Usage in an RDBMS

To illustrate and identify a unique key and a foreign key in a relational database, a sample student information table is shown.

First Name	Last Name	Student ID	Postal Code
Sam	Jones	22122	78003
Mary	Smith	22198	72008

Attributes in this table include First Name, Last Name, Student ID, and Postal Code. Tuples exist for Sam and Mary. The cell that identifies the Student ID for Sam contains the value 22122. The attribute that uniquely identifies each student, and is therefore the key, is the Student ID. The Postal Code is a foreign key.

To highlight the significance of a foreign key in a relational database, a sample postal code table is shown.

Postal Code	City	State
72008	Anytown	Texas
78003	Thistown	New York
78009	Mytown	Tennessee

The Postal Code in the cell for Sam is 78003. By using this foreign key, the postal code table can be accessed and Sam is found to be living in Thistown, New York.

For example, if the entry in the postal code table for 78003 was removed, the reference in the student information table for Sam's Postal Code would be invalid. Before any entry can be removed from a table, the DBMS verifies its use as a foreign key in another table. If it exists as a foreign key, it cannot be removed until all table references are deleted.

Example: Normalization

During the process of creating relational databases, removing redundant data is essential. An illustrated sample grade table is shown.

Last Name	Student ID	Class	Instructor	Term	Grade
Jones	22122	Math 101	Haddad	Spring 2012	A
Smith	22198	Science 101	Chan	Spring 2012	B
Smith	22197	Science 102	Cham	Spring 2012	B

In this relational database format, a single table maintains all of the relationships. However, the problem here is that there is no control over the information. Smith actually took two classes, but it appears that two different Smiths took two classes because the Student ID contains an error in the second Smith entry.

It is also important to note that the instructor name "Chan" might be misspelled in the second instance as "Cham." Normalization will help alleviate this problem. Creating multiple tables is part of the solution. In these simple examples, the asterisk (*) indicates the key.

Student Table

Last Name	Student ID *
Jones	22122
Smith	22198

Class Table

Class *	Instructor	Title
Math 101	Haddad	Intro to Algebra
Science 101	Chan	Earth Science
Science 102	Chan	Biology

Instructor Table

Instructor *	First Name
Haddad	Allen
Chan	Wu

A compound key is used in the Grade Table so that only one grade is recorded per student for each class. Student ID validation is possible by using the foreign key, Student ID, to match the Student Table. The Class foreign key is matched against the Class Table.

Grade Table

Student ID *	Class *	Term *	Grade
22122	Math 101	Spring 2012	A
22198	Science 101	Spring 2012	B
22198	Science 102	Spring 2012	B

For reporting purposes, it is possible to merge the tables to create a Grade Statement.

Grade Statement

Student Name	Class	Instructor	Term	Grade
Jones	Intro to Algebra	Allen Haddad	Spring 2012	A
Smith	Earth Science	Wu Chan	Spring 2012	B
Smith	Biology	Wu Chan	Spring 2012	B

Object-Oriented Programming Terminology

OOP uses objects to perform functions or house information and includes a series of specific terms.

OOP Term	Description/Example
Class	**Description:** A *class* defines the general characteristics of a type of object, including attributes, fields, and operations. A class should be somewhat self-defining. **Example:** The idea of a restaurant could be considered a class. The attributes are the menu items. The operations are the methods of food preparation and service. The allowed inputs are the raw materials, cooks, food servers, and customers. The allowed outputs are the meals that are produced from the menu, which will vary.
Object	**Description:** An *object* is a specific instance of a class. An object is a specific implementation of a class. It inherits its attributes from the class and defines specific values for each attribute. **Example:** Using the restaurant class as an example, a particular restaurant object might be a pizza parlor or an Asian restaurant. They are both restaurants in the general sense, but they produce completely different results.
Modularity	**Description:** *Modularity* isolates all object processes within the object. For programming implementation, the object becomes a single testing entity. If the module works as described in the specification, it is assumed that it will work well with other modules that call upon its services. **Example:** In the restaurant example, modularity assumes that all food is prepared on site. If you have to wait for food to be prepared in another restaurant and then be delivered to your eating location, you would not be pleased.
Method	**Description:** The *method* describes an object's abilities—what the object can do. In OOP, a method generally affects only one particular object. **Example:** The cook method in a pizza parlor will result in a different product set than that created when the cook method is executed in an Asian restaurant.
Encapsulation	**Description:** *Encapsulation* conceals or masks the functional details of a class from the calling objects. **Example:** Most restaurants do not readily release their recipes. When you go to a restaurant, you order the food from the menu. The processes used in food preparation are hidden from view.

OOP Term	Description/Example
Abstraction	**Description:** *Abstraction* generalizes classes to the highest, most appropriate level needed to use them. **Example:** If you are hungry, you might choose to go to a restaurant. If you are craving Northern Italian-style pizza, you would modify the level of abstraction to meet your needs for the specific type of pizza you desire. If you have no preference and want any variety of pizza, your highest level of abstraction would be a pizza parlor.
Polymorphism	**Description:** *Polymorphism* occurs when classes are treated as equivalents and are referred to in identical terms. **Example:** The class might have a method to order_food(). The order_food() method used in a restaurant with a wait staff involves communicating to the server in person. In a restaurant without servers, such as a carry-out restaurant, you communicate through the telephone. The resulting service is the same, but the implementation of the order_food() method is different.
Polyinstantiation	**Description:** *Polyinstantiation* is when a single class is instantiated into multiple independent instances. This can be used for security purposes when you want two different users of the system to get different answers even if they ask the same question. **Example:** Two customers come into your restaurant and both order sausage pizzas. One is a good friend so you make a wonderful Chicago-style deep-dish sausage pizza. The other is your competitor from up the street, so even though he ordered the same thing, you bake up a frozen pizza so he cannot learn your trade secrets.

Levels of Integrity

Database integrity ensures that data stored within a database is accurate and valid and not unknowingly altered or deleted. It is often referred to as *ACID integrity* to represent the four principal areas of integrity assurance: atomicity, consistency, isolation, and durability.

Referential integrity is a type of database integrity that ensures proper maintenance of all table values that are referenced by the foreign keys in other tables.

Entity integrity requires that each tuple has a unique primary key that is not null, thereby assuring uniqueness.

ACID Integrity Terminology

Each ACID integrity term is an instrumental method for ensuring authenticity and reliability of database information.

ACID Integrity Term	Description
Atomicity	*Atomicity* is a DBMS guarantee that all tasks associated with a transaction reach completion. If the DBMS cannot complete all tasks, then it guarantees that none of the tasks will be completed. Therefore, no partial results are maintained in the database.
Consistency	*Consistency* requires database stability before and after a transaction.
Isolation	Within a DBMS, *isolation* occurs when transactions and database processes cannot discern, or see, what is occurring in other, simultaneous transactions. Intermediate results of one transaction cannot affect the progress or status quo of another transaction.
Durability	*Durability* guarantees that a transaction will maintain stability, and not be undone, once the user is notified of its completion.

Database Views

If you want to ensure data integrity, it is typically not a good idea to give users unfettered access to the database or to allow them to write unrestricted queries. Instead, it is better to build a front-end application that provides a constrained interface. This database view will limit what they are able to see. It may even include logic that will allow certain types of information based on their login. A reference monitor can be built into the front end. The user should not be able to bypass the RM and access data directly.

Data Warehousing

Definition:

A *data warehouse* is a pre-processed database that contains information about a specific subject from various sources, and is used for subsequent reporting and analysis.

Once data warehouses are created, they are not updated. If updates are required, another warehouse is created. This is to protect the value of the data if subsequent comparison reports are necessary.

Example: Voter Information

Political parties often create data warehouses containing voter information. This information is obtained from voter registration files. It is combined with census information, property tax information, vehicle registration information, and other data sources. This warehouse can then be used to perform an analysis of voting populations within precincts to create lists for political canvassing and other uses.

Pre-Processed Structured Databases

When creating warehouses, it is often necessary to pre-process the information to create data-consistent coding. For example, one information source in the warehouse might store telephone numbers as alphabetic data that include dashes, such as 212-555-1123. Another data source might store phone numbers in a numeric format, such as 2125551123. By pre-processing the information, a consistent phone number storage arrangement is determined and implemented.

Data Mining Techniques

Data mining is the practice of analyzing large amounts of data to locate previously unknown or hidden information. By using the techniques of inference and aggregation, a lot can be learned from the data. This is a very important function for any organization as it provides information used to make better decisions; for example, making decisions to provide the best products and services. In the wrong hands, inference and aggregation might allow people to learn things that would normally not be available to them.

Data Mining Technique	Description
Inference	A data miner reviews data trends and formulates predictions about the subject matter.
	For example, inference can be used to study the incidence of cancer in large populations. By comparing symptoms and disease incidents, it is possible to infer that some symptoms are better indicators of the disease's presence than others.
Aggregation	The summarization of information found in the data repository can be used for different purposes. Summarizing information rather than exposing the data directly enables different groups of users to make inferences by only looking at information they are authorized to see.
	For example, aggregation can also help in the study of a population's cancer incidence. By examining patient data and aggregating mortality information, it is possible to ascertain the average remaining lifetime of the population when considering the overall life span determined from the aggregation.
	Users are collecting data classified at a lower level to make inferences about data that would be classified at a higher level.

Database Vulnerabilities

An array of database vulnerabilities should be considered to avert disclosure risks, maintain confidentiality, and ensure data integrity.

Database Vulnerability	Cause(s)
Access control bypass	Database administrators (DBAs) can bypass normal application security and gain direct access to database information. This presents a security risk as unaudited and unedited updates might occur.

Database Vulnerability	Cause(s)
Aggregation	The unauthorized release of information that is accumulated from the database can present a serious risk. For example, releasing the number of hours of experienced downtime for major combat aircraft within the last month might cause grave damage to national security. The downtime of each aircraft, by itself, may not be a serious issue, but a combination of all downtimes might create a severe threat.
Improper view restrictions	A *view* is a user portal into a database. Views are often restricted based on need to know or least privilege. With databases, there may be a way to negotiate an established view for a group of users by using programming techniques, such as an SQL injection attack, to gain access when it is not authorized.
DoS	When massive databases are scanned row by row in search of nonexistent data, a denial of service (DoS) outcome may be produced. This type of vulnerability can be threatened either intentionally or inadvertently. Poorly designed queries may result in a DoS when an unexpected system load occurs.
Deadlocks	A *deadlock* occurs when one transaction requires the use of a resource that is locked by another transaction. This often transpires when two or more transactions are waiting on resources locked by a separate transaction.
	If a program reads a row in update mode, the row is locked until the update is complete. Other users have to wait until the lock is released. Deadlocks can also occur if two transactions are waiting on each other's locked rows.

Database Security Mechanisms

Database systems contain various embedded security features that help deter unauthorized database access.

Database Security Mechanism	Description
Lock controls	To control concurrent access to a single row in a table, database systems implement lock controls. Though necessary, lock controls can produce deadlocks.
Other DBMS access controls	Additional DBMS access controls include: • View-based access controls. • Grant and revoke access controls. • Security for object-oriented databases.
Metadata controls	*Metadata* is information that describes specific characteristics of data, such as origin, condition, content, and/or quality. In object-oriented systems, controlling access to metadata limits what users can discover about information available through objects.

Database Security Mechanism	Description
Data contamination controls	Bounds checking, data typing, data length restrictions, and well-formed transactions are all methods used to control data contamination in the database.
OLTP controls	*Online transaction processing (OLTP)* presents issues related to concurrency and atomicity. If a user attempts to buy the last copy of a book at an online bookstore at the same time another user is making the same purchase, who gets the book? Row locking, atomicity, and logging are all used to ensure that only one book is sold and that the record of that sale is permanently recorded should the system fail.
Noise and perturbation	Artificial data is inserted to act as noise in order to confuse the users that should not have access. Legitimate users will have the noise filtered out. *Perturbation* is the intentional addition of spurious data into database fields with the intention of defeating inference attacks.
Cell suppression	*Cell suppression* involves intentionally hiding cells containing highly confidential information. The cells may be suppressed for everyone or they might be suppressed based on the ID of the user accessing the data. The database needs to allow for statistical analysis without allowing access to personally identifiable information (PII) information so a certain amount of cell suppression is enforced.
Partitioning	The logical splitting apart of a database into independent parts. This is sometimes done for performance but it can also increase security by limiting what information is made available.

ACTIVITY 7-3
Discussing Database System Security

Scenario:
In this activity, you will discuss database system security.

1. **Which of the following statements describes a database system?**

    a) A mechanism that attempts to mimic or emulate the process of human intelligence by implementing algorithms that cause the system to learn about its environment and make decisions based on its learning.

    b) A standardized format for storing information in a computer system so that this information can be efficiently accessed by applications.

    c) A program that uses knowledge-based techniques to support human decision making, learning, and action.

    d) A set of related information organized within a software framework for ease of access and reporting.

2. **What is the appropriate description for each database system model?**

___	Hierarchical Database Management Model	a.	This model is implemented using pointers to other database elements so that traversing information in the database requires the use of pointers to locate subsequent entries.
___	Network Database Management Model	b.	In this model, data is accessed by gaining entry to the database component as a closed environment.
___	Relational Database Management Model	c.	This model allows a designer to create connections among the various database components.
___	Object-Oriented Database Model	d.	This model is implemented in a tree structure with internal database links to higher-level elements.

3. **What is the appropriate description for each database interface language?**

___	ODBC	a.	Allows the incorporation of documents, graphics, sound files, and other formatted information into a parent document.
___	JDBC	b.	A document description language that simplifies the presentation of database information in various formats.
___	XML	c.	A mechanism that allows Java-based programs to access databases transparently.
___	OLE DB	d.	Provides a standard API that allows programmers to access any database from any platform.

4. **What is the appropriate description for each of the database terms?**

___	Table	a. A column or field in a database.
___	Tuple	b. The intersection, or value, of a row and column in a database.
___	Attribute	c. A row, or record, in a database.
___	Cell	d. An attribute that provides a unique value in a tuple or row that uniquely identifies that row.
___	Key	e. A set of rows and columns that contains related information.
___	Foreign key	f. A cell value in one table that refers to a unique key in a different table.

5. **When using an RDBMS, if an entry was removed from one table but not from the others, which of the following statements describes how an invalid entry can be updated or removed correctly?**

   a) First, the RDBMS must verify the usage as a foreign key in other tables. Next, if it exists as a foreign key, then it cannot be removed until all the table references are deleted first.

   b) First, every table's attributes must be updated to include new key values. Next, the subsequent tables must be updated to match the new foreign key references.

6. **Which of the following OOP terms isolates all object processes within the object?**

   a) Object

   b) Method

   c) Modularity

   d) Encapsulation

   e) Abstraction

7. **True or False? Referential integrity ensures that data stored within a database is accurate and valid, not altered or deleted.**

   ___ True

   ___ False

8. **What is the appropriate description for each ACID integrity term?**

___	Atomicity	a. Guarantees that a transaction will maintain stability, and not be undone, once the user is notified of its completion.
___	Consistency	b. A DBMS guarantees that all tasks associated with a transaction have reached completion.
___	Isolation	c. Occurs when transactions and database processes cannot discern, or see, what is occurring in other, simultaneous transactions.
___	Durability	d. Requires database stability before and after a transaction.

9. **Which one of the following is a pre-processed database that contains information about a specific subject from various sources, and is used for subsequent reporting and analysis?**

   a) RDBMS

   b) Data mine

   c) Data warehouse

10. **True or False? Data mining is the process of sifting through and analyzing large amounts of data to locate previously unknown or hidden information.**

    ___ True

    ___ False

11. **What is the appropriate description for each database vulnerability?**

___	Access control bypass	a.	When a group or individual is granted established or impartial access to unauthorized information.
___	Aggregation	b.	The unauthorized release of information that is accumulated from the database.
___	Improper view restrictions	c.	When one transaction requires the use of a resource that is locked by another transaction.
___	DoS	d.	When DBAs can circumvent normal application security and gain direct access to database information.
___	Deadlocks	e.	When massive databases are scanned row by row in search of non-existent data so that the databases cannot respond to legitimate requests.

12. **What is the appropriate description for each database security mechanism?**

___	Lock controls	a.	Bounds checking, data typing, data length restrictions, and well-formed transactions are all methods used to control data corruption in the database.
___	Other DBMS access controls	b.	View-based access controls, grant and revoke access controls, and security for object-oriented databases.
___	Metadata controls	c.	Manages concurrent access to a single row in a table.
___	Data contamination controls	d.	Presents issues related to concurrency and atomicity.
___	Online transaction processing controls	e.	Information that describes specific characteristics of data, such as origin, condition, content, and/or quality.

Lesson 7 Follow-up

In this lesson, you analyzed application security by applying software configuration management strategies, software controls, and database system security mechanisms. Recognizing the application development methods that ensure data integrity and protect data from external attacks, and employing the applicable software development and change processes will help you to efficiently implement application security in your organization.

1. **Will you be responsible for the application security at your corporation?**

2. **Do you work with applications or databases in your organization that have specific security such as financial systems?**

8 | Cryptography

Lesson Time: 4 hour(s), 30 minutes

Lesson Objectives:

In this lesson, you will analyze cryptography characteristics and elements.

You will:

- Identify and apply cipher technology.
- Apply symmetric-key cryptography.
- Identify asymmetric-key cryptography.
- Analyze hashing and message digests.
- Identify email, Internet, and wireless security options.
- Identify cryptographic weaknesses.

Introduction

As an information systems security professional, you have managed the security practices of your organization to control access to data, secure data networks, and safeguard data transmissions. Now, you can focus on protecting your organization's data. In this lesson, you will analyze the characteristics and elements of cryptography to ensure the confidentiality of your information.

The business world is inherently competitive. The first company to market a new product or technology is uniquely positioned to become the industry leader. This makes it difficult for competitors to enter the field and capture any appreciable market share. To keep sensitive company information private, data security is extremely important. Your ability to encrypt your organization's data is vital to protecting its information and attaining business goals.

This lesson supports content found in the Cryptography domain of the CISSP® certification.

TOPIC A
Ciphers and Cryptography

Your organization's applications and databases are protected against internal errors and external attacks. You have analyzed the risks associated with your security and determined that all are within acceptable levels. Now, you need to ensure that your company's confidential information stays that way. In this topic, you will identify and apply cipher technology.

As an information systems security professional, maintaining the integrity of your organization's data is a critical responsibility. Similarly, ensuring timely and reliable access to data for authorized users is a key mandate. However, in addition to integrity and availability, it is important to achieve confidentiality to properly enforce each principle of the information security triad. Data security through encryption ensures confidentiality. Learning to apply a basic cipher is your key to implementing more sophisticated ciphers and increasing the security of your organization's data.

Cryptography

Definition:

Cryptography is the analysis and practice of information concealment for the purpose of securing sensitive data transmissions. It uses techniques such as encryption and decryption to control the privacy and legibility of valuable information. Cryptography is used extensively in computer security and other technical applications, such as ATM cards and electronic commerce.

Example:

Figure 8-1: Cryptography.

Example: Magnetic Tape Data

When magnetic tapes are transported from one location to another, the information stored in them should be encrypted to safeguard the information stored on them. The processes used to encrypt and decrypt the information on the tapes are the result of the study of cryptography.

Encryption

Definition:

Encryption is a security technique that converts data from an ordinary, intelligible state known as *cleartext* or *plaintext* form, into coded, or *ciphertext* form. Only authorized parties with the necessary *decryption* information can decode and read the data. Encryption can be one-way, which means the encryption is designed to hide only the original message and is never decrypted. Or, it can be two-way, in which the encoded message can be transformed back to its original form and read.

Example:

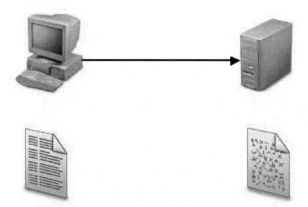

Figure 8-2: *Encryption.*

Example: A Simple Encrypted Message

The following example demonstrates how the content of a plaintext message cannot be easily determined once the message is encrypted.

● Plaintext message: Attack at Dawn

● Encrypted message: `i8xfe zieam 5e3xy`

Ciphers and Algorithms

Definition:

An encryption *algorithm* is the rule, system, or mechanism used to encrypt data. A *cipher* uses an algorithm to encrypt, decrypt, or hash information. Algorithms can be simple mechanical substitutions, but in electronic cryptography, they are generally complex mathematical functions. The stronger and more complex the algorithm, the more difficult it is to break the encryption. In symmetric and asymmetric encryption, the algorithm is used with a key to accomplish the encryption or decryption.

Example:

Figure 8-3: Ciphers and algorithms.

Example: A Simple Encryption Algorithm

A letter-substitution cipher, in which each letter of the alphabet is systematically replaced by another letter, is an example of a simple encryption algorithm.

The Avalanche Effect

The *avalanche effect* is a process found in a cipher that causes a very small change in the plaintext to produce a very large change in the ciphertext.

Encoding

Encoding is sometimes included in discussion on encryption but it really is something different altogether. Encoding is simply changing the format of information not in order to hide it, but to make it easier to transport or store. One of the best examples of encoding is Morse code. Even though "… --- …" might seemed encrypted, anyone that knows Morse code can easily understand it and translate it to "SOS." It is only changed into dots and dashes to make it easier to send across the wire.

Cryptographic Keys

Definition:

A cryptographic *key* is a specific piece of information that is used with an algorithm to perform encryption and decryption. Keys have various lengths depending on the cryptographic algorithm used and the amount of protection required for the encrypted data. A different key can be used with the same algorithm to produce different ciphertext. Without the correct key, the receiver cannot decrypt the ciphertext even with a known algorithm. The more complex the key, the stronger the encryption.

Example:

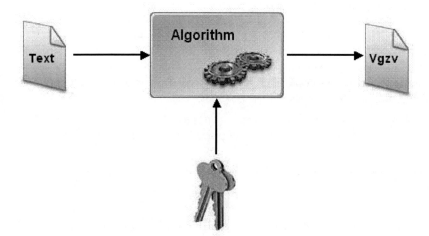

Figure 8-4: Cryptographic keys.

Example: A Simple Encryption Key

In a simple letter-substitution algorithm, the key might be "replace each letter with the letter that is two letters following it in the alphabet." If the same algorithm were used on the same cleartext but with a different key—for example, "replace each letter with the one three letters before it"—the resulting ciphertext would be different.

Example: A 128-Bit Key

The following example represents a 128-bit key.

01000100001000111110100101011010000111110001011101100010101100011

01111101101000111000100101011010010100010001011101100010101100011

Because this is difficult to read, it is frequently represented with text that looks like this:

d8Zxin7T92mH4jpz

With 8 bits in each character or byte, 16 characters are used to represent a 128-bit key.

In general, the longer the key, the more secure the encryption. On the other hand, the longer the key, the more computationally expensive the encryption will be. Also, different types of encryption will need significantly different key lengths to be sufficiently secure. While 256-bit symmetric encryption is very secure, you would need key lengths approaching 2,048 in asymmetric encryption for the same level of assurance.

Cryptography and the CIA Triad

Cryptography is essentially used to maintain and protect the three principles of the information security CIA triad.

Security Principle	Cryptographic Protection Method
Confidentiality	Cryptography ensures confidentiality by encrypting information to hide the content of encrypted files and data from everybody but the intended recipient.

Security Principle	Cryptographic Protection Method
Integrity	Cryptography ensures integrity when a modification to the encrypted data can be identified. If encrypted data cannot be decrypted using the proper mechanism, it signifies that the encrypted data has been modified, either purposefully or accidentally, during the transmission of information. Whatever the reason, if integrity has been compromised, the data should not be used.
Availability	Cryptography ensures availability by using encrypted credentials when establishing identity and authorization. Many logon processes use specific functions to hide real password values.

Additional benefits of cryptography include:

● Non-repudiation: Being able to verify that a sender or recipient is genuine and that the message has not been modified is increasingly important. With the proper exchange of keys and certificates, this level of assurance can be gained.

● Authentication: Can help ensure that a user or system is trusted.

The Cryptography Process

While there are many different cryptographic methods, the process used in cryptography is universal.

1. Start with the plaintext.

2. Select an encryption method and key.

3. Encrypt the plaintext into ciphertext.

4. Transport or store the ciphertext until needed.

5. Decrypt the ciphertext using a key to display the original plaintext.

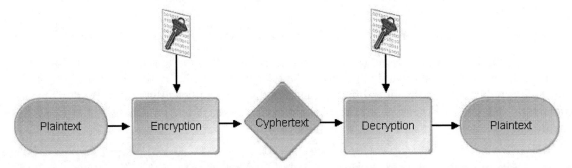

Figure 8-5: *The cryptography process.*

Cryptosystems

Definition:

A *cryptosystem* is the general term for the hardware and/or software used to implement a cryptographic process. Cryptosystems implement ciphers to encrypt and decrypt sensitive information. *Cryptanalysis* is the study of cryptosystems with the intent of breaking them, and the *work factor* is the amount of time needed to break a cryptosystem.

Early on, cryptosystems were based in hardware. Today, they can be implemented more efficiently in software due to the complexity of algorithms. However, the software still requires a hardware platform to operate.

 Cryptology is the study of both cryptography and cryptanalysis.

Example:

During World War II, the Germans used a hardware device called the Enigma to encrypt and decrypt messages.

During this period, the United States had their own encryption device called SIGABA and the Japanese had the Purple machine. Each country had huge cryptanalysis efforts during the war. The United States and Great Britain had some success breaking the Enigma and Purple machines. SIGABA was unbroken and remained classified until 1996.

Figure 8-6: *The Enigma.*

Cipher Evolution

The historical evolution of ciphers began thousands of years ago, progressing from early, simplistic processes to more complex processes.

Cipher Era	Description
Early or manual ciphers	Early ciphers were implemented manually. For example, in Sparta, the Spartans wrapped paper or leather around a staff and then wrote a message on the paper or leather down the length of the staff. When the paper or leather was unwrapped, the message was hidden. To decrypt the message, it was wrapped around a staff of an identical diameter and made readable again.
Mechanical era	Hardware-based cryptosystems are implemented without the use of software. The use of mechanical cypherdisks like those found in the Enigma marked the beginning of the mechanical era. During this period, devices sped up the encryption and decryption processes.

Cipher Era	Description
Software or modern era	Software-based cryptosystems rely on computer software to implement a cryptographic process. In the past, it was often necessary for those doing the encryption and decryption to understand the process, even with mechanical assistance. Today, the software era allows the process to be performed with little or no user knowledge. By following simple instructions, the user can perform the encryption and decryption processes.
The future	The future of cryptography is quantum cryptography. Although it might not be ready to have its own era named after it, there is a lot of excitement about quantum cryptography. It is based on the idea that any time you measure something, you have in fact made slight alterations to the object. By measuring light particles as they pass through a device, nearly impossible-to-break keys can be created.

 Two books on cryptography and computer security written for a general audience are *The Code Book* by Simon Singh and *Secrets and Lies* by Bruce Schneier.

The Ideal Cipher

In 1949, the American mathematician and electrical engineer Claude Shannon described the ideal cipher in terms of usability and secrecy. For usability, a cipher must provide an environment where keys and algorithms are simple and easy to implement. Errors should not propagate and the ciphertext should not be longer than the plaintext. For secrecy, Shannon assumed that the enemy knows the system. Because of this theory, the secrecy of the key is vital to the protection of the information. Shannon's work was very similar to publications by Auguste Kerckhoff in the 19th century. Kerckhoff's principle states, "The method must not need to be kept secret, and having it fall into the enemy's hands should not cause problems."

Shannon suggested that the ideal cipher would thwart statistical analysis. The ciphertext and the plaintext must be statistically independent in addition to the ciphertext and the key.

Diffusion and Confusion

While creating the ideal cipher may be impossible at times, it is possible to approximate it. Shannon proposed using techniques such as diffusion and confusion to approximate the ideal cipher. *Diffusion* refers to the creation of a complex cipher by mixing up the plaintext during the encryption process. *Confusion* refers to the creation of a complex cipher by mixing up the key values during the encryption process.

Substitution

Definition:

Substitution is a technique that replaces parts of a message or cryptographic output to hide the original information. Substitution occurs during processing within the cipher algorithm, where predefined bit patterns in the intermediate output are replaced with substitute patterns. When decrypted, the substitute patterns are identified and the original patterns are reinstated.

Example: Predefined and Substitute Patterns

The following table represents the substitution of predefined patterns.

Predefined Pattern	Substitute Pattern
anAnt	Xyzzy
Z1Dr5	At3vl

Transposition/Permutation

Definition:

Transposition, or permutation, is the process of rearranging parts of a message or cryptographic output to hide the original information. The original message or key may be the subject of the transposition process. Transposition may also occur during the operation of the cipher algorithm.

Example: Simple Transposition

With an input value of "This is the time to attack" and a transposition rule of 1,8,19,26,21,7,3..., your transposed value will be "T okasi…"

The characters in the input value are transposed, or reorganized, based on the rule provided. The first character in the input is the first character in the output, the eighth character in the input is the second character in the output, and so on. While this example illustrates character-based transposition, most algorithms use a bit-based transposition process.

Alternative Ciphers

There are simpler, alternative ciphers available that are used to hide information rather than to disguise information by standard encryption methods.

Alternative Cipher	Description
Steganography	*Steganography* hides information by enclosing it in other files such as a graphic, movie, or sound file. Steganography can be used to hide information in a picture by replacing the low-order bits of each byte in the picture with elements from the hidden information. The hidden information is spread throughout the host image. Special software is used to insert and extract the secret.
Watermark	A *watermark* is an embedded mark or image that acts similarly to a steganographic process. The watermark identifies the source of the image for copyright protection and other uses.

Alternative Cipher	Description
Code book	A *code book* is a book or booklet that contains a series of codes that are used to represent common words or phrases that might be used in communications. For example, a message might be encoded as follows:
	`A9BCX ZZYZZ THIDE 5TB2A`
	When referencing the code book, the five letter/number codes translate into the following message:
	`A9BCX`—Enemy
	`ZZYZZ`—On
	`THIDE`—Left
	`5TB2A`—Flank
	The secrecy of the code book ensures the secrecy of the system. Code books are generally used for one day only. After that, they are destroyed and never reused.
One-time pad	A *one-time pad (OTP)* is the only provable, secure encryption tool that can be used. The OTP contains a very long, non-repeating key that is the same length as the plaintext. The key is used one time only and is then destroyed.

ACTIVITY 8-1
Discussing Ciphers

Scenario:

In this activity, you will discuss applications for cipher technology to understand how to implement more sophisticated ciphers and increase the security of your organization's data.

---

1. **A security technique that converts data from an ordinary, intelligible state known as cleartext or plaintext form into coded or ciphertext form is known as:**

    a) Cryptography.

    b) Algorithm.

    c) Encryption.

    d) Cryptosystem.

---

2. **True or False? Without the correct key, the receiver can decrypt the ciphertext if the algorithm is known.**

    ___ True

    ___ False

---

3. **Place the universal cryptography process in order.**

    Transport or store the ciphertext until needed.

    Encrypt the plaintext into ciphertext.

    Start with the plaintext.

    Select an encryption method and key.

    Decrypt the ciphertext using a key to display the original plaintext.

---

4. **True or False? A work factor is the study of cryptosystems with the intent of breaking them.**

    ___ True

    ___ False

---

5. **Which era in the cipher evolution allowed the implementation of a cryptographic process to be performed with little or no user knowledge?**

    a) Software

    b) Mechanical

    c) Early

    d) Late

---

6. **What are the characteristics of the ideal cipher that Claude Shannon described in terms of usability and secrecy?**

7. **During processing, where does substitution occur?**

   a) Within the key

   b) Within the password

   c) Within the plaintext

   d) Within the cipher algorithm

8. **Which one of the following occurs during the transposition process?**

   a) Cryptographic output is replaced to hide the original information.

   b) Cryptographic output is rearranged to hide the original information.

   c) Cryptographic output is encrypted using a cipher algorithm.

   d) Cryptographic output is decrypted using a cipher algorithm.

9. **What is the appropriate description for each alternative cipher method?**

   ___ Steganography

   ___ Watermark

   ___ Code book

   ___ One-time pad

   a. An embedded image that identifies the source of the image for copyright protection and for other uses.

   b. A picture that hides information by replacing the low-order bits of each byte in the picture with elements from the hidden information.

   c. A tool that contains a very long, non-repeating key that is the same length as the plaintext.

   d. Used in a series to represent common words or phrases that might be used in communication.

TOPIC B
Symmetric-Key Cryptography

You have analyzed the application of basic ciphers. In a perfect world, this simple encryption would be sufficient to provide data confidentiality and integrity. Unfortunately, the world is not perfect, so data must constantly be subjected to ever increasing methods of security. In this topic, you will apply a symmetric-key cryptography method that is most relevant to ensuring your organization's data security.

As you know, cryptography is akin to locking a message and providing the key to only those authorized to open the lock. While the locks may be the same, a secure key is critical to ensure the confidentiality of your information. Your ability to select an appropriate symmetric-key cryptography method will provide you the assurance that your keys are unique and secure.

Symmetric Encryption

Definition:

Symmetric encryption or *shared-key encryption* is a two-way encryption scheme in which encryption and decryption are both performed by the same secret key. The key can be configured in software or coded in hardware. Then, the key must be securely transmitted between the two parties prior to encrypted communications. This need for secure key exchange leads to the largest challenge of symmetric encryption. Symmetric encryption is relatively fast, and suitable for encrypting large data sets, but is vulnerable if the key is lost or compromised. Adding to the confusion, a symmetric key is sometimes called a secret key or private key because of the absolute need to protect the key from exposure.

Example:

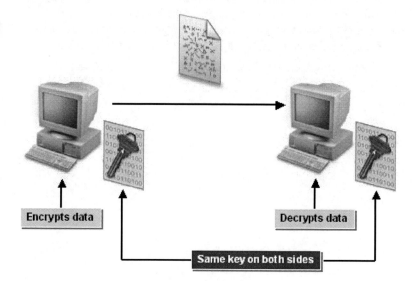

Encrypts data

Decrypts data

Same key on both sides

Figure 8-7: Symmetric-key cryptography.

Cipher Types

The two major categories of symmetric encryption ciphers each provide for confidentiality, integrity, and availability.

Cipher Type	*Description*
Stream cipher	

A *stream cipher* is a type of symmetric encryption that encrypts data one bit at a time. Each plaintext bit is transformed into encrypted ciphertext. Stream ciphers generate a keystream that is Exclusive ORed (XORed) with each bit to output the ciphered text. These algorithms are very fast to execute. The ciphertext is the same size as the original text, which can aid the cryptanalyst in breaking the cipher. This method produces fewer errors than other methods, and when errors occur, they affect only one bit.

For a stream cipher to be effective, the key stream should be as random as possible and should not have repetitious patterns. If the key stream values do repeat, they should be long enough to dismiss easy guesswork. Modern stream ciphers are extremely fast and can be implemented in hardware modules.

RC4 is an example of a stream cipher. Created in 1987 by Ron Rivest, it can use a key from 8 bits to 2,048 bits with a usual keysize of 40 to 256 bits.

Cipher Type	Description

Block cipher

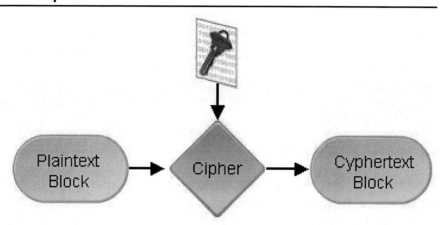

A *block cipher* encrypts data a block at a time, often in 64-bit or 128-bit blocks. It is usually more secure, but is also slower, than stream encryption.

The Digital Encryption Standard (DES) is an example of a block cipher. A 64-bit block of plaintext is encrypted with a 64-bit key, resulting in a 64-bit block of ciphertext.

Without using techniques such as transposition and substitution, cleartext blocks with identical content may be encrypted to the identical ciphertext. For this reason, block ciphers are strengthened by using an iterative process where multiple rounds of substitution, diffusion, and other functions are performed from four to 32 times. Or they may be strengthened through *chaining,* in which the results of one cipher step change the encryption process for the next cipher step.

XOR

XOR is a binary math operation that tests to see whether two inputs are the same as or different from each other. The result is 0 if the inputs are either both 0s or both 1s. The result is 1 if one input is a 0 and the other is a 1. The following table shows this logic.

Text	10010101
Key	01010101
Cipher text	11000000

Key Clustering

Key clustering is the result of two different keys encrypting the same cipher text.

Initialization Vectors

Definition:

An *initialization vector (IV)* is a string of bits that may be used with a symmetric cipher and a key to produce a unique result when the same key is used to encrypt the same cleartext. The IV is used to reduce the likelihood that identical ciphertext will be created when the identical cleartext is encrypted. IVs may be calculated using time factors, such as synchronized clocks, or by using a pre-shared value. The IV may be as large as a block in a block cipher or as long as the key in a stream cipher.

Example: IV Implementation

Using the key `abcdefghijklmnopqrstuvwxyz`, the plaintext message "Attack at Dawn" will be encrypted as `i8xfe zieam 5e3xy`. If encrypted again, the message "Attack at Dawn" will result in the same encrypted message.

If an IV is used with the key, the resulting encrypted message will be different. For instance:

● Plaintext message: Attack at Dawn

● IV: `i8j3k0x12axejq9drfwxyqkdszzy` (generated using a time base such as a clock)

● Key: `abcdefghijklmnopqrstuvwxyz`

● Encrypted message: `aqn7e zy8n2 qplm5`

Symmetric Encryption Algorithms

There are many available symmetric encryption algorithms.

Symmetric Algorithm	Description
DES	The *Data Encryption Standard (DES)* is a block algorithm that uses a 64-bit block and a 64-bit key. The key is actually only 56 bits with 8 bits of parity. It is a fairly weak encryption process that has been broken in many different brute force attacks.
	DES is a one of a family of ciphers named after Horst Feistel, who created early ciphers at IBM.
	DES is not secure in itself. It is used in different block cipher modes to gain security.
2DES	*Double DES (2DES)* is the same algorithm as DES with the exception that the encryption process is repeated twice in an attempt to strengthen the output. Analysis has shown that 2DES is no more secure than the original DES.
3DES	*Triple DES (3DES)* uses the DES algorithm but employs three keys to encrypt the same information in three processes. An alternative to 3DES with three encryptions (EEE) is to first encrypt with one key, decrypt with a second key, and then encrypt with a third key (EDE).
IDEA	The *International Data Encryption Algorithm (IDEA)* is a block cipher first proposed in 1991. It is used in Open PGP.

Symmetric Algorithm	Description
AES	Adopted in 2002, the *Advanced Encryption Standard (AES)* is a symmetric block cipher that has been approved by the U.S. government for encrypting Secret and Top Secret information. AES is often referred to as the Rijndael candidate because it was selected in a competition among many different algorithms. Vincent Rijmen and Joan Daemen developed the algorithm and combined their names to create the name of the AES competition submission. AES uses 128-bit blocks and keys of 128, 192, and 256 bits in length. The AES cipher does not use the Feistel processes but implements a substitution-permutation network.
RC2, 4, 5, and 6	The *Rivest Cipher (RC)* algorithms are a series developed by Ronald Rivest. All have variable key lengths. RC2 is a fixed-size block cipher. RC4 is a stream cipher. RC5 and RC6 are variable-size block ciphers.
Blowfish	*Blowfish* is a freely available 64-bit block cipher algorithm that uses a variable key length. It was developed by Bruce Schneier.
CAST-128	*CAST-128*, named after its developers, Carlisle Adams and Stafford Tavares, is a symmetric encryption algorithm with a 128-bit key. It was one of the contenders in the AES competition.

Symmetric Algorithm Issues

There are specific key issues that should be considered when implementing symmetric encryption algorithms.

Issue	Description
Transportation	Transportation must be accomplished using secure procedures to protect the secrecy of the keys.
Number of keys	To ensure that only the sender and receiver can encrypt and decrypt the data using symmetric algorithms, each sender and receiver pair needs to have a unique key to safeguard the information they send to each other. If there were 10 individuals in a secure environment and each of the 10 individuals needed to send truly secure information to each of the other nine individuals, the number of keys required can be calculated by using the following formula: Number of keys = [n * (n − 1)] / 2 With 10 individuals, the formula would be [10 * (10 − 1)] / 2 or (10 * 9) / 2 or 45. Managing 45 keys is a difficult task, especially considering that each key requires: • Proper maintenance. • Frequent modification. • Secure communication to each individual.

The DES Standard Process

Block ciphers that follow the DES standard include several process phases.

DES Process Phase	Description
Expansion	Each 64-bit block is split into two 32-bit half-blocks. Each 32-bit half-block is expanded to 48 bits by duplicating some of the bits.
Key mixing	Each 48-bit half-block is XORed with one of the subkeys. Sixteen 48-bit subkeys are created from the main key, resulting in one key for each round.
Substitution	After the key-mixing process, a series of substitutions are performed to mask the original data values. The substitutions result in 32 4-bit blocks called *S-boxes*.
Permutation	Following the substitution phase, the 32 4-bit blocks are arranged based on a pre-defined scrambling process. This is called the *P-box*.

 The process of expanding, substituting, and creating permutations provides DES an approximation of Claude Shannon's ideal cipher.

Symmetric Algorithms Overview

Each symmetric algorithm has distinct values that are associated with individual characteristics.

Algorithm	Characteristics	Values
DES	Block size	64 bits
	Key size	56 bits plus 8 parity bits
	Number of rounds	16
	Subkey generation	Left circular shift
	Round transformations	Permutation and substitution
2DES	Block size	64 bits
	Key size	112 bits
	Number of rounds	32
	Subkey generation	Left circular shift
	Round transformations	Permutation and substitution
3DES	Block size	64 bits
	Key size	168 bits
	Number of rounds	48
	Subkey generation	Left circular shift
	Round transformations	Permutation and substitution

Algorithm	Characteristics	Values
Blowfish	Block size	64 bits
	Key size	Variable (32–448 bits)
	Number of rounds	16
	Subkey generation	PI, XOR, 521 executions
	Round transformations	Addition modulo, XOR
RC2	Block size	64 bits
	Key size	Variable (8–1,024 bits)
	Number of rounds	18
	Subkey generation	Mixing and "mashing"
	Round transformations	Addition modulo, XOR, AND, complement, left circular shift
RC5	Block size	Variable (32, 64, 128 bits)
	Key size	Variable (0–2,040 bits)
	Number of rounds	Variable (0–255)
	Subkey generation	Computed array founded on the base of natural logs (e) and the golden ratio (1.61803...)
	Round transformations	Addition modulo, XOR, left circular shift
IDEA	Block size	64 bits
	Key size	128 bits
	Number of rounds	8
	Subkey generation	XOR, addition modulo, multiplication modulo
	Round transformations	Multiplication addition structure
CAST-128	Block size	64 bits
	Key size	40–128 bits
	Number of rounds	16
	Subkey generation	S-box substitutions based on round transformations
	Round transformations	Addition modulo, subtraction modulo, XOR, left circular shift
AES	Block size	128, 192, 256–128 are official AES bits; 192 and 256 bits were in the Rijndael submission
	Key size	128, 192, 256 bits
	Number of rounds	10, 12, or 14
	Round transformations	Non-linear layer, linear mixing layer, key addition layer

Block Cipher Modes

There are several block cipher modes that are used for symmetric encryption.

Block Cipher Mode	Description
ECB	The *Electronic Code Book (ECB)* mode breaks the plaintext down into 64-bit blocks and then encrypts each block separately. Duplicate plaintext blocks cause the same encryption result. This is beneficial for encrypting small amounts of data, which are seen in electronic transactions.
CBC	In *Cipher Block Chaining (CBC)* mode, 64-bit plaintext blocks are XORed with a 64-bit IV and then encrypted using the key. The resulting ciphertext is then chained to the next ciphering round, where it replaces the IV and helps to mask the contents of the second data block. This process is continued until the last block is encrypted. A potential concern with CBC is that errors will propagate.
CFB	In *Cipher FeedBack (CFB)* mode, the IV is first encrypted using the key and then XORed with the plaintext to create the ciphertext. In the second step, the ciphertext from the first step is encrypted with the key. The resulting encrypted information is XORed with the second plaintext block, and the ensuing ciphertext is chained to the third step, where it is encrypted. CFB is a stream mode technique.
OFB	In *Output FeedBack (OFB)* mode, the IV is encrypted with the key and then chained to the next block's encryption step. Each encryption step encrypts only the result of the first IV's previous encryption.
CTR	*Counter (CTR)* mode uses a counter to provide the IV. The counter encryption can be performed in parallel, rather than serially, because the numbers used for the IV can be predetermined. Errors do not propagate. The 802.11i standard for wireless encryption supports AES in CTR mode.

Key Management

There are many different factors that should be considered when managing cryptographic keys.

Key Management Factor	Description
Key control measures	Determines who has access to keys and how they are assigned.
Key recovery	Recovers lost keys.
Key storage	A secure repository for key assignment records.
Key retirement/destruction	How keys are removed from use and how they are destroyed.
Key change	The process of changing keys to systems on a periodic basis.
Key generation	Generates random keys for better data protection.
Key theft	What to do when keys have been compromised.
Frequency of key use	Limits the time that keys are used and the frequency of key reuse.

Key Management Factor	Description
Key escrow	Provides law enforcement and other agencies authorized access to encrypted information; keys may have to be stored at other locations. To do so, key escrow is used. *Key escrow* involves splitting the key into multiple parts and storing each part with a separate escrow agency. When a law enforcement agency receives approval to obtain the escrowed keys through a court order, the agency contacts the key escrow agency and acquires each of the parts.

An additional escrow method called *Fair Cryptosystems* allows the key to be split into "N" parts. All "N" parts are required to re-create the initial key, but each "N" key can verify that it is part of the original key without divulging its information. |

ACTIVITY 8-2
Discussing Symmetric-Key Cryptography

Scenario:

In this activity, you will discuss symmetric-key cryptography to help determine the method that is most relevant to ensuring your organization's data security.

1. **What are some characteristics of symmetric encryption?**

2. **True or False? A stream cipher is usually more secure, but it is also slower than block encryption.**

   __ True

   __ False

3. **Which one of these is used to reduce the likelihood that identical ciphertext will be created?**

   a) One-time pad

   b) Symmetric encryption

   c) Initialization vector

   d) Two-way encryption scheme

4. **What is the appropriate description for each symmetric encryption algorithm?**

__	DES	a.	A freely available 64-bit block cipher algorithm that uses a variable key length.
__	AES	b.	A block algorithm that uses a 64-bit block and a 64-bit key.
__	Blowfish	c.	A block cipher that uses 128-bit blocks and keys of 128, 192, and 256 bits in length.
__	CAST-128	d.	A block cipher first proposed in 1991 and used in Open PGP.
__	IDEA	e.	A symmetric encryption algorithm with a 128-bit key.

5. **To accomplish transportation, what must be used when considering the implementation of symmetric encryption algorithms?**

_____

6. **What is the appropriate description for each phase of the DES standard process?**

____	Expansion	a.	Thirty-two 4-bit blocks are arranged based on a predefined scrambling process.
____	Key mixing	b.	Each 64-bit block is split into two 32-bit half-blocks.
____	Substitution	c.	After the key-mixing process, these are performed to mask the original data values.
____	Permutation	d.	Each 48-bit half-block is XORed with one of the subkeys.

7. **What is the appropriate description for each block cipher mode?**

____	ECB	a.	The IV is encrypted with the key and then chained to the next block's encryption step.
____	CBC	b.	The IV is first encrypted using the key and then XORed with the plaintext to create the ciphertext.
____	CFB	c.	This breaks the plaintext down into 64-bit blocks and then encrypts each block separately.
____	OFB	d.	This uses a counter to provide the IV.
____	CTR	e.	64-bit plaintext blocks are XORed with a 64-bit IV and then encrypted using the key.

8. **What is the appropriate description for each key management factor?**

____	Key control measures	a.	Determining who has access to keys and how they are assigned.
____	Key recovery	b.	The process of altering keys to systems on a periodic basis.
____	Key storage	c.	Creating random keys for better data protection.
____	Key generation	d.	The process of splitting a key into multiple parts and then storing each part at a different location.
____	Key escrow	e.	Salvaging lost keys.
____	Key change	f.	A secure repository for key assignment records.

TOPIC C
Asymmetric-Key Cryptography

While using a single key to encrypt a message is a good form of security, it has its drawbacks, such as ensuring that both parties agree to and know the key. Asymmetric encryption was a response to the challenges of symmetric key exchange. It is based on work done in the 1970s by Whitfield Diffie and Martin Hellman. An information systems security professional should address these concerns and consider improvements to data security. In this topic, you will identify asymmetric-key cryptography and apply the best method most relevant to the needs of your organization.

Securing your organization's data is an important task. The single key of symmetric-key cryptography methods is a powerful tool at your disposal. However, when dealing with extremely sensitive data, advanced encryption may be necessary. Selecting an asymmetric-key cryptography method allows you to employ all the levels of encryption necessary to ensure the security of your organization's information.

Asymmetric Encryption

Definition:

Asymmetric encryption is a two-way encryption scheme that uses two different keys. Asymmetric encryption was designed to solve the problems of key distribution and key management found in symmetric encryption.

A 1976 paper named "New Directions in Cryptography" formed the basis for most public-key encryption implementations, including Rivest, Shamir, and Adleman (RSA). It introduced the idea of using two different keys to achieve secure communication. The keys would be generated simultaneously, and one key would be used to encrypt and the other would be used to decrypt. In implementations, the user keeps one key, which becomes the private key, and the other key becomes the public key and can be freely distributed.

Asymmetric algorithms are based on using a one-way function. The one-way function ensures that the same key cannot decrypt its encrypted messages. For instance, a public key cannot decrypt what has been encrypted with a public key, only a private key can.

Asymmetric encryption is based on factoring very large prime numbers. Multiplying two very large prime numbers together is easy. Trying to factor them is much more difficult. For example, 727 * 757 = 550,339. If all you know is the number 550,339 and you needed to figure out what two numbers created it, the problem is much more difficult. This example also uses very small prime numbers. Actual numbers used by products like RSA are one hundred or more digits long.

Example:

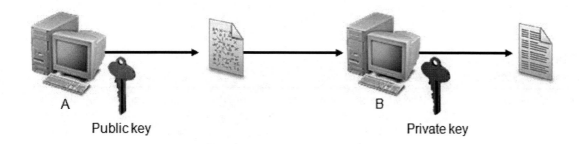

A   Public key

B   Private key

Figure 8-8: *Asymmetric encryption.*

Asymmetric Encryption Keys

Unlike symmetric encryption, the mainstay of asymmetric encryption is using public and private keys. The *private key* is kept secret by one party during two-way encryption. Because the private key is never shared, its security is relatively maintained.

The *public key* is given to anyone. Depending on the application of the encryption, either party may use the encryption key. The other key in the pair is used to decrypt. Only the public key in a pair can decrypt data encoded with the corresponding private key, and vice versa.

Key generation is the process of generating a public and private key pair using a specific application.

Asymmetric Encryption Benefits and Limitations

Asymmetric encryption has helped eliminate a major shortcoming of symmetric cryptography. Because the public key is available to anyone, it can be sent using email or other non-secure modes. Key management in an asymmetric environment is the responsibility of each individual. People can generate their own private and public key pairs, maintaining private key confidentiality and freely distributing their public keys.

However, asymmetric algorithms are limited in the amount of processing required to encrypt and decrypt. The mathematical processes involved are complex. Public-key creation is reasonably simple, but it is computationally infeasible to generate the private key from the public key. Asymmetric algorithms take thousands of times more processing power than symmetric algorithms.

Key length is another issue. Asymmetric keys are much longer than symmetric keys. If a symmetric algorithm requires a 256-bit key, an asymmetric algorithm might use a 2,048-bit key for the same level of confidentiality assurance.

Hybrid Cryptography—Symmetric and Asymmetric Algorithms

Symmetric and asymmetric algorithms are used concurrently to provide secure communications. For example, you can use RSA, an asymmetric algorithm, for endpoint authentication and validation, while using the Triple DES (3DES) or Advanced Encryption Standard (AES), which are symmetric algorithms used for confidentiality.

Asymmetric Encryption Applications

Asymmetric key encryption can be applied to sensitive data in different ways.

Asymmetric Encryption Application	Description
Confidentiality	*Confidentiality* or *secrecy* is supported when the sender encrypts using the recipient's public key and the receiver decrypts using the recipient's private key. Only the recipient can decrypt a message that is encrypted with the public key. This provides increased confidentiality.
Integrity	*Integrity* is supported when the sender encrypts using the sender's private key and the receiver decrypts with the sender's public key. If the message is altered in transport, the decryption will not succeed.
Non-repudiation	Non-repudiation is also supported when the sender's public key is used to decrypt the message. Because only the associated sender's private key can create content that can be decrypted using the sender's public key, this confirms the identity of the sender.

Asymmetric Encryption Algorithms

There are three algorithms that are specific to asymmetric encryption.

Asymmetric Algorithm	Description
RSA	The *Rivest Shamir Adleman (RSA)* algorithm was designed in 1978 by Ron Rivest, Adi Shamir, and Len Adleman at Massachusetts Institute of Technology (MIT), and was the first successful algorithm for public-key encryption. The algorithm has a variable key length and block size and is based on factoring the product of two large prime numbers. It is still widely used and is considered highly secure if it employs sufficiently long keys. Today, there is no computational method available to perform it quickly.
Elgamal	*Elgamal* is a public-key encryption algorithm developed by Taher Elgamal. It is based on functions using discrete logarithms.
ECC	The *elliptic curve cryptography (ECC)* algorithm is a method of public-key encryption. It is based on additional developments in discrete logs and requires shorter keys than other public-key algorithms.

Diffie-Hellman Key Exchange

Diffie-Hellman is a method that provides for secure key exchange.

Managing private keys for symmetric algorithms is difficult. Diffie-Hellman key exchange permits the sender and receiver to establish a shared secret (symmetric) key over an insecure communications channel. Once the secret key has been exchanged, the key can be used to encrypt subsequent communications using a symmetric key cipher. Diffie-Hellman is an asymmetric encryption algorithm typically used to generate and share keys that are subsequently used by symmetric encryption algorithms like 3DES and AES. In other words, 3DES and AES, both symmetric algorithms, encrypt with session keys generated by Diffie-Hellman, an asymmetric algorithm.

 In 2002, the algorithm's name was changed to Diffie-Hellman-Merkle to credit Ralph Merkle's contribution to the creation of public-key cryptography.

Digital Certificates

Definition:

A *digital certificate* is an electronic document that associates credentials with a public key. Both users and devices can hold certificates. The certificate validates the certificate holder's identity and is also a way to distribute the holder's public key. A server called a *certificate authority* (CA) issues certificates and the associated public/private key pairs.

Example:

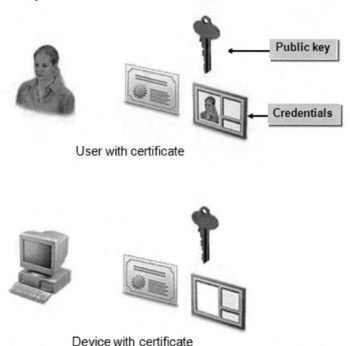

User with certificate

Device with certificate

Figure 8-9: *Digital certificates.*

Public Key Infrastructure

Definition:

A *public key infrastructure (PKI)* is a cryptographic system that is composed of a CA, certificates, software, services, and other cryptographic components for the purpose of enabling the authenticity and validation of data and/or entities. The PKI can be implemented in various hierarchical structures, and can be publicly available or maintained privately by an organization.

Example:

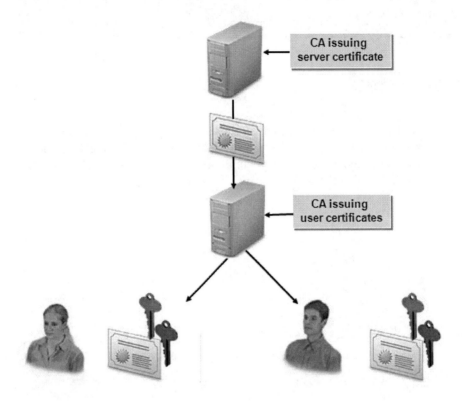

Figure 8-10: *PKI.*

PKI Components

A PKI contains several components.

- Digital certificates, to verify the identity of entities.

- One or more CAs, to issue digital certificates to computers, users, or applications.

- A *registration authority (RA)*, responsible for verifying users' identities and approving or denying requests for digital certificates.

- A *certificate repository database*, to store the digital certificates.

- A *certificate management system*, to provide software tools to perform the day-to-day functions of the PKI.

The PKI Process

When using the PKI, the first step is to obtain a public and private key pair from the CA. The public key is retained by the CA and a certificate is then issued to the individual. That certificate, standardized as an X.509 version 3 certificate, is also available to anyone who wishes or needs to verify that the public key provided is the actual key of the individual supplying it. The CA certifies the identity.

The PKI process also includes procedures for revoking certificates when they expire or when the security of the private key is in doubt.

Certificate Information

Certificates contain the following information:

- Version
- Serial Number
- Algorithm ID
- Issuer
- Validity
- Not Before
- Not After
- Subject
- Subject Public Key Info
- Issuer Unique Identifier (Optional)
- Subject Unique Identifier (Optional)
- Extensions (Optional)
- Certificate Signature Algorithm
- Certificate Signature, to determine certificate validity

Certificate Revocation List

A *Certificate Revocation List (CRL)* is a list of certificates (or, more accurately, their serial numbers) that have been revoked, are no longer valid, and should not be relied on by any system user. The list enumerates revoked certificates along with the reason or reasons for revocation. The dates of certificate issue, and the entities that issued them, are also included. In addition, each list contains a proposed date for the next release. When a potential user attempts to access a server, the server allows or denies access based on the CRL entry for that particular user.

A CRL is generated periodically after a clearly defined time frame, and may also be generated immediately after a certificate has been revoked. The CRL is always issued by the CA, which issues the corresponding certificates. All CRLs have a (often short) lifetime in which they are valid and during which they may be consulted by a PKI-enabled application to verify a counterpart's certificate prior its use. To prevent spoofing or denial of service (DoS) attacks, CRLs are usually signed by the issuing CA and therefore carry a digital signature. To validate a specific CRL prior to relying on it, the certificate of its corresponding CA is needed, which can usually be found in a public directory.

An alternative to CRL is the Online Certificate Status Protocol (OCSP). It is a newer method for obtaining the revocation status of an digital certificate from a server using an HTTP request. OCSP requests use less bandwidth and provide faster confirmation on the validity of the certificate.

ACTIVITY 8-3
Discussing Asymmetric-Key Cryptography

Scenario:

In this activity, you will discuss asymmetric-key cryptography to help determine the method most relevant to the needs of your organization.

1. **True or False? Asymmetric encryption is a two-way encryption scheme that uses two different keys and are based on the use of a one-way function with a trapdoor.**

   ___ True

   ___ False

2. **Which statement is true about an asymmetric private encryption key?**

   a) It contains fewer bits than the public key.

   b) It is kept secret by one party during two-way encryption.

   c) A specific application is used to generate only private keys.

   d) A specific application is used to generate only public keys.

3. **How can public-key encryption support secrecy? How can it support integrity?**

4. **What is the appropriate description for each asymmetric encryption algorithm?**

___ RSA	a.	A method of public-key encryption that requires shorter keys than other public-key algorithms.
___ Elgamal	b.	Has a variable key length and block size and is based on factoring the product of two large prime numbers.
___ ECC	c.	A public-key algorithm based on functions using discrete logarithms.

5. **True or False? A digital certificate validates the certificate holder's identity and is also a way to distribute the holder's private key.**

   ___ True

   ___ False

6. **The PKI consists of which one or more of the following components?**

    a) Software

    b) Network protocols

    c) CAs

    d) Certificates

7. **Which one of these PKI components is responsible for verifying users' identities and approving or denying requests for digital certificates?**

    a) Certificate repository database

    b) Certificate management system

    c) Certification authorization system

    d) RA

8. **Which one or more of the following is included in the PKI process?**

    a) Procedures for revoking certificates when they expire

    b) Procedures for creating network user accounts

    c) Procedures for revoking certificates when the security of the private key is in doubt

    d) Procedures for key escrow

TOPIC D
Hashing and Message Digests

You have identified both symmetric- and asymmetric-key cryptography and selected the encryption method that best protects your data. Next, it is important to further implement these encryption schemes and techniques as building blocks to create more complex encryption systems.

Although standard public and private key encryption systems are useful methods for protecting sensitive data, it is not always feasible to encrypt and decrypt an entire file that may be several gigabits in size. Instead, you can use hashing and message digests to reduce the amount of information that has to be decrypted and verified. Hashing is concerned with protecting the integrity of your documents and transmissions. It is frequently used with other forms of encryption to provide an integrity component, while symmetric or asymmetric encryption provides the confidentiality.

Hashing

Definition:

Hashing is one-way encryption that transforms cleartext into ciphertext. The resulting ciphertext is never decrypted and is called a *hash, hash value,* or *message digest.* It may seem odd that it is never decrypted but it can perform its function just the same. Because the cleartext can be hashed again at any point in time and be compared to the original hash, you will know if there has been any change to the integrity of the cleartext. The input data can vary in length, whereas the hash length is fixed. It is possible to break a hash through brute force. With a large password or a large file, the likelihood of finding the correct password for file contents through brute force is improbable.

The message digest can be either keyed or non-keyed. When keyed, the original message is combined with a secret key sent with the message. When non-keyed, the original message is hashed without any other mechanisms.

 Collision occur when a hash function generates identical output from two different inputs.

Example:

Figure 8-11: *Hashing.*

Hashing in Password Protection

Hashing is used in a number of password authentication schemes. When a password is entered into a computer system for user authentication, rather than store the password in readable form, most systems use a one-way hashing function to encode the password for system storage. Although a hash is created from the raw data, that data cannot be obtained from the hash.

Because hashing algorithms are publicly known, the protective nature of the hash is its one-way function. When a user attempts to access the computer with a specific password, the password is hashed using the same algorithm and the stored hash value is compared to the new hash. If the values match, the password is correct. If they do not match, the password entered is incorrect. Because hashing does not require the use of keys, there is nothing to share.

Hashing in File Transmission and Verification

If a 20-gigabyte (GB) file needs to be transported to another location, it is critical to ensure that the file contents are correct. This can be accomplished by first encrypting the file prior to forwarding, and then decrypting it once it arrives at its destination. Successful decryption indicates that the file has not been modified in the transmission process. An excessive amount of time is required for file encryption and decryption.

To limit the time frame for content verification, a message digest can be computed. Using a hashing algorithm, a 168-bit hash can be generated that represents the entire 20-GB file. The hash and the file are then transmitted to the desired destination. Once received, a new hash is created and, if the original hash and the destination hash match, it can be assumed that the file was not modified during transmission.

Salting the Hash

Adding a salt to the hash helps to create randomness. If two identical pieces of plaintext were hashed without a salt, they would generate the same hash value. By adding random data with the original plaintext, the system will generate unique hash values.

Digest and Hashing Algorithms

Some common encryption algorithms are used for message digests and hashing.

Digest/ Hashing Algorithm	Description
MD2, 4, and 5	The *Message Digest (MD)2*, *MD4*, and *MD5* algorithms each produce a 128-bit message digest. They were created as a series by Ronald Rivest, with each algorithm improving upon its predecessor. **MD2:** ● Developed in 1989 ● Optimized for 8-bit computers **MD4:** ● Developed in 1990 ● Optimized for 32-bit computers **MD5:** ● Developed in 1991 ● Optimized for 32-bit computers ● An enhanced MD4—Although slightly slower than MD4, it consists of supplementary, efficient safety mechanisms that increase security
HAVAL	The *HAVAL* algorithm is a modification of MD5. It produces hashes of variable lengths: 128 bits, 160 bits, 192 bits, 224 bits, and 256 bits.
SHA versions 1, 256, 384, and 512	The *Secure Hash Algorithm (SHA)* algorithm is modeled after MD5 and is considered the stronger of the two. It is used with the Digital Signature Algorithm (DSA). SHA includes four updated algorithms. SHA-1 produces a 160-bit hash value, while SHA-256, SHA-384, and SHA-512 produce 256-bit, 384-bit, and 512-bit digests, respectively.

 As of this writing, the National Institute of Standards and Technology (NIST) has completed the submission process for a new version of SHA. All the entries have been submitted and evaluated and five finalists were chosen. These final five algorithms will be publicly reviewed before the final replacement algorithm is named in 2012.

Message Authentication Code Algorithms

Message authentication codes perform cryptographic functions similar to hashing.

Authentication Code Algorithm	Description
MAC	The *message authentication code (MAC)* uses a shared secret key to encrypt a file and then takes the last block of encrypted data and sends it as an authentication code along with the unencrypted file. At the destination, the receiver encrypts the file again with the secret key and compares the last block of the file with the sent authentication code. If they match, the data is assumed to have been unmodified.
	This process is sometimes called a *message integrity code (MIC)* or a *modification detection code (MDC)*. However, a MIC does not imply the use of a secret key, and therefore must be transmitted in an encrypted form to ensure message integrity.
HMAC	The *hash message authentication code (HMAC)* creates a hash of a file that is then encrypted for transmission. The file is transported with the encrypted hash value. When the file is received at its destination, the hash is re-created. The decrypted hash is then compared to the new hash.

Digital Signatures

Definition:

A *digital signature* is a message digest that has been encrypted again with a user's private key. The digital signature is appended to a message to identify the sender and the message. When the message is received, the digital signature is decrypted, with the user's public key, back into a message digest. The recipient then rehashes the original message and compares it to the sender's hash. If the two hash values match, the digital signature is authentic and the message integrity is confirmed.

Example:

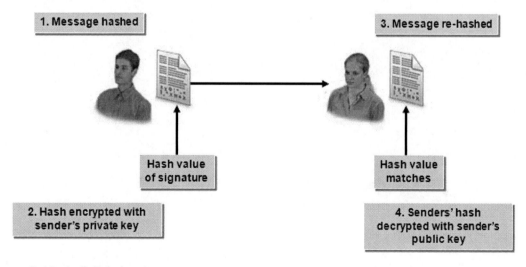

1. Message hashed
2. Hash encrypted with sender's private key
   - Hash value of signature
3. Message re-hashed
4. Senders' hash decrypted with sender's public key
   - Hash value matches

Figure 8-12: A digital signature.

Digital Signature Non-Repudiation

Determine the information source by signing a hash or any other data with a private key. If it is possible to decrypt the information with the sender's public key, the sender has been verified, thus resulting in non-repudiation. Non-repudiation exists when the sender cannot deny his or her association with a data transmission.

Encryption of the Hash

It is important to remember that a digital signature is a hash that is then itself encrypted. Without the second round of encryption, another party could easily:

1. Intercept the file and the hash.
2. Modify the file.
3. Re-create the hash.
4. Send the modified file to the recipient.

ACTIVITY 8-4
Discussing Hashing and Message Digests

Scenario:
In this activity, you will discuss message digests and hashing so that you better understand how to utilize these cryptographic functions.

1. After one-way hashing encryption transforms cleartext into ciphertext, what is the result?

2. What are some other names for a hash?

3. True or False? A message hash is always combined with a secret key that is sent with the message.

   ___ True

   ___ False

4. Which one of these digest/hashing algorithms includes four updated algorithms?
   a) HAVAL
   b) SHA
   c) MD5

5. Compare and contrast the use of a MAC to the use of a message digest.

TOPIC E
Email, Internet, and Wireless Security

Now that you are familiar with the concepts of hashing and message digests and have applied hashing algorithms and digital signatures, you should use this information to secure specific systems in your network. It is important to address the security of email message transmissions and Internet and wireless data exchange. In this topic, you will identify email, Internet, and wireless security options.

Email is a quick and inexpensive method to exchange information. Its widespread use also makes it a target of those who would threaten the integrity and confidentiality of your data. Similarly, business organizations have grown increasingly reliant on the Internet and wireless access, resulting in security issues and vulnerabilities that affect daily information transactions. Simplicity translates to poor access control and virtually nonexistent source identification. Your knowledge of email systems and security is imperative to protecting your organization's email, Internet, and wireless communications.

Encryption and Email Security

These are some standard applications of encryption that are specific to securing email.

Email Security Method	Description
PGP	*Pretty Good Privacy (PGP)* is a publicly available email security method that uses a variation of public-key cryptography to encrypt emails: the sender encrypts the contents of the email message and then encrypts the key that was used to encrypt the contents. The encrypted key is sent with the email, and the receiver decrypts the key and then uses the key to decrypt the contents. PGP also uses public-key cryptography to digitally sign emails to authenticate the sender and the contents.

PGP is built on of a web-of-trust model rather than a traditional PKI infrastructure. In the web-of-trust, you collect certificates from people you trust. For example, you might decide that because you trust Alice and Alice trusts Bob, that you too can trust Bob. |
| PEM | *Privacy-Enhanced Mail (PEM)* is a standard that provides for the secure exchange of email over the Internet. PEM applies various cryptographic techniques to allow for confidentiality, sender authentication, and message integrity. The message integrity characteristics allow the user to ensure that a message has not been altered during transport from the sender. The sender authentication allows a user to verify that the received PEM message is definitely from the individual who sent it. The confidentiality feature allows a message to be kept secret from individuals who are not included in the message address. |

Email Security Method	Description
MIME and S/MIME	*Multipurpose Internet Mail Extension (MIME)* is an internal labeling process used to define the type of attachment files that are found in an email. MIME is used to identify graphic formats, music formats, movie formats, and other file formats that may be included in an email message.
	Secure/MIME (S/MIME) is an extension of MIME that prevents attackers from intercepting and manipulating email and attachments by encrypting and digitally signing the contents of the email using public-key cryptography. S/MIME ensures that the email that is received is the same email that was sent and that its contents are the original contents included by the sender.

Encryption and Internet Security

There are various methods that protect Internet information without requiring individual file encryption and decryption.

Internet Security Method	Description
Link encryption	*Link encryption* is an Internet security device that is attached to each end of a transmission line to encrypt and decrypt data. It provides encryption at Layer 2 of the Open System Interconnection (OSI) model.
	For example, if two routers are connected via a leased line, a link encryption device can be attached to the circuit at each end of the line. When information leaves the router, it is encrypted by a link encryption device and then decrypted when it is received at the router.
IPsec	*Internet Protocol security (IPsec)* is a set of open, non-proprietary standards that can be used to secure data as it travels across the network or the Internet. IPsec uses an array of protocols and services to provide data authenticity and integrity, anti-replay protection, non-repudiation, and protection against eavesdropping and sniffing. IPsec works at Layer 3 of the OSI model.
	IPsec enables information to travel in two modes: transport mode or tunnel mode.
	● *Transport mode* protects the information in a payload of an IP datagram. The original IP addresses are preserved, making it possible to determine the structure of the internal network.
	● *Tunnel mode* allows the encryption of the original IP datagram and the entire payload. Creating the tunnel removes the ability to view any of the information regarding the original networks because that information has been encrypted.
Upper-layer encryption	Various security protocols, such as Secure Sockets Layer (SSL), Transport Layer Security (TLS), Hypertext Transfer Protocol Secure (HTTPS), and Secure Shell (SSH), can be used to implement encryption in the upper layers of the OSI model.

The IPsec Process

IPsec is not a protocol per se, but rather a framework that uses various protocols to achieve the desired result. It is hybrid encryption using a combination of hashing, symmetric, and asymmetric encryption.

Whether transport or tunnel mode is used, IPsec requires that certain processes occur to be successful. IPsec uses two capabilities to deliver confidentiality and integrity. Confidentiality is provided through the use of an Encapsulated Security Payload (ESP) header, which provides information about the encrypted part of the IPsec messages. Integrity and authentication are handled by the Authentication Header (AH). However, it is important to note that ESP can also handle authentication and integrity. In fact, ESP could be used by itself to provide all three services (confidentiality, integrity, authentication [the CIA triad]), making the AH optional.

Before IPsec can connect between the two ends of a connection, it must first agree on the services to provide. The agreement is made during a process called the Security Association (SA). Two different SAs are required: one for sending and another for receiving. The security association includes:

● Negotiating the time limit for the SA.

● The mode (tunnel or transport).

● The ESP encryption algorithm, key, and initialization vector (IV).

● The ESP authentication algorithm and key.

● The AH authentication algorithm and key.

● A sequence number counter.

Periodic renewal of the security association ensures that both ends stay connected so the communication may continue.

Internet Key Exchange in IPsec

IPsec does not use public key infrastructure (PKI) for key exchange. It uses a process called the *Internet Key Exchange (IKE)*. IKE is a combination of two protocols; the Internet Security Association and Key Management Protocol (ISAKMP) and OAKLEY. OAKLEY is named for the developer of the protocol and does the key negotiation. ISAKMP defines the available infrastructure for the key management process.

Encryption and Wireless Security

Common wireless security protocols use various encryption methods.

Wireless Security Protocol	Algorithm
WEP	Wired Equivalent Privacy (WEP) was the first encryption method used to protect wireless data. In WEP, a single key was used to authenticate with the wireless access point and to encrypt and decrypt the information during transmission.
	WEP employed the Rivest Cipher 4 (RC4) stream cipher. Standard 64-bit WEP used a 40-bit key and a 24-bit initialization vector (IV). Since the 24-bit IV was always the same, key breaking was an easy task. Eventually, 128-bit and 256-bit WEP keys were allowed, which strengthened the security of WEP-based wireless traffic.

Wireless Security Protocol	Algorithm
WPA	Wi-Fi Protected Access (WPA) improved protection by using the RC4 algorithm and implementing a 128-bit key with a 48-bit IV.
	WPA includes a message integrity code (MIC) to check for any manipulated packets. It also features the *Temporal Key Integrity Protocol (TKIP)* algorithm, which changes the keys on packets for each packet exchange and helps secure wireless computer networks. IVs are generated for each frame that is sent in the wireless network.
WPA2	WPA2 is implemented with the Advanced Encryption Standard (AES). Replay attacks are controlled using a CTR in the header of the wireless frames. Pre-shared keys may be used, but for enterprise environments, Remote Access Dial-In User Service (RADIUS) servers and the Extensible Authentication Protocol (EAP) provide better authentication. WPA2 is also referred to as 802.11i.

Wireless Access Protocol

The *Wireless Access Protocol (WAP)* is not associated with data encryption. It is a protocol associated with the implementation of mobile phone, smartphone, and personal digital assistant (PDA) applications that access the Internet.

For example, the iPhone uses WAP when retrieving web-based information from an Internet or mobile phone service provider.

IPsec/VPN

When security is necessary, organizations may also choose to use an IPsec/Virtual Private Network (VPN) environment in addition to the wireless encryption. In this environment, the data is best encrypted by IPsec and then further encrypted for wireless transmission using one of the wireless security methods.

ACTIVITY 8-5
Discussing Email, Internet, and Wireless Security

Scenario:

In this activity, you will discuss email, Internet, and wireless security options.

1. **What can Pretty Good Privacy (PGP) be defined as?**

2. **What can Secure Multipurpose Internet Mail Extensions (S/MIME) be defined as?**

3. **Which one of the following is an Internet security device that is attached to each end of a transmission line to encrypt and decrypt data?**

   a) Link encryption

   b) IPsec

   c) HTTPS

   d) WPA

4. **Match each wireless access protocol with its appropriate description.**

___ WEP	a.	Uses the RC4 algorithm and the TKIP algorithm
___ WPA	b.	Uses RC4 for encryption
___ WPA2	c.	Uses the AES algorithm

TOPIC F
Cryptographic Weaknesses

You have determined a security strategy for email and Internet communications within your organization. While this helps address the problem of securing transmitted data, other prevention methods should be considered to protect the confidentiality and integrity of your electronic data. The potential for cryptographic deficiencies and limitations presents additional risk concerns. In this topic, you will identify weaknesses in cryptographic processes.

Because business organizations today are ever reliant on sharing and accessing confidential information electronically, data security maintenance is a continuous undertaking. Even when all proper safeguards are implemented and protection is enforced, setbacks and threats can still occur that endanger system reliability and permeate security. This means that mitigating cryptographic security concerns is a requirement for protecting data integrity. Your ability to determine and recognize cryptographic shortcomings and system frailties will serve to reduce the risk of security compromises to your data.

Encryption-Based Attacks

There are several common encryption-based attack categories.

Encryption Attack Type	Description
Birthday attack	A *birthday attack* exploits a paradox in the mathematical algorithms used to encrypt passwords. This type of attack takes advantage of the probability of different password inputs producing the same encrypted output, given a large enough set of inputs. It is named after the surprising statistical fact that there is a 50% chance that any two people in a group of 23 will share a birthday.
Dictionary attack	A dictionary attack automates password guessing by comparing encrypted passwords against a predetermined list of possible password values. Dictionary attacks are only successful against fairly simple and obvious passwords, because they rely on a dictionary of common words and predictable variations, such as adding a single digit to the end of a word.
Replay attack	A *replay attack* can be used to bypass the encryption protecting passwords while in transit. If the encrypted password can be captured and then replayed, the attacker may be able to gain access to a system without ever having access to the password itself.
Side channel attack	A *side channel attack* targets the cryptosystem by gathering information about the physical characteristics of the encryption and then exploiting them. For example, by timing the transfer of encryption key information, an attacker might be able to determine the length of the key.
Factoring attack	A *factoring attack* attempts to determine the prime numbers used in asymmetric and symmetric encryption as a means to break cryptosystems. This attack theory was discovered by RSA Laboratories when it developed the RSA Factoring Challenge as an effort to research and explore computational number theory and integer factorization using semiprimes, or numbers with two prime factors. Although the challenge was discontinued in 2007, it was extraordinarily successful in testing the cryptanalytic strength of both asymmetric- and symmetric-key algorithms.

For more information on RSA factorization and factoring attacks, visit **www.rsa.com/rsalabs/ node.asp?id=2189**.

Cryptanalysis Methodologies

Cryptographic attackers can employ several variants of man-in-the-middle attacks to determine encryption keys and break cryptosystems.

Cryptographic Attack	Description
Ciphertext-only	The attacker has several ciphertext samples of messages encrypted with the same algorithm and, possibly, the same key. The intent is to find the encryption key. Once the key for one message is determined, the other messages may be decrypted.
Known plaintext	The attacker has a copy of the plaintext and ciphertext for one or more messages. The intent is to find the correct key. Messages often have a common format with salutations and closings. With this knowledge, the attacker can use a limited amount of information to figure out the encryption key.
Chosen plaintext	The attacker has a copy of the plaintext and ciphertext for one or more messages, but chooses to work with only a selected part of the plaintext when attempting to break the system. The intent is to find the correct key. By manipulating the key, a portion of the message may be decoded and eventually the entire key may be recovered.
Chosen ciphertext	The attacker has a copy of the plaintext and ciphertext for one or more messages, but chooses to work with only a selected part of the ciphertext when attempting to break the system. The intent is to find the correct key. By manipulating the key, a portion of the message may be decoded and eventually the entire key may be recovered.

Frequency Analysis

Frequency analysis is a method for breaking encryption when simple substitution algorithms are used. Letters used in a particular linguistic alphabet appear in certain words based on a given frequency. For example, in English, the most often used letter is E. If an encrypted document contains a number of Vs approximately equal to the frequency of E in typical plaintext samples, the V may be replaced with E in all instances to derive the original message. Other frequency replacements may be used.

Reverse Engineering

In cryptography, *reverse engineering* is the process of analyzing and determining the structure, function, and operation of a cryptosystem based on system output and other external characteristics. If an attacker can gain enough information about system functionality or about key-generation techniques, or can observe enough encrypted data, it may be possible to reverse engineer the process and break the system.

Reverse Engineering Algorithms

Oftentimes, it is not necessary to reverse engineer the algorithms used in asymmetric and symmetric encryption because the algorithms are published for all to see. By allowing everyone to observe how the algorithms work, stronger algorithms are produced because weaknesses can be identified and repaired early in the implementation.

Random Number Generator Vulnerability

A *random number generator (RNG)* is a device that is used to create keys and to perform cryptographic functions. If the RNG is biased, meaning it does not generate truly random numbers, the distribution of the keys created using the biased RNG is also biased. This weakness can lead to the use of statistical analysis to break the key-generation process, which can then lead to a reduced amount of time needed to determine keys that will decrypt encrypted files.

Temporary Files Vulnerabilities

Temporary files are often used in the process of encrypting or decrypting large amounts of data. Temporary files present a security risk in that the files contain remnants of the encryption or decryption process. Access to temporary storage areas on computers should be controlled to limit temporary file exposure to unauthorized users.

ACTIVITY 8-6
Discussing Cryptographic Weaknesses

Scenario:
In this activity, you will discuss weaknesses in cryptographic processes.

1. **What is the appropriate description for each cryptographic attack?**

   ____ Ciphertext-only

   ____ Known plaintext

   ____ Chosen plaintext

   ____ Chosen ciphertext

   a. Once knowledge of a common message format is obtained, the attacker can use a limited amount of information to figure out the encryption key using a copy of the plaintext and ciphertext.

   b. Once the key for one sample encrypted message is determined, the attacker can decrypt the other messages using samples of messages encrypted with the same algorithm.

   c. Once the key is manipulated, the attacker can decode a message and uncover the entire key working with part of the ciphertext.

   d. Once the key is manipulated, the attacker can decode a message and uncover the entire key working with part of the plaintext.

2. **Which one of these encryption-based attacks exploits weakness in the mathematical algorithms used to encrypt passwords?**

   a) Factoring attack

   b) Dictionary attack

   c) Birthday attack

   d) Frequency analysis

3. **What is a good example of how frequency analysis is conducted?**

4. **True or False? Reverse engineering is a cryptographic process of analyzing and determining the structure, function, and operation of a cryptosystem.**

   ___ True

   ___ False

5. **What type of security risk do temporary files present?**

   a) The files exploit the probability of different plaintext inputs producing the same encrypted output.

   b) The files contain biased random numbers that could be used during statistical analysis to decrypt files.

   c) The files contain remnants of the encryption or decryption process.

Lesson 8 Follow-up

In this lesson, you analyzed cryptographic characteristics and elements; applied cryptographic practices, processes, methods, and standards; and identified cryptographic weaknesses to ensure your information's CIA triad. Because data security assurance is fundamental to privacy maintenance, it is important to use proactive defense strategies that properly counteract threats to your information resources and intellectual property. Your ability to effectively encrypt your organization's data to protect its information will help to ensure its competitive edge and capacity to attain desired business goals.

1. **Given this information on cryptography, where do you see the need for cryptography in your organization? Would you apply cryptography? At what level?**

2. **What industries do you see having the highest need for encryption? Do you work in this type of industry?**

9 | Physical Security

Lesson Time: 3 hour(s)

Lesson Objectives:

In this lesson, you will analyze physical security.

You will:

- Apply physical access control.

- Identify physical access monitoring systems and tools.

- Identify physical security methods.

- Analyze facilities security.

Introduction

Protecting organizational information systems and their assets involves more than employing cryptosystems and implementing cryptographic techniques. Tackling the challenges of physical security to preserve your organization's intellectual and personnel assets is a primary concern for information systems security professionals. In this lesson, you will analyze physical security controls, and design strategies, tools, and techniques.

Protecting your organization's physical resources from intruders, natural disasters, and internal threats is vital to the success of your company. Applying effective physical security to these resources will help you ensure a safe environment for employees, data, equipment, and the facility itself.

Protecting the physical safety of your employees is the most important work that you do. Protecting life trumps all other security concerns. Physical security can be tied back to all aspects of the CIA triad. By controlling the physical aspects of security, you are protecting the confidentiality of documents and facilities, the integrity of your systems, and most importantly, the availability of your buildings, systems, records, and employees.

This lesson supports content found in the Information Security Governance & Risk Management and Physical (Environmental) Security domains of the CISSP® certification.

TOPIC A
Physical Access Control

Like intellectual property and information resources, your organization's physical resources need protection from internal and external forces. Applying physical security measures to your organization begins with controlling which individuals have access to your building. In this topic, you will apply physical access control.

Controlling physical access to your organization's facility is as important to your company's success as controlling access to internal resources and data. Vandalism, property destruction, or theft can occur if unauthorized personnel or intruders are able to freely enter your building's premises. Controlling physical access to your company's facility will help you to properly counteract or avert violations and maintain security.

Much of the work done here will be of the preventive and detective types of physical controls. It is important to back them up with the proper administrative and technical controls.

What Is Physical Security?

Physical security refers to the implementation and practice of various control mechanisms that are intended to restrict physical access to facilities. In addition, physical security involves increasing or assuring the reliability of certain critical infrastructure elements such as electrical power, data networks, and fire suppression systems. Challenges to physical security may be caused by a wide variety of events or situations, including:

● Facilities intrusions.

● Electrical grid failures.

● Fire.

● Personnel illnesses.

● Data network interruptions.

Physical Protection Areas

There are several fundamental resource areas in an organization that require a high level of protection.

Physical Protection Area	Description
Physical plant	The physical plant area of protection is spread across an entire facility. In most cases, there are central control areas that require protection in addition to systems that encompass entire buildings or even a campus. Areas to be protected include: ● Heating, ventilation, and air conditioning (HVAC) systems. ● Electrical sources and lines. ● Fire detection and suppression systems. ● Lighting. ● Doors. ● Windows. ● Fences. ● Plumbing.
Computer facilities	Computer facilities include server rooms and data centers. Maintaining security in these areas by limiting access to only authorized individuals is a vital component of an overall security policy.
Data network	The data network protection area includes network hardware and wiring and the areas in which they reside. Network hardware includes routers, switches, firewalls, cabling, and wireless access points. This hardware should be protected in the same manner as other computer facilities to provide security against various attack vectors.
Personnel	People are a key asset that should be protected in any circumstance when physical security is involved. **Safety of personnel is a key issue for the CISSP® test.** In addition to protecting personnel, one must also form a defense against both electronic and physical attacks from authorized and unauthorized personnel.

Physical Threats

The physical threats a security specialist faces can come from many different areas.

Physical Threat	Description
Internal	Carnegie Mellon University (CMU) and the Central Intelligence Agency (CIA) have reported that 85% of security problems, whether they are physical or logical threats, come from within the organization. It is important to always consider what is happening inside of the organization, especially when physical security is concerned. For example, disgruntled employees may be a source of physical sabotage of important security-related resources.
External	It is impossible for any organization to fully control external security threats. An external power failure is usually beyond the security specialist's control because most organizations use a local power company as their source of electrical power. However, the risks posed by external power failures may be mitigated by implementing devices such as an Uninterruptable Power Supply (UPS), a battery backup, or a generator.

Physical Threat	Description
Natural	Although natural threats are easy to overlook, they can pose a significant threat to the physical security of a facility. Buildings and rooms that contain important computing assets should be hardened against likely weather-related problems including tornados, hurricanes, snow storms, and floods.
Man-made	Whether intentional or accidental, people can cause a number of physical threats. For example, a backhoe operator may accidentally dig up fiber optic cables and disable external network access. On the other hand, a disgruntled employee may choose to exact revenge by cutting the fiber optic cable on purpose. Man-made threats can be internal or external.

Layered Protection

In physical security, layered protection is a mechanism that begins from the perimeter, or outermost boundary of a facility, and continues inward through the building grounds, entry points, and interior. It uses physical access controls such as fences, intrusion detection systems (IDSs), surveillance devices, locks and badges, or smart cards to create distance and deter intruders from entering a building.

One major concern of physical security and your layered defense strategy is inadequate design. For example, imagine your company purchased a building and had very little input on its design. In this instance, you will need to account for the inadequacies and reinforce them where you can. On the other hand, perhaps you are in a multi-tenant building and have very little or no control of the perimeter of the building. Then, you will need to pay extra attention to your internal design choices.

Physical protection works at four levels:

1. Deter
2. Detect
3. Delay
4. Respond

If an unauthorized person can bypass one physical control layer, like the perimeter of a building, the next control layer should provide more deterrence for access. Each layer should implement its own physical access controls. In addition, multiple levels can implement the same physical access control, such as locks for building, office, server, and similar entry points.

Layered protection in physical security is the equivalent of defense in depth in logical or organizational security.

Layered Protection Areas

There are three areas that are often involved in a layered protection scheme.

Layered Protection Area	Description
Perimeter access	The perimeter is the first layer of defense. At the perimeter, fences, gates, lighting, intrusion detection devices, dogs, and guards are among the techniques that can be used as protective measures. Perimeter security is a visible and immediate deterrent to casual troublemakers, while more advanced perimeter security measures can provide a significant and delaying obstacle for determined attackers, giving security and police more time to respond.
Facility access	Restricting facility access to authorized personnel has become a standard practice in most industries. Like paper financial records, computers and networks are at their most vulnerable when an individual can gain direct, physical access to the sensitive information or hardware. Controlling access to the entire facility limits potential access to vital or important information or hardware that may not be within a secure area and enhances the personal security of employees and visitors. Facility access is controlled by using guards, locks, access devices, man traps, gates/doors, and good design.
Secured area access	Within the facility, specific areas should be designated as secured areas. These areas are home to highly sensitive and vital business information and/or technology assets. Admission to these areas should be tightly controlled and monitored at all times. Access to secured areas is controlled by secured doors, locks, strengthened walls, and other similar methods.

Physical Access Barriers

Barriers are protective devices in a number of categories that seek to limit physical access to a space.

Physical Access Barrier	Description
Fencing	The first barrier that is often considered is a fence. Fences are used for three different purposes.

- A fence that is 3 to 4 feet high does not eliminate access but can be used to clearly mark a property line. It may keep trespassers out of the area but will not dissuade determined attackers.

- A fence that is 5 to 6 feet high may not keep determined attackers out of the area; however, the difficulty of overcoming a barrier of this height will serve as a deterrent for most people.

- A truly deterrent fence is 8 feet high and has barbed or razor wire at the top. Few people will attempt to cross this type of barrier.

- Very high security areas may provide multiple fences with a "no-man's" land in between. The area between may also be filled with razor wires and sensors. Strain-sensitive cabling can also be wound into the fence to detect an intruder climbing or cutting the fence. This will keep out all but the most determined intruders.

- Fences need gates. These gates will be perceived as a weak spot. Make sure your gates match the security level of your fencing. Gates are evaluated as Class I through IV by Underwriters Lab (UL) 325.
  - Class I: Residential usage; covering one to four single-family dwellings.
  - Class II: Commercial usage where general public access is expected; a common application would be a public parking lot entrance or gated community.
  - Class III: Industrial usage where limited access is expected; one example is a warehouse property entrance not intended to serve the general public.
  - Class IV: Restricted access; this includes applications such as a prison entrance monitored either in person or via closed circuitry.

Physical Access Barrier	Description
Walls	External and internal walls should be constructed in such a way that they prevent individuals from trying to gain access through them. Solid concrete walls with embedded reinforcements are excellent barriers and are well suited to use as external walls. Walls have the added advantage/disadvantage that they obstruct views. This can be an advantage because it keeps people from seeing into an area, but can quickly turn into a disadvantage if the intruder has breached the wall and is no longer visible. Internal walls, especially those surrounding a secure area, need to be solid and difficult to penetrate. Standard drywall is considered inadequate for security but it can be improved by including mesh between two layers of drywall. Fire codes often define the fire protection levels for walls, and most walls should have the protection capability to withstand a fire for at least one hour.
Doors	Doors must have sufficient locks to defeat penetration attempts. Secure areas should have solid doors that meet the same fire protection level as the walls.
Windows	Windows present a number of different security issues. Ideally, secured areas will not have windows. They can break easily, and even with protective wire meshes or unbreakable glass, it is not difficult to access a space using a window. If windows are necessary, the strongest possible protection must be provided. Be sure to take into account local fire codes.

Physical Access Barrier	Description
Lighting	Lights are not a true barrier; however, the visibility that they provide represents a deterrent control against entry into an area. Lights can be used to illuminate large areas, such as the perimeter of a building or a fence.
	The lights that are present should allow either a video camera or a guard to see potential intruders. Lights should also be used in entryways, easing the identification of an individual at a door.
	Lighting can also act as a detective control. The amount of lighting will vary by area. For example, the areas around buildings should meet the illumination requirement of producing two foot candles of light at a height of 8 feet. This guideline is known as the 2x8 rule or the 8x2 rule. Lighting in a parking facility might be as high as 5 foot candles.
	Lighting is also important for video surveillance purposes. In this case, it should shine outwards from the building to illuminate the intruder's face. Lighting that points back towards the building can cause glare and reduce the effectiveness of cameras.
	Lighting may also be triggered by a physical IDS. If the system identifies an attacker, trip or glare lights are activated in the area of intrusion. Because of their brightness intensity, these lights tend to momentarily blind and disorient an intruder.
Bollards	*Bollards* are obstacles designed to stop a vehicle. They are strategically placed to provide a physical barrier. They may be as simple as a concrete post or large concrete planters. Designs that are more sophisticated might include carefully planted trees and even sculptures designed to withstand impact.

Lock Types

Locks are one of the most obvious and necessary methods of securing various facilities and objects, such as doors, windows, gates, computers, and network equipment.

Lock Type	Description
Key lock	Key locks require keys to open them. They are easily picked by experts, but may include a ward, or obstruction, in the keyhole to prevent uncut keys from opening the locks. Key locks typically use pin tumblers, interchangeable cores, or wafers under springs used for tension. The body and bolt of the lock should be made of substantial materials to withstand bolt cutters and hack saws.
	Physical key protection is essential to control manual lock security and safeguard entry systems. Keys are often marked with a "do not duplicate" indicator that informs key manufacturers to ensure key protection.
Deadbolt lock	Deadbolt locks are keyed locks that incorporate a bolt into the door frame for added security when used with an alternate type of lock. If the same key is used as the tumbler lock in the door, the protection against lock picking is minimal. Additional protection is gained by making it harder to kick down the door.

Lock Type	Description
Keyless lock or cipher lock	Keyless locks do not require keys to unlock them. A keyless lock typically has a keypad or push buttons that open the lock when the correct access code is entered. These are not very secure because they frequently have a small number of combinations and can show wear patterns that reveal the combination.
Combination lock	Combination locks are keyless locks that use a sequence of numbers in a specific order to open the lock. The combination may be provided at the time of lock manufacturing or may be programmable by the user. A combination lock may be electronic and can include a digital display. Combination values should be protected to control combination lock security and safeguard entry systems.
Intelligent keys	Keys that have chips embedded provide higher levels of protection. The lock can recognize the key and provide access control decisions based on user, time, and more.

Device Locks

Device locks protect mobile and desktop computing devices and peripherals that are easy to steal without detection. Device locks include cable locks to anchor laptops and peripherals to desks, chairs, and so on; power switch control covers; port controls; and slot locks or brackets. Device locks can be keyed or keyless.

Key Control

A lock is only as good as the security of the keys that unlock it. If too many keys are floating around or unknown keys exist, security is greatly compromised. In many cases, master keys exist to unlock many different locks. Master keys must be controlled very carefully. Knowing exactly which locks they will and will not affect is very important. High security areas will need to use locks with different, or no, master keys.

Key control systems should take into account factors like key identification, key issuance, key returns, no-returned keys, and master keys. This is clearly defined in policies, procedures, and guidelines. To make sure keys can be accounted for, it is necessary to perform key audits.

Facility Control Devices

Advanced systems are available to provide physical access controls beyond simple barriers and locks.

Facility Control Device	Description
Automatic access control	Automatic access controls may use cipher keypads, access control cards, or other types of controls to identify authorized users. The door lock may be electrically activated or may be manually activated by turning a handle. Automatic systems can also log the access events of those who pass through a door or gate.

Facility Control Device	Description
Card entry systems	Card entry systems use cards that may be similar in size and shape to a credit card to identify the individual attempting access. These cards have a magnetic stripe containing identifying information. This magnetic stripe is read by the reader as the card is swiped through it. Proximity cards transmit radio signals containing the card ID to a receiver when held close to the receiver.
Biometric entry systems	Biometric identification systems utilize unique facets of individuals to identify them. Examples of biometric identification systems include retina or iris scanners, fingerprint scanners, or hand geometry sensors. These devices require a central system that contains a database of unique identification information for each individual in the system. Once the biometric scan is completed and the identity has been verified, an automatic door lock may be opened.
Security guards	While not sophisticated electronic systems, security guards can monitor critical checkpoints and verify identification, allow or disallow access, and log physical entry occurrences. They also provide a visual deterrent and can apply their own knowledge and intuition to potential situations. Although guards are effective resources for controlling facility security, maintaining security guard patrols requires a considerable amount of investment. Patrol times can be lengthy, and shift costs as well as uniform and equipment expenses can be high. Due to the expensive nature of security patrol implementations and the possibility of unreliable guard behavior, an organization may consider precautions and counteractive measures. Many facilities require guards to use devices that record their locations and activities to ensure and verify proper surveillance practices.
Man traps	A *man trap* is a physical entry portal with two doors, one on each end of a secure chamber. An individual enters a secure area through an outer door. The outer door must be closed before an inner door can open. Identity is sometimes verified before an individual enters the secure area through the first door, and other times while they are confined to the secure area between the two doors.
IDS	IDSs are used to identify unauthorized access attempts to a physical facility. These systems use various detection methods such as infrared sensors, sound sensors, and motion detectors. If an attempt to access a physical area is detected, an alarm is sent to a monitoring station and sirens, lights, and other alerting systems can be activated.
Alarms and responses	Alarms activated by unauthorized access attempts require quick responses. Locally stationed security guards or police may respond to alarms. These responding individuals may trigger access control devices in the facility to automatically lock.

ACTIVITY 9-1
Discussing Physical Access Control

Scenario:

In this activity, you will discuss physical access control. This will help you understand how to properly counteract or avert violations and maintain security by controlling physical access to your company's facility.

1. **Which one of the following physical protection areas includes network hardware and wiring along with the areas in which they reside?**

    a) Personnel

    b) Physical plant

    c) Data network

    d) Computer facilities

2. **The computer facility's physical protection area includes which of the following?**

    a) Protection from electronic and physical attacks from authorized or unauthorized personnel

    b) Server rooms and data centers

    c) Routers, switches, firewalls, cabling, and wireless access points

    d) Lighting, doors, windows, fencing, and plumbing

3. **Give some examples of internal and external man-made threats.**

4. **Which one of the following is generally considered to be the first layer of defense in a layered protection scheme?**

    a) Standard access

    b) Secured area access

    c) Facility access

    d) Perimeter access

5. **Why is lighting considered a physical barrier?**

6. **In secure areas, which of the following physical access barriers should meet the same fire protection standards as walls?**

    a) Doors

    b) Fencing

    c) Locks

    d) Windows

7. **Which one or more of the following are examples of a biometric entry system?**

    a) Hand geometry sensors

    b) Iris scanners

    c) Motion detectors

    d) Fingerprint sensors

8. **Which one of the following facility control devices is a physical entry portal with two doors on either end of a secure chamber?**

    a) IDS

    b) Man traps

    c) Card entry systems

    d) Alarms and responses

9. **Why might you choose a keyed over a keyless lock?**

10. **For which of the following layered protection areas would a fence typically be used?**

    a) Standard access

    b) Secured area access

    c) Facility access

    d) Perimeter access

TOPIC B
Physical Access Monitoring

Controlling physical access to your company's facility provides the first line of defense in protecting employees, networks, and equipment. The next phase in applying physical, organizational security is providing adequate surveillance of the facility and grounds. In this topic, you will identify systems and tools for monitoring physical access.

Once people are inside your facility, you need to observe their activity. Surveillance is key to protecting your organization's systems from data access by unauthorized personnel. Monitoring people's movement in and out of the facility will help you ensure that your organization is protected from unwanted threats.

Facility Control Systems

A *facility control system* is a set of support information services that are combined with physical security protection processes.

Facility Control System Component	Description
Entry restriction	Identification and authentication information is maintained for authorized individuals. Much in the same way user IDs and passwords are stored and then used to restrict access to a computer system or network, the facility control system verifies identifications and uses authentication data to ensure the integrity of that verification.
Exit restriction	In an ideal world, anyone who scanned their badge to enter would also scan their badge to exit. However, it is unlikely that the fire marshal will make that an absolute requirement. Trapping users in a burning building would violate the most important tenet of all, to protect human life. Although scan outs can be encouraged and turnstiles can be installed, there is almost always a provision for exiting without scanning. For example, in a high security environment, you may disable all badges that were not scanned on exit at midnight. This would require the user to see a guard to get in the following day.
Intrusion detection	Unauthorized access attempts are identified. Repeated attempts to enter a door using incorrect identification and/or authentication information should send an alert to a monitoring station.
Activity logging	Information for all entryways and exits, as well as for access denials or unusual activity, is logged. These logs can be used to determine which individuals are currently in the facility, prior facility access, and areas where problems have occurred.
	One advantage to activity logging is that it can help to control bad habits by exposing individual behavior to security personnel. A related potential threat is known as *tailgating*, whereby an individual closely follows someone else into a secure environment with the intent of avoiding authentication by the control system. When the unauthorized individual attempts to leave, the control system can flag the incident as unusual and alert security personnel.

Perimeter Intrusion Detection Systems

In a layered protection strategy, securing the facility's perimeter is the first line of defense. A perimeter intrusion detection system (PIDS) senses changes in an environment, such as an individual approaching a building or touching a vehicle.

Although perimeter controls such as fences help to delineate physical boundaries and deter attacks, they can be penetrated. In other cases, it may be impossible to install fencing or other security measures due to local building codes or community standards. A PIDS can supplement other perimeter security controls or provide a strong level of security in the absence of other security measures.

PIDS Types

There are several types of PIDSs that help monitor security disturbances.

PIDS Type	Description
Motion sensor	A *motion sensor* uses movement to detect a perimeter approach or a presence inside a controlled area. It can detect human and animal movement, and be unintentionally triggered by natural events like wind.
	Many motion sensors are implemented using a beam of light or radio signal. A sensor that is positioned opposite the signal emitter detects a break in the beam and generates an alert.
	Motion sensors come in two forms:
	● *Infrared devices*—Emit a beam of infrared light that is sensed by the receiver. These devices have a limited distance of operation.
	● *Microwave systems*—Emit a narrow beam of low-intensity radio signals that are sensed by the receiver. These systems are used in situations where the coverage areas are too large for effective infrared device detection.
Pressure-sensitive sensor	A *pressure-sensitive sensor* detects pressure when weight, such as a human or animal body, is applied to the device. Pressure sensors often have the capability to set low- and high-sensing thresholds. In a highly secure area, a perimeter fence is commonly surrounded by crushed gravel within its interior zone. If the fence is defeated, pressure-sensitive sensors are typically embedded in the gravel as a second line of defense.
Heat detector	A *heat detector* is installed to measure temperature increases emitted from a heat source such as a human, fire, or animal. It can detect a fire before it flames, it does not require a line-of-sight to the monitoring area, and it is not susceptible to wind or natural events.
Proximity detector	A *proximity detector* is installed to emit a calculable electrical field while in use. Also called a capacitance detector, it measures the change in the electrical field caused when an individual or animal approaches the sensor. Typically, it sounds an alarm if triggered and protects specific objects, such as artwork, cabinets, or a safe, rather than an entire space.
Vibration detector	A *vibration detector* is installed to measure vibrations caused by breaking glass, collisions with solid objects, or footsteps. It may be unintentionally triggered by natural events like wind.

PIDS Type	Description
Magnetic detector	A *magnetic detector* is installed to measure changes in a magnetic field. It reacts to conductors like keys or coins. For example, a wand used in airport security screening is a magnetic detector.
Photometric detector	A *photometric detector* is installed to detect a change in the light level in a designated area, specifically a windowless room or area. It emits a beam that is expected to hit a receiver. If it does not, an alarm sounds.

Surveillance Systems

Definition:

A *surveillance system* is a physical security mechanism that monitors designated internal and external areas of a facility for unusual behavior or a potential intruder. Video surveillance occurs through visual human detection or through visual recording devices. Audio surveillance occurs through sophisticated listening devices. Both of these methods are used to detect abnormal activity or undesirable conditions.

Example:

Figure 9-1: *A video surveillance camera.*

Types of Surveillance Systems

There are several types of surveillance systems that effectively monitor the physical security of a facility.

Surveillance System Type	Description
Video	Most of today's video monitoring systems have switched from videotape to complete digital archival and retrieval systems. The key to successful video surveillance, however, is in assessing the total facility security needs to ensure the most effective placement of cameras, lighting, and recording devices.
	Closed-circuit television (CCTV) is a visual recording device that uses video cameras to transmit images to monitors and video recorders. CCTV surveillance levels include detection, recognition, and identification.
	A CCTV system typically consists of a camera (or cameras), transmission media, and a monitor. In addition, lenses of various lengths are available to provide wide-area coverage for physical security and surveillance. Lenses can be a fixed length for reduced cost or zoom for more control. Zoom is most helpful when guards are able to manage it remotely. Lenses might have automatic irises to allow for changing light levels. This is especially important if guards have the ability to raise light levels if they sense an intrusion. Otherwise, the increased light might make the cameras ineffective. Pan Tilt Zoom (PTZ) cameras provide the most control but at a much higher cost. Today's sophisticated digital cameras require less lighting to illuminate the monitoring area and generate highly visible images. CCTV systems may include video motion sensors, pre-programmed computer activation, and alarms.
Security patrol	Highly secure facilities, such as military installations and prisons, have guard stations with armed security personnel at all times to provide surveillance, deterrence, and security enforcement. They are equipped with monitoring devices, alarm systems, and so on. Guards, or some type of security personnel, are employed by most large businesses to provide deterrence and safeguard employees from intruders or other unwanted activity. Security guards may be company employees or contract personnel who are bonded, trained, and certified, or licensed if necessary.
Security dogs	Dogs provide an effective, rapid response mechanism against trespassers or other disturbances. Barking dogs are helpful in identifying threats to alert security guards who need to respond. While dogs cannot actually remove suspicious individuals, they employ scare tactics that encourage intruders to vacate the premises or delay escape until human guards can respond to a particular situation.

Surveillance System Type	Description
Audio	Audio surveillance includes recording systems or listening devices that provide eavesdropping capabilities. Military, government, and law enforcement agencies all use different forms of audio surveillance. Surveillance transmitters, surveillance recorders, audio monitoring equipment, covert room transmitters, and listening devices can be used to monitor and collect evidence on suspected intruders or suspicious activity. • Lithium transmitters have features such as remote activation and voice activation. • Digital transmitters can send data bursts via encryption, voice, or computer. • Concealable transmitters can be used for undercover surveillance and tracking capabilities. • Phone transmitters can monitor phone and room conversations.

Physical Access Logs

Physical access logs are maintained by access control systems and by security guards. These logs record individual entry to and exit from facilities and controlled areas. Security guards can maintain logs on paper or through a special computer application; facility control systems create logs automatically. In addition to entry and exit logging, some organizations use radio frequency identification (RFID) or other technologies to track individuals as they move around monitored facilities.

A physical access log should clearly identify:

● The name of the individual attempting access.

● The date and time of access.

● The access portal or entry point.

● The user ID entered to attempt access.

● The location of access to internal spaces, if required.

● Unsuccessful access attempts, including those during unauthorized hours.

Alarm Systems

Alarm systems are used to alert responders; depending on the alarm, systems can be triggered manually, passively, or by IDS notification.

Alarm System Type	Description
Lights	Trip and glare lighting deters intruders. Flashing indicators and revolving lights are used to attract the attention of responders to problematic locations. High-intensity strobe lights are very effective for identifying and startling intruders.

Alarm System Type	Description
Bells and sirens	Bells and sirens promptly alert responders to security disruptions. Specific sounds are associated with certain disturbances that provide triggers for individuals to respond accordingly. For example, when a fire alarm sounds, most people are conditioned to exit a building through the closest marked exit. Alert bells and sirens related to non-fire activities should include a different sound identifier than a fire alarm.
Local activation/local response	Alarm systems in this category are triggered by a local event and have local responders present. An intrusion detection alarm caused by the unauthorized opening of a door could sound a local alarm; a local responder would then be responsible for researching the problem and providing a remedy. An example would be the doors to jetways at airports. Each door is alarmed. If someone opens the door without using the keypad, a local alarm is sounded at or near the door. Airport police would respond to secure the door.
Local activation/remote response	A residential home alarm could be considered a local activation/remote response system because the alarm is activated locally, in the home, and it immediately generates a remote response when the alarm company calls the home owner to follow up on the triggered alarm.
Remote activation/local response	In some cases, a local problem will be reported from a remote location. An alarm management system may be installed off site that requires remote monitoring by company staff or a third party. When a problem occurs in the facility, the alarm is sounded at the remote site, and a message or call is placed to local responders.
Remote activation/remote response	Alarms and responses can also be handled remotely. For example, in a campus setting, the organization might have an agreement that all alarms from the on-campus fire detection system are sent directly to the municipal fire department. The fire department can then respond directly to the site of the alarm. Campus personnel do not need to call in the alarm or take any action other than evacuating the area.

ACTIVITY 9-2
Discussing Physical Access Monitoring

Scenario:

In this activity, you will discuss systems and tools for monitoring physical access.

1. **Which of the following facility control system components can help identify unauthorized access attempts?**

   a) Access verification

   b) Activity logging

   c) Entry restriction

   d) Intrusion detection

2. **Maintaining identification and authentication information for authorized individuals is a part of which of the following facility control system components?**

   a) Entry restriction

   b) Intrusion detection

   c) Activity logging

   d) Surveillance

3. **In a layered protection strategy, while protecting a facility's perimeter, which of the following does the PIDS sense?**

   a) Unauthorized access to the facility

   b) Changes in the environment

   c) Keypad inaccuracy

   d) Theft

4. **What is the appropriate description for each PIDS type?**

___	Motion sensor	a. Emits a calculable electrical field in which changes are measured.
___	Pressure-sensitive sensor	b. Measures vibrations caused by breaking glass, collisions with solid objects, or footsteps.
___	Heat detector	c. Measures changes in a magnetic field.
___	Proximity detector	d. Detects pressure when weight is directly applied to the device.
___	Vibration detector	e. Measures temperature increases emitted from a heat source such as a human, fire, or animal.
___	Magnetic detector	f. Detects a change in the light level in a designated area, specifically a windowless room or area.
___	Photometric detector	g. Uses movement to detect a perimeter approach or presence inside a controlled area.

5. **Surveillance can occur through which one or more of the following?**

   a) Audio recording devices

   b) Trip and glare lighting

   c) Visual human detection

   d) Visual recording devices

6. **True or False? Physical access logs are maintained by access control systems and by security guards.**

   ___ True

   ___ False

7. **A smoke detector in an unattended warehouse sends an alarm directly to the local municipal fire department. This is an example of which one of the following?**

   a) Local activation/local response

   b) Remote activation/local response

   c) Remote activation/remote response

   d) Bells and sirens

TOPIC C
Physical Security Methods

Controlling and monitoring physical security access are two effective countermeasures to potential physical security threats and vulnerabilities. The next phase in applying physical security is addressing how to protect valuable resources within your facility. In this topic, you will identify different methods, policies, and controls for ensuring physical security.

Organizational personnel require procedures to guarantee their protection from dangerous objects and disastrous events. Establishing effective physical security methods will help you to ensure the safety of company resources and data in addition to the security of your personnel.

Restricted Work Areas

You may need to implement extra security in some areas to protect the content of information stored in those areas. You can implement a variety of security options to create a restricted work area when this protection is needed.

● Secured areas should be restricted to authorized individuals with the proper level of access or clearance.

● Simple options for securing areas include adding additional locks or lighting, and keeping an entry and exit log.

● More advanced protection for secured areas includes strengthened walls, stronger floors and ceilings, heavier doors, and other hardening to protect the area's contents.

● Access control and closed-circuit television (CCTV) systems may be used to further safeguard secured areas.

● The use of mobile phones, smartphones, personal digital assistants (PDAs), cameras, and external computing devices can also be restricted or denied depending on the circumstances.

Unauthorized Information Disclosure

Consider an area where national security documents are stored and used; by controlling physical access, the disclosure of information is limited to only those with access to the controlled area. When access is limited, it is easier to trace the source of unauthorized disclosure. If the list of people with access privileges was larger, it would be more difficult to locate the origin of disclosure. In many secured areas, it is difficult to transport unauthorized information into or out of the space.

Media Risks

Physical computer media such as magnetic tapes, CD-ROM or DVD-ROM media, removable Flash drives, removable Universal Serial Bus (USB) or FireWire disk drives, internal hard disks, and camera or phone memory chips all require protection. A primary risk when dealing with media is the highly portable nature of most media types, which means that it is easy to remove a piece of media from a controlled area. Media are also vulnerable to loss and damage. Therefore, any media that contains secured information should be labeled appropriately, accounted for, and restricted in movement and relocation.

Media Protection Methods

One way to help protect computer media is to ensure that the individuals associated with them know that someone is watching and regularly monitoring activity.

Media Protection Method	Description
Two-man rule	The *two-man rule* is a technique that requires the presence of two individuals at all times to monitor behavior when certain criteria are met. These criteria vary and can include: ● The nature of the information being accessed. ● When certain activities are underway. ● When particular systems or media are in use.
Media inventories	Frequent media-specific inventories will help identify missing items.
Media storage access	Logging access to media storage areas helps identify who might be responsible for media removal.
Portable media encryption	Any protected information that is transferred onto portable media must be encrypted, making unauthorized access to that stored information more difficult.
Portable media status	The status and whereabouts of any portable media containing secured information must be carefully tracked and logged.

Personnel Controls

The personnel who have been given access to a specific location are also a physical security concern. Proper administrative practices include background investigations, sound hiring practices, periodic performance reviews, and establishing security clearances. Security does not end once an individual has been granted access; managing secured areas and the personnel that have access to them is a key part of physical security.

As a general rule, people should be granted access to physical facilities in the same way that they are granted access to information: by applying the concepts of least privilege and need to know. Individuals should be given access to only those areas where they have a need to access information or a need to perform job duties. Therefore, individuals without clearances and a clear need to know should not be allowed entry into a secured physical space without the proper escort and supervision.

Unintentional Disruptions

There is probably little need for a clerical staff person to have access to a heating, ventilating, and air conditioning (HVAC) control system or a server room. However, if an element of curiosity leads such a person to this kind of restricted area with control panels, his or her actions may potentially cause a disruption of service or an unexpected disaster.

Personnel Safety Issues

The International Information Systems Security Certification Consortium, or (ISC)², highlights in their publications that personnel safety is the primary goal of physical security. Organizational security policies and procedures should clearly stress the vital importance of keeping valuable personnel resources safe in any emergency situation. Your policies should state and enforce specific personnel safety priorities.

Emergency Policy Types

While organizations may choose to create different emergency policies, they should adhere to specific guidelines of interest.

Emergency Policy Type	Description
Intrusion response policy	This policy provides direction as to how to respond to a physical intrusion. An intrusion response policy does not describe exactly how to respond; it describes expected responses.
	An intrusion response policy might read:
	● "In the event of forced physical entry into any corporate facility, the local police department must be immediately notified of such an occurrence."
	The policy does not state who is required to make the notification or how to do it, as this would be a procedure; however, it does set an expectation of what must happen and when it must happen.
Fire policy	Fire policies provide directions similar to intrusion response policies. A fire policy might include a statement similar to this:
	● "All corporate facilities will be equipped with fire detection systems that comply with local fire codes."
	While it may seem obvious that compliance with this policy will be enforced by local fire codes, it does illustrate that corporate management is making an effort in their policies to highlight the importance of the policy in general. This demonstrates that certain legal principles are being followed to protect the corporation from lawsuits.
Natural emergency policy	In the event of a natural disaster, it is important that a corporation has an appropriate response policy. For example:
	● "Each corporate facility will have hardened areas for use by personnel in the case of natural disasters like tornados or severe thunderstorms."

Emergency Response Procedures

Procedures are used to implement policies and may be specific to either a local or global environment.

Emergency Response Procedure	Description
Evacuations	Mandatory evacuation of employees to safe locations in the event of a general emergency.
Restricted building re-entry	Prohibiting employees from retrieving property following a building evacuation after a severe storm. This will protect them from a potential building collapse.
General employee notification	After a disaster, employees are often unsure of what to do next. Procedures should clearly outline response expectations to a disaster based on where employees are located. For example: • "If an employee is at home, the employee should do this..." • "If an employee is on the way to work and is notified of an emergency, the employee should do this...." Oftentimes, calling trees are used whereby senior management notifies lower-level management, who then notifies their subordinates, until all individuals are informed. The policy should also include information about how to conduct an exercise to periodically test the notification system.
Accounting for employees	During any emergency situation, it is necessary to know where each employee should be and where each one actually is. This helps disaster responders locate missing people.
Key staff and organization notification	When incidents occur, key staff such as corporate management and internal emergency response teams should be notified as quickly as possible. They will initiate the local response to the emergency. They will also evaluate the situation and determine which of the following responders will be required. • Press—A single individual should be appointed as the communications liaison between the organization and the press. This helps eliminate potential confusion that can often arise when several sources provide information. • Fire—In many locations, the fire service is the first responder. Fire department contact procedures should include telephone numbers and proper notification practices such as providing location information, addresses, building numbers, and so on. • Gas and electric—Some disasters require that gas and/or electric services be shut off. Contact information should be easily located in the disaster response procedures. • Emergency responders—Other responders might include ambulance services, telecommunication providers, cleanup services, and so on.
Training, drills, and exercises	Local fire codes require fire drills so that individuals understand their responsibilities and the correct responses to a given situation. Ideally, training for other emergency procedures should be offered as well. Frequent drills and exercises will assure that the organization's employees' safety is a high-priority concern.

ACTIVITY 9-3
Discussing Physical Security Methods

Scenario:

In this activity, you will discuss different methods, policies, and controls for ensuring physical security.

1. **What are the levels of protection you can employ to create a restricted work area?**

2. **Which one of these media risks necessitates special protection such as locked storage and media labeling?**

    a) Accidental erasure of secure information

    b) The highly portable nature of most media types

    c) The possible overwrite of secure information

    d) Unauthorized viewing of secure information

3. **What is the definition of the two-man rule?**

    a) Requiring the presence of two people to move media from one location to the next

    b) Requiring that once media is moved, two people must authorize the new location of the media

    c) Requiring the presence of two people to monitor behavior when criteria are met

    d) Requiring that once media is created, two people must make copies of it for security reasons

4. **True or False? Once an authorized individual has been granted access to a secure location or to secure information, security is no longer needed.**

    ___ True

    ___ False

5. **What is the primary goal of physical security outlined by the (ISC)²?**

    a) Facility safety

    b) Perimeter safety

    c) Information safety

    d) Personnel safety

6. **True or False? The intrusion response policy states who is required to make a notification and how the notification should be made in the event of forced physical entry into any corporate facility.**

    ___ True

    ___ False

7. **A calling tree is an example of which one of the following emergency response procedures?**

    a) Accounting for employees

    b) General employee notification

    c) Key staff and organization notification

    d) Training, drills, and exercises

TOPIC D
Facilities Security

Establishing appropriate physical security methods reduces vulnerabilities in accessing restricted areas, protects sensitive data stored on electronic media, and validates the effectiveness of emergency procedures. Now, you need to complete the final phase of applying physical security: selecting and designing a facility that minimizes exposure to physical threats and vulnerabilities. In this topic, you will analyze methods, controls, and rules for designing secure facilities.

Imagine what would happen if a fire started in a building that did not have fire detection or suppression systems. The building and all of its housed resources, possibly including some personnel, would go up in flames. Cultivating a secure facility by implementing an effective design scheme will help you to provide a secure and safe work environment for your employees and information system assets.

Facility Design Issues

An often-overlooked component of layered defense for facilities is facility layout and design. When designing a new facility or performing significant renovations, there are several factors that should be considered. One design issue involves the availability of critical infrastructures and services, such as electrical power, communications connections, and water supply. Although it may seem more efficient from an initial cost perspective to have all utilities and services enter the building in the same place and to have all controls for these systems in the one location, you need to consider disaster scenarios, including:

- Install separate lines to the building for utilities.
- Ensure there are redundant lines for utilities.
- Install a backup power supply or generator.
- Use separate routes for utility lines and communications lines within the building.
- Make sure that the HVAC system in the building is adequate to keep employees comfortable and equipment safe.

Facilities Protection Categories

There are many protection factors to consider when physically securing a building facility.

Facility Protection Category	Description
Service entry points	If all services enter a building at the same point, this point becomes a tempting target for attack, which is a major weakness in a facility's physical security. If all services are controlled from one location with no redundancy, this location is also a significant weak point.
	Water and sewer lines should be protected from tampering. Electrical and communications lines should enter the building from different locations. You should also consider duplicating electrical and network connections for redundancy.

Facility Protection Category	Description
Service protection	Backup power supplies or generators should be in place to maintain the security system and allow for the controlled shutdown of vital computer assets.
	Once water, sewer, power, and communications lines enter a building, they still need to be protected. Water and sewer lines should not be routed over computer or communications areas. Power and communications lines should not be routed over or under spaces that are not sufficiently protected from intrusion.
	Placing an Ethernet jack in a reception area that is not constantly monitored may allow unauthorized individuals access to the network. The use of wireless networks provides a similar threat but with a much wider scope.
Electronic protection	Computer and server rooms and telecommunications closets must have adequate heating, ventilating, and air conditioning (HVAC) support. The devices operated in these areas often generate a good deal of heat, and adequate cooling and ventilation is vital to their short-term and long-term efficiency and reliability.
	You should not use rooms that are not specifically designed or modified for the housing of computer or network equipment. This is because the HVAC and power capabilities of the room may not be up to the task of maintaining proper environmental conditions for this equipment.
	In addition, computer and server rooms also require positive ventilation. The air pressure inside these rooms should be higher than the external air pressure. In this case, if a room's door is opened, the air is forced out rather than brought in. This keeps pollutants out of the room, therefore increasing the equipment's life span and preventing harmful dust, gasses, or vapors from entering the controlled area.

Power Issues

Power problems can create security issues in two ways. First, physical security in an organization is often enabled by devices that use electrical power. Secondly, the computers, routers, switches, and other devices used to store and access information also require power. Thus, the loss of power or the presence of other power issues can be catastrophic. These issues often lead to non-availability of data or resources and can potentially cause data loss or corruption.

Types of Power Problems

Power setbacks can occur in many forms with varying degrees of severity and energy loss.

Power Problem	Description
Blackout	A *blackout* involves a complete loss of power.
Brownout	A *brownout* is a long-term, low-voltage power failure. It is called a brownout because the lights dim during the event.
Sag	A *sag* is a momentary low-voltage power failure.
Spike	A *spike* is a short-term, high-voltage power malfunction.

Power Prob-lem	Description
Surge	A *surge* is a long-term, high-voltage power malfunction.
In-rush	An *in-rush* power problem is a surge or spike that is caused when a device is started that uses a great amount of current.

Power Protection Systems

There are a number of protection systems that can restore power to some operational capacity, decrease failures, or monitor power sources.

Power Protection System	Description
UPS	An *Uninterruptible Power Supply (UPS)* is a device that continues to provide power to connected circuits when the main source of power becomes unavailable. Most UPS devices are battery operated. They are meant for temporary use and are intended to support computer systems until they can be powered off normally. Power is likely to be interrupted when the batteries or other power sources are discharged.
Generators	A *generator* creates its own electricity through the use of motors. Generators provide long-term power and are often started while a UPS system supports equipment through the initial power loss. Generators can fail when the motor fuel runs out or when a mechanical failure occurs.
Surge/spike protectors	A *surge/spike protector* is a device that provides power protection circuits that can reduce or eliminate the impact of surges and spikes.
Power line monitors	A *power line monitor* is used to evaluate the source of electrical power. The monitors report information such as voltage levels and power utilization. A monitor can help solve various electrical problems when working with the local power provider.

Environmental Issues

Environmental controls are a very important part of ensuring the reliability of computer and network resources. Computer equipment is subject to problems when the environment they are used in is not well controlled. Changes in temperature and humidity can lead to static electricity or component corrosion. Water and fluids can damage computer equipment to the point of destruction, and too much heat can corrupt data and damage hardware.

Environmental Controls

There are certain systems and devices that can be implemented to help control a facility's physical environment.

Environmental Control	Description
HVAC systems	A *heating, ventilation, and air conditioning (HVAC) system* controls the environment inside a building.
	• Humidity and temperature control—Most experts recommend that temperatures in a computer facility should be in the range of 65 to 75 degrees. In an effort to save energy, and money, this number is rising. Vendors are now testing equipment to run in data centers with temperatures as high as 85. This would be uncomfortable for humans, but many data centers are unoccupied or lightly occupied. The relative humidity in the facility should be between 40% and 60%. High and low temperatures and humidity can damage equipment. Low humidity causes static electricity; high humidity causes corrosion.
	• Positive air pressure is a must. Air should be forced from the data center and server rooms to keep contaminants out. Filters on HVAC systems keep dust to a minimum and must be changed regularly. Ultraviolet (UV) light is used to fight bacteria, germs, and viruses. Intakes for the HVAC systems should be hard to access and protected with filters to prevent the introduction of contaminants.
	• To ensure that HVAC systems are running properly, it is important to monitor them both locally and remotely.
Pipes and drains	Pipes and drains have a potential for leaking or backing up. To reduce the possibility for costly mistakes, pipes and drains must be clearly marked.
	• Pipes that are exposed in stairwells and other locations should be plainly marked with their contents. A pipe marked "Water" does not clarify the issue because it may contain scalding hot water used in a heating system, or cold water used in an HVAC chiller. Steam pipes, fuel pipes, and other piping require clear, explicit markings.
	• The location of pipe shutoff valves should also be indicated, as well as the direction in which to turn the shutoff valves. Performing periodic shutoffs helps to ensure correct shutoff functioning.
	• Drains that are found in facilities should be positive drains that do not allow substances to back up onto the floor from the drain source.
Lighting	In emergency situations, lighting is essential. Local building codes often require battery-operated emergency lighting in commercial buildings. The emergency lights should be tested for normal operation on a monthly basis.

Fire Prevention Methods

The first rule of fire protection is fire prevention. Local fire codes specify the fire prevention practices required or expected by the community. Periodic fire drills are one typical requirement. Other requirements might include:

- The elimination of storage items and trash in fire stairwells.
- The specifications of fire extinguisher types used in a facility.
- The type of fire suppression system used in a building.

Fire Detection Methods

Various fire detection systems are used to identify the threat of a fire. They can detect a temperature level and produce an alert when that temperature is reached. They can also detect the rate of change in temperature and report when the rate of change is high enough to suspect the presence of a fire.

- Smoke detectors sense the presence of smoke by using various scientific methods such as testing for particles in the air.
- Heat sensors are triggered either when a target temperature is reached or when there is a high rate of increase in temperature.
- Flame detectors use optical sensors to record incoming radiation in the infrared (IR) and UV wavelengths.

Commercial fire detection systems are often connected to a central reporting station where the location of the suspected fire is indicated. In some cases, the detection system or monitoring station is connected directly to a fire department.

Once a fire is detected, the first rule of fire safety is to call the fire department and evacuate the facility. Only trained personnel should attempt to fight a fire when their safety is not threatened.

Hand-Held Fire Extinguishers

In some cases, small fires may be extinguished using hand-held fire extinguishers. All fires are caused by the presence of fuel, heat, and oxygen. Extinguishers are designed to remove one or more of the components so that the fire goes out. However, because all fires are not fueled in the same way, fire extinguishers are not universal. They vary according to the type of fire and extinguishing agent used. Since class A, B, and C can be put out using the same type of powder, it is possible to manufacture an extinguisher to address all three types. All fire extinguishers should be inspected on a regular basis.

Extinguisher Classes and Fire Types

The following table describes the class of extinguishers and the types of fires they are meant to extinguish.

Class	Type of Fire	Agent Used	How to Remember
A	Common combustibles like wood, paper, and so on	Water, soda acid, multi-purpose dry powders	Common combustibles create *Ash*

Class	Type of Fire	Agent Used	How to Remember
B	Liquids and fuels	CO_2, gas, foam, multi-purpose dry powders	Liquids are stored in *Barrels*
C	Electrical fires	CO_2, gas, multipurpose dry powders	Electricity moves in *Circuits*
D	Combustible metals	Class D dry powder	Metal fires are *Dangerous*
K	Kitchen fires	Wet chemical	K is for *Kitchen*

Water-Based Extinguishers

Water-based systems of various types are used to extinguish fires in most areas of a building.

Water-Based System Type	Mode of Operation/Considerations
Wet pipe	**Mode of Operation:** Water is stored in the pipes at all times. When a given temperature is reached, a heat-sensitive vial in the sprinkler head will break, releasing the water. Different vials with different sensitivities can be used in different areas. **Considerations:** Pipes may leak due to corrosion or freezing. If a sprinkler head malfunctions, water can damage the surrounding area.
Dry pipe	**Mode of Operation:** Pipes are filled with compressed air. If there is a loss of air pressure, the valve will open, filling the pipe with water. Because pipes are not filled with water until a fire is detected, there are fewer concerns with freezing or accidental leaks. Sprinkler heads are individually activated like the wet pipes. **Considerations:** No leakage and no unexpected discharge unless the fire system malfunctions.
Preaction	**Mode of Operation:** Preaction requires two separate actions to happen before discharging. First, a fire is detected. Second, an alarm is activated. There may be a short delay between the alarm and the release of the water to allow time for people to leave the area. **Considerations:** Same considerations that apply to dry pipes. Incurs higher costs to purchase and install.
Deluge	**Mode of Operation:** High output sprinklers in wet or dry pipe systems that saturate the affected area. The sprinklers are always open and when the system is activated, it delivers water to all sprinkler heads. **Considerations:** Not used in computer facilities due to high water output. May be appropriate in areas where extensive fire damage is expected.

Fire Suppression in Computer Facilities

Fires in computer facilities are especially dangerous. The damage done to computers is extremely expensive, and the chemicals used in the machines may emit toxic substances. It is not practical to fight these fires with small extinguishers or to douse fires with water. Special gasses are used to extinguish fires in computer facilities.

Fire Extinguishing Gasses

The first fire extinguishing gas used in large-scale computer fires was Halon. Halon, however, is full of chlorofluorocarbons, which are ozone-depleting substances. The Montreal Protocol of 1989 banned production and installation of Halon systems effective January 1, 1994. Systems already in place could continue to use Halon but it is becoming increasingly difficult to find it to replenish the system. New substances are available that can replace Halon for large computer fires, including FM-200, Inergen, argon, and FE-13.

ACTIVITY 9-4
Discussing Facility Security

Scenario:

In this activity, you will discuss methods, controls, and rules for designing secure facilities.

1. **Which one of the following is an often overlooked component of layered defense for facilities?**

   a) The number of employees in the facility

   b) The time of day that the facility is accessed

   c) The facility layout and design

   d) The location of the facility

2. **Which one of the following should be in place to maintain the security system and allow for the controlled shutdown of vital computer assets?**

   a) Positive ventilation

   b) Backup power supplies and generators

   c) Water and sewer lines

   d) Additional computer systems

3. **True or False? The air pressure inside computer and server rooms should be lower than the external air pressure.**

   ___ True

   ___ False

4. **What is the appropriate description for each power problem?**

___	Blackout	a. A short-term, high-voltage power malfunction.
___	Brownout	b. A complete loss of power.
___	Sag	c. A long-term, low-voltage power failure.
___	Spike	d. A momentary low-voltage power failure.
___	Surge	e. A surge or spike that is caused when a device is started that uses a great amount of current.
___	In-rush	f. A long-term, high-voltage power malfunction.

5. **Which one of the following power protection systems is a device that provides instant power to connected circuits when the main source of power becomes unavailable?**

    a) UPS

    b) Generator

    c) Surge/spike protector

    d) Power line monitor

6. **Environmental controls are an important part of ensuring the reliability of which one or more of the following?**

    a) Ventilation systems

    b) Computer resources

    c) Network resources

    d) Utility systems

7. **What is the first rule in fire protection?**

    a) Fire prevention

    b) Fire detection

    c) Fire suppression

    d) Fire evacuation

8. **Which one or more of the following are fire detection systems?**

    a) Fire extinguishers

    b) Flame detectors

    c) Heat sensors

    d) Smoke detectors

9. **True or False? Fire extinguishers are universal and can be used to put out all types of fires.**

    ___ True

    ___ False

10. **Which of the following was designed to extinguish fires in computer facilities?**

    a) Hand-held fire extinguishers

    b) Water

    c) FM-200

    d) Sand

11. **Which one of the following water-based extinguishers is not used in computer facilities due to high water output?**

   a) Wet pipe

   b) Dry pipe

   c) Preaction

   d) Deluge

Lesson 9 Follow-up

In this lesson, you analyzed the physical security controls, design strategies, tools, and techniques that assist in preserving your information systems and assets. Your company's success depends on the protection of its physical resources. Intruders, natural disasters, and internal threats can emerge at any time and target the safety and security of your facility, office, or workspace. Applying effective physical security to your organization's resources helps you ensure and sustain a safe environment for employees, data, and equipment.

1. **Has your company ever experienced a power failure? What type was it? What system was implemented or could be implemented to secure the area or be used as a countermeasure?**

2. **What kind of physical security controls does your organization have in place? Does your company have emergency policies and procedures in place for dealing with physical threats? Are you familiar with them?**

10 | Operations Security

Lesson Time: 2 hour(s), 15 minutes

Lesson Objectives:

In this lesson, you will analyze operations security.

You will:

- Apply operations security control.
- Identify operations security auditing and monitoring.
- Identify threats and violations.

Introduction

You have identified and applied physical security controls, measures, and best practices to help protect your organization's information systems. To completely secure your information systems, you need to control your hardware and media, as well as the people who access and administer them. In this lesson, you will analyze the processes, tools, strategies, and techniques for implementing operations security.

An organization's business operations depend on the security of its critical data, resources, and assets to thrive in today's technological environment. Intrusive threats and attacks that compromise the confidentiality, integrity, and availability of information can happen at any time if they are not properly detected, counteracted, and mitigated. A thorough understanding of operations security will allow you to effectively control the hardware, media, and user access privileges for continued secure system functionality.

This lesson supports content found in the Operations Security domain of the CISSP® certification.

TOPIC A
Operations Security Control

Exercising control over business-critical tasks, such as information processing and system administration, on a daily basis is as important to your organization's overall security as controlling access to data and systems. Operations security seeks to safeguard information assets by controlling the way data is accessed and processed in business organizations. In this topic, you will apply the mechanisms, practices, and techniques that help control operations security.

Security policies and procedures for all of your information systems can only be effective if you have a means to enforce them within your organization. You need to develop controls for each area of operational security, including hardware, media, systems, and personnel. Establishing these controls allows you to enforce your policies and protect the operating environment from threats and violations. To ensure that the controls are effective, auditing is a very important part of operations security.

Operations Security

Operations security (OPSEC) is a structured process of denying adversaries critical information about business capabilities and plans by identifying, controlling, and protecting indicators associated with sensitive business functions. While tactical and strategic security deals with mid- and long-term issues, OPSEC is near-term. OPSEC focuses on answering the question, "What do I need to do now, this week, or possibly this month to protect the enterprise?"

 OPSEC was initially developed by the U.S. Armed Forces during the Vietnam conflict to protect national security and prevent intelligence leaks. The CISSP Operations Security domain builds on the original work done by the armed forces, and takes a similar approach to protecting assets while realizing you have adversaries even in the business world.

The OPSEC Process

The OPSEC process includes a series of specific action items that help to minimize or eradicate adversary exploitation attempts.

Action Item	Description
Identifying critical information	Any information that is determined to be vital to an adversary is deemed critical. Once this information is identified, protecting it becomes the first priority. This ensures that all remaining action items adhere to the OPSEC process of securing only the vital information specified. Identification of critical information is an ongoing activity. Information can become more critical or less critical over time. As you add systems or make acquisitions you will need to account for any critical information. Even data that is no longer actively used might still be highly desired by a competitor and needs to be protected as critical information.

Action Item	Description
Analyzing threats	The task of researching and analyzing adversarial intelligence, organizational counterintelligence, and open source information to recognize the potential adversaries that may threaten critical, unclassified information. Analyzing threats is also an ongoing activity. New threat agents will continuously emerge. Constant vigilance is a requirement for operations security.
Analyzing vulnerabilities	Operations issues are evaluated to identify vulnerabilities that could expose critical information. Once determined, the vulnerabilities are compared with and measured against the adversary's intelligence-gathering capacity. This information will prove helpful in performing the threat analysis.
Assessing risk	Risk assessment is a two-step process: 1. Evaluating the likelihood of a threat exposing a vulnerability will determine the risk. 2. When the risk has been calculated the organization can determine what would be an appropriate OPSEC response.
Applying suitable OPSEC measures	The selected OPSEC measures are employed after the risk assessment is integrated into OPSEC plans for future business functions and activities.

Operations Security Roles

There are many different operations security roles that are involved in detailing and enforcing permissions and access capabilities. As you are assigning users to different roles, you should still be concerned with least privilege, separation of duties (SoD), job rotation, and more. Operations security is also aware that with more privileged accounts, more access typically follows. It is critical that auditing and systematic reviews are performed to validate that the appropriate level of trust is applied.

Operations Security Role	Description
User	Users rely on data owners to authorize and grant them access privileges. Users' security roles involve safeguarding the information they can access and protecting their access credentials. Users should be regularly trained on correct and standardized security practices and be made aware of potential security threats.
Group	It is much easier to apply rights and permissions to groups of users than to individuals. There is a risk however, because as groups get larger, it is less likely that each member of the group requires the same privileges. Group membership audits and reviews can help identify privilege creep.
Operator	Operators are system users that typically have a tightly defined role to maintain the systems. Backup operators, router and switch operators, and print server administrators are all critical users but should have very limited and tightly controlled permissions, only slightly exceeding that of a regular user.

Operations Security Role	Description
System administrator	System administrators are responsible for implementing the proper operating environment for applications and users. Their security roles are often related to the principle of availability. Maintaining uptime, backing up and restoring data, and protecting applicable assets are all part of a system administrator's operational duties. System administrators also maintain new software and hardware development awareness and provide this information to security administrators well in advance. Administrator accounts should only be used when performing tasks that require them. Administrators should use regular user accounts for their normal day-to-day activities. Administrator accounts may require longer passwords with more frequent changes and should always be changed when an administrator leaves.
Security administrator	Security administrators are responsible for operational security issues such as maintaining passwords and other authentication mechanisms, reviewing logs, operating and configuring firewalls, and reviewing patches and software updates for security vulnerabilities. Security administrators may also be responsible for maintaining and tracking audit trails and log files. These records can act as a vital source for solving security issues after threat exposure. All precautions mentioned for the system administrator will apply here as well. In fact, the accounts might have even tighter controls and be subject to more rigorous audits.

Operations Security Protection Areas

Security administrators are commonly responsible for performing specialized functions to support OPSEC protection areas.

Operations Protection Area	Description
Security clearance	Security levels for data are established with assistance from the data owner. A list of users who require data access must then be cleared. The clearance process is well defined within the U.S. federal government. In commercial enterprises, access to client data, medical data, and business records is based on company policy. While a formal clearance process may not be required, frequent reviews of who is allowed access versus who is currently receiving access is necessary.

Operations Protection Area	Description
Password and password management	When a new user needs to be added to the system, the security administrator typically authenticates him or her and provides a temporary password. During the first logon, the new user is required to change the password. Policies also determine a user's password change requirements as well as the password strength.
	Password management policies specify local requirements. If a particular password is too long, it is tempting for the user to write it down. This should certainly be a violation of the password policy, but it is unlikely that the security administrator will know it has happened. If passwords are used lengthy and are shared by users, the password can become common knowledge. Short passwords are subject to being broken using password-cracking tools or brute force. It is more difficult for users to guess and learn passwords that recurrently change. For all these reasons, a password policy must appropriately define passwords and inform users how to react and respond to password disclosure. Some organizations will even do cube audits where they check to see if users are writing down passwords.
Account characteristics	Accounts may have different characteristics depending on the functions performed and the security level required for those functions. While CISSP® is technology and software neutral, the way Microsoft® deals with account characteristics is a useful example. In the Microsoft® Windows® environment, users are assigned to groups that each have specific characteristics, some of which include the following:
	● Administrators—The administrator account is at the highest level; administrators have the ability to perform all functions.
	● Server operators—Can log on locally, perform backup and restore operations, change the system time, and shut down systems.
	● Account operators—Can create new groups and delete groups, create and delete accounts, and access all user information.
	● Print operators—Can change device drivers, add new devices, and manage printers.
	Other Windows account characteristics include the user name, the user password, the user password age limits, and the account status.
Special privileges	Based on need to know and least privilege, and with the advice and consent from data owners, special security privileges may be granted to users. With these privileges, users can run special applications to repair systems or to fix database problems. Special privileges should be limited in duration and special accounts should be managed carefully.

Security Profiles

Definition:

A *security profile* is a description of the security-relevant information about each user or protected element in a system. A security profile for a user in a Windows environment will include the user name, user group assignments, password, and password strength requirements.

Example:

Group assignments

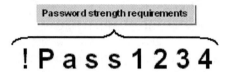

!Pass1234

Figure 10-1: A security profile.

System Security Characteristics

Other system security characteristics include user permissions for files and directories, user permissions for accessing printers and other peripheral devices, and user permissions for adding and deleting hardware and software. These permissions are associated with the group to which the user is assigned.

Operations Security Best Practices

There are many security-related best practices that help organizations implement OPSEC solutions.

Best Practice	Description
Redundancy	*Redundancy* is using more than one resource to maintain availability. For example, two separate electrical sources from two different power grids can keep a system up and running should one of the grid sources fail. Another example involves using the Redundant Array of Independent Disks (RAID) 1 or RAID 5 to allow for recovery from a single drive fault.
	As you look for ways to make systems more redundant, you first should look for the components that are most likely to fail, such as servers, hard drives, and power supplies. As you solve the potential failure of a single device inside the server, you then move up the chain. If you have a single critical server, like an email server that could fail, you might want to use a second server to create a cluster. If the servers are all plugged into a single UPS, you have another potential single point of failure and you should address that and then move on to the circuits that your UPS connects to. Can you have redundant power? If you can justify the cost, you can continue looking further and further up until you have redundant data centers.
Fault tolerance	*Fault tolerance* is a system property in which a single component fault does not cause a complete system failure. Fault tolerance is often enabled through redundancy.
Backup and restore	Backups ensure the restoration of data in the event of data loss caused by unexpected disasters. When systems fail or lose data, backups can be restored or copied back to the original systems.
	Backups can be stored locally to give you fast access to restoring files, but then you risk having them destroyed in the same disaster that might destroy the data center. Backups kept offsite will be slower to recover but will be available in nearly any emergency situation.
Material safeguarding	Safeguarding classified materials entails developing and implementing policies, guidelines, standards, and procedures that specify how to maintain the confidentiality of classified information. Access controls, either physical or logical, are at the heart of this process. The first step is deterring unauthorized individuals from accessing classified materials.
Material destruction	Destroying classified materials is a required operations security activity. With governmental activities, there is a set of standards that determines methods for destroying various types of classified information. Corporations have adopted many of these same standards. Destruction specialists must have a clearance level that matches the level of destroyed material. They must also follow specific processes that include:

- Degaussing—Reducing or eradicating magnetic storage devices using very powerful magnetic fields. Traditional hard drives and backup tapes are good candidates for degaussing. Optical disks and newer solid state storage are not good candidates as they are not affected by magnet fields.
- Drive wiping by writing binary zeros on an entire drive using approved processes. Different levels of secure wiping require multiple writes to each sector of the hard drive. Seven is a typical number for sensitive material.
- Complete physical destruction of media through incineration, shredding, or pulping.

Best Practice	Description
Material reuse	It is possible that the media erasure process could leave readable data in places where there could be swap files or hidden files, slack space, or unused or vacant cluster space remaining on a disk. This is because file deletion does not actually delete a file but removes pointers to it. Programs can undelete a file and retrieve the deleted information. If it is necessary to reuse media, systems can force a true deletion and data wipe if the proper options are used.
Sensitive media handling	Sensitive media must be handled appropriately. This includes proper marking, proper storage, and proper handling and transporting.
	Media marking:
	Mark or label each piece of portable physical media with the following information at a minimum:
	<ul><li>Creation date</li><li>File name</li><li>Operating system</li><li>Classification</li><li>Retention factor or lifetime of the data</li><li>Backup system used</li></ul>
	Unmarked data is assumed to be a part of public domain.
	Media storage:
	Media should be stored in the same environment where it is used. It should be under lock and key to prevent unauthorized access. As the useful life of the information is extended, it can be moved from online to nearline using magnetic tape or virtual tape systems implemented on a disk. As it continues to age, media data can be moved completely offline, which extends retrieval time but still maintains availability. In all storage situations, labeling and marking is necessary. Employ sufficient safeguards to maintain the confidentiality and integrity of the data.
	Media handling:
	Media handling requires constant and rigorous management. Media in transit must be protected at the same level and to the same degree as media stored in a facility. Temperature control is also vital: media must be protected from extreme cold, heat, and humidity. When transported outside of storage facilities, media should be encrypted if it contains sensitive or classified information. Transfer-of-control logs, hand receipts, or other methods that identify who maintains control over information are required.
Declassification	As risks associated with the disclosure of classified information are reduced, the information can be declassified. The data owner determines the point in time of declassification. Security administrators are required to follow the local standards for declassification.
Misuse prevention	Access controls are used to prevent the misuse of data. Additional techniques such as need to know and least privilege, along with audit reviews, reduce the chances of misuse.

Best Practice	Description
Record retention	Corporate policy and legal and regulatory requirements dictate how to retain data records. Because it is difficult to attain legal and regulatory compliance, the corporate legal departments must assume advisory roles and act as internal consultants to ensure adherence to these standards. Failing to properly retain information can result in fines and imprisonment.

Operations Security Control Categories

The operations security process uses many different security controls. These different controls will fall into the security control categories in the same way that access controls do. It seems like the information in the operations security domain overlaps with the other domains and it does so intentionally. It is important then to remember that operations security is especially concerned with the near-term controls.

Security Control Category	Description
Preventative	*Preventative controls* are used to prevent unauthorized access or data modification. Enforcing user IDs and passwords used to authenticate authorized users is an example of a preventative measure.
Detective	*Detective controls* are used to discover the location of unauthorized access infiltration or unauthorized access attempts. An intrusion detection system (IDS) is an example of a detective control.
Corrective	*Corrective controls* are intended to remedy problems caused by security setbacks. Restoring file backups is an example of a corrective measure.
Directive	*Directive controls* provide guidance. A corporate security policy is an example of a directive control.
Recovery	*Recovery controls* help to correct a security problem by returning the system to a secure state. If a system fails, for example, trusted recovery is performed to restore security.
Deterrent	*Deterrent controls* encourage compliance with security guidelines and practices. An acceptable use policy would be an example of a deterrent control.
Compensating	*Compensating controls* mitigate the lack of another control. Employing a security guard in addition to a sophisticated physical IDS is an example of a compensating measure.

Operations Security Control Methods

There are many methods that help control operational security.

Security Control Method	Description
SoD	Separation of duties (SoD) monitors task implementation based on the specific responsibilities of authorized personnel. For example, users do not set up security profiles and security administrators do not perform system administrator functions.
Need to know	The need-to-know method manages individual information access based on job scope and job function requirements.
Least privilege	Least privilege helps regulate security by limiting individuals' capabilities to what is specifically needed for them to perform their jobs.
Job rotation	Job rotation involves rotating individuals between different organizational jobs to provide them with knowledge about different procedures and job responsibilities. It also creates a foundation for cross-training that increases employee availability in the organization.
Mandatory vacations	Mandatory vacation policies enforce a minimum amount of consecutive vacation days each year, which allows management ample time to audit employee activities.
Antivirus and anti-malware management	Antivirus and anti-malware signatures and software require constant monitoring and updating to remain current. It is important to monitor and audit the software to make sure it is being distributed and used effectively.
Audit	Auditing enables security administrators to identify problem areas by reviewing user and system activities. Auditing is also required for legal purposes.
Closed shop	A *closed shop* is a security control method in which only authorized users are allowed access to system information. Users will need to have appropriate security clearance and need to know for the information on the system.
Change control	*Change control* is a formal process of tracking hardware and software changes to ensure they are properly authorized and implemented, and that they follow procedural specifications.
Configuration management	Maintaining the correct hardware and software for critical systems requires careful configuration management. Any changes will be implemented with proper change control and reflected in the configuration documents for the system.
Patch management	In addition to watching the vendor's sites for patches, the patch administrator might also want to watch independent sites like the following: ● www.sans.org ● www.cert.gov ● nvd.nist.org For example, Microsoft supports automated patch management in its products through its security updates feature. Local security administrators can configure how security-related updates made available through Microsoft's Windows Update website are downloaded and distributed within their enterprises .

ACTIVITY 10-1
Discussing Operations Security Control

Scenario:

In this activity, you will discuss the mechanisms, practices, and techniques that help control operations security.

---

1. **OPSEC deals with which of the following issue types?**

   a) Near-term

   b) Breaches in progress

   c) Mid-term

   d) Long-term

---

2. **What is the core purpose of OPSEC?**

---

3. **What is the appropriate description for each operations security action item?**

   ___ Identifying critical information

   ___ Analyzing threats

   ___ Analyzing vulnerabilities

   ___ Assessing risk

   ___ Applying suitable OPSEC measures

   a. Identifying vulnerabilities through a business planner examination, pinpointing viable OPSEC measures for each.

   b. Employing selected measures after integrating a risk assessment into OPSEC plans for future business functions and activities.

   c. Recognizing potential adversaries through research and analysis of adversarial intelligence, organizational counterintelligence, and open source information.

   d. Determining whether data is vital to an adversary, which makes that information critical.

   e. Identifying and comparing probable indicators against an adversary's intelligence-gathering capacity.

---

4. **Which one or more of the following are operations security roles involved in detailing and enforcing permissions and access capabilities?**

   a) System administrator

   b) Security administrator

   c) User

   d) Password manager

---

5. **Which one of the following operations security protection areas assigns users to groups that have specific characteristics?**

   a) Special privileges

   b) Password and password management

   c) Account characteristics

   d) Security clearance

6. **Which one or more of the following describes a security profile?**

   a) A description of security-relevant information for protected system elements.

   b) A system-generated report that lists security information for each system on a network.

   c) A repository for items such as user name and user-specific password strength requirements.

   d) A description listing all the hardware and software used within an organization.

7. **Which of the following best practices describes a system property in which a single non-functioning component does not cause a complete system failure?**

   a) Misuse prevention

   b) Backup and restore

   c) Record retention

   d) Fault tolerance

8. **Which of the following best practices involves deterring unauthorized individuals from accessing classified materials as the first step?**

   a) Material destruction

   b) Material safeguarding

   c) Material reuse

   d) Sensitive media handling

9. **A corporate security policy is an example of which one of the following operations security control categories?**

   a) Detective

   b) Directive

   c) Deterrent

   d) Compensating

10. **True or False? Enforcing user IDs and passwords used to authenticate authorized users is an example of a corrective security control category.**

    ___ True

    ___ False

11. **What is the appropriate description for each security control method?**

___	SoD	a.	Manages individual information access based on job scope and job function requirements.
___	Need to know	b.	Monitors task implementation based on the specific responsibilities of authorized personnel.
___	Least privilege	c.	Enforces a minimum of one week of time off per year, allowing management ample time to audit employee activities.
___	Job rotation	d.	Limits individuals' capabilities to the lowest level specifically needed by them to perform their jobs.
___	Mandatory vacations	e.	Creates a foundation for cross-training that increases employee availability in the organization.

12. **What is the appropriate description for each additional security control method?**

___	Antivirus management	a.	Tracks hardware and software changes to ensure they are properly authorized and implemented, and that they follow procedural specifications.
___	Audit	b.	Monitors and updates malware prevention signatures and software.
___	Closed shop	c.	Allows only authorized users access to system information.
___	Change control	d.	Identifies problem areas by reviewing user and system activities.

TOPIC B

Operations Security Auditing and Monitoring

Operations security controls provide procedures to protect valuable information assets from loss, theft, or attack. To be effective, operations security controls need a system of checks and balances to ensure proper implementation, review, and correction. Security auditing and monitoring provides the tools and techniques to oversee operations security controls. In this topic, you will identify auditing and monitoring techniques to properly ensure operations security.

Your organization has gone to great lengths to protect its systems and resources. Security policies define expected behavior, but do little to support enforcement. Operational controls intend to provide enforcement, but lack a means of detection. Only a thorough understanding of system monitoring and audits will provide you with the means to observe and report system activity, and thereby enforce your security objectives. While system monitoring is usually done in-house, security audits will be a combination of in-house and third party. It is especially important in security audits that the auditors are independent. This does present a challenge as these auditors may have access to critical information. It will be extremely important to have carefully prepared contracts and signed non-disclosure agreements.

Security Auditing

Definition:

Security auditing is the practice of recording security-relevant events in an audit file for future analysis. It can be internal or external and focuses on system-, application-, and user-level events. The analysis may be used to locate activities that violate corporate policies or track user activities to diagnose system problems or security issues. Audit logs should be enabled by the security administrator, who selects the security-relevant events, such as system logins, which are placed in the audit log. The type and number of events helps to determine the quantity of entries that will be registered in the audit log.

Example:

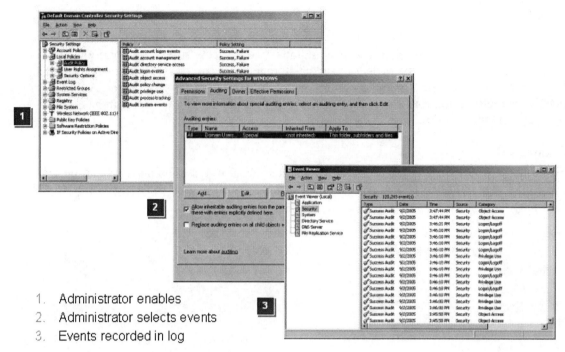

1. Administrator enables
2. Administrator selects events
3. Events recorded in log

Figure 10-2: Security auditing.

Example: System Break-ins

To determine the steps taken in a recent system break-in, a security analyst performs an audit log analysis to determine who accessed the file, when it occurred, and what system was used for file access.

Audit Log Protection

Audit logs and their content should always be protected from manipulation to ensure that they contain an accurate portrayal of system activities. Protection methods include using a write-only medium wherein entries are noted in writing but cannot be deleted or modified. There should be special permissions necessary to clear the audit log. The clearing of the audit log should also show up as a record in the audit log. Audit log monitoring systems should immediately notify the system or security administrator when a log file is cleared. Audit logs can be written to tape or disk media. Encryption helps protect audit log information, and creating hashes of audit logs aids in detecting changes. Audit log access is typically restricted to security administrators or organization auditors.

Full Logging

Creating log files can lead to excessive media usage. One logging technique involves logging everything. Once the log contains everything, analysts and auditors can review any or all of the log entry types as the need arises. However, with more log entries created, more media space will be required to store the files. The resulting cost may be extreme and unacceptable to management. This can also lead to an intentional or unintentional denial of service (DoS). In many systems, if the security audit logs fill up, the system will stop responding to additional requests as a way of protecting itself from a request it cannot log. If an intruder can fill the log with bogus entries, they may create a basic DoS or possibly even bring crash the system.

Clipping Levels

Definition:

A *clipping level* is a logging technique that provides an alternative to the log-all methodology to reduce the size of log files. If a security administrator selects an extraordinary quantity of audit events that require a great deal of media storage space, he or she can create a clipping level to set a limit on the generated number of log records for a given incident. Although clipping levels help decrease and minimize the size of an audit file, they may eliminate the required amount of log records.

Example:

For example, if a user attempts to log in to a system 40 times, a clipping level can be set to reduce the logging to the first three attempts. In this case, it may be sufficient to refrain from recording the last 37 attempts.

Repeated login   Full log   Set clipping level   Reduced log size
attempts

Figure 10-3: *Setting a clipping level.*

Security Audit Events

Security audit events are based on policy and recorded system activity. Log entries contain a variety of useful information for tracking activities, which commonly includes:

- Identification of the event.
- Time of the event.
- Identification of the individual or process causing the event.

System-Level Audit Logs

Audit logs can be generated at the system level to record the following activities:

- Login attempts
- Login successes
- Login failures
- Logouts
- Application accessing
- File creations
- File deletions
- File modifications
- User account creations
- User account modifications
- User account deletions

Application or Database Audit Logs

Audit logs can also be created by applications or databases to record the following activities:

- Transactions processed
- Data status before transactions
- Data status after transactions
- Transaction failure information
- Transaction backout information

Security Monitoring

Definition:

Security monitoring is the practice of monitoring operations controls to identify abnormal computer activity. It uses intrusion detection, penetration testing, and violation processing to track operational events to watch for unusual or unauthorized activity. Active operations security practices include a need to constantly monitor the security-relevant elements of a system. These aspects include both logical and physical elements.

Example:

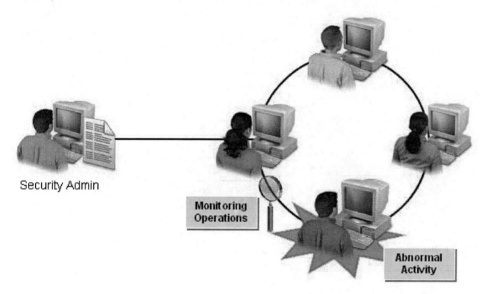

Figure 10-4: *Security monitoring.*

Example: Periodic Audit Reviews

Audit reviews comprise one form of security monitoring that is required on a periodic basis according to policy, legal, or regulatory requirements. Frequently analyzing intrusion detection system (IDS) logs, firewall logs, and system access logs is useful for identifying areas that require further analysis and access control improvements.

Example: Periodic Physical Access Reviews

Analyzing physical access control systems is essential for determining areas in need of strengthening or method improvement. For example, when repeated attempts are made to enter a facility's back door, installing a fence surrounding the building protects unauthorized access.

Violation Analysis

Definition:

Violation analysis, also called *violation processing* or *violation tracking*, is a security monitoring technique that tracks anomalies in user activity. It uses established clipping levels or activities outside normally expected ranges to analyze repetitive mistakes, individuals who exceed their authority, and patterns that indicate serious intrusion attempts.

Example: A Login Anomaly

A user who typically logs on close to the start of the work day suddenly logs on at 10:00 pm. This could indicate an attempt to gain inappropriate access after hours when there is less supervision. Or it could be a benign instance of an employee coming in late to finish a work task.

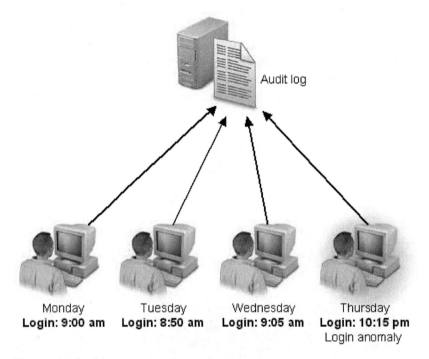

Monday	Tuesday	Wednesday	Thursday
Login: 9:00 am	**Login: 8:50 am**	**Login: 9:05 am**	**Login: 10:15 pm** Login anomaly

Figure 10-5: *A login anomaly.*

Violation Factors

Log analyses help to identify patterns of activity that indicate security issues that require further investigation and research.

Violation Factor	Description
Source	Understanding the origin of violations provides information to help identify problem areas. For example, successful logins may originate from a user's normal system while abnormal login attempts may come from several other systems. Nevertheless, evidence indicates that all of these systems are in the same physical location. Visually monitoring the area may help identify the individual making unauthorized access attempts.

Violation Factor	Description
Frequency	The regularity of events can help determine the level of risk associated with a particular violation. Thirty thousand improper access attempts may represent a severe threat pattern whereas three access attempts may present a risk, but one with a very low threat incidence.
Severity	The severity of the violation may depend on who, where, and how the attempted violation was performed. For example, physical attempts to access a computer facility represent a high-level security risk with the probability of severe consequences, whereas attempts to access an office supply storage room may yield less severe consequences.
Response	In all cases, the response to security violations must be measured by the risk associated with the violation. Thirty thousand access attempts in one hour will present high risk whereas three access attempts will present low risk. A measured response based on risk allocates the right assets to the right problem.

ACTIVITY 10-2
Discussing Operations Security Auditing and Monitoring

Scenario:
In this activity, you will discuss auditing and monitoring techniques used to properly ensure operations security.

1. **Which one or more of the following events does security auditing focus on?**

   a) System-level

   b) Application-level

   c) User-level

   d) Organizational-level

2. **True or False? Security audit event log entries contain information such as the identification of the event, the time of the event, and the identification of the individual or process causing the event.**

   ___ True

   ___ False

3. **Security monitoring uses which one or more of the following to track operational events for unusual or unauthorized activity?**

   a) Penetration testing

   b) Intrusion detection

   c) Violation prevention

   d) Violation processing

4. **What is the purpose of violation analysis?**

5. **Which one of the following violation factors addresses the likelihood and level of consequences for a security violation?**

   a) Severity

   b) Source

   c) Frequency

   d) Response

TOPIC C
Operational Threats and Violations

You identified system auditing and monitoring techniques that help to implement and manage operations security controls. The final phase in ensuring operations security is acknowledging and attending to unauthorized internal and external system intrusions. In this topic, you will identify threats and violations that endanger system security.

Attacks on your systems, whether intentional or unintentional, can escalate in frequency and severity if they are not detected, acted on, and resolved. If a hacker penetrates your network and gets away with it, it is likely that subsequent violations will occur. Effectively handling operations security threats and violations ensures the confidentiality, integrity, and availability of critical information resources for your business operations. If the organization is large enough or the work is sensitive enough, it may be appropriate to develop an internal incidence response team. Smaller organizations may rely on contracts with companies specializing in security incident response.

Security Threats

Operations security threats come in many forms and target any number of elements in the security spectrum.

Threat Type	Security Target
Disclosure	Disclosure targets confidentiality because it exposes private business information without authorization.
Destruction	If data is destroyed, its availability is compromised because it is no longer accessible to authorized parties.
Interruption of service	Service interruptions disrupt continuous system operations and, therefore, disable the availability of critical data.
Corruption and modification	When electronic data is altered or damaged and extensive errors are revealed, it directly impacts information integrity.
Theft	Theft is a human threat that targets confidentiality and availability by confiscating computer equipment and assets, interrupting system communications, overriding access privileges, and retrieving private data without authorization or permission.
Espionage	The act of espionage is a human-intelligence threat that affects confidentiality, integrity, and availability by obtaining private, or secret, information through physical or electronic means without the information owner's authorized consent.
Hackers and crackers	Hacking and password cracking are human-based security threats that target confidentiality, integrity, and availability by detecting and exploiting system flaws, acquiring or prohibiting unauthorized system access, and recovering password data.
Malicious code	Because malicious code is designed to deliberately penetrate access rights and privacy, and damage computer systems, its intrusive nature has a destructive impact on data confidentiality, integrity, and availability.

Security Violations

Definition:

A *security violation* is a breach of security regulations or policies that may or may not result in a system compromise. Security violations may be intentional or unintentional, may or may not result in damage, and should be reported to the appropriate authorities for action. Violations may be criminally prosecuted, regardless of their severity.

Example: Unauthorized Access

An example of a security violation is an unauthorized employee entering a building. This is a security violation even if the employee does not do any damage or harm to the facility.

User Accountability

User accountability is the driving force behind information systems security violations. Users are responsible for their own behavior and are expected to adhere to the organization's security policies for computers and networks that they can access. The significance of security violations depends upon malice and the attitudes of the individuals who commit the violations, rather than whether or not information was actually compromised.

Security Violation Types

Security violations can manifest themselves and occur in two key areas.

Violation Type	Description
Physical	Physical violations include the following activities: • Unauthorized physical access to a facility • Stealing media or equipment • Damaging equipment • Disconnecting electrical or communications services
Logical	Logical violations include the following activities: • Cracking passwords using brute force • Perpetrating man-in-the-middle attacks • Inserting a virus or worm into a computer network • Compromising a user password or authorization method • Obtaining access information through a social engineering attack

Incident Responsiveness

Once a security violation has been identified, a simple or complex response must be initiated to return the system to a secure state.

Incident Response Step	Description
Detection	Incident response starts with incident detection. Determining what has happened, when it happened, and if it is continuing to happen, are key first steps. Using audit logs, IDS, and real-time monitoring will all be helpful. Coordinating information from multiple sources can also help identify if other systems are also at risk.
Containment	Containing the incident is critical. Taking the system offline while leaving it powered on will be helpful for forensic purposes. Having trained forensic investigators is important. It is easy for untrained people to miss critical information—or worse—delete critical information.
System cleaning	The system must be cleansed of all attacks to restore it to its normal, secure operating condition. A trusted recovery can be performed by: ● Using virus removal tools. ● Restoring corrupted systems. ● Reloading software and data. Each of these trusted recovery techniques should be chosen according to the nature and state of the attack.
Reporting and documenting	It is important to report the incident in the appropriate way. You may have obligations to report it to law enforcement or simply report it to internal auditors. Follow up with documentation in order to help prevent future incidents.
Assessing training and awareness	Discovering and identifying existing threats, such as social engineering attacks or the physical presence of unauthorized individuals on facility premises, may indicate the need for more intensive security awareness and training. A thorough analysis of security violations can provide the necessary information to develop a training and awareness program.
Evaluating protection	Performing an additional violation analysis is useful when evaluating the current level of protection for logical and physical assets. By pinpointing security gaps and violation sources, process improvement steps can be determined to implement robust defense mechanisms that heighten and stabilize security.
Vulnerability testing	Vulnerability testing further facilitates protection improvements because it can identify system flaws and severe or mild problem areas in logical and physical security.

ACTIVITY 10-3
Discussing Threats and Violations

Scenario:

In this activity, you will discuss threats and violations that endanger system security.

1. **What is the appropriate description for each OPSEC threat?**

    ___ Disclosure

    ___ Destruction

    ___ Interruption of service

    ___ Corruption and modification

    a. Continually disrupting system operations, disabling the availability of critical data.

    b. Compromising availability of data because it is no longer accessible to authorized parties.

    c. Exploiting information integrity by altering or damaging electronic data.

    d. Exposing private business information without authorization.

2. **What is the appropriate description for each additional OPSEC threat?**

    ___ Theft

    ___ Espionage

    ___ Hackers and crackers

    ___ Malicious code

    a. Individuals who detect and exploit system flaws to acquire or prohibit unauthorized system access and password data.

    b. Using unauthorized software to penetrate access rights and privacy and to damage data confidentiality, integrity, and availability.

    c. Confiscating computer equipment and assets that target confidentiality and availability.

    d. Confiscating private information through physical or electronic means, affecting confidentiality, integrity, and availability.

3. **True or False? Security violations may result in criminal prosecution, regardless of their severity.**

    ___ True

    ___ False

4. **Which one or more of the following activities are included in logical violations?**

   a) Cracking passwords using brute force

   b) Disconnecting electrical or communications services

   c) Obtaining access information though a social engineering attack

   d) Stealing equipment

5. **Why is assessing training and awareness an appropriate response to a security violation?**

Lesson 10 Follow-up

In this lesson, you analyzed the processes, tools, strategies, and techniques for implementing operations security. Intrusive threats and attacks that compromise the confidentiality, integrity, and availability of critical information can happen at any time if they are not properly detected, counteracted, and mitigated. Effectively controlling vital operations security elements such as hardware, media, and user access privileges allows you to ensure strong and secure system functionality.

1. **Has your organization ever experienced a major breach in security? Were you aware of the security-relevant policies prior to or only after the event?**

2. **How does OPSEC differ from other security planning areas that you are familiar with, covered by the CISSP exam?**

11 | Business Continuity and Disaster Recovery Planning

Lesson Time: 3 hour(s)

Lesson Objectives:

In this lesson, you will apply Business Continuity and Disaster Recovery Plans.

You will:

- Analyze business continuity planning.

- Identify the Business Continuity Plan implementation.

- Identify the fundamental elements of a Disaster Recovery Plan.

- Identify the DRP implementation.

Introduction

Knowing the organizational resources you need to protect, identifying who can and who cannot have access to your company's resources, and implementing available control mechanisms to alleviate potential threats are important responsibilities for information systems security professionals. Equally important is protecting your organization's resources from natural or other outside influences. In this lesson, you will apply plans to protect your business in the event of a minor disruption or complete natural disaster.

Planning your responses to natural or man-made disasters is essential to maintaining critical business processes. By staying proactive and performing effective business continuity and disaster recovery planning, you can ensure that your business continues to operate in the face of disastrous events.

This lesson supports content found in the Business Continuity and Disaster Recovery Planning domain of the CISSP® certification.

TOPIC A
Business Continuity Plan Fundamentals

Business Continuity Plans are important safeguards against all kinds of organizational threats and violations. Now, you can address how to ensure that your organization's business processes are protected from internal and external disaster by planning ahead, estimating the possible damages that could occur, and implementing appropriate controls. The real key is planning ahead. These plans need to be written and tested before disaster strikes. There are too many stories about businesses that lacked Business Continuity Plans and never survived the initial disaster, or if they did survive the initial disaster, were not able to survive the next one to three years. In this topic, you will analyze the development schemes, contingency requirements, and disaster identification involved in business continuity planning.

Business continuity planning is instrumental in determining the success of your organization by providing an immediate, accurate, and measured response to a disaster. There is no greater concern than identifying how to maintain business processes following disruptive events and system interruptions. Your ability to effectively sustain business processes after a crisis will help to ensure the availability of critical systems and resources until regular conditions are reinstated.

Business Continuity Plans

Definition:

A *Business Continuity Plan (BCP)* is a policy that defines how an enterprise will maintain normal day-to-day business operations in the event of business disruption or crisis. The intent of the BCP is to ensure the survival of the business entity by preserving key documents, establishing decision-making authority, communicating with internal and external stakeholders, protecting and recovering assets, and maintaining financial functions. The BCP should address infrastructure issues such as maintaining utilities service, utilizing high-availability or fault-tolerant systems that can withstand failure, and creating and maintaining data backups. The BCP should also account for the protection of the employees, contractors, temps, visitors, and any other people that might be present. The protection of human life will trump all other concerns. The BCP must be reviewed and tested on a regular basis. The creation and maintenance of a BCP is going to require senior management support. They should be fully informed of the plan and any changes to the plan.

Example:

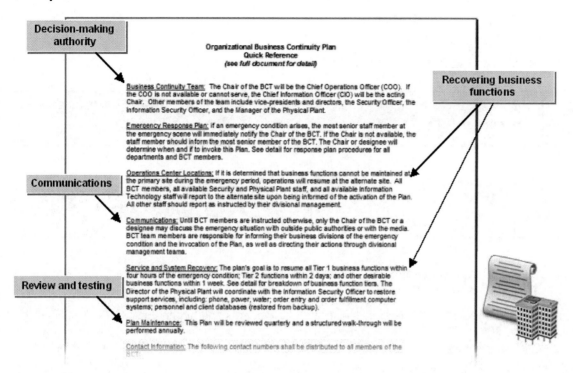

Figure 11-1: A BCP.

BCP and DRP

While some organizations consider a BCP and a Disaster Recovery Plan (DRP) the same thing, they are distinct in the CISSP material. You may consider the DRP as a component of the BCP but they are still separate plans. The BCP is a larger over-arching document that prepares a company for disaster. The DRP is what is initiated when disaster strikes and brings the company out of the disaster.

There is not always a firm distinction between the terms BCP and DRP. The website **www.isc2.org** used to distinguish between DRPs and BCPs; however, in its current materials, it allows for them to be separate plans or two components of the same plan. You may find that some consider the DRP to be a subset of the overall BCP and that it is not a separate plan.

The NFPA Business Planning Framework

The National Fire Protection Association (NFPA) provides stipulations, standards, and practices for IT- and business continuity-related management. NFPA released a document titled "Standard on Disaster/Emergency Management and Business Continuity Programs," or NFPA 1600, that supplies the designated framework for BCP documents. Although it details a BCP's content requirements, it does not present any details about the BCP creation processes. It offers the following "Ten Professional Practice Areas:"

1. Project Initiation and Management.
2. Risk Evaluation and Control.
3. Business Impact Analysis.
4. Developing Business Continuity Strategies.
5. Emergency Response and Operations.
6. Developing and Implementing BCPs.

7. Awareness and Training Programs.

8. Maintaining and Exercising BCPs.

9. Public Relations and Crisis Communications.

10. Coordination with Public Authorities.

 For more information on BCP framework standards, visit **www.nfpa.org/assets/files//PDF/NFPA16002010.pdf**.

 These development steps are a general description of what should happen in an organization to assist in creating a working BCP. If an organization is without a BCP, it is likely that it could take months or even years to fully write and test a plan.

NIST SP 800-34

In 2002 (updated 2010), the National Institute of Standards and Technology (NIST) Special Publication 800-34 Rev. 1 outlined the steps required for what they refer to as contingency planning. These steps include:

1. Developing the contingency planning policy statement.

2. Conducting a business impact analysis.

3. Identifying preventive controls.

4. Developing recovery strategies.

5. Developing an information technology (IT) contingency plan.

6. Planning testing, training, and exercises.

7. Planning maintenance.

 For more information on NIST contingency planning, visit **http://csrc.nist.gov/publications/PubsSPs.html** and click the PDF file for SP 800-34 Rev. 1 to download.

Project Management Applications

In evaluating the contingency planning steps, it is important to note that each step contains general statements that can be applied to any project management activity. These include:

1. Starting the plan.

2. Evaluating the impact of the proposed activity.

3. Developing the project.

4. Testing and implementing the solution.

5. Maintaining the project for success.

Disruptive Events (Threats)

A BCP should address various types of disruptive events that can target the continuity of daily business operations. First, identify the potential threats. Next, identify the assets that are exposed to the threat. The likelihood of the threat destroying your assets is the risk. Perform continual risk analysis to find ways to avoid, mitigate, transfer, or accept the risk.

Disruptive Event	Description
Natural hazards	Natural hazards such as earthquakes, tornados, hurricanes, floods, lightning strikes, and tsunamis can all disrupt, stall, or completely halt business activities. Many of these are localized threats. A hurricane is of little concern in the Upper Midwest of the USA. Tornadoes, on the other hand, are very much a threat. These threats also have very different impact zones. A hurricane covers a very wide, somewhat predictable path; a tornado has a very unpredictable, narrow path. This has implications when doing risk analysis.
Human-caused	Human-caused hazards may be unintentional or intentional. Human errors can cause accidental mishaps such as file deletion and poor transaction processing. Intentional hazards occur when individuals damage or disrupt activities through vandalism, theft, or fraud. Unintentional hazards will frequently be inside your organization. Intentional attacks can come from inside or outside your organization.
Technology-caused	While technology-caused hazards may seem human based, this category is often more difficult to identify because it is related to hardware or software that can malfunction due to hardware failures or poor programming practices. Although natural and human-caused hazards are generally easy to perceive and detect, software and hardware hazards are not as obvious; nevertheless, they are just as dangerous.

Business Impact Analysis

Definition:

A *business impact analysis (BIA)* is a BCP phase that identifies present organizational risks and determines the impact to ongoing, business-critical operations and processes if risks are actualized. BIAs contain vulnerability assessments and evaluations to determine risks and their impact. BIAs should include all phases of the business to ensure a strong business continuation strategy. The BIA will also help identify the systems that need to be recovered most quickly, should there be a disaster. This information will be inserted into the DRP.

Example:

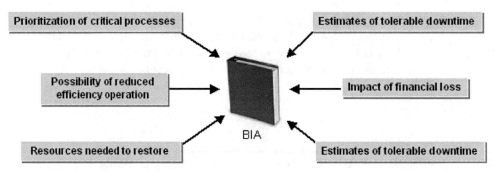

Figure 11-2: A BIA.

Example: Flood Impact

As a risk is identified, an organization determines the chance of risk occurrence and then determines the quantity of potential organizational damage. If a roadway bridge crossing a local river is washed out by a flood and employees are unable to reach the business facility for five days, estimated costs to the organization need to be assessed for lost manpower and production.

BIA Organizational Goals

A BIA is designed and developed to achieve several organizational goals, which include:

● Ensuring the health and safety of employees, responders, and others.

● Enabling continuous company operations that include property, infrastructure, and facilities.

● Maintaining the continuous delivery of goods and services to customers.

● Providing a safe workplace environment should a disaster occur.

The BIA Process

The BIA process involves a series of four phases.

1. Project planning and development

2. Data collection

3. Application and data criticality assessment

4. Data analysis to assess vulnerabilities and other key business factors

Critical Business Processes

Definition:

A *critical business process* is an activity that, if not recovered, can lead to business loss or failure. Critical business processes are determined during the BIA by senior management based on actual impact rather than on internal political practices. The analysis should include the identification of key personnel on whom the processes depend. Critical processes may have sub-processes; if any one process or sub-process fails, the entire business may lose its sustainability and cease to operate successfully.

Example:

Figure 11-3: *Shipping orders is a critical business process.*

Example: Product Development

In a medical supplies manufacturing business, product development is a critical business process. This process may also include, and depend upon, a variety of critical sub-processes, such as:

- Ordering supplies.
- Receiving supplies.
- Managing inventory.
- Maintaining production lines.
- Controlling the quality of manufactured products.
- Warehousing.
- Shipping.
- Billing.
- Processing orders.

Vulnerability Assessments

A *vulnerability assessment* is a BIA phase that focuses on financial and operational loss impact and locates threat exploitation indicators in an organization. Vulnerability assessments identify the security weaknesses of each threatened asset and determine the cost of removing those vulnerabilities.

 Vulnerability assessments are not just related to information technology (IT) but to all facets of an organization.

Vulnerability-Assessed Threats

Some examples of vulnerability-assessed threats may include the following:

- If a business is located next to railroad tracks and a train derails, leaking toxic fluids, the business might be forced into inactivity for a number of days.

- If key manufacturing staff express their plans to strike, they may threaten to damage equipment beforehand to heighten the impact of their impending actions.

- A key supplier may be unable to provide raw materials for the production of an organization's principle products.

Vulnerability Tables

A simple table is often a strategic tool for completing a vulnerability assessment.

Vulnerability	Identification Source	Risk of Occurrence (1 = Low; 5 = High)	Impact Estimate (US Dollars)	Mitigation
Flood damage	Physical plant	1	$25,000	Standing order for sandbags
Electrical failure	Physical plant	2	$100,000	Generator, UPS
Flu epidemic	Personnel	4	$200,000	Flu shots

Using a table allows planners to identify potential threats or vulnerabilities, record the possible impact, and then prioritize mitigation efforts. Mitigation helps reduce the impact of an exploited vulnerability. A loss of power has a relatively high risk with a reasonable mitigation effort, consisting of a one-time expenditure to purchase a backup generator.

If there were two additional columns in the table, the assessment would be more useful.

Vulnerability	Cost of Mitigation	Vulnerability Impact Post Mitigation
Electrical failure	$500	$0

By adding these extra columns, business continuity planners would be able to evaluate the vulnerabilities, propose mitigation, and evaluate the vulnerabilities by the residual risks after mitigation.

Maximum Tolerable Downtime

Definition:

Maximum tolerable downtime (MTD) is the longest period of time that a business outage may occur without causing serious business failures. Each business process can have its own MTD, such as a range of minutes to hours for critical functions, 24 hours for urgent functions, 7 days for normal functions, and so on. MTDs vary by company and event.

 It is quite possible you will see other similar sounding terms like maximum tolerable outage, maximum tolerable period of disruption, and others. They all essentially mean the same thing, at least as far as the CISSP material is concerned.

Example:

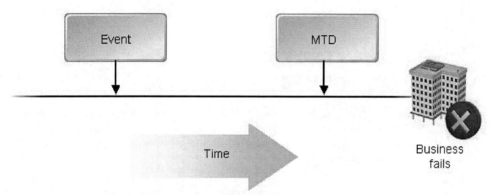

Figure 11-4: MTD.

Example: Medical Equipment Suppliers

The MTD limits the amount of recovery time that a business has to resume operations. An organization specializing in medical equipment may be able to exist without incoming manufacturing supplies for three months because it has stockpiled a sizeable inventory. After three months, the organization will not have sufficient supplies and may not be able to manufacture additional products, therefore leading to failure. In this case, the MTD is three months.

Recovery Point Objectives

The *Recovery Point Objective (RPO)* is the point in time, relative to a disaster, where the data recovery process begins. In IT systems, it is often the point in time when the last successful backup is performed before the disruptive event occurs. It is the amount of time or data that you can afford to lose. If you are doing nightly backups that start at midnight and you have a complete data disaster at 11:00 pm, you will lose all data created during that day. It is important to individually determine an acceptable RPO for different systems and data stores.

For example, if the last backup was executed Sunday afternoon and the failure occurs on the following Tuesday, then the RPO is Sunday afternoon. The latest backup is restored and processing begins to recover all activity from Sunday afternoon to the Tuesday failure point.

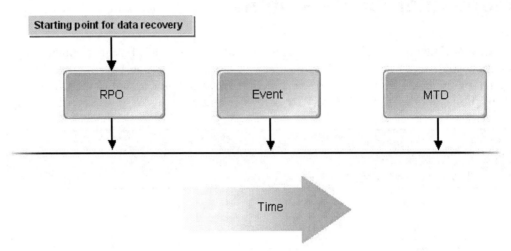

Figure 11-5: An RPO.

Recovery Time Objectives

The *Recovery Time Objective (RTO)* is the length of time within which normal business operations and activities can be restored following a disturbance. It includes the necessary recovery time to return to the RPO point, and reinstate the system and processing to their current status. The RTO must be achieved before the MTD.

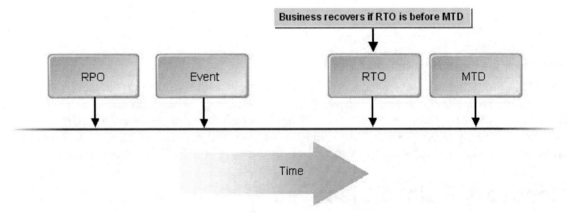

Figure 11-6: An RTO.

RPO/RTO Optimization

Ideally, the RPO and RTO should be zero or as near to zero as is economically feasible. That is, a failure can be immediately recovered. Although a near-zero RPO/RTO solution is extremely expensive, it is necessary in some circumstances. Airline reservation systems and stock market trading systems require the implementation of a near-zero RPO/RTO solution. In other cases, if the impact of a loss is less severe, a lower-cost solution can be used.

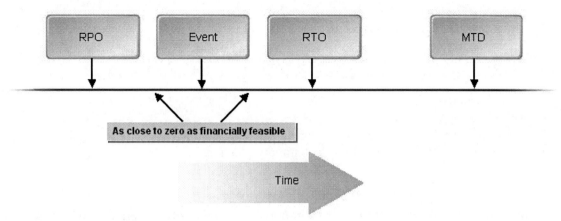

Figure 11-7: RPO/RTO optimization.

Cost of Recovery vs. Cost of Loss

When determining disaster response, the cost of recovery should be weighed against the cost of loss. In many cases, it is not justifiable to spend more on system recovery if the cost of system loss is minimal. Although recovery costs should be need based, they should not, necessarily, exceed the cost of loss.

However, loss is often difficult to identify. While it might be possible to quantify the loss in sales of non-produced items, there may be other areas of loss that are not as obvious, such as:

- Failing to maintain competitive advantages.
- Contract violations and associated penalties.
- Failing to maintain reputation.
- Revenue loss.
- Productivity loss.
- Delayed income.
- Failing to meet legal requirements.

A complete analysis should include these types of issues when determining recovery requirements.

ACTIVITY 11-1
Discussing Business Continuity Planning

Scenario:

In this activity, you will discuss the development schemes, contingency requirements, and disaster identification involved in business continuity planning.

---

1. **There is a BCP in effect at your corporation. As the security administrator, you are responsible for ensuring that this policy coincides with the organization's everyday needs. To accomplish this, you plan to review and test the BCP:**

   a) Once every five years.

   b) At least monthly.

   c) Only when business operations change.

   d) At least annually.

---

2. **Place the BCP development phases in order from first to last.**

   Initiate the plan creation process and set goals.

   Determine how to prevent the events.

   Determine the impact of various events to the business.

   Provide updates to the solutions and plans.

   Check to see if the solutions actually work.

   Determine what to do if the events cannot be prevented.

---

3. **Your organization is located in an area where there is a threat of hurricanes. As a member of the BCP team, you need to determine what effect there would be if a hurricane halted business activities at your corporation. What BCP phase is this an example of?**

   a) Critical business processes

   b) BIA

   c) MTD

   d) RPO

---

4. **Your organization is located in a major shipping port at the edge of large lake. Therefore, the building is susceptible to damage in the event of flooding, a cargo spill, or a maritime collision. As the security administrator, you need to conduct an investigation to identify the areas of the building with the highest level of risk associated with these threats, then calculate the cost of providing additional protection in case of this type of emergency. Which one of these BCP concepts does this represent?**

   a) Critical business processes

   b) MTD

   c) Vulnerability assessment

   d) Recovery point objectives

5. **You work for a major urban newspaper. Brainstorm a list of critical and non-critical business processes for your organization.**

6. **You work for a local chain of auto repair shops. You are responsible both for the design and the budgeting for your company's BCP. Will you recommend a near-zero RTO/RPO? Why or why not?**

TOPIC B
Business Continuity Plan Implementation

Analyzing the effects of system downtime and determining how to build a BCP are essential to identifying the overall impact of a potential disaster on your organization's business processes. Now you are ready to assemble your team and key players and implement a BCP. In this topic, you will identify team responsibilities and evaluation, testing, and maintenance strategies for implementing an effective BCP.

While business continuity planning jump starts operational recovery efforts and business impact analyses focus on the effects of system downtime due to a disaster, no progress can be made without implementing the BCP within your organizational infrastructure. Once your plan is prepared, you should conduct rigorous evaluations and testing. This type of regime will help you confirm that you developed an appropriate BCP that ensures system resilience and maintains critical business processes after a potential crisis.

Program Coordinators

Definition:

The *program coordinator* is the individual responsible for implementing and controlling the BCP. The program coordinator maintains the long-term plan and determines when the process modifications are required based on business operation changes. The program coordinator must receive senior management support to be effective. In addition to receiving support, the program coordinator must keep senior management informed on the progress and testing of the BCP. If seen as a low-level administrator, the program coordinator may not obtain the necessary support from the organization to complete the BCP.

Example:

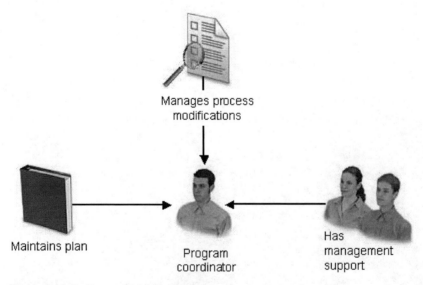

Manages process
modifications

Maintains plan

Program
coordinator

Has
management
support

Figure 11-8: Program coordination.

Program Coordinator Duties

The program coordinator should hold periodic meetings to evaluate the BCP, and verify that copies of the BCP are available to management and staff when needed. Printed hard copies should be stored in different onsite locations as well as at a convenient offsite location for easy accessibility. BCPs should only be stored on computers as documentation, not for operational purposes.

The Advisory Committee-BCP Team

Definition:

The *Advisory Committee-BCP team* is a group of individuals from varying backgrounds within the community who assemble to create the BCP and assist in plan maintenance. The team typically includes senior management members, business partners, security and IT professionals, company personnel, and legal representatives. The team should be composed of decision makers who can influence the process objectively. When an organization has multiple satellite branches or offices, it is important to include remote business associates in the business planning process, either as part of an overall enterprise team or as a location-specific team.

Example:

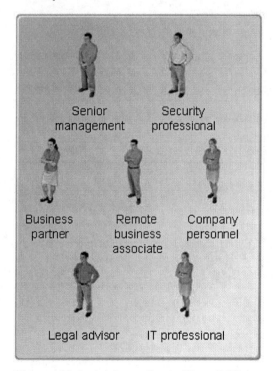

Figure 11-9: Advisory Committee–BCP team members.

BCP Team Responsibilities

The BCP team is responsible for an array of activities, which include:

- Determining threats and vulnerabilities.
- Providing probability estimates of threats and vulnerabilities.
- Performing a business impact analysis (BIA) based on evaluated threats and vulnerabilities, and probability estimates.
- Prioritizing recovery efforts based on critical business activities that affect the overall survival of the organization.
- Evaluating alternate sites that could be used in an emergency.
- Determining action plans in the event of a disaster.
- Writing policies, guidelines, standards, and procedures on BCP implementation.
- Testing the BCP.
- Making sure legal requirements are fulfilled during the disaster process.

BCP Contents

To properly implement a BCP, it should contain specific content that is consistent throughout the organization. This includes:

- A statement of policy from senior management that defines the BCP's vision and mission.
- A statement of authority that authorizes the BCP team to operate.
- The roles and responsibilities of the plan's team members.
- Plan goals, objectives, and evaluation methods.
- Applicable laws, regulations, authorities, and/or industry codes of practice.
- A budget and project schedule.
- Records management practices.

 For more information and general guidance on BCP content objectives, visit **http://www.nfpa.org/aboutthecodes** and click the link for NFPA 1600.

Records Management

Maintaining a thorough record-keeping process is essential for two purposes:

1. It documents team activities for historical purposes.
2. It documents activities for due diligence to demonstrate that standard business processes were considered during plan development. This type of documentation would be necessary for insurance or audit purposes.

Business Plan Evaluations

The BCP development process must include an evaluation phase to ensure targeted objectives, time efficiency, and cost effectiveness. The BCP team should evaluate:

- The plan's coverage adequacy in all areas of the business.
- Threat and vulnerability identification.
- Prioritization of proper responses to business needs.
- Training and plan testing.
- Communications methods.
- BCP team staffing and time allocations.
- The frequency and methods for plan updates.

Business Plan Testing

When testing a BCP, various methods can be employed.

BCP Testing Method	Description
Reviewing contents	Because they are familiar with BCP construction, plan developers review the BCP's contents. However, because of their involvement as developers, they often have a limited view of corporate needs that can cause biased opinions.
Analyzing the business continuity solution	Senior management and division and department heads perform an additional analysis to ensure that the business continuity solution fulfills organizational recovery requirements. Because these individuals view the process from a corporate standpoint, they help to confirm that the BCP properly meets expectations.
Using checklists	Checklists confirm whether the BCP meets pre-determined, documented business needs.
Performing walkthroughs	Walkthroughs specifically focus on each BCP process phase. Planners and testers walk through the individual steps to validate the logical flow of the sequence of events.
Parallel testing	This test is used to ensure that systems perform adequately at the alternate offsite facility, without taking the main site offline.
Conducting simulations	Simulations effectively test the validity and compliance of the BCP. In a simulation, each part of the planning process is exercised, with the exception of replicating and causing an outage. Although calls are made and specific actions are taken, the real event response is simulated.
	Simulations are instrumental in verifying design flaws, recovery requirements, and implementation errors. By identifying these solution discrepancies, process improvements can be applied that help ensure high-level plan maintenance.
Full interruption testing	This test mimics an actual business disruption by shutting down the original site to test transfer and migration procedures to the alternate site, and to test operations in the presence of an emergency.

Business Plan Maintenance

Durable plan maintenance hinges on continual process improvements that are determined throughout the testing phase. To adequately maintain the BCP, it should be reviewed yearly for any necessary changes. Evaluation and test results should be included in the review process to improve any areas of deficiency. If any business units or departments have major changes in processes, products, or IT, the BCP should be updated to accommodate these modifications.

The Business Continuity Process

The business continuity process includes several steps to properly resume business operations after a disruptive event.

Business Continuity Step	Description
Assess level of impact	You will need to determine if the disruption is a temporary condition from which the business will naturally recover without incident, or if it is a disaster that will require activation of the DRP.
Begin continuity operations	The BCP should contain detailed steps regarding methods for implementing continuity operations. This is the initiation of the DRP. There will be an established process to declare the disaster and the disaster recovery team will begin their work. An operations manager should be appointed to oversee the situation and manage communications.
Notify stakeholders	Stakeholders should be informed of a significant business disruption. They may consist of senior management, board members, affected managers and employees, service providers, and potentially, suppliers. Clients should be informed if the disruption will noticeably affect services or product deliveries.

ACTIVITY 11-2
Discussing BCP Implementation

Scenario:

In this activity, you will discuss team responsibilities and evaluation, testing, and maintenance strategies for implementing an effective BCP.

1. **You work for a large multi-national corporation. As the Chief Security Officer, you have been asked to chair the BCP advisory team for the company headquarters. Who might you invite to join the team?**

2. **The advisory committee has met for its monthly meeting and you have left the meeting with a beta-level draft of the BCP. You have been charged with evaluating the BCP prior to implementation. What are some examples of items that you will be evaluating?**

3. **You and your colleague have just performed a walkthrough of the plan that would be put in effect in the event of damages to your portside building from a maritime collision within the port area. The two of you think that you need to perform more rigorous tests to ensure the effectiveness of the BCP. What are some other testing methods you might want to recommend?**

4. High water conditions in the harbor have caused shore flooding and made it impossible for your employees to report to work. Civil authorities have notified you first because you are on record as the primary emergency contact for your company. What actions should you take?

_____

TOPIC C
Disaster Recovery Plan Fundamentals

You have implemented a BCP to protect your business from internal or external disruptions so that your critical systems can continue functioning as normally as possible. However, even in cases where business activities seem to be operating smoothly, you also need a plan to rebuild your organization in the event of a disaster. In this topic, you will identify the fundamental elements of a DRP.

The adage "prior planning prevents poor performance" is no truer than when dealing with how a disaster impacts your business. Successful disaster recovery is only possible with a plan in place that defines the actions to be taken in response to an emergency. Appropriately defining disaster recovery strategies will help prepare you and your organization to effectively respond to a calamitous event.

Disaster Recovery Plans

Definition:

A *Disaster Recovery Plan (DRP)* is a policy that defines how people and resources will be protected in the case of a natural or man-made disaster, and how the organization will recover from the disaster. The DRP can include a list of individuals responsible for recovery, an inventory of hardware and software, and a series of steps to take to respond to the disaster and rebuild affected systems.

Example:

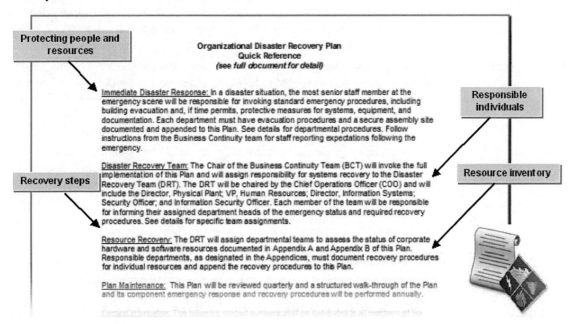

Figure 11-10: A DRP.

Response Conditions

While the BCP determines how to eliminate or mitigate risks, threats, and vulnerabilities, the DRP focuses on responses to exploitations that have caused a disastrous event. For example, an organization may be aware that a flood washed out a major bridge in its business area 10 years ago. Therefore, a DRP might be created that addresses flood possibilities and implements an expected organizational response system. The plan may designate a solution wherein two alternate travel routes are suggested when such a disaster is declared. If this is the case, the plan should include an effective communication scheme to inform all employees, business partners, customers, and suppliers of possible washout delays and commuting alternatives.

Disaster Recovery Strategy Considerations

There are several factors to take into consideration when an organization develops a disaster recovery strategy.

Disaster Recovery Factor	Description
Risks	As a DRP is created, residual risks must be considered. ● People—The DRP must, at all costs, ensure the safety of the organization's people. Employee-related issues such as transportation, housing, food, sanitation, heating, cooling, and so on should always be considered. Failure to include these factors may decrease morale and counteract cooperation when needed. ● Places—Determining a relocation scheme, if and when needed, is also an issue. While a backup site might be inexpensive, it may also present a high risk if it is located in a less desirable area, or if it is lacking the same protection profile as the original site. Transportation and utilities that match those used at the original site should be acquired for the backup location. ● Things—Essential items such as office supplies, information technology (IT) equipment, and raw materials need to be protected to ensure and sustain individual performance, productivity, and efficiency as well as the continuation of business operations.
Cost vs. benefits	A recovery strategy may be highly effective but include a cost factor that the organization cannot afford. On the other hand, a simple, cost-effective solution may be found if the organization expends more time and effort up front. Goals and cost factors should be carefully weighed and considered to ensure an effective DRP.
Prioritization	When making a recovery decision, business needs should be ranked in order of importance to prioritize recovery efforts. Because business-critical processes are determined during BCP preparation, the DRP can use the same list to identify which processes to recover first. The prioritization list should be widely published so that there are no surprises when disaster strikes. Disasters can bring out the best and the worst in people. If the owner of a critical system finds out during the disaster that their particular system has been rated low priority and they are going to have to wait hours—and possibly even days—to get up and running, it can make a difficult situation nearly intolerable.

Disaster Recovery Priority Levels

Each DRP should define the immediacy and priority of a particular incident to initiate the appropriate level of response.

Priority Level	Description
Short-term	This priority level prompts a rapid response. In most cases, short-term responses are necessary for business-critical processes. For example, in a production facility, if a production line is unavailable, it must be possible for staff to continue receiving orders so that products can be shipped upon availability.
Mid-term	This priority level initiates a quick response. For example, during a flood, four tractor-trailer rigs are damaged. Although these vehicles are necessary for product shipments, the organization has 18 more operational rigs that can deliver manufactured goods.
Long-term	This priority level suspends response efforts for a period of time. For example, an organization may determine that, over time, it will be necessary to renovate the company cafeteria. However, given all the other existing issues that require urgent attention, management decides that the renovation project is not an immediate priority and puts it on hold.
Not required	This priority level defers response efforts indefinitely. For example, an employee basketball court that is used during the lunch hour for recreation is not a critical resource. Because this is an optional activity that does not require a prioritized response assignment, it should not be included in a priority list.

Disaster Recovery Response Approaches

No matter how big or small, each disaster requires an appropriate response approach to mitigate the impact on people, data, and equipment.

Response Approach	Description
Short-term	Some solutions are considered short-term if they represent a stop-gap measure to be replaced in the future. ● Mirrored sites—A mirrored site has all the features and functions of the primary site. Because the mirrored site has the current hardware, software, and data, if the primary site fails, the mirrored site can resume operations with a minimum RTO, often in seconds. The mirrored site is expensive to implement but has the highest level of recovery in the shortest amount of time. Mirrored sites are also called redundant sites or dual data center sites. ● Shared location—In a shared location, the company shares processing capabilities with another company. Because the site is not owned by the company with the disaster, the shared location may not be available when needed. This is also known as a reciprocal site. In either a mirrored site or shared location, the objective is to use the site temporarily and return to normal production as soon as possible.

Response Approach	Description
Long-term	Long-term approaches are useful when a decision is made to return to business as usual. To complete long-term approaches, a substantial investment in time and resources is necessary.
	● Relocation—Relocating to a completely different facility may be necessary if the damage to the primary site is extensive. As a long-term solution, this is beneficial if the new site is compatible with the old site; that is, if it has similar transportation and infrastructure support and the employees collectively agree with the move. Building costs are limited to a new build-out of the existing facility.
	● Rebuilding—Rebuilding the primary site is typically a costly and time-consuming proposition. The old site must be cleared and declared free of environmental issues. Building plans are then created and the local zoning board grants their approval. Once the building is complete, business operations can resume.

Backup Strategies

There are several backup strategies you can choose from, depending on business needs and backup costs.

Backup Strategy	Description
Tape/disk backup	Full backups, incremental backups, and differential backups can all be used to back up tape and disk data. You should choose the method that best suits your needs.
Mirrored backup	With mirrored backups, each write to a disk drive is reproduced on another drive found in another location. The backup storage device is connected via a high-speed data network. When a write is issued to the local disk drive, a separate write is sent to the remote site. Only when both writes are acknowledged by both disk drives will processing continue.
Remote journaling	In disaster recovery, remote journaling is a less expensive backup strategy than a mirrored backup because it only captures the transaction as opposed to all data modifications. Upon the failure of a central site, the latest backup can be restored at the remote site. The journal is used to process transactions that were not in the most recent backup.
Electronic vaulting	In disaster recovery, electronic vaulting helps to transfer backup volumes to an offsite location. After the backup medium is produced, it is copied to a remote site. Should the primary site fail, a copy of the vaulted data is prepared and sent to the remote site for restoration and resumed production.

Certified Information Systems Security Professional (CISSP)®: Third Edition

Data Restoration Strategies

When you need to recover a system using incremental backups, the last full backup is restored, followed by all incremental backups restored in their order of creation. With differential backups, the last full backup and only the last differential backup are restored. This minimizes the number of different restore operations.

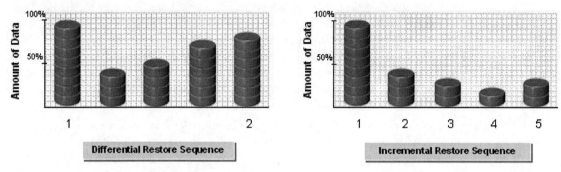

Figure 11-11: *Data restoration strategies.*

Alternate Sites

As part of a DRP, an organization can maintain various types of alternate, or backup, sites that can be used to restore system functioning.

Alternate Site Type	Description
Hot site/mirror site	A *hot site*, or *mirror site* is a fully configured alternate network that can be quickly put online after a disaster. A hot site is an exact duplicate of the primary processing location.
	In most cases, staffing at the hot site will be similar if not identical to the primary site. The viability of a hot site is tested by disconnecting the primary site from the hot site and observing whether the processing switchover is successful. Airline reservation centers, stock brokerages, and clearinghouses require the use of hot sites because they cannot tolerate any extended downtime and need a Recovery Point Objective (RPO) of nearly zero.
	An example of a hot site would be a secondary operations center that is fully staffed and in constant network contact with the primary center under normal conditions.

Lesson 11: Business Continuity and Disaster Recovery Planning **353**

Alternate Site Type	Description
Warm site	A *warm site* is a location that is dormant or performs non-critical functions under normal conditions, but which can be rapidly converted to a key operations site if needed.
	Warm sites are often provided as a service with high investment costs by third-party vendors that own the hardware and operating location. Communications capabilities should match those of the primary site as closely as possible. The viability of a warm site is tested by confirming the successful transportation and installation of software and data from the primary site. The RPO can be days long or up to a week depending on the traveling distance and time required for installation.
	An example of a warm site might be a customer service center that could be quickly converted into a network-maintenance facility, if needed.
Cold site	A *cold site* is a predetermined alternate location where a network can be rebuilt after a disaster.
	A cold site can be a space in a facility with appropriate power, environmental controls, and communications facilities. To use a cold site, an organization should order and install new hardware, transport the data and software to the location, hook up communications, and then begin operation.
	The RPO for a cold site can be up to weeks or months depending on hardware availability and installation speed. Although this is the least expensive alternative, it does present serious implementation problems. There is generally no effective way to test a cold site installation.
	An example of a cold site might be nothing more than a rented warehouse with available power and network hookups, where key equipment could be moved and installed in the event of a disaster.
Portable site	A *portable site* is a mobile site that can be operated anywhere should a disaster occur. It houses computer hardware, networking capabilities, and communications equipment to restore and maintain business operations. It may be located outside the primary site while it is in repair and recovery mode, which minimizes travel for employees who are involved in a disaster.
	For instance, large vans and trailers are often used as portable sites in which mirroring is performed to maintain up-to-date data in installed hardware. When a disaster is imminent, the computers can be relocated to a designated alternate location.
	In most cases, portable sites only support extremely critical applications. The downside is the high cost factor of acquiring and maintaining the vans and trailers, as well as the limited recovery capability presented by this solution.

ACTIVITY 11-3
Discussing DRP Fundamentals

Scenario:

In this activity, you will discuss the fundamental elements of a DRP so you and your organization can effectively respond to a calamitous event.

1. **Your company has implemented a BCP and charged your team with responsibility for the DRP for your organization. What are some examples of items that you will need to include in your organization's DRP?**

2. **During the DRP development, you took the list of critical business processes that were itemized for your company's BCP and ranked them in order of business need. Which disaster recovery factor is this an example of?**

3. **You have met with the BCP/DCP team and have discussed several backup strategies that will be utilized in the event of a disaster. The advisory committee has decided that, in an effort to protect company data, you will be transferring backup volumes to an offsite location. In the event of an emergency, a copy of this saved data will be prepared and sent to the remote site so that it can be restored. Which backup strategy is this an example of?**

4. **Your company's main trunk phone line goes down in an electrical storm. Customers cannot call and place orders. What priority level would you assign this?**

    a) Short-term

    b) Mid-term

    c) Long-term

    d) Not required

5. **How might you deal with the loss of the phone line?**

6. **The storm damaged pavement in the employee parking lot. There is still adequate parking, but some employees may have a longer walk to the building until the area is re-paved. How would you prioritize this issue?**

   a) Short-term

   b) Mid-term

   c) Long-term

   d) Not required

7. **How would you deal with the parking lot issue?**

TOPIC D
Disaster Recovery Plan Implementation

Now that you are familiar with the various aspects and strategies of a DRP, you need to determine the effectiveness of your plan for your organization. In this topic, you will identify team responsibilities, process requirements, and testing techniques for implementing an effective DRP.

The development of a DRP is key to allowing your organization to rebound after an influential catastrophe. However, even the best plans are sometimes not enough to ensure recovery. Functional testing is required to validate your strategies. Thoroughly testing your DRP will verify its credibility for implementation and help you restore operations and revitalize your organization's business environment in the face of a disaster.

Recovery Team

Definition:

The *recovery team* is a group of designated individuals who implement recovery procedures and control recovery operations in the event of an internal or external disruption to critical business processes. The recovery team provides immediate response in an emergency and restores critical business processes to their normal operating capacity, at the remote or recovery site, once key services and information systems are back online. The team primarily focuses on meeting the RTO without exceeding the MTD. Team members might include systems managers, systems administrators, security administrators, facilities specialists, communications specialists, personnel staff, and legal representatives.

Example:

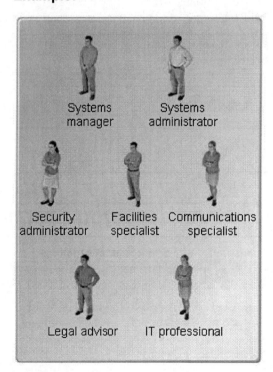

Figure 11-12: The recovery team.

Salvage Team

Definition:

The *salvage team* is a group of designated individuals who restore the primary site to its normal operating environment. The salvage team cleans, repairs, salvages, and assesses the viability of the primary business-processing infrastructure once the disaster is over. To restore operations at the original site, team members should create a restoration plan, seek budget approval, and then, with the permission of senior management, begin salvage and restoration activities.

Example:

Figure 11-13: *The salvage team.*

Disaster Recovery Evaluation and Maintenance

Your DRP development process should include an evaluation phase to ensure its effectiveness. You can use evaluation techniques similar to those used to evaluate a BCP. After the plan has been completed, you should review it at least yearly and make any maintenance-level changes required based on the results of the review as well as the results of periodic testing.

Disaster Recovery Testing

Every DRP should be tested periodically as part of its implementation.

DRP Testing Method	Purpose
Checklist and desktop	With a checklist or desktop test, a team of experts evaluates the DRP to verify its validity and identify gaps. While this is an inexpensive testing option, it is not as thorough as other tests, like walkthroughs or simulations.
Offsite restoration	This testing method involves transporting software, data, and personnel to an offsite location, such as a warm site, and installing and operating the systems as if a disaster has occurred. Therefore, this method effectively tests the plan's viability and identifies areas for improvement.
Mirrored site cutover	The easiest way to test DRP processes is to cut over from the primary site to the hot, or mirror, site and operate from the hot site. This is the ultimate test of success that measures the recovery team's ability and the procedures used to sustain operations at the secondary location.

The Disaster Recovery Process

The disaster recovery process includes several steps to properly resume business operations after a disruptive event.

Disaster Recovery Step	Description
Begin emergency operations	The DRP should contain detailed steps regarding specific emergency services. An incident manager should be appointed to assume control of the situation and ensure personnel safety.
Notify stakeholders	Stakeholders should be informed of a business-critical disaster. They consist of senior management, board members, investors, clients, suppliers, and employees.
Assess damage	A damage assessment should be conducted to determine the extent of incurred facility damages, to identify the cause of the disaster if it is unclear, and to estimate the amount of expected down time. This assessment can also determine the appropriate response strategy. For instance, a full recovery to a remote site may not be warranted if damage is limited to parts of the business that do not threaten operational functioning or survival.
Assess facility	It is necessary to assess the current facility's ability to sustain the function of being the primary location of operation. If the facility has been adversely affected and has suffered significant losses, relocating to an alternate site may be the best option.

ACTIVITY 11-4
Discussing DRP Implementation

Scenario:

In this activity, you will discuss team responsibilities, process requirements, and testing techniques for implementing an effective DRP so you can restore operations and revitalize your organization's business environment in the face of a disaster.

1. After a flood at your business, you need someone to respond immediately to ensure everyone's safety and get the business operating at your remote site. What team will you send in?

2. In addition to alerting the team, what other actions should you take to respond to this disaster?

3. The business is operating again. Now you need someone to assess the water damage to carpeting and floors, what it will cost to replace them, and to oversee the restoration. What team will you send in?

4. The DRP process has been evaluated. The advisory committee has decided that, to complete the validation of the DRP, an offsite test will be conducted, including evaluations of software, data, and personnel. At this warm site, operations will proceed as if a disaster has occurred, and will test the DRP and pinpoint areas needing improvement. Which disaster recovery testing method is this an example of?

5. What disaster recovery evaluation method could you implement to fully validate that the DRP will enable you to sustain operations in the event of a real disaster?

Lesson 11 Follow-up

In this lesson, you applied BCP and DRP to protect your business in the event of a minor disruption or complete natural disaster. Planning your responses to natural or man-made disasters will help you maintain critical business processes and ensure that your business continues to operate in the face of these types of events.

1. **Have you ever experienced a business disruption based on any of the event categories in this lesson? Was it a natural- or human-caused event?**

2. **How did you and your organization handle the business disruption?**

12 | Legal, Regulations, Compliance, and Investigations

Lesson Time: 2 hour(s)

Lesson Objectives:

In this lesson, you will identify legal issues, regulations, compliance standards, and investigation practices relating to information systems security.

You will:

● Identify how to comply with laws and regulations that pertain to your work as a computer information security professional.

● Identify proper computer crime incident response processes and techniques.

Introduction

During business continuity planning, you analyzed the impact a disaster would have on your organization. With reasonable assurance that operations will continue in the event of a disaster, you can now focus on ensuring that business functions will continue when faced with a legal, regulatory, or investigative battle. In this lesson, you will identify legal issues, regulations, compliance standards, and investigation practices relating to information systems security.

If your organization experiences a criminal attack, you need to be aware of the relevant laws, regulatory standards, and compliance protocols, as well as how to conduct proper investigations, in order to respond quickly, legally, and effectively. Analyzing and identifying these rules and principles will help you to ensure that your organization successfully handles, from a legal and investigative perspective, an attack from any source.

 The information included in this lesson is not legal advice but is based on generally accepted legal principles and published guidelines.

This lesson supports content found in the Legal, Regulations, Investigations, and Compliance domain of the CISSP® certification.

TOPIC A

Computer Crime Laws and Regulations

To completely protect your organization, it is critical to address how computer crimes impact your company's bottom line. The first step is to understand the legal landscape that surrounds you and how it affects you in your capacity as an information systems security professional. In this topic, you will identify how to comply with laws and regulations that pertain to your work as a computer information security professional.

It is no surprise to find that the frequency and severity of computer crimes continues to rise. While evaluating your information systems, you realize the business impact that computer crimes can have on your organization's productivity and finances. It is difficult to effectively function without fully understanding the legal constraints that pertain to you and your obligations under the laws. To properly protect your organization against crimes, and ensure that employees abide by all relevant laws and regulations, you need to determine what computer crime laws and regulations apply to computer offenses.

Common Law

Definition:

Common law is a set of unwritten but well-understood and normally accepted principles of justice. Many legal systems in the Western world are based on the principle of common law. Common law is often determined by court decisions or on decisions made by a sovereign. Each common law affects all future decisions. If previous decisions do not pertain to a particular case, a judge has the authority to create a new law, known as a *precedent*. Common law systems are most often seen in countries that originated with British law, including the United States, the United Kingdom, Canada, and former colonies of the British Empire.

Example: Common Law Marriage

Throughout history, common law marriage has been recognized in many countries. In the U.S., approximately 13 states still recognize a couple as being legally married under common law, even in the absence of a marriage license or marriage ceremony, if they meet certain requirements; however, the specific requirements vary from state to state.

The Prudent Person Rule

Historically known as the prudent or reasonable man rule, the *prudent person rule* is a standard or principle used in common law that suggests that adequate protection is the protection that a prudent man would use under normal circumstances. For example, the prudent person standard requires that funds may be invested only in securities by a fiduciary entrusted with these funds. This person would only be interested in investing his or her capital if he or she was to receive a good return of income, and if his or her capital would be preserved in the meantime.

Statutory Law

Definition:

Statutory law, or *statute law*, is written law comprised of *statutes* passed by federal, state, and local legislatures defining day-to-day laws and how bodies of government function. Statutory law is interpreted by the judiciary and often includes a process known as *codification*, wherein laws, rules, and regulations are documented and grouped by subject.

Statutory laws come in two varieties: criminal and civil. *Criminal law* governs individual conduct that violates government laws enacted for public or societal protection. *Civil law* governs a wrong committed against a business or individual that results in damage or loss to that business or individual.

Example: Right Against Self-Incrimination

The 5th Amendment to the U.S. Constitution grants individuals the right to refuse to answer a question or make a statement that would establish if they committed a crime or were involved in criminal activity. This is known as the right against self-incrimination.

Types of Statutory Offenses

There are two types of statutory offenses in the U.S. legal system.

Statutory Offense Type	Prosecution and Penalty Characteristics
Criminal	A criminal act is one that is considered to be an offense against society as a whole, and as such has been prohibited by law. Criminal offenses may or may not have specific victims. An example of a criminal statutory offense could be a hacker breaking into a computer system who commits a crime based on federal and state laws. The case is brought by the local district attorney and is tried in local courts. The penalty is often a fine, jail time, or both. Guilt in a criminal case is determined by a high standard such as **"beyond a reasonable doubt."**
Civil	Civil offenses recognize that damage has been done to one party by another party. The lawsuit is brought by the damaged party and the damage must be proven in court. The penalties in civil law cases are fines, court costs, and attorney fees. Guilt in a civil case may be determined by a lower standard such as by **"preponderance of the evidence."** For example, if a group of individuals has been damaged by their company inadvertently leaking personal information, there might be no violation of law, but they might choose to sue the company to recover damages under civil law. Civil law uses *tort law* to identify what legal harm constitutes and to create the means for recovering damages in the case of intentional malicious acts or accidents.

Administrative Law

Definition:

Administrative law, or *regulatory law,* is the law set by regulatory agencies. In the United States, the executive branch oversees administrative law, regulatory agencies execute it, and the judicial branch interprets it. Once laws are passed expressing the will of the legislature, it is the job of the executive branch to develop appropriate regulations and guidelines for organizations to follow.

If the regulations are violated, the regulatory agency can bring a suit against the violator in an administrative law court. The administrative law judge weighs the presented evidence and rules for the party who presents sufficient evidence to sway the judge.

Example: OSHA Regulatory Law

An Act of Congress was used to create the Occupational Safety and Health Administration (OSHA) and provide it a mandate to oversee and enforce workplace safety. OSHA, which is an executive branch department, created and issued appropriate guidelines for safety-related issues, such as specific guidelines for dealing with biohazards.

Intellectual Property Law

Intellectual property law protects the rights of ownership of ideas, trademarks, patents, and copyrights, including the owners' right to transfer intellectual property and receive compensation for the transfer.

Intellectual Property Law	Description
Patent	A *patent* is a legal protection provided to unique inventions. The patent protects the item's creator from competition for a given period of time. Patent protection is considered to be very strong, but at the same time, it is the responsibility of patent owners to protect their patents. In the United States, patents must be filed within one year of the first production of the patented item. Patents last for 20 years in the United States. Once the patent has expired, the patent enters the public domain.
Trademark	A *trademark* is a design or phrase used to identify unique products or services. In the U.S., a trademark lasts for 10 years and may be renewed for an additional 10-year period by filing an affidavit of use. Coca Cola® is a registered trademark along with its traditional bottle shape. The ® is a registered trademark while ™ is an unregistered trademark.
Copyright	A *copyright* protects an original artistic work, such as one by an author or musician. Copyright protection is not as strong as patent protection but the length of protection is much greater. The lifetime of the copyright varies. Normal copyrights exist for 70 years past the death of the creator. Those items copyrighted by corporations, or where the identity of the original author is hidden, last for 95 years after publication, or 120 years after the first use, whichever comes first.

Intellectual Property Law	Description
Trade secret	A *trade secret* is an item that requires protection that, if lost, would severely damage the business. In order to be provided legal protection, the trade secret must be properly secured and protected. The formula for the spices used by a fried chicken company might be considered a trade secret. It is the responsibility of the organization to protect their own trade secrets. Non-disclosure agreements are a common method to enforce a trade secret.
Licensing	To use a creator's protected materials, users are generally required to obtain *licensing*. Software manufacturers protect their products by mandating and issuing licensed copies for consumer purchase. Violating the licensing provision may result in civil or criminal charges.

International Protection from WIPO

In other parts of the world, intellectual property protection is provided by general principle agreements among various countries and controlled through the World Intellectual Property Organization (WIPO). WIPO is a specialized organization under the United Nations.

International protection of intellectual property varies due to different legal systems and interpretation of laws in those jurisdictions. For example, under WIPO, a patent must be obtained before the patented product is used in commerce. There is no one-year grace period as found in the U.S. The general principle concerns first to file rather than first to invent.

For more information on WIPO, visit **www.wipo.int**.

Information Privacy Law

Information privacy law protects the information of private individuals from malicious disclosure or unintentional misuse. With the increased ability to collect and store personally identifying information (PII) there has grown a need to try to protect this data.

 Privacy laws are becoming more common around the world and it will be important for the CISSP candidate to be familiar with some of the more common privacy laws. Privacy laws are a mixture of state common law, federal and state statutes, and constitutional law.

Information Privacy Law Act	Description
Privacy Act of 1974	The *Privacy Act of 1974* was mandated in response to the abuse of privacy during the Nixon administration. It protects the privacy of individual information held by the U.S. government. It applies to all personal information, provides for restrictions on individual access, and enforces penalties for unauthorized disclosure.
FERPA	The *Family Educational Rights and Privacy Act (FERPA)* was passed in the same session of Congress as the Privacy Act of 1974. This law protects the privacy of educational information held in any federally funded institution of higher learning. After FERPA was passed, the practice of mailing grade reports from a university or college to a student's parents was prohibited.

Information Privacy Law Act	Description
ECPA	The *Electronic Communications Privacy Act (ECPA)* of 1986 made it a crime to snoop into employee activities while using electronic communications devices unless the employees were notified in advance that the monitoring might take place. It also enforced the requirement for legal authorization of wiretaps and other government monitoring practices.
HIPAA	The *Health Insurance Portability and Accountability Act (HIPAA)* of 1996 was originally intended to protect people with health insurance when they transferred from one company to the another. In 2003, legislation was written to modify HIPAA and add a privacy component. The privacy component now protects a class of information called Protected Health Information (PHI). PHI is any information that can identify a particular patient and includes a patient's medical record or payment history.
GLBA	The *Gramm-Leach-Bliley Act (GLBA)* of 1999 protects the privacy of an individual's financial information that is held by financial institutions and others such as tax preparation companies. A privacy standard was set and rules were created to safeguard the information and provide penalties in the event of a violation.
COPPA	The *Children's Online Privacy Protection Act (COPPA)* of 1998 was written to protect the online privacy of children. Restrictions provided by COPPA included the right to opt out of any information sent by a provider, to limit the amount and type of information collected from children, and to require parental consent for any information provided to children. COPPA implementation, however, has no real way of controlling childrens' access because there is no true method of identifying any user consistently when accessing the Internet.
USA PATRIOT Act	In response to the attacks of September 11, 2001, U.S. Congress passed the *Uniting and Strengthening America by Providing Appropriate Tools Required to Intercept and Obstruct Terrorism (PATRIOT) Act* of 2001. This legislation increased the governmental ability to wiretap and control financial transactions used to fund terrorism. From an information security perspective, the government could collect information from the Internet using a blanket subpoena.
SOX Act	After the accounting scandals and the failures of many large companies in the early 2000s, the *Sarbanes-Oxley (SOX* or *Sarbox) Act* of 2002 was passed to help control how corporations report about and audit themselves. One of the major record-keeping requirements of SOX is the need to keep long-term email, voicemail, and instant messaging records in corporations.

International Protection from EU Privacy Laws

The European Union (EU) provides many different, individual privacy protections regarding personal data processing. The principle EU publication covering privacy, known as Directive 95/46/EC, can be found at **www.cdt.org/privacy/eudirective/EU_Directive_.html**.

Computer Crime Law

Early on, the U.S. government's main focus of protection was the area of privacy. Eventually, the use of online systems and the advent of the hacker lead to computer crime law legislation.

Computer Crime Law Act	Description
CFAA	The *Computer Fraud and Abuse Act (CFAA)* of 1984 was passed to protect government systems from illegal access or from exceeding access permissions. It was amended in 1994, in 1996, and in 2001. The amendments evolved from new concerns that had developed over the intervening time period and extended coverage to new types of attacks. Final coverage addresses computers in interstate commerce. Activities that are prohibited include retrieving information without authorization, trafficking passwords, sending viruses or worms to infect computers, and so on.
CSA	The *Computer Security Act (CSA)* of 1987 was enacted when the federal legislature recognized that the government was not doing enough to protect computer systems. Key requirements of CSA were to fulfill training needs and plan developments for information and systems security. CSA was replaced by FISMA.
NIIPA	As threats to computer security expanded, the passage of the *National Information Infrastructure Protection Act (NIIPA)* in 1996 targeted some of these new threats, creating legal remedies for hacking, stealing trade secrets, and damaging systems and information. In particular, it targeted Internet infrastructure security.
FISMA	The *Federal Information Security Management Act (FISMA)* of 2002 was passed to remedy the evolutionary nature of information systems security in the federal government. Some of the act's key provisions require organizations to: <ul><li>Define the boundaries of a system to be protected and then identify the types of information found within that system.</li><li>Document system information and perform a risk assessment to identify areas requiring additional protection.</li><li>Protect systems using an identified set of controls and certify systems before use. An operating approval is issued upon certification.</li><li>Continuously monitor systems for proper operation.</li></ul>

Federal Sentencing Guidelines

Violators of the acts protecting government information systems are subject to federal sentencing guidelines set forth by the U.S. Sentencing Commission. These guidelines specify recommended sentences. Rather than allow individual judges to set sentences for these types of crimes, specific sentence limits are provided to the judge. Additionally, the sentencing guidelines mandate that criminals have an opportunity to be informed of the risks involved in crimes against federal systems.

The federal sentencing guidelines can be seen in full-text form at **www.ussc.gov**.

Compliance

Compliance refers to the awareness of and adherence to relevant laws and regulations that are set forth by and apply to a particular corporation, public agency, or organizational entity. Compliance requirements evolve with the legal landscape. With the recent downfall of large corporations in the U.S., laws like Sarbox, HIPAA, and GLBA place an organization's burden of compliance at the top tier of management.

Security professionals are often not fully versed in compliance requirements. They should consult with legal department heads and representatives to determine if any new requirements exist and then determine the right course of action to properly comply with the changes.

Liability

Definition:

Liability is a legal responsibility for any damage caused by one individual or company to another. Organizations must protect themselves from legal liability by complying with applicable laws and regulations, by following the prudent person rule when making decisions, and by exercising due diligence, also known as due care. The legal concept of *due diligence* or *due care* establishes the generally recognized expectations of behavior that companies or entities in a given industry must adhere to when performing normal business functions.

Example: Liability and Due Diligence

A company that wants to acquire another company must use due diligence to prove that they looked into the company's financial and business status to ensure action in the interest of protecting their shareholders. If the company's stock fell after the acquisition and shareholders could demonstrate that the company had not performed proper due diligence prior to the purchase, it is possible that the shareholders could successfully sue for financial damages in civil court. In the computer realm, a company might be held liable for an employee's loss of personal information if the company cannot demonstrate that it practiced due care while responding to a security breach.

Internal Audits

An organization's audit department is an important ally in the detection of computer crimes. Internal audit departments review processes, logs, and transactions to ensure compliance with generally accepted principles of operational and regulatory requirements. Organizations like banks, savings and loans, and security traders are required to comply with federal, state, and local laws and regulations. An important function of the audit department is to verify compliance.

External Audits

Certain enterprises are also required to submit to an audit by an external auditing organization. The purpose of the external audit is to again validate and verify compliance and provide additional oversight. Recently, the use of external auditors associated with the accounting firms used by the organization has caused insurmountable problems. The problems could be traced back to a lack of separation of duty. Consequently, regulations have been devised that enforce the use of external auditors not directly affiliated with the accounting firm used by a particular organization.

Foundation Documents

Whether internal or external, the audit process is supported by a set of guidelines provided by federal and state regulators. The audit guidelines are often in checklist form. Auditors use these checklists to verify compliance to the stated requirements.

Best Practices

The audit process is typically accompanied by a set of best practices. *Best practices* are commonly accepted activities related to business operations.

Best practices are often documented in industry publications and books related to the operation of networks, computers, auditing, and the like. Hardware and software vendors also provide best practice guidance to their customers on websites or in other forms of documentation.

Best practices are often the foundation of the concept of the prudent person rule. If everyone does it, it must be prudent.

Governmental Oversight Resources

Federal and state governments provide documentation to organizations to help ensure systems protection as well as legal ramifications if adequate protection is not supplied. The National Institute for Science and Technology (NIST) created a document that contains an exhaustive list of government publications dealing with information technology (IT) security.

The Department of Defense (DoD) directives are another source of guidance. Under that umbrella, there are documents from the Director of Central Intelligence (DCI), the National Security Agency (NSA), and others.

 For more information on government-enforced IT security, visit **http://csrc.nist.gov/publications/CSD_DocsGuide.pdf**.

 For more information on DoD issuances, visit **www.dtic.mil/whs/directives**.

ACTIVITY 12-1
Discussing Computer Crime Laws and Regulations

Scenario:

In this activity, you will discuss how to comply with laws and regulations that pertain to your work as a computer information security professional.

1. **In the case of common law, if a prior decision does not adhere to a certain case, a judge can create which type of new law?**

   a) Procedure

   b) Precedent

   c) Tort

   d) Codification

2. **Which one of the following types of law is passed by federal, state, and local legislatures?**

   a) Administrative law

   b) Common law

   c) Intellectual property law

   d) Statutory law

3. **Which one of the following types of laws defines what constitutes legal harm and creates means for damage recovery from intentional malicious acts or accidents?**

   a) Administrative law

   b) Codification

   c) Tort law

   d) Criminal law

4. **How many types of statutory offenses are known in the U.S. legal system? What are some prosecution and penalty characteristics of these offenses?**

5. **Which branch of the U.S. government is responsible for developing appropriate regulations and guidelines, within the law, for businesses to adhere to?**

   a) Executive branch

   b) Legislative branch

   c) Judicial branch

6. **What is the appropriate description for each intellectual property law?**

   ___ Patent

   ___ Trademark

   ___ Copyright

   ___ Trade secret

   ___ Licensing

   ___ Privacy

   a. Legal protection of creator's materials that are usually issued in copies for purchase.

   b. Legal protection of artistic work that lasts for 70 years past the death of the creator.

   c. Legal protection or secrecy of an individual's information maintained by a legal principle.

   d. Legal protection of an item that, if lost, would severely damage the business and must be properly secured and protected.

   e. Legal protection of a phrase or design used to identity a product that lasts for 10 years but can be renewed using an affidavit.

   f. Legal protection of an invention that lasts for 20 years.

7. **What is the appropriate description for each information privacy law?**

   ___ Privacy Act of 1974

   ___ FERPA

   ___ ECPA

   ___ HIPAA

   a. Protects the privacy of educational information held in any federally funded institution of higher learning.

   b. Protects the privacy of any health insurance information that can identify a patient, including medical records or payment history.

   c. Protects the privacy of employee activities during the use of electronic communications devices unless employees are notified in advance that monitoring will be taking place.

   d. Protects the privacy of individual information held by the U.S. government.

8. **What is the appropriate description for each additional information privacy law?**

___	GLBA	a.	The requirement of large corporations to keep long-term records of email, voicemail, and instant messaging to control how the corporations report about and audit themselves.
___	COPPA	b.	Protects the privacy of children online, requiring parent consent for any information collected from children or provided to children over the Internet.
___	USA PATRIOT Act	c.	Protects the privacy of an individual's information held by financial institutions or tax preparation companies.
___	SOX Act	d.	Allows the government to take additional measures, such as wiretaps and the control of financial information, to combat terrorism.

9. **Which one of the following computer crime laws is in effect to fulfill training needs and plan developments for information and systems security?**

   a) CFAA

   b) CSA

   c) NIIPA

   d) FISMA

10. **Which one of the following computer crime laws particularly targets Internet infrastructure security?**

    a) CFAA

    b) CSA

    c) NIIPA

    d) FISMA

11. **True or False? Understanding and interpreting compliance laws is the responsibility of the security professional in an organization.**

    ___ True

    ___ False

12. **Which one or more of the following are terms for the general expectation of company behavior while performing normal business functions?**

    a) Liability

    b) Compliance

    c) Due care

    d) Due diligence

13. **What are some examples of tasks that internal and external audit departments perform?**

_____

TOPIC B
Computer Crime Incident Response

You have identified how to comply with laws and regulations that pertain to your work as a computer information security professional. Implementing computer laws and using the legal resources available to you to protect your organization's information systems provides you with a solid foundation if you suspect a computer crime has occurred. Next, it is time to consider how you would react if you were directly affected by a computer-related crime. In this topic, you will identify proper computer crime incident response processes and techniques.

The reliability of the evidence collected during an investigation is essential to the success of any future legal proceeding. The intangibility of computer crimes makes the burden of evidence all the more critical. To ensure that your evidence is reliable and admissible in a court of law, you must understand how to appropriately perform investigations and collect substantial proof when incidents of computer crime arise.

Computer Crime

Definition:

A *computer crime* is a criminal act that involves using a computer as the source or target, instead of an individual. It can involve stealing restricted information by hacking into a system, compromising national security, perpetrating fraud, conducting illegal activity, or spreading malicious code. It may be committed via the Internet or a private network.

Example:

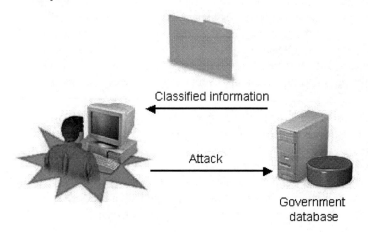

Classified information

Attack

Government database

Figure 12-1: A computer crime.

Examples of typical computer crimes include unauthorized access to a computer or network, distributing illegal information via a computer network, and stealing classified information stored on a computer. Phishing and other similar social engineering attacks, if they involve illegal activity, can be categorized as computer crimes.

Computer Crime, Liability, and the Prudent Person Rule

Successful computer crimes may exist in areas where adequate security protections, as determined by the prudent person standard, are not in use. For example, in a high-crime area, a prudent man would ensure that doors and windows are secure before leaving home, otherwise a computer might be stolen. A prudent person would also use virus protection and firewall protection on a computer attached to the Internet.

In cases where crimes are committed and the prudent person rule is not employed, a liability may arise. For example, when magnetic tapes are transported and stolen, it is commonly known that the contained information has been leaked to the public. A prudent person would encrypt the data on the magnetic tape to protect it. If the data is not encrypted, therefore releasing personal information, the holder of the information is liable for any damages incurred to those individuals affected by the leak.

While the concept of liability does not weigh on the facts of a crime and associated legal procedures, it does weigh on the impact to the organization when a crime is committed.

The Computer Criminal Incident Response Process

There are multiple phases in the criminal incident response process, some of which are unique.

Criminal Incident Response Phase	Description
Response capability	Organizations will often form a computer crime or incident response team. These individuals are trained in the proper collection and preservation techniques for computer crime response.
Incident handling	The first order of business in incident response is to determine the events that actually occurred. The incident response team assesses whether a crime or incident actually happened and to what extent a system or process was damaged.
Triage	*Triage* is a medical term that indicates the priority of patient treatment. In an emergency room, the most severe cases are seen first. In a computer crime-related scenario, once the team has analyzed the situation and determined the incidents, they implement a triage approach by responding to the situation based on criticality. If multiple events are occurring, the most serious event will be handled first and the remaining events will be intercepted based on risk priority.
Investigative	When the response team has identified the problem, the investigative process begins. The investigation can be performed by internal team members. The risk of an internal investigation is that the internal team may not be trained sufficiently and may damage or not collect evidence that is present. An organization may request the services of consultants who are highly skilled at computer crime and incident investigations. These individuals are expensive in terms of cost, but do not overlook evidence because of their advanced training and experience.
	Local law enforcement is another investigative source. Police departments have become more skilled at computer crime investigations and often have access to resources above and beyond the corporation or consulting organization. However, there are a few liabilities with police investigations. With internal investigators or consultants, the priority of action is determined by the organization. Police personnel are often overburdened. Their priorities are primarily based on community need, not company need. They are also subject to restrictions set forth by the 4th Amendment and other evidence-gathering laws.

Criminal Incident Response Phase	Description
Containment	If possible, even before the investigation begins, it is necessary to secure the scene. No one should approach computers, touch keyboards, nor turn on or off any device. Doing so may damage evidence. You should also not disconnect any wires, remove any peripheral devices, or do anything to change configurations or shut down operating systems. Trained investigators understand how to capture evidence from systems without compromising the system security or damaging evidence.
Analysis and tracking	Once evidence has been gathered, the forensic analysts begin examining the facts and determining what does or does not constitute substantial proof. As with all evidence, the chain of custody must be maintained and the evidence must be tracked to ensure that it remains useful. Disk drives often need to be duplicated before analysis. Common backup methods are not sufficient to protect evidence. A forensic copy is required, which reproduces all bits from all areas of a disk drive to a second drive. An actual full duplication of the original drive is obtained.
Recovery	The next step is to recover the system. After obtaining the drive's forensic copy, the original system can be returned to operating condition. This may require restoring backup files, reprocessing transactions, and auditing the system to discover any additional problems.
Repair	If a system has been damaged, it may be necessary to repair the problem. Replacing damaged components or systems helps to preserve the evidence of a crime.
Debriefing and feedback	Once the recovery is complete, the team should tell management about the event, report on the executed activities, and suggest the best course of action to reduce the likelihood of repetitive incidents. There may also be a disclosure requirement. Some crimes must be disclosed to regulatory bodies and law enforcement, which is a statutory requirement that cannot be overlooked. Failure to disclose this type of information is also considered a crime.

The Evidence Life Cycle

The evidence life cycle involves the gathering of evidence and the process of application. A piece of evidence can potentially go through these steps:

1. Discovery and recognition
2. Protection
3. Recording
4. Collection
5. Identification
6. Storage and preservation
7. Transportation
8. Presentation in court
9. Return to victim or owner

Evidence Collection Techniques

Once a crime has been committed, if evidence is uncovered, it must be secured and properly recorded and collected. Collecting evidence about cybercrimes requires special training and collection methods that differ from physical crimes. This task is best left to professionals who have been trained in the proper practices. Novices can often damage or remove all traces of evidence if they approach evidence gathering the wrong way. Trained investigators know that everything is evidence. They are cautious and careful about what they collect and how they collect it.

Evidence Types

Each type of evidence is important in a criminal investigation, because any piece of evidence may have a enormous impact on the outcome of the case.

Evidence Type	Description
Best	*Best evidence* is required to be admissible in a court of law. Any copies of the evidence are not admissible if the original exists.
Secondary	*Secondary evidence* is a copy of an original document. This is not as admissible in court as best evidence.
Direct	*Direct evidence* is received from the testimony of an individual who observed the crime or activity. Furthermore, it can be evidence that clearly indicates that the crime was committed and proves the case on its own merits.
Conclusive	*Conclusive evidence* is permanent evidence that cannot be disputed. In a court of law, conclusive evidence overrides all other types of evidence.
Opinion	*Opinion evidence* is characterized into the following types: • Expert: Involves stating an opinion based upon facts and expertise. • Non-expert: Involves stating an opinion only based upon fact.
Corroborative	*Corroborative evidence* is gathered from multiple sources that can support other types of evidence in a court of law.
Circumstantial	*Circumstantial evidence* is gathered from multiple sources to infer a conclusion in a court of law.
Hearsay	*Hearsay evidence* is presented by an individual who was not a direct observer but who heard, or received word, about the event from others. Computer records are considered hearsay because they cannot directly testify. A judge decides if computer records can be used in court depending on the reliability of the evidence.
Demonstrative	*Demonstrative evidence* is used to demonstrate or explain events. The use of a model to explain how a computer crime was committed is considered demonstrative evidence.

Chain of Evidence

Definition:

The *chain of evidence* is the record of evidence history from collection, to presentation in court, to return or disposal. In security terms, the chain of evidence is used as a legal control to provide for the accountability and integrity of evidence. Physical evidence is often bagged and sealed to protect it, if it is small enough.

The record should contain information about the evidence, such as the description, dimensions, markings, and serial numbers, who obtained the evidence, what the evidence is, when and where the evidence was obtained, who secured the evidence, and who had possession of the evidence.

The improper handling of evidence or the destruction of the chain of custody information may lead to the inadmissibility of the evidence in court.

Example:

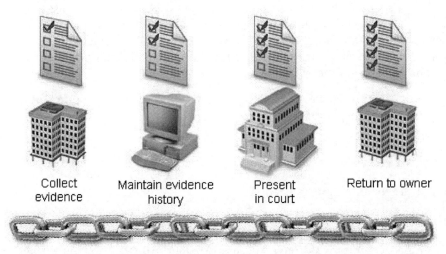

| Collect evidence | Maintain evidence history | Present in court | Return to owner |

Figure 12-2: The chain of evidence.

Example: Computer Removal

When computer crimes are reported, one of the first response activities is removing computers from the crime location. They are tagged with a chain of custody record to begin the process of making the evidence secure for future presentation in court.

The Five Common Rules of Evidence

For evidence to be admissible in court, certain rules must be followed. However, the rules of evidence are not consistent among countries or even among various court systems in the United States. There are five common rules that govern the admissibility of evidence in both criminal and civil court proceedings.

Common Rule of Evidence	Description
Reliable	The evidence presented is consistent and can lead to a common conclusion.
Preserved	The chain of custody records help with preservation and identification.

Common Rule of Evidence	Description
Relevant	The evidence must pertain to the case at hand.
Properly identified	The chain of custody records help with preservation and identification.
Legally permissible	Determined by the judge and the rules of evidence of a particular court.

 For more information regarding U.S. Federal Rules of Evidence, visit **www.law.cornell.edu/ rules/fre/**

Admissibility Considerations

For evidence to be used, it must be collected in legal ways. If law enforcement agencies are involved in gathering evidence, the collection must not violate the 4th Amendment to the U.S. Constitution. Illegal search and seizure is not allowed. If evidence is gathered internally, the 4th Amendment does not apply, but the court must be assured that the collection practices safeguard the accuracy and integrity of the evidence.

The courts prefer original documents. However, if an original document has been destroyed or damaged, or cannot be obtained for legal reasons, the court may admit copies of documents.

If a company uses monitoring to collect evidence on their employees, the provisions of the Electronic Communications Privacy Act (ECPA) apply. Employees must be notified in advance of the monitoring practice and agree in writing to the monitoring. ECPA violations can result in criminal prosecution of the monitoring organization.

Log files are often the foundation of electronic evidence. The admissibility of log files is dependent upon their protection from modification. A simple way to ensure that protection is to write the log files to restricted volumes with limited access. Another method is to create a hash of the log files to prove that they have not been altered. Additionally, log files must be evaluated and reviewed periodically to be used as evidence. Log files that have not been audited and verified will be excluded from the court.

Surveillance Techniques

Many different techniques can be used for surveillance depending on the situation.

Surveillance Technique	Description
Protocol analyzers	*Protocol analyzers*, or *sniffers*, are used to intercept and record computer network traffic. They can gather all information passed through a network, or selectively record certain types of transactions based on the address of the devices in question or the protocols and applications used. These records may be used as indirect evidence in an investigation. Sniffer monitoring is subject to ECPA guidelines.

Surveillance Technique	Description
CCTV	Closed-circuit television (CCTV) can be placed in strategic locations in an organization to record the movement or actions of employees. The captured information may be stored on videotape or on a computer system for later analysis in a criminal investigation. In some cases, the videotape may record the key strokes of a suspected computer criminal to convey the actual details of the crime that was committed. Sufficient storage space and/or tapes are required to house the information for a long period of time.
Wiretaps	Wiretaps are also subject to ECPA, even if done by the company. Law enforcement wiretaps require a subpoena.
Security personnel	The visibility of security guards often serves as an important source of surveillance, as they can act as a deterrent. They can monitor and see what is happening, alert management to certain situations, and report on observations of potential criminal incidents.

Surveillance Law Violations

Legal restrictions apply to surveillance practices. ECPA limits the monitoring and recording of conversations. The 4th Amendment restricts illegal searches and seizures. State and local laws may also add restrictions based on privacy. In all cases, an expectation of privacy may limit what can be collected using surveillance methods.

Search and Seizure

Organizations may be able to collect evidence within the boundaries of their buildings. The corporate legal department should be consulted as to the limits of company authority. Newly hired employees should be informed of the limits of the expectation of privacy within the company. They should sign a statement of acceptance of company surveillance policies and acknowledge the limits on their privacy while at the workplace.

Law Enforcement Searches

When law enforcement responds to a criminal act, they are restricted by the laws in the jurisdiction. They cannot violate the law in gathering evidence. Should they violate the law, the evidence they gather may be excluded from the ensuing court case, and other evidence gathered based on the illegally obtained evidence may also be excluded.

Fruit of the poisonous tree is the legal doctrine established to deter law enforcement from employing illegal practices when collecting criminal evidence. The concept of the doctrine derives from the theory that any information gained from a tainted evidence source is likewise contaminated.

Enticement vs. Entrapment

While not directly related to search and seizure, the methods used to attract repeat criminals must also be legally employed. One concept is the use of *enticement,* which is the practice of attracting criminals to repeat a particular illegal act as a means to catch them. There is also *entrapment,* which is the practice of capturing an individual at a crime scene who did not have criminal intentions to perform an illegal act. For instance, a secure website with a history of being hacked could employ a covertly monitored button with the label "click here to gain unauthorized access to this server." That label might amount to entrapment of the person who clicks it, since it would tend to lure both those without criminal intent and the criminally minded to click on it and commit a digital trespass. The same button on the same secure website instead labeled "authorized access only" is more likely to be construed as enticement.

Computer Forensics

Computer forensics is a specialized field dedicated to the analysis of computer-based evidence. Forensic experts can use numerous methods to obtain evidence specific to computer systems. This includes:

- Analyzing software for the presence of viruses or worms.

- Obtaining forensic copies of disk drives.

- Analyzing disk drive areas for hidden information including slack space, deleted files, and unallocated space.

- Analyzing network traffic to locate criminal activity.

- Shutting down systems without losing evidence.

Digital or Electronic Evidence

Forensic analysts are trained to search for digital evidence. They have the tools to find information in disk locations that are not available using normal operating system access methods.

For example, when a file is deleted from a disk drive, the pointer to the file is removed from the directory, but the contents of the file are still stored on the disk. A forensic analyst can undelete the file and view the contents.

ACTIVITY 12-2
Discussing Computer Crime Incident Response

Scenario:

In this activity, you will discuss proper computer crime incident response processes and techniques to appropriately perform investigations and collect substantial proof when incidents of computer crime arise.

---

1. **What are some examples of typical computer crimes?**

---

2. **What is the appropriate description for each computer criminal incident response process?**

____	Response capability	a. Determination of events and assessment by an incident response team.
____	Incident response and handling	b. Response to a computer crime-related situation based on criticality.
____	Triage	c. Securing the scene of the incident as to not damage evidence.
____	Investigative	d. Identification, examination, and inspection of a problem by either an internal response team or local law enforcement.
____	Containment	e. Formation of an incident response or computer crime team by an organization.

3. **What is the appropriate description for each additional computer criminal incident response process?**

____	Analysis and tracking	a. Replacing damaged components or systems to aid in the preservation of crime evidence.
____	Recovery	b. Informing management of the incident and suggesting the next best course of action to reduce the possibility of future events from occurring.
____	Repair	c. Examination of facts and evidence by forensic analysts.
____	Debriefing and feedback	d. The restoration of backup files, reprocessing transactions, and auditing the system to return the system to operating condition.

4. **True or False? Collecting evidence about cybercrimes requires different and special training methods.**

    ___ True

    ___ False

5. **What is the appropriate description for each evidence type?**

___	Best	a.	A copy of an original document that is not as admissible in court as is best evidence.
___	Secondary	b.	Permanent evidence that cannot be disputed.
___	Direct	c.	Classified into either the expert or non-expert types.
___	Conclusive	d.	Required to be admissible in a court of law.
___	Opinion	e.	Received from the testimony of an individual that witnessed the crime.

6. **What is the appropriate description for each additional evidence type?**

___	Corroborative	a.	Presented by someone who was not in direct observation of a crime.
___	Circumstantial	b.	Used to explain events that took place during the crime.
___	Hearsay	c.	Gathered from multiple sources that support other types of evidence in a court of law.
___	Demonstrative	d.	Gathered from multiple sources to infer a conclusion in a court of law.

7. **What are the phases of the chain of evidence?**

8. **What are five common rules of evidence?**

9. **True or False? An organization never has the right to collect evidence within the perimeter of their buildings, due to having the same level of restriction as law enforcement.**

    ___ True

    ___ False

10. **What are some of the ways that forensic experts can obtain computer system-specific evidence?**

Lesson 12 Follow-up

In this lesson, you identified legal issues, regulations, compliance standards, and investigation practices relating to information systems security. Responding quickly, legally, and effectively to illicit organizational attacks depends on your knowledge and application of relevant laws, regulatory standards, compliance protocols, and investigative procedures. Recognizing the specifications and criteria of these rules and principles will help you and your organization successfully monitor compliance adherence and manage legal conflicts and investigations in the event of misconduct or an attack.

1. **In your industry, are you subject to any of the aforementioned computer-related laws, or do other laws apply to your organization?**

2. **Have you ever participated in a cybercrime investigation?**

Follow-up

Good work! You analyzed a broad range of information systems security subjects that are organized into 10 domains covered on the CISSP exam.

Now, you can effectively control access to data and information systems to protect organizational assets from potential threats. Your understanding of how network systems and telecommunications work will help you to properly secure those technologies. In addition to applying sound security management and best practices on the job, you can effectively control applications and systems development security to reduce system vulnerability in distributed or centralized environments. Using cryptography, you are now better prepared to disguise information using keys and algorithms to ensure its integrity, confidentiality, and authenticity.

Additionally, you can efficiently implement operations security through proper identification of resources, auditing, and monitoring. You are now ready to handle business interruptions and protect critical business processes by performing effective business continuity planning. You identified how to apply appropriate physical security measures to protect your company's assets and resources. Finally, you have a stronger foundation for understanding legal issues, regulations, compliance requirements, investigations, and ethics and how they relate to computer crimes and forensics.

What's Next?

Now that you have completed this course, you may want to continue your professional development by preparing for the CISSP certification exam and acquiring exam certifications in other security-related fields such as CISM, CEH, or CHFI. Once you have achieved your CISSP status, you will need to earn Continuing Professional Education (CPE) credits. You can earn these credits by attending security classes, security seminars, chapter meetings, and a wide variety of other activities. You will need to earn 120 credits over three years with at least 20 credits earned each year.

A | Mapping CISSP® Course Content to the (ISC)² CISSP Exam Objectives

The following table will assist you in mapping the CISSP® course content to the (ISC)² CISSP certification exam objectives.

Exam Objective Domain	CISSP Lesson and Topic References
Domain 1.0: Access Control	
● Control access by applying concepts/ methodologies/techniques	Lesson 1: Topics A and B
● Understanding access control attacks	Lesson 1: Topic C
● Assess effectiveness of access controls	
● Identify and access provisioning lifecycle	Lesson 1: Topic B
Domain 2.0: Telecommunications and Network Security	
● Understand secure network architecture and design	Lesson 2: Topic A
● Securing network components	Lesson 3: Topic B
● Establish secure communications channels	Lesson 3: Topic B
● Understand network attacks	Lesson 3: Topic B
Domain 3.0: Information Security Governance & Risk Management	
● Understand and align security functions to goals, mission and objectives of the organization	Lesson 4: Topic A
● Understand and apply security governance	Lesson 4: Topic A
● Understand and apply concepts of confidentiality, integrity, and availability	Lesson 4: Topic A
● Develop and implement security policy	Lesson 4: Topic A
● Manage the information life cycle	Lesson 4: Topic A
● Manage third-party governance	Lesson 4: Topic A

Exam Objective Domain	CISSP Lesson and Topic References
● Understand and apply risk management concepts	Lesson 6: Topic A
● Manage personnel security	Lesson 9: Topic C
● Develop and manage security education, training and awareness	Lesson 5: Topic B
● Manage the security function	Lesson 4: Topic A
Domain 4.0: Software Development Security	
● Understand and apply security in the software development life cycle	Lesson 7: Topic A
● Understand the environment and security controls	Lesson 7: Topics A, B and C
● Assess the effectiveness of software security	Lesson 7: Topics A
Domain 5.0: Cryptography	
● Understand the application and use of cryptography	Lesson 8: Topics A and E
● Understand the cryptographic lifecycle	Lesson 8: Topic B
● Understand encryption concepts	Lesson 8: Topic A
● Understand key management processes	Lesson 8: Topic B
● Understand digital signatures	Lesson 8: Topic D
● Understand non-repudiation	Lesson 8: Topic C
● Understand cryptanalytic attacks	Lesson 8: Topic F
● Use cryptography to maintain network security	Lesson 8: Topic E
● Use cryptography to maintain application security	Lesson 3: Topic C
● Understand PKI	Lesson 8: Topic C
● Understand certificate related issues	Lesson 8: Topic C
● Understand information hiding alternatives	Lesson 8: Topic A
Domain 6.0: Security Architecture and Design	
● Understand the fundamental concepts of security models	Lesson 2: Topic A
● Understand the components of information system security evaluation	Lesson 2: Topic C
● Understand the capabilities of information systems	Lesson 2: Topic A
● Understand the vulnerabilities of security architectures	Lesson 2: Topic A

Exam Objective Domain	CISSP Lesson and Topic References
● Understand software and system vulner-abilities and threats	Lesson 1: Topic C
● Understand countermeasure principles	Lesson 1: Topic B
Domain 7.0: Operations Security	
● Understand security operations concepts	Lesson 10: Topic A
● Employ resource protection	Lesson 10: Topic A
● Manage incident response	Lesson 10: Topic C
● Implement preventative measures against attack	Lesson 10: Topic C
● Implement and support patch management and vulnerability management	Lesson 10: Topic A
● Understand change and configuration man-agement	Lesson 7: Topic A
● Understand system resilience and fault tolerant requirements	Lesson 3: Topic D
Domain 8.0: Business Continuity and Disas-ter Recovery Planning	
● Understand business continuity require-ments	Lesson 11: Topic A
● Conduct business impact analysis	Lesson 11: Topic A
● Develop a recovery strategy	Lesson 11: Topic A
● Understand disaster recovery process	Lesson 11: Topics A and B
● Exercise, assess and maintain the plan	Lesson 11: Topics B, C, and D
Domain 9.0: Legal, Regulations, Investiga-tions, and Compliance	
● Understand legal issues that pertain to information security	Lesson 12: Topics A and B
● Understand professional ethics	Lesson 6: Topic B
● Understand and support investigations	Lesson 12: Topic B
● Understand forensic procedures	Lesson 12: Topic B
● Understand compliance requirements and procedures	Lesson 12: Topic A
● Ensure security in contractual agreements and procurement processes	Lesson 4: Topic A
Domain 10.0: Physical (Environmental) Secu-rity	
● Understand site and facility design consid-erations	Lesson 9: Topics A and B

Exam Objective Domain	CISSP Lesson and Topic References
● Support the implementation and operation of perimeter security	Lesson 9: Topic A
● Support the implementation and operation of internal security	Lesson 9: Topic B
● Support the implementation and operation of facilities security	Lesson 9: Topic D
● Support the protection and securing of equipment	Lesson 3: Topic D
● Understand personnel privacy and safety	Lesson 9: Topic A

Lesson Labs

Lesson labs are provided as an additional learning resource for this course. The labs may or may not be performed as part of the classroom activities. Your instructor will consider setup issues, classroom timing issues, and instructional needs to determine which labs are appropriate for you to perform, and at what point during the class. If you do not perform the labs in class, your instructor can tell you if you can perform them independently as self-study, and if there are any special setup requirements.

Lesson 1 Lab 1

Discussing Information Systems Access Control

Activity Time: 20 minutes

Scenario:

In this lab, you will discuss information systems access control to ensure that you can keep information system resources secure. It contains questions that may be similar to the types of questions you will see on the CISSP® exam.

1. **Which of the following attributes is associated with confidentiality?**

   a) Keeping information free from unauthorized disclosure

   b) Keeping information accurate

   c) Keeping information unavailable when users need it

   d) Keeping information locked in a safe

2. **Which of the following attributes is associated with integrity?**

   a) Keeping information free from unauthorized disclosure

   b) Keeping information accurate

   c) Keeping information available when users need it

   d) Keeping information in one piece, in an integral form

3. **Which of the following attributes is associated with availability?**

   a) Keeping information free from unauthorized disclosure

   b) Keeping information accurate

   c) Keeping information available when users need it

   d) Keeping information in a place where people can use it

4. **Which of the following is NOT an attribute of the reference monitor?**

   a) It must be tamper proof.

   b) It must be always invoked.

   c) It must be referred to consistently.

   d) It must be compact and verifiable.

5. **A reference monitor controls access by _____ to _____.**

   a) Users, data

   b) Subjects, objects

   c) Programs, information

   d) Administrators, permissions

6. **Least privilege is a security concept that requires that a user:**

   a) Is limited to only those functions required to do his or her job.

   b) Is given at least administrator privileges.

   c) Has privileges equal to all other users in his or her department.

   d) Is able to keep information secret and is therefore trusted with information.

7. **I&A is commonly known as:**

   a) Information and audit.

   b) Installation and activation.

   c) Intrusion and aptitude.

   d) Identification and authentication.

8. **In order to maintain accountability, which of the following is NOT necessary?**

   a) Unique identification

   b) Authorization for various activities

   c) A good accounting system

   d) Audit

9. **Restoring a backup after a system failure is an example of which of the following access control categories?**

   a) Compensating

   b) Corrective

   c) Recovery

   d) Preventative

10. **The use of a security policy to define management intention is an example of which access control type?**

    a) Administrative

    b) Physical

    c) Technical

    d) Preventative

11. **An access control matrix creates a relationship between:**

    a) Objects and servers.

    b) Objects and subjects.

    c) Objects and data.

    d) Subjects and people.

12. **MAC requires the use of:**

    a) Access control matrices.

    b) Permissions such as read, write, and modify.

    c) Security labels.

    d) Security parameters.

13. **Information classified as Secret has been found to have a risk of disclosure that would cause what kind of damage to national security?**

    a) None

    b) Grave

    c) Substantial

    d) Serious

14. **The type of access control used on a router or firewall to limit network activity is:**

    a) Discretionary.

    b) Rule-based.

    c) Role-based.

    d) Mandatory.

15. **All of the following are examples of devices with constrained interfaces EXCEPT which one?**

    a) An ATM.

    b) A normal PC with a normal keyboard.

    c) An airport check-in kiosk.

    d) A gas pump at a gas station.

16. **A passphrase is often known as a:**

    a) Virtual password.

    b) Secondary password.

    c) Password replacement.

    d) Phrase to trick hackers.

17. **A biometric device uses which of the following factors to authenticate an identity?**

   a) Human

   b) Artificial

   c) Transitory

   d) Transactional

18. **The CER provides information about:**

   a) The number of hackers crossing from white hat to black hat status.

   b) A comparison of Type I and Type II errors.

   c) The place where Type I and Type II errors are equal.

   d) The value of a biometric measurement.

Lesson 2 Lab 1
Discussing Security Architecture and Design

Activity Time: 20 minutes

Scenario:

In this lab, you will discuss security architecture and design so that you can enforce various levels of confidentiality, integrity, and availability within your organization. It contains questions that may be similar to the types of questions you will see on the CISSP® exam.

1. **In a processor, operating systems run in which of the following states?**

   a) Operator

   b) User

   c) Application

   d) Supervisor

2. **Which one of the following is memory that can be read but difficult to write?**

   a) RAM

   b) ROM

   c) Cache

   d) Virtual

3. **Virtual memory uses which of the following techniques to function properly?**

    a) Swapping

    b) Slipping

    c) Partitioning

    d) Slicing

4. **In a PC with a single processor, which technique is used to make the processor appear to be running many programs at one time?**

    a) Multiprocessing

    b) Process slicing

    c) Multitasking

    d) Multiuser mode

5. **Which one of the following security models is used to detect covert channels?**

    a) Information Flow

    b) BLP

    c) Chinese Wall

    d) Biba

6. **Which one of the following security models is used primarily for maintaining confidentiality?**

    a) Information Flow

    b) BLP

    c) Clark-Wilson

    d) Biba

7. **The star (*) property deals with:**

    a) Writing to objects.

    b) Reading from objects.

    c) Labeling confidential information.

    d) The asterisk principle of security management.

8. **Conflict of interest is controlled by which of the following models?**

    a) Biba

    b) BLP

    c) Brewer-Nash

    d) Harrison-Ruzzo-Ullman

9. **The TCB is made up of which of the following?**

   a) Hardware, software, applications

   b) Hardware, software, firmware

   c) Hardware, software, memory

   d) Hardware, applications, access control lists (ACLs)

10. **Which one of the following is a definition of a backdoor?**

    a) An unauthorized entry point into an application or operating system

    b) An exit point from a program

    c) A place to insert Trojan horse programs into an application

    d) A place used to examine how a program is working

11. **In what security mode must all users have proper security clearance, formal access approval, a signed NDA and a valid need to know for all information on the system?**

    a) Compartmented

    b) System-high

    c) Multilevel

    d) Dedicated

12. **Which TCSEC level requires the first use of MAC?**

    a) A1

    b) B1

    c) C1

    d) D1

13. **Which evaluation process is the latest and includes international evaluations?**

    a) TCSEC

    b) TNI

    c) ITSEC

    d) Common Criteria

14. **In security, C&A stands for:**

    a) Certification and accreditation.

    b) Classification and authentication.

    c) Categorization and allocation.

    d) Confidentiality and authority.

15. **C&A includes a risk evaluation and an approval to operate. The approval to operate is made by the DAA, or the:**

    a) Dedicated Approval Activity.

    b) Designated Approving Authority.

    c) Determination of Activity Approval.

    d) Diagnostic Activity Authority.

16. **Program failures caused by information leaking from the memory of one program into the memory of an adjacent program is called:**

    a) Race condition.

    b) Buffer overflow.

    c) Buffer overrun.

    d) Race overflow.

17. **Which of the following defines the separation between the trusted and untrusted part of a system?**

    a) Security kernel

    b) Kernel security

    c) Security perimeter

    d) Perimeter security

18. **Which one of the following is an integrity security model?**

    a) Biba

    b) BLP

    c) Information Flow

    d) Harrison-Ruzzo-Ullman

19. **When should security considerations be included in the design of a system?**

    a) At the beginning of the process

    b) During the first security review

    c) After implementation

    d) Throughout the entire system development process

20. **What part of the security environment is the innermost part implemented in an operating system?**

    a) TCB

    b) Security perimeter

    c) Security kernel

    d) Security capsule

21. **Untrusted components installed as patches to an operating system or program cause:**

    a) TCB failures.

    b) Login failures.

    c) Process failures.

    d) Hardware failures.

Lesson 3 Lab 1

Discussing Network and Telecommunications Security

Activity Time: 20 minutes

Scenario:

In this lab, you will discuss network and telecommunications security to help you understand how to control user access to information and focus on building network systems that provide a secure environment to share and distribute information. It contains questions that may be similar to the types of questions you will see on the CISSP® exam.

1. **Which one of the following is the correct sequence of elements in the OSI model?**

    a) Physical, Network, Application, Presentation

    b) Physical, Network, Presentation, Application

    c) Network, Physical, Presentation, Application

    d) Application, Network, Physical, Presentation

2. **Which OSI layer ensures that the receiver can accurately interpret the information being transmitted?**

    a) Presentation

    b) Application

    c) Network

    d) Transport

3. **Half-duplex communication is similar to using a:**

    a) Telephone.

    b) Walkie-talkie.

    c) Super highway.

    d) Radio station.

4. **A network used in a setting where multiple buildings are connected or associated together is called a:**

    a) LAN.

    b) WAN.

    c) GAN.

    d) CAN.

5. **Which of the following devices functions primarily at Layer 2 of the OSI model?**

    a) Hub

    b) Router

    c) Switch

    d) Gateway

6. **All devices are connected to a central device that performs a traffic distribution function. In this scenario, what type of topology is in use?**

    a) Star

    b) Bus

    c) Ring

    d) Mesh

7. **How many layers are found in the TCP/IP model?**

    a) 3

    b) 4

    c) 6

    d) 7

8. **Which technology used for network access is replacing common modems with a digital transmission method provided by a telephone company?**

    a) DSL

    b) Cable modem

    c) ATM

    d) SONET

9. **The protocol used to translate IP addresses to MAC addresses is:**

    a) ARP.

    b) DNS.

    c) DHCP.

    d) APAP.

10. **A host-to-host protocol that provides reliable delivery of data is:**

    a) UDP.

    b) ICMP.

    c) TCMP.

    d) TCP.

11. **Which one of the following is not a data transfer protocol?**

    a) FTP

    b) TFTP

    c) ICMP

    d) HTTP

12. **Which of the following protocols replaces Telnet and provides higher security levels?**

    a) SSH

    b) SSL

    c) TLS

    d) STelnet

13. **WAP is a protocol that deals with:**

    a) Wireless access to an Ethernet network.

    b) Securing wireless networks.

    c) Wireless access to data networks using mobile phone technology.

    d) Wireless access using IPsec.

14. **CHAP uses how many steps to authenticate to the dial-in service?**

    a) 1

    b) 2

    c) 3

    d) 4

15. **As a wireless security protocol, what does WEP stand for?**

    a) Wi-Fi Encrypted Privacy

    b) Wired Equivalent Privacy

    c) Wireless Equivalency Protocol

    d) Working Encapsulation Protocol

16. **Which one of the following is a network topology where each device is connected to every other device?**

    a) Mesh

    b) Ring

    c) Bus

    d) Star

17. **Which protocol is not used for routing on a logical network?**

    a) Ethernet

    b) IPX

    c) Appletalk

    d) IP

18. **What device is used to move data between dissimilar physical layer protocols at Layer 3 of the OSI model?**

    a) Hub

    b) Router

    c) Switch

    d) Gateway

19. **An IPv4 address has how many bits?**

    a) 16

    b) 24

    c) 32

    d) 48

20. **Ethernet networks always use which type of address?**

    a) Logical

    b) IP

    c) TCP

    d) MAC

Lesson 4 Lab 1

Discussing Information Security Management Goals

Activity Time: 20 minutes

Scenario:

In this lab, you will discuss information security management goals to help you understand how to ensure that security issues are aligned with business objectives. It contains questions that may be similar to the types of questions you will see on the CISSP® exam.

1. **Who is ultimately responsible for protecting the assets of an organization?**

    a) Data custodian

    b) Senior management

    c) IT department head

    d) Security administrator

2. **Which one of the following is part of the CIA triad?**

    a) Authentication

    b) Applicability

    c) Availability

    d) Authenticity

3. **Confidentiality is maintained if:**

    a) Unauthorized users gain unauthorized access.

    b) Important information does not leak out of the system.

    c) Access to information is given only to authorized users.

    d) Rumors about people do not spread in the company.

4. **Which one of the following is not a physical control?**

    a) A fence that deters intruders

    b) A policy detailing which physical controls to use

    c) Guard dogs roaming the property at night

    d) Lighting of doors and parking areas

5. **A pre-employment screening for a highly sensitive position should evaluate all of the following EXCEPT:**

   a) Drug use.

   b) Financial problems.

   c) Reference checks.

   d) Food preferences.

6. **A risk management team should include which of the following personnel?**

   a) Legal staff

   b) Physical plant staff

   c) Security staff

   d) Staff from throughout the organization

7. **Risk, as it applies to CISSP, is best defined as:**

   a) Taking a chance without knowledge of a predetermined outcome.

   b) The likelihood of a threat taking advantage of a vulnerability.

   c) A gamble with many chances of failure.

   d) The loss of income when someone becomes ill and has no insurance.

8. **Which is the most likely threat?**

   a) Hurricanes

   b) Tornados

   c) Disgruntled employees

   d) Water leaks in the computer room

9. **Systems are under the most threat from:**

   a) Insiders.

   b) Outsiders.

   c) Hackers.

   d) Crackers.

10. **Having multiple security schemes deployed in a hierarchical model is called:**

    a) Modular defense.

    b) Structural defense.

    c) Defense in depth.

    d) Hardened defense.

11. **Security policies represent:**
    a) Operational instructions for implementing security.
    b) Tactical instructions for implementing security.
    c) Procedures specified by senior management.
    d) High-level objectives specified by senior management.

12. **Information classification is determined by the:**
    a) Custodian.
    b) User.
    c) Coordinator.
    d) Owner.

13. **When a risk is mitigated it is:**
    a) Removed with 100% certainty.
    b) Reduced, often to an acceptable level.
    c) Estimated, but not removed.
    d) Not changed in any way.

Lesson 5 Lab 1

Discussing Information Security Classification and Program Development

Activity Time: 20 minutes

Scenario:

In this lab, you will discuss the security classification of information and security program development to help you understand how to transform these goals into a workable security program. It contains questions that may be similar to the types of questions you will see on the CISSP® exam.

1. **Military classification includes all of the following terms EXCEPT:**
    a) Secret.
    b) Public.
    c) Confidential.
    d) Top Secret.

2. **Who is responsible for keeping records of access to classified information?**

   a) Data owner

   b) Data classifier

   c) Data custodian

   d) Data destroyer

3. **Which one of the following is an example of physical access control?**

   a) Using passwords for authentication

   b) Using permissions on files

   c) Using a cipher lock on a door

   d) Using an encryption protocol

4. **Who is responsible for the overall organizational security policy?**

   a) CEO

   b) CSO

   c) CIO

   d) COO

5. **Which document type is used to document steps taken in a process?**

   a) Policy

   b) Procedure

   c) Guideline

   d) Baseline

6. **Which document type is used to document required implementations or uses of a tool?**

   a) Policy

   b) Procedure

   c) Standard

   d) Baseline

7. **Who is responsible for implementing the security program of an organization?**

   a) Everyone

   b) Security department

   c) Senior administrators

   d) IT department

8. **Which type of planning deals with long range goals?**

    a) Tactical

    b) Organizational

    c) Operational

    d) Strategic

9. **The organization is planning to change to a new authentication process within 18 months. What type of plan would be used for this implementation?**

    a) Tactical

    b) Organizational

    c) Operational

    d) Strategic

10. **Which classification level used by the U.S. military suggests that grave damage to national security will result from an unauthorized disclosure of information?**

    a) Top Secret

    b) Secret

    c) Confidential

    d) Unclassified

11. **What type of training content would be typical for all employees to receive?**

    a) Discussions on the development of an encryption algorithm

    b) Instructions on configuring an enterprise firewall

    c) Discussions on social engineering threats

    d) Instructions on setting a clipping level for server log files

12. **A guideline is used to provide:**

    a) The minimum security required in a system or process.

    b) A required implementation practice.

    c) The steps to complete a specific task.

    d) A suggested implementation practice.

13. **Which role in an organization is responsible for determining how to implement the security policies?**

    a) Everyone

    b) Security department

    c) Senior administrators

    d) IT department

14. **Who is responsible for the proper destruction of classified media?**

   a) Individual users

   b) CFO

   c) Data custodian

   d) IT media librarian

15. **What determines the classification of data or information?**

   a) Cost to safeguard

   b) Risk of disclosure

   c) Damage to national assets

   d) The individual data owner

16. **At a minimum, how often should users receive security training?**

   a) Every week

   b) Every month

   c) Once a quarter

   d) Once a year

17. **Information access is allowed based on which one of the following principles?**

   a) SoD

   b) Need to distribute

   c) Need to analyze

   d) Need to know

18. **To avoid confusion, commercial organizations should use a classification scheme that is:**

   a) The same as the military.

   b) Specific to the organization.

   c) The standardized commercial scheme found in industry publications.

   d) Modeled after a successful company in the same industry.

19. **In an organization, what is the best reason why a security policy should be implemented if there is not one currently in place?**

   a) A policy can help the organization.

   b) A policy makes good business sense.

   c) A policy is not required.

   d) A policy is always necessary.

20. **A plan that details the penetration testing activities for the next three months is considered:**

    a) Operational.

    b) Tactical.

    c) Strategic.

    d) Organizational.

21. **Security policies are developed to protect all of the following assets except which one?**

    a) Data

    b) Employees' homes

    c) Facilities

    d) People

Lesson 6 Lab 1
Discussing Risk Management and Ethics

Scenario:

In this lab, you will discuss risk management criteria and ethical codes of conduct to help you understand how to identify risk factors as well as distinguish between ethical and unethical behavior standards. It contains questions that may be similar to the types of questions you will see on the CISSP® exam.

1. **The process of determining the potential damage or exposure from a threat is:**

    a) Threat analysis.

    b) Impact analysis.

    c) Risk analysis.

    d) Outcome analysis.

2. **Failure to manage risks effectively can result in which one of the following?**

    a) Violation of the DAD triad

    b) Violation of the CIA triad

    c) Violation of the MAC triad

    d) Violation of the SLA triad

3. **The critical first step in risk analysis is to:**

   a) Identify the vulnerabilities.

   b) Identify the assets to protect.

   c) Identify the attackers.

   d) Identify the countermeasures.

4. **A vulnerability is:**

   a) A lack of a safeguard.

   b) A lack of a threat.

   c) A lack of a risk.

   d) A lack of an asset.

5. **Which one of the following is not a way to manage risk?**

   a) Avoidance

   b) Reduction

   c) Acceptance

   d) Substantiate

6. **Which one of the following is a way to transfer risk?**

   a) Give the asset to someone else

   b) Hire more security personnel

   c) Buy insurance for an asset

   d) Strengthen the physical security used to protect the asset

7. **Which one of the following is the least precise method used to value assets?**

   a) Asset management system

   b) Accounting system

   c) Insurance value

   d) Delphi estimates

8. **Which of these is an unintentional man-made threat?**

   a) A mistake

   b) Giving passwords to coworkers

   c) Habitually leaving classified documents on a desk, unprotected, as a normal practice

   d) Posting a password on a chat room

9. **Which of the following presents the greatest threat to security?**

   a) Hackers

   b) Employees

   c) Crackers

   d) Spam artists

10. **Which one of the following risk analysis methods is based on numerical analysis of historical incidents?**

    a) Qualitative

    b) Subjective

    c) Quantitative

    d) Objective

11. **Which risk analysis method is based on objective measures?**

    a) Qualitative

    b) Quantitative

    c) Numerical

    d) Scientific

12. **Qualitative risk analysis uses which one of the following methods?**

    a) Delphi

    b) Mind meld

    c) Book value analysis

    d) Structured walkthrough

13. **Which one of the following would not be classified as a vulnerability?**

    a) No virus scanning software

    b) Windows in the computer room

    c) Water lines over a computer room

    d) Cipher locks on the computer room door

14. **The term ARO is used to describe the:**

    a) Actual Risk Outcome.

    b) Activity Reduction Overview.

    c) Annualized Rate of Occurrence.

    d) Action Review Outline.

15. **The EF is used to:**

    a) Determine how many employees will come down with the flu.

    b) Estimate the loss of an asset as a percent should a threat occur.

    c) Account for the damage the sun can do to a CD or DVD-ROM if overexposed.

    d) Determine the cost of replacing film damaged by an X-ray machine.

16. **Which one of the following factors is not involved in calculating the ALE?**

    a) ARO

    b) AF

    c) AV

    d) EF

17. **The SLE is calculated by multiplying the:**

    a) Effective value times the actual loss.

    b) The EF times the AV.

    c) The AV times the ARO.

    d) The EF times the SLO.

18. **The ALE = $400,000. The EF = 20%. The SLE = $4,000,000. What is the AV?**

    a) $44,000,000

    b) $80,000,000

    c) $20,000,000

    d) $2,000,000

19. **The ALE = $400,000. The EF = 20%. The SLE = $4,000,000. What is the ARO?**

    a) Once every 10 years

    b) 10 times a year

    c) Once every 100 years

    d) 10 times in 10 years

20. **In determining which safeguard to use, the cost of the safeguard must be:**

    a) More than the ALE.

    b) Equal to the ALE.

    c) Less than the ALE.

    d) Equal to or less than the ALE.

21. **The IAB ethics are found in:**

    a) RFC 1087.

    b) RFC 1099.

    c) RFC 3089.

    d) RFC 1888.

22. **Which ethics statement requires users to refrain from wasting Internet resources?**

    a) IAB ethics

    b) (ISC)^2 ethics

    c) ADA ethics

    d) IEEE ethics

23. **Violating the (ISC)^2 ethics can lead to:**

    a) Money fines from the (ISC)^2.

    b) Removal of the CISSP designation.

    c) A letter of reprimand from the (ISC)^2.

    d) Criminal prosecution from the (ISC)^2.

Lesson 7 Lab 1
Discussing Application Security

Activity Time: 20 minutes

Scenario:

In this lab, you will discuss application security and apply software configuration management strategies, software controls, and database system security mechanisms to help you understand how to address software development, operation, and maintenance. It contains questions that may be similar to the types of questions you will see on the CISSP® exam.

1. **At which stage of the software product development process should security concerns be addressed?**

    a) During the entire product life cycle

    b) At the beginning of the process

    c) During the programming

    d) When testing begins

2. **Which one of the following statements is true about proprietary software?**

   a) Copies of the source code are normally made available to the buyers.

   b) The software is available at no cost to the user.

   c) The software source is closed and users cannot inspect the code for problems.

   d) Users cannot trust the vendors of proprietary software.

3. **A milestone is used in which one of the following software development models?**

   a) Spiral

   b) Circular

   c) Block step

   d) Waterfall

4. **Which software development model uses an iterative development process, which includes risk analysis, requirements specifications, prototyping, and testing?**

   a) Spiral

   b) Circular

   c) Block step

   d) Waterfall

5. **The concept of foreign keys is found in which one database type?**

   a) Structured

   b) Relational

   c) Hierarchical

   d) Object oriented

6. **Which one of the following is the open standard for communicating from any computer language to any database system?**

   a) ODBC

   b) JDBC

   c) XML

   d) HTTP

7. **The ACID elements of database transactions are used to protect which one database feature?**

   a) Confidentiality

   b) Availability

   c) Integrity

   d) Authentication

8. **If a database transaction is said to be durable, what is the one resulting transaction?**

   a) It will backed out if the transaction fails.

   b) It will cause a secure state in the database.

   c) It will be separated from all other transactions in the database.

   d) It will not be backed out if the user has been informed that the transaction is complete.

9. **Which statement is not true of a data warehouse?**

   a) It is a database containing information about a specific subject.

   b) The information is pre-processed.

   c) The information in the warehouse is constantly updated.

   d) A data warehouse is useful for reporting and analysis.

10. **Which one of the following techniques is used by data mining to derive useful information?**

    a) Index gleaning

    b) Aggregation

    c) Interference

    d) Scanning

11. **When transaction A is waiting for transaction B to finish, and transaction B is waiting for transaction A to finish, one state exists, which is called a:**

    a) Hidden lock condition.

    b) Process lockup.

    c) Deadlock.

    d) DoS attack.

12. **Which one of the following is used in a database to limit what data a user can see?**

    a) Views

    b) Scopes

    c) Ranges

    d) Subsets

13. **Function points are used to:**

    a) Estimate the size of a program.

    b) Detail each step in the program development cycle.

    c) Indicate the work factor in creating a manual procedure.

    d) Evaluate the levels of sophistication or maturity found in an organization's software.

14. **Metadata is:**

    a) Metropolitan population statistics used in data analysis.

    b) Large clumps of data found in a data warehouse.

    c) Data about data.

    d) Intermediate data selected prior to creating reports.

15. **A tuple is:**

    a) A row in a database.

    b) A column in a database.

    c) The intersection of a row and column in a database.

    d) The content of a cell in a database.

16. **What is a requirement of referential integrity?**

    a) A foreign key can be deleted even if it is used in another table.

    b) A foreign key cannot be deleted if it is used in another table.

    c) Keys may be created using any foreign language.

    d) Normalization rules are always followed.

17. **Normalization usually requires the:**

    a) Removal of redundant data.

    b) Use of flat files.

    c) Addition of redundant data to simplify data access.

    d) Addition of columns to tables for data recovery.

18. **The term encapsulation is most often used with which one of the following database forms?**

    a) Relational

    b) Object-oriented

    c) Hierarchical

    d) Network

19. **When an operation is first verified as allowable and then later replaced with another illegal operation, which one of the following vulnerabilities has been exploited?**

    a) TOC/TOU

    b) Race condition

    c) Malformed input

    d) Object reuse

20. **Which element of a database operating environment is ultimately responsible for overall system security?**

    a) Database

    b) Operating system

    c) Programming language

    d) Security kernel

Lesson 8 Lab 1
Discussing Cryptography

Activity Time: 20 minutes

Scenario:

In this lab, you will discuss the characteristics and elements of cryptography to ensure the confidentiality of your information. It contains questions that may be similar to the types of questions you will see on the CISSP® exam.

1. **The original message found before encryption and after decryption is called the:**

    a) Ciphertext.

    b) Plaintext.

    c) Cipherstream.

    d) Originstream.

2. **An algorithm that results in a large change in the encrypted data from a small change in the original message exhibits which one of the following?**

    a) Tsunami effect

    b) Hurricane effect

    c) Land slide effect

    d) Avalanche effect

3. **If it is possible to prove the identity of the sender of a message, which one of the following principles is in effect?**

    a) Origination identity principle

    b) Non-repudiation

    c) Hashed message control

    d) Strong identification

4. **When a public key is used to encrypt data and a private key is used to decrypt it, the data in transit is assured:**

   a) Confidentiality only.

   b) Availability.

   c) Integrity and confidentiality.

   d) Integrity only.

5. **Symmetric-key cryptography uses which of the following key types?**

   a) Secret

   b) Public

   c) Private

   d) Confidential

6. **The work factor is:**

   a) The amount of time needed to encrypt a file.

   b) The amount of time needed to decrypt a file.

   c) The amount of time needed to scrub a hard drive.

   d) The amount of time needed to break a cryptosystem.

7. **What is the effective key length used with 3DES?**

   a) 64 bits

   b) 40 bits

   c) 112 bits

   d) 168 bits

8. **Which one of the following is the most recently adopted symmetric algorithm?**

   a) IDEA

   b) AES

   c) 3DES

   d) CAST-128

9. **Public-key encryption was developed by:**

   a) Diffie and Hellman.

   b) Merkle and Adams.

   c) Tavares and Rivest.

   d) Rivest and Merkle.

10. **What item allows an encryption algorithm to be successfully reused?**

   a) Algorithm

   b) Users

   c) Key

   d) Computer system

11. **Which computer logical function is the basis of most cryptosystem algorithms?**

   a) XORed

   b) And

   c) Not

   d) Exclusive nor

12. **Which one of the following is not a hashing algorithm?**

   a) MD5

   b) SHA

   c) HAVAL

   d) RC4

13. **Which one of the following encryption algorithms is not used to protect Wi-Fi networks?**

   a) WEP

   b) WAP

   c) WPA

   d) WPA2

14. **IPsec uses which of the following processes to exchange keys?**

   a) IKE

   b) PKI

   c) SA

   d) BRP

15. **The process using all possible values of a key to attempt to break a cryptosystem is called:**

   a) Brute force.

   b) Atomic attack.

   c) Superscan.

   d) Key dictionary attack.

16. **A process used to break simple substitution ciphers by studying the uses of various letters in a language is called:**

    a) Letter analysis.

    b) Vocabulary distribution.

    c) Selective letter analysis.

    d) Frequency analysis.

17. **Which is true about random number generators used in encryption and decryption?**

    a) They are always 100% random in their output of numbers.

    b) They always rely on clock pulses, which are random on most computers.

    c) They can be checked against a second generator using the same processes.

    d) They are not truly random and can present weaknesses in the algorithms used.

18. **Who proposed the ideal cipher?**

    a) Claude Shannon

    b) Shannon Clarke

    c) Ron Rivest

    d) Desmond Lucipher

Lesson 9 Lab 1

Discussing Physical Security

Activity Time: 20 minutes

Scenario:

In this lab, you will discuss physical security controls, design strategies, tools, and techniques to tackle the challenges of physical security to preserve your organization's intellectual and personnel assets. It contains questions that may be similar to the types of questions you will see on the CISSP® exam.

1. **Physical threats to security come from all of the following areas EXCEPT:**

    a) Internal activities.

    b) External activities.

    c) Computer-generated activities.

    d) Natural disasters.

2. **Which one of the following is not typically used in a layered protection scheme for physical threats?**

   a) Perimeter access controls

   b) Facility access controls

   c) Logical (computer) access controls

   d) Secured area access controls

3. **A fence that is three to four feet high is used to:**

   a) Deter determined attackers.

   b) Keep most people out because it is hard to climb.

   c) Delimit the property line and keep out casual trespassers.

   d) Provide the most effective boundary control.

4. **When using lighting to deter or identify intruders the usual illumination is:**

   a) Two foot candles of illumination at eight feet high.

   b) Eight foot candles of illumination at 20 feet high.

   c) A flash system to blind the intruder and freeze him/her in place.

   d) Room-level lighting.

5. **A door securing an area must have the same fire protection capability as:**

   a) The walls of the secured area.

   b) The other doors in the building, regardless of where they are located.

   c) The closest external door.

   d) The windows of the secured area.

6. **The security of a manual lock is enforced by all of the following EXCEPT:**

   a) The security of the key.

   b) The lights used around the lock location.

   c) The strength of the lock components.

   d) The key distribution policies and processes.

7. **Which one of the following physical safeguards is most effective in identifying a threat?**

   a) Guard dog

   b) Physical IDS

   c) Human guard

   d) CCTV

8. **If it is necessary to determine if a person has crossed a barrier, but it is not practical to use lights, which system might be most effective in a large area?**

   a) CCTV

   b) Pressure sensitive sensors

   c) Human guard

   d) Motion sensors

9. **Which one of the following is useful in determining who entered a given area of the facility?**

   a) CCTV

   b) Card entry systems

   c) Manual locks

   d) IDSs

10. **What is the principal goal for any physical security system?**

    a) Safeguard human life

    b) Safeguard corporate property

    c) Safeguard information

    d) Safeguard computer systems

11. **In a computer facility, at what levels should HVAC systems maintain humidity?**

    a) 40% to 80% relative humidity

    b) 40% to 45% relative humidity

    c) 20% to 40% relative humidity

    d) 40% to 60% relative humidity

12. **Automatic fire detection systems use all of the following methods EXCEPT:**

    a) Rate of temperature rise.

    b) Temperature level.

    c) Presence of smoke.

    d) Human determination.

13. **A type B fire extinguisher is used to put out which one of the following types of fires?**

    a) Paper

    b) Liquids and fuels

    c) Electrical

    d) Kitchen

14. **Halon has been outlawed as a fire-extinguishing gas. Which of the following chemicals is a preferred replacement?**

    a) Kryptonite

    b) H2O

    c) Chlorofluorocarbon

    d) FM-200

15. **A fire control system that does not charge the system with water until a fire is detected is called a:**

    a) Wet pipe system.

    b) Damp pipe system.

    c) No-water system.

    d) Dry pipe system.

16. **Which one of the following systems is not used in a computer area because of the amount of water discharged?**

    a) Wet pipe

    b) Dry pipe

    c) No-water

    d) Deluge

17. **Which one of the following is a momentary high-voltage power problem?**

    a) Spike

    b) Sag

    c) Brownout

    d) Surge

18. **What method might be a traditional approach that is still useful in developing and employing an employee notification system?**

    a) Emails

    b) Instant messages

    c) Calling trees

    d) Emergency networks

19. **In looking at building design, secure areas of a building should be located:**

    a) Near an exit for easy egress in an emergency.

    b) Close to external walls next to the street.

    c) In the center of the building with reinforced walls and ceiling.

    d) Close to the restroom facilities for convenience.

20. **When granting access to a physical area, which one of the following is not a determining factor?**

   a) Need to know

   b) Least privilege

   c) Two-man rule

   d) Access control cost

Lesson 10 Lab 1
Discussing Operations Security

Activity Time: 20 minutes

Scenario:

In this lab, you will discuss operations security and processes, tools, strategies, and techniques for implementing operations security. It contains questions that may be similar to the types of questions you will see on the CISSP® exam.

1. **Operations security deals with which type of need?**

   a) Strategic

   b) Tactical

   c) Mid-term

   d) Day to day

2. **Who determines which users can access which data?**

   a) Security administrator

   b) IT administrator

   c) Data owner

   d) CEO

3. **Which of these is a risk associated with changing passwords infrequently?**

   a) They are often written down.

   b) They are targets for social engineering.

   c) They may be guessed or broken by brute force.

   d) They increase physical vulnerabilities.

4. **A user has been granted special privileges to modify data due to a programming error. Which one or more of the following should be performed to safeguard data in the system during this time?**

   a) Remove any security controls protecting the date to make it easier to modify.

   b) Remove access control shortly after the modification is complete.

   c) Remove the special privileges immediately after the modification has been made.

   d) Disable auditing so as to not interfere with the ability to modify the program.

5. **What is a security profile?**

   a) A description of the security-relevant information about each user or protected element in the system.

   b) The description of the security kernel in the system architecture design document.

   c) The collection of permissions for each user that is stored in the system access control log.

   d) A written description of the policy for granting access to resources.

6. **Fault tolerance is implemented by using what?**

   a) Redundant hardware

   b) Employee briefings on personality quirks

   c) Extra security guards and CCTV to protect the facility

   d) Reset buttons and switches on computer consoles and HVAC systems

7. **A directive operations security control might be found in which one of the following documents?**

   a) Security policy

   b) Guideline

   c) Procedure

   d) Baseline

8. **A facility that only allows authorized users is called:**

   a) An impenetrable facility.

   b) A closed shop.

   c) An open shop.

   d) A secure bastion.

9. **In a security context, what are mandatory vacations used for?**

   a) To reward good employees

   b) To ensure that all employees get a chance for some time off throughout the year

   c) To allow auditing of employee activities

   d) To reduce payouts at employee termination

10. **A system that is used to track user and program activity is called:**

    a) A system tracker.

    b) An event monitor.

    c) An activity log.

    d) An audit log.

11. **What security level should the audit logs have?**

    a) Modification ability for anyone

    b) Violation alarm notice

    c) Restricted access for any company personnel

    d) Encryption to protect the contents

12. **Evaluating an audit log to locate conditions that might indicate a security issue due to repeated mistakes is called what?**

    a) Violation analysis

    b) Log review

    c) Error determination

    d) Activity review

13. **A response to a repeated error found in an audit log should be measured and determined by which of these?**

    a) The person committing the error.

    b) The security risk associated with the error.

    c) The lack of training of the user committing the error.

    d) The cost of a severe response to the situation.

14. **Theft of information targets which of these CIA areas?**

    a) Confidentiality and integrity

    b) Integrity and availability

    c) Confidentiality and availability

    d) Confidentiality only

15. **What is one of the best ways to ensure the operational security of the organization?**

    a) Lock systems down so no security errors will occur.

    b) Provide frequent, ongoing security training to personnel.

    c) Conduct vulnerability testing to locate shortcomings.

    d) Hire an outside contractor to control security.

16. **With trusted recovery, the system is ensured to:**

    a) Restore backups automatically, without assistance.

    b) Recover from a failure to be restored to a secure state.

    c) Recheck the TCB for normal operation.

    d) Support recovery from small problems.

17. **Which of the following typically dictates how often audit log reviews are conducted?**

    a) Laws

    b) Corporate policy

    c) Financial information

    d) Regulations

18. **SoD would allow which of these pairs to work together in completing each others' tasks?**

    a) Audit and administration

    b) Security and users

    c) Programmers and software testers

    d) None of these pairs should work together

19. **A hacker has been found trying to obtain data from a swap file area on a disk drive. What is this type of activity known as?**

    a) Object pilfering

    b) Subject extraction

    c) Dumpster diving

    d) Object reuse

20. **Which of the following require constant follow-up to ensure the latest versions are available and used?**

    a) Operating system complete releases

    b) Virus signature files

    c) Password encryption algorithms

    d) Corporate security policies

Lesson 11 Lab 1

Discussing Business Continuity and Disaster Recovery Planning

Activity Time: 20 minutes

Scenario:

In this lab, you will discuss plans to protect your business in the event of a minor disruption or complete natural disaster to protect your organization's resources from natural or other outside influences. It contains questions that may be similar to the types of questions you will see on the CISSP® exam.

1. **What is the purpose of a BCP?**

    a) To take care of one-time disasters.

    b) To ensure the business continues after a disruption or crisis.

    c) To identify key players in the business.

    d) To keep key business documents available when needed.

2. **Which of these is the most important aspect to consider for ensuring BCP success?**

    a) Senior management is involved and supports BCP creation.

    b) All aspects of the organization are studied carefully.

    c) The impact for all types of interruptions is understood.

    d) Physical security is continued.

3. **Which of these is a top consideration for a BCP?**

    a) Safety of personnel

    b) Safety of hardware

    c) Safety of software and information

    d) Safety of the facility

4. **Who should the BIA team include?**

    a) Senior management only

    b) Security management team

    c) IT management team

    d) Individuals from all parts of the organization

5. **What is MTD?**

   a) The longest period of time that the business can suspend functioning without the business failing.

   b) The longest time a server can fail without needing to be rebooted.

   c) The tolerance the users show when a system fails.

   d) The time a server takes to restore a failed backup.

6. **The RPO is often related to which one of the following?**

   a) The last restore of the system.

   b) The last backup of the system.

   c) The point at which the system fails.

   d) The point at which the system is recovered.

7. **If the RTO extends beyond the MTD, what is likely to happen?**

   a) The users become more upset.

   b) The customers are unhappy with the business.

   c) The business is likely to fail.

   d) The cost of doing business expands exponentially.

8. **If the RPO and RTO are nearly zero, what financial impact might be felt?**

   a) Near-zero RPOs and RTOs are very expensive to support.

   b) Near-zero RPOs and RTOs are cheap because downtime is minimal.

   c) Near-zero RPOs and RTOs are revenue neutral and have no financial impact.

   d) Near-zero RPOs and RTOs are moderately expensive to support.

9. **Which of these is a critical business process?**

   a) A process that if it were to sustain a loss or damage, it could lead to business failure

   b) A process that takes too much money from other processes

   c) An essential security function

   d) A process that is related to every other function in the business

10. **Which of these is the most important factor for a BCP coordinator to have?**

    a) Enough funds

    b) Enough contact with other employees

    c) A thorough knowledge of all parts of the business

    d) A high level of support from top management

11. **Which one of the following is not a typical item that the BCP team must incorporate?**

   a) Determine threats and vulnerabilities

   b) Prioritize recovery efforts

   c) Document BCP plans

   d) Restore operations

12. **Which of these is a BCP testing method that verifies system functioning at an alternate site without disrupting business operations?**

   a) Reviewing BCP contents

   b) Walkthroughs

   c) Parallel testing

   d) Full interruption testing

13. **Which of these is a BCP review that involves desk checking?**

   a) Simulation

   b) Checklist

   c) Walkthrough

   d) Full interruption

14. **How often should a BCP be reviewed and revised?**

   a) Once a year only

   b) With major changes to business operations

   c) Twice a year

   d) When senior management decides

15. **When the BCP fails to mitigate risks and a disaster occurs, which plan is implemented?**

   a) BCP

   b) ARP

   c) DCP

   d) DRP

16. **Why is a mirrored site the best when recovery time is considered?**

   a) A mirrored site is a complete copy of the original and has a very short recovery time should a disaster occur.

   b) A mirrored site is inexpensive since it uses an exact mirror located at the original site.

   c) A mirrored site has little benefit because of the cost and distance to move equipment and people.

   d) A mirrored site is easy to set up and maintain.

17. **An incremental backup strategy is one that requires a full backup followed by which of these?**

    a) Periodic backups that do not reset the archive bit

    b) Periodic backups that reset the archive bit

    c) Periodic backups of files selected by the backup operator

    d) Occasional backups performed as necessary based on administrator decisions

18. **The objective of the DRP team is to begin operating within the time limit of which of these?**

    a) RPO

    b) RTO

    c) MTD

    d) MDT

Lesson 12 Lab 1

Discussing Legal, Regulations, Compliance, and Investigations

Activity Time: 20 minutes

Scenario:

In this lab, you will discuss legal issues, regulations, compliance standards, and investigation practices relating to information systems security so you understand how to ensure that business functions will continue when faced with a legal, regulatory, or investigative battle. It contains questions that may be similar to the types of questions you will see on the CISSP® exam.

1. **In a criminal investigation, what is considered evidence?**

    a) Computer disks

    b) Computer hardware

    c) Program source files

    d) Program code

2. **Computer-generated evidence is considered to be:**

    a) Direct.

    b) Demonstrative.

    c) Hearsay.

    d) Differential.

3. **Which one of the following should not be included in an evidence record?**

    a) Who collected it

    b) Where it was collected

    c) When it was collected

    d) The replacement cost of the evidence

4. **In what circumstances can copies of documents not be used as evidence?**

    a) If the original was destroyed

    b) If the original cannot be subpoenaed

    c) If the original has been damaged

    d) If the copy was seized illegally

5. **When can audit logs be used as evidence?**

    a) If they have been periodically reviewed as part of their collection process

    b) If they have not been subject to a clipping level

    c) If the logs have been written to media, disallowing modifications

    d) If the lawyers certify their correctness

6. **It is best for a forensic analysis to be performed by whom?**

    a) Local security analysts

    b) Trained professional forensic analysts

    c) Local police departments

    d) Local college professors

7. **Which amendment of the U.S. Constitution prohibits illegal search and seizure?**

    a) 4th Amendment

    b) 2nd Amendment

    c) 9th Amendment

    d) 22nd Amendment

8. **Which law prohibits the monitoring or interception of electronic communications without notice to employees or those who will be monitored?**

   a) ECPA

   b) Network Interception, Monitoring and Data Act

   c) Privacy Act of 1974

   d) Home Secrecy Act

9. **In a criminal investigation, what is enticement used for?**

   a) To trap a person who is not intending to perform a criminal act

   b) To coax a criminal into performing a criminal act that they are intending to do

   c) To trick a person into stealing computer hardware left laying on a table

   d) To prevent a criminal from performing a criminal act

10. **Which one or more of the following locations can be used to hide evidence on a disk drive?**

    a) Slack space

    b) Disk driver

    c) Disk controller

    d) File Allocation Table

11. **Which of the following are considered external auditors?**

    a) Employees of the company being audited who work in the external audit department.

    b) Employees of the company being audited who do not work in the internal audit department.

    c) A group that verifies compliance with laws, regulations, and policies but are not employees of the audited company.

    d) Accounting experts who also know about security issues.

12. **The penalty for violating civil law consists of which of the following?**

    a) A jail term.

    b) A cash fine.

    c) A cash fine and jail term.

    d) A jail term, court costs, and lawyer fees.

13. **The evidence standard of "beyond a reasonable doubt" is used to determine guilt in which type of case?**

    a) Civil case

    b) Administrative law case

    c) Statutory case

    d) Criminal case

14. **A patent is a legal protection of what?**

    a) A written work of an author.

    b) An invention.

    c) A mark identifying a product.

    d) A trade secret.

15. **A trademark is protected for how many years in the United States?**

    a) 5 years

    b) 20 years

    c) 10 years

    d) 40 years

16. **Which act protects the privacy of health-related information?**

    a) ECPA

    b) SOX Act

    c) GLBA

    d) HIPAA

17. **What does the Computer Fraud and Abuse Act of 1984 protect?**

    a) Federal government systems

    b) State systems

    c) Personal computer systems

    d) Commercial computer systems

18. **Which law replaced the Computer Security Act?**

    a) FISMA

    b) NIIPA

    c) FERPA

    d) COPPA

19. **Which one of the following is not usually considered a computer crime?**

    a) Phishing

    b) Hacking

    c) Cracking

    d) Identity theft

20. **Who protects intellectual property in an international setting?**

    a) WIPO

    b) IPPO

    c) POPI

    d) KIPSW

Solutions

Lesson 1

Activity 1-1

1. **Which of the access control models is generally considered the most restrictive?**

   a) DAC

   ✓ b) MAC

   c) RBAC

   d) Constrained Interface

2. **Another name for the information security triad is:**

   a) The FBI triad.

   b) The ISS triad.

   ✓ c) The CIA triad.

   d) The IST triad.

3. **Which one of these represents the property of keeping an organization information accurate, without error, and without unauthorized modification?**

   a) Availability

   ✓ b) Integrity

   c) Confidentiality

   d) Accountability

4. **What is the appropriate description for each data access process?**

_d_	Least privilege	a.	The limitation of access based on rules provided through the identification of the entity attempting to access an object.
_a_	Access control services	b.	The process of determining and assigning privileges to various resources, objects, and data.
_c_	SoD	c.	A division of tasks between different people to complete a business process or work function.
_b_	Access control	d.	The security principle that limits the access of information to the minimum necessary.

5. **Which one or more access control categories are sufficient to maintain the CIA triad?**

    ✓ a) Detective

    ✓ b) Preventative

       c) Compensating

    ✓ d) Corrective

6. **Which one of the following access control services determines the capabilities of a subject when accessing the object?**

       a) Accountability

    ✓ b) Authorization

       c) Audit

       d) I&A

7. **Which one of the following access control types covers personnel security, monitoring, user and password management, and permissions management?**

       a) Corrective

       b) Physical

    ✓ c) Administrative

       d) Technical

8. **What is the appropriate description for each security term?**

_e_	Confidential	a.	Information that is not classified.
_b_	Secret	b.	Disclosure could cause serious damage.
_d_	FOUO	c.	Information protected with the highest level of security.
_c_	Top Secret	d.	Unclassified information that may be exempt from mandatory release.
_a_	Unclassified	e.	Disclosure could cause damage.
_f_	SBU	f.	Warrants a degree of protection and administrative control.

9. **True or False? A separation of duties policy would require a division of tasks between different people to complete a business process.**

    ✓ True

    ___ False

10. **Restricting access to objects based on the sensitivity of the information contained in the objects is an example of:**

    ✓ a) MAC.

    b) DAC.

    c) RBAC.

    d) ACL.

11. **Which one of the following non-discretionary access control techniques limits a subject's access to objects by examining object data so that the subject's access rights can be determined?**

    a) Rule-based

    b) Role-based

    c) Time-based

    ✓ d) Content dependent

Activity 1-2

1. **True or False? For identification to be useful, it is sufficient for each identity to be recognizable to the system.**

    ___ True

    ✓ False

2. **What one or more methods are used to authenticate an identity?**

    ✓ a) Something you have

    b) Somewhere you have been

    ✓ c) Something you are

    ✓ d) Something you know

3. **What is the appropriate description for each authentication method?**

a	Something you know	a.	An authentication factor that uses passwords and password variants.
c	Something you have	b.	An authentication factor that uses a personal attribute such as fingerprints.
b	Something you are	c.	An authentication factor that uses a physical device such as a magnetic strip.

4. **Which one of the following authentication methods is necessary to safeguard systems and facilities in high-security environments?**

    a) A token

    b) A PIN

    c) Biometrics

    ✓ d) Multifactor authentication

5. **Though single sign-on can be convenient, what is a potential security problem?**

    ✓ a) It can allow an unauthorized user access to all systems.

    b) It can allow hackers through the firewall.

    c) It can allow an unauthenticated user access to secure facilities.

    d) If you forget your user ID and password, you will not have access to any systems.

6. **Which one of the following access control administration methods involves distributing the process to localized parts of the enterprise?**

    a) Centralized

    b) Hybrid

    ✓ c) Decentralized

    d) RADIUS

Activity 1-3

1. **What is the simplest way to attack an access control system?**

    a) Break into a building.

    b) Social engineering.

    ✓ c) Capture a user ID and steal a password.

    d) Guess a password through a brute force process.

2. **What is the appropriate description for each software-based attack method?**

_d_	DoS	a.	Programs such as malware, spyware, viruses, and worms may cause system failures or malfunctions.
_a_	Malicious software	b.	Information left on media after erasures or deletions.
_c_	Sniffer	c.	A protocol analyzer is used to capture user IDs and passwords.
_b_	Data remanence	d.	Limits or eliminates the user's ability to access the network and/or data.

3. **What is the appropriate description for each additional software-based attack method?**

_d_	Dictionary attack	a.	Passing electrons through a wire or over the radio to leak protected information.
_e_	Trapdoor	b.	Attempting to access a system by trying every possible combination of a password or PIN number.
_b_	Brute force	c.	Reclaiming information from media thought to be erased.
_a_	Emanation	d.	A set of predefined words from a dictionary to crack a password.
_c_	Object reuse	e.	Accessing a program or operating system through a hidden entry point.

4. **An attack where an attacker pretends to be someone else to hide his or her actual identity is known as:**

   ✓ a) Spoofing.

   b) Shoulder surfing.

   c) Theft.

   d) Guessing.

5. **True or False? The audit function is the principal function for monitoring access.**

   ✓ True

   ___ False

6. **The controlled use of attack methods to test the security of a system or facility is known as** *penetration testing* .

7. **Which one of the following penetration test process phases includes gaining more detailed information about the selected or potential target?**

   a) Vulnerability

   b) Network scanning

   ✓ c) Enumeration

   d) Reconnaissance

8. **True or False? War dialing locates and then attempts to penetrate wireless systems.**

   ___ True

   ✓ False

Lesson 1 Follow-up

Lesson 1 Lab 1

1. **Which of the following attributes is associated with confidentiality?**

   ✓ a) Keeping information free from unauthorized disclosure

   b) Keeping information accurate

   c) Keeping information unavailable when users need it

   d) Keeping information locked in a safe

2. **Which of the following attributes is associated with integrity?**

   a) Keeping information free from unauthorized disclosure

   ✓ b) Keeping information accurate

   c) Keeping information available when users need it

   d) Keeping information in one piece, in an integral form

3. **Which of the following attributes is associated with availability?**

   a) Keeping information free from unauthorized disclosure

   b) Keeping information accurate

   c) Keeping information available when users need it

   ✓ d) Keeping information in a place where people can use it

4. **Which of the following is NOT an attribute of the reference monitor?**

   a) It must be tamper proof.

   b) It must be always invoked.

   ✓ c) It must be referred to consistently.

   d) It must be compact and verifiable.

5. **A reference monitor controls access by _____ to _____.**

   a) Users, data

   ✓ b) Subjects, objects

   c) Programs, information

   d) Administrators, permissions

6. **Least privilege is a security concept that requires that a user:**

   ✓ a) Is limited to only those functions required to do his or her job.

   b) Is given at least administrator privileges.

   c) Has privileges equal to all other users in his or her department.

   d) Is able to keep information secret and is therefore trusted with information.

7. **I&A is commonly known as:**

   a) Information and audit.

   b) Installation and activation.

   c) Intrusion and aptitude.

   ✓ d) Identification and authentication.

8. **In order to maintain accountability, which of the following is NOT necessary?**

   a) Unique identification

   b) Authorization for various activities

   ✓ c) A good accounting system

   d) Audit

9. **Restoring a backup after a system failure is an example of which of the following access control categories?**

   a) Compensating

   b) Corrective

   ✓ c) Recovery

   d) Preventative

10. **The use of a security policy to define management intention is an example of which access control type?**

    ✓ a) Administrative

    b) Physical

    c) Technical

    d) Preventative

11. **An access control matrix creates a relationship between:**

    a) Objects and servers.

    ✓ b) Objects and subjects.

    c) Objects and data.

    d) Subjects and people.

12. **MAC requires the use of:**

    a) Access control matrices.

    b) Permissions such as read, write, and modify.

    ✓ c) Security labels.

    d) Security parameters.

13. **Information classified as Secret has been found to have a risk of disclosure that would cause what kind of damage to national security?**

    a) None

    b) Grave

    c) Substantial

    ✓ d) Serious

14. **The type of access control used on a router or firewall to limit network activity is:**

    a) Discretionary.

    ✓ b) Rule-based.

    c) Role-based.

    d) Mandatory.

15. **All of the following are examples of devices with constrained interfaces EXCEPT which one?**

    a) An ATM.

    ✓ b) A normal PC with a normal keyboard.

    c) An airport check-in kiosk.

    d) A gas pump at a gas station.

16. **A passphrase is often known as a:**

    ✓ a) Virtual password.

    b) Secondary password.

    c) Password replacement.

    d) Phrase to trick hackers.

17. **A biometric device uses which of the following factors to authenticate an identity?**

✓ a) Human

b) Artificial

c) Transitory

d) Transactional

18. **The CER provides information about:**

a) The number of hackers crossing from white hat to black hat status.

b) A comparison of Type I and Type II errors.

✓ c) The place where Type I and Type II errors are equal.

d) The value of a biometric measurement.

Lesson 2

Activity 2-1

1. **True or False? Because the TCB ensures system security through the implementation of security policies, protection against system-wide deficiencies is guaranteed.**

___ True

✓ False

2. **Which of the following descriptions best explains the function of the security perimeter?**

a) It acts as a physical barrier to the TCB.

b) It determines access to objects by subjects.

✓ c) It separates the trusted and untrusted parts of a computer system.

d) It implements the RM in an operating system.

3. **What is the order of the process steps for designing, developing, and implementing a computer system?**

_2_ Firmware or software development

_3_ Software protection design

_1_ Hardware design

4. **Which of the following statements best describes the primary objective for implementing layered protection?**

a) It eliminates the risk of security infringements.

b) It manages the security of computer components.

✓ c) It creates a series of layers that impede penetration attempts.

5. **What is the appropriate description for each hardware component?**

_c_	CPU	a.	Devices that provide input to and output from a computer system.
_e_	Primary storage	b.	Software modules that interface between an operating system and I/O devices.
_g_	Secondary storage	c.	Executes security instructions that allow a computer system to successfully operate.
_d_	Virtual memory	d.	A category of storage that uses random access disks to temporarily store information needed by the operating system and application programs.
_a_	I/O	e.	A common term used for memory based on its immediate availability as an information storage location.
_f_	Computer bus	f.	The set of physical connections between devices that are attached to a computer's motherboard.
_b_	Drivers	g.	A means of storage that keeps information for long periods of time and at great volumes.

6. Which one or more categories form the software architecture of a computer system?

✓ a) Operating systems

   b) Firmware

   c) Appliances

✓ d) Application programs

7. Which software category is the first line of defense in a computer system?

✓ a) Operating system

   b) Application program

8. Which of the following techniques allows several programs to appear to operate simultaneously in a single-processor computing system?

   a) Threading

✓ b) Multitasking

   c) Multithreading

9. True or False? Multiprocessing facilitates an operating system's capacity to support more than one processor and allocate tasks between processors.

✓ True

___ False

10. Which one of the following items is software that is used on hardware devices to control their elementary functions?

   a) Microcontroller

   b) CPU

   c) Spyware

✓ d) Firmware

11. **What is the order of the phases that occur when access rights are evaluated in a distributed system architecture?**

   _3_ RM authorization of data access

   _2_ RM authorization on the client device to access the network and use the RM on the server

   _1_ Extension of the TCB from separate machines to the distributed environment

12. **Which one or more of the following security models are integrity models?**

   a) BLP

   b) Lattice

   ✓ c) Biba

   ✓ d) Clark-Wilson

13. **There are times when a user is prevented from accessing specific data on a computer because of competing system information. A user's access to additional information may be dependent upon the discontinuation of active data access. Which security model does this represent?**

   a) Harrison-Ruzzo-Ullman

   b) Graham-Denning

   c) Non-Interference

   d) Information Flow

   ✓ e) Brewer-Nash

Activity 2-2

1. **What is the appropriate description for each TCB vulnerability?**

_d_	Maintenance hooks	a.	Vulnerabilities in which two processes try to access and modify information at the same time.
_b_	TOC/TOU exploits	b.	Make use of a weakness in the TCB where access is granted at one point in time and used much later on.
_a_	Race conditions	c.	Move too much information into a program memory area.
_c_	Buffer overflows	d.	Methods that are placed in operating systems and applications used for maintenance during development that can be used for unauthorized access.

2. **What is the order of the process steps when performing a trusted recovery?**

   _3_ Verify that all security-relevant items are correct

   _1_ Operate and run the system in single user mode to ensure file recovery

   _4_ Provide system availability for multiuser or network access

   _2_ Restore missing or corrupt files to obtain the most recent backups

3. **Which data recovery process potentially produces an insecure system environment?**

   a) Trusted recovery

   ✓ b) Untrusted recovery

4. **What is the appropriate description for each type of security mode?**

d	Dedicated	a.	All users must have a proper clearance for the highest level of data classification on the system, formal access approval for all information they will access on the system, a signed NDA for all information they will access on the system, and a valid need to know for some of the information on the system.
b	System-high	b.	Users are required to have a proper security clearance, formal access approval, a signed NDA, and a valid need to know for some information on the system.
a	Compartmented	c.	All users must have proper security clearance for information they will access on the system, formal access approval, a signed NDA, and a valid need to know for some information on the system.
c	Multilevel	d.	All users must have proper security clearance, formal access approval, a signed NDA, and a valid need to know for all information on the system.

Activity 2-3

1. **Which of the following acronyms applies to the first national standard for system security evaluations?**

   a) DoD

   ✓ b) TCSEC

   c) TDI

   d) TNI

2. **What is the appropriate description for each TCSEC objective?**

   d   Policy

a. This objective requires access to specific types of reference materials, such as the Security Features User's Guide, the Trusted Facility Manual, and test and design records.

   c   Accountability

b. There are two types of this security objective: mechanisms and continuous protection.

   b   Assurance

c. This objective includes three requirements: identification, authentication, and auditing.

   a   Documentation

d. There are two types of this security objective: mandatory and discretionary.

3. **What is the appropriate description for each information systems security standard?**

   d   ITSEC

a. This security standard was developed in Europe, the United States, and Canada as a replacement for TCSEC and ITSEC. Protection profiles are produced by systems consumers and describe system protection expectations.

   a   Common Criteria

b. This security standard began as a British Standard. It is now the current international standard for information systems security.

   c   CMMI

c. This security standard was created to rate the quality of software. The evaluation process reviews the methods involved in producing the software.

   b   ISO 27002

d. This security standard evaluates TOE systems. Evaluations include functionality and assurance.

4. **What is the order of the first six phases of the security C&A process?**

   1 Establishing a preferred level of security

   2 Defining a specific environment for system use

   4 Evaluating network system security

   6 Comparing evaluations to security requirements

   5 Evaluating physical security

   3 Evaluating individual system security

Lesson 2 Follow-up

Lesson 2 Lab 1

1. **In a processor, operating systems run in which of the following states?**

    a) Operator

    b) User

    c) Application

    ✓ d) Supervisor

2. **Which one of the following is memory that can be read but difficult to write?**

    a) RAM

    ✓ b) ROM

    c) Cache

    d) Virtual

3. **Virtual memory uses which of the following techniques to function properly?**

    ✓ a) Swapping

    b) Slipping

    c) Partitioning

    d) Slicing

4. **In a PC with a single processor, which technique is used to make the processor appear to be running many programs at one time?**

    a) Multiprocessing

    b) Process slicing

    ✓ c) Multitasking

    d) Multiuser mode

5. **Which one of the following security models is used to detect covert channels?**

    ✓ a) Information Flow

    b) BLP

    c) Chinese Wall

    d) Biba

6. **Which one of the following security models is used primarily for maintaining confidentiality?**

    a) Information Flow

    ✓ b) BLP

    c) Clark-Wilson

    d) Biba

7. **The star (*) property deals with:**

   ✓ a) Writing to objects.

   b) Reading from objects.

   c) Labeling confidential information.

   d) The asterisk principle of security management.

8. **Conflict of interest is controlled by which of the following models?**

   a) Biba

   b) BLP

   ✓ c) Brewer-Nash

   d) Harrison-Ruzzo-Ullman

9. **The TCB is made up of which of the following?**

   a) Hardware, software, applications

   ✓ b) Hardware, software, firmware

   c) Hardware, software, memory

   d) Hardware, applications, access control lists (ACLs)

10. **Which one of the following is a definition of a backdoor?**

    ✓ a) An unauthorized entry point into an application or operating system

    b) An exit point from a program

    c) A place to insert Trojan horse programs into an application

    d) A place used to examine how a program is working

11. **In what security mode must all users have proper security clearance, formal access approval, a signed NDA and a valid need to know for all information on the system?**

    a) Compartmented

    b) System-high

    c) Multilevel

    ✓ d) Dedicated

12. **Which TCSEC level requires the first use of MAC?**

    a) A1

    ✓ b) B1

    c) C1

    d) D1

13. **Which evaluation process is the latest and includes international evaluations?**

    a) TCSEC

    b) TNI

    c) ITSEC

    ✓ d) Common Criteria

14. **In security, C&A stands for:**

    ✓ a) Certification and accreditation.

    b) Classification and authentication.

    c) Categorization and allocation.

    d) Confidentiality and authority.

15. **C&A includes a risk evaluation and an approval to operate. The approval to operate is made by the DAA, or the:**

    a) Dedicated Approval Activity.

    ✓ b) Designated Approving Authority.

    c) Determination of Activity Approval.

    d) Diagnostic Activity Authority.

16. **Program failures caused by information leaking from the memory of one program into the memory of an adjacent program is called:**

    a) Race condition.

    ✓ b) Buffer overflow.

    c) Buffer overrun.

    d) Race overflow.

17. **Which of the following defines the separation between the trusted and untrusted part of a system?**

    a) Security kernel

    b) Kernel security

    ✓ c) Security perimeter

    d) Perimeter security

18. **Which one of the following is an integrity security model?**

    ✓ a) Biba

    b) BLP

    c) Information Flow

    d) Harrison-Ruzzo-Ullman

19. **When should security considerations be included in the design of a system?**

    a) At the beginning of the process

    b) During the first security review

    c) After implementation

    ✓ d) Throughout the entire system development process

20. **What part of the security environment is the innermost part implemented in an operating system?**

   a) TCB

   b) Security perimeter

   ✓ c) Security kernel

   d) Security capsule

21. **Untrusted components installed as patches to an operating system or program cause:**

   ✓ a) TCB failures.

   b) Login failures.

   c) Process failures.

   d) Hardware failures.

Lesson 3

Activity 3-1

1. **Which one or more of the following items must be included in a data network?**

   ✓ a) Network protocol

   ✓ b) Network adapter hardware and drivers

   c) Network application

   ✓ d) Network media

2. **Which of the following reference models is a theoretical framework for the exchange of data between any two points on a telecommunications network?**

   a) Data service model

   b) TCP/IP model

   ✓ c) OSI model

   d) Data network model

3. **Which one of the following OSI model layers is not correct?**

   a) Layer 7: Application

   ✓ b) Layer 3: Physical

   c) Layer 6: Presentation

   d) Layer 2: Data Link

   e) Layer 5: Session

4. **Which model was developed in the late 1960s from a project sponsored by DARPA to design the Internet's protocols?**

    ✓ a) TCP/IP model

    b) OSI model

    c) ISO model

    d) IPX/SPX

5. **What is the appropriate description for each TCP/IP model layer?**

b	Network Access	a.	Supports application-to-application information transfers using port numbers to identify the applications.
c	Networking	b.	Handles the physical networking requirements of generating frames on a cable, fiber, or wireless network.
a	Host-to-Host	c.	Creates logical networks using IP network addresses.
d	Application	d.	Begins the process of sending information using application programs, then ends the process at the destination device or application.

6. **A multinational company with offices all over the world needs to communicate. What type of network will this be?**

    a) CAN

    ✓ b) WAN

    c) MAN

    d) LAN

7. **What is the appropriate description for each network component?**

b	Router	a.	A networking device that connects various network segments based on hardware addresses.
a	Switch	b.	A networking device used to connect multiple networks that employ the same protocol.
d	Firewall	c.	A networking device that supports many different types of network functions.
c	Appliance	d.	A software program or hardware device that protects networks from unauthorized data by blocking unsolicited traffic.

8. **What is a type of data network topology in which all devices are connected to a central device that performs a traffic distribution function?**

   The star network topology.

9. **What is a type of data network topology in which all devices are connected to all other devices?**

   The mesh network topology.

10. **Which one of the following is a connection-oriented protocol used in the TCP/IP model?**

    a) UDP

  ✓ b) TCP

    c) IP

    d) DNS

11. **True or False? Data services are combinations of hardware and software dedicated to managing network functions and resources.**

  ✓ True

  __ False

Activity 3-2

1. **Which one of the following remote access technologies uses secure transport protocols like IPsec to transfer information from a remote client over the Internet?**

    a) Dial-up

    b) Ethernet

    c) Wireless

  ✓ d) VPN

2. **Which one of the following actions is a capability of the PPTP remote access protocol?**

    a) Supporting automatic configuration using the associated LCP

  ✓ b) Encapsulating PPP packets for remote delivery over the Internet to the target network

    c) Identifying the beginning and end of an IP datagram

    d) Securing wireless transmissions over the 802.11 networks

3. **True or False? Wi-Fi Protected Access (WPA) is the latest advancement of the wireless protection protocols.**

  __ True

  ✓ False

Activity 3-3

1. **What is the appropriate description for each network attack method?**

e	DoS	a.	Causes network over-utilization by filling networks with unwanted email messages.
a	Spam	b.	A malware or malicious program that attaches itself to another program.
b	Virus	c.	Unauthorized software that masquerades as legitimate software.
d	Worm	d.	An independent malware program capable of duplicating itself to other devices in the network.
c	Trojan horse	e.	Causes excessive use of network resources and excludes user access to resources by causing a server overload or failure.

2. **A user calls the help desk complaining that there is a strange application on his computer. Upon further investigation, you discover that he had downloaded what he thought was a music application, but was actually some type of unauthorized software. Which of the following attacks could this be?**

    a) Spam

    b) DoS

    c) Worm

    ✓ d) Trojan horse

3. **Your users cannot access a server and you notice almost 100% network saturation. Which of the following attacks might be underway?**

    a) Spam

    ✓ b) DoS

    c) Worm

    d) Trojan horse

4. **Which one of the following security protocols is an upgraded version of SSL?**

    ✓ a) TLS

    b) S-SSL

    c) HTTPS

    d) S-HTTP

5. **Which of the following network security mechanisms detects unwanted network attacks and alerts an administrator to the event?**

    a) Firewall

    b) ACL

    c) IPS

    ✓ d) IDS

6. **Your company uses an IP mobility application and you want your roaming wireless remote users to be able to access the company network securely. Which one of the following remote access mechanisms will you check?**

   a) TACACS

   b) RADIUS

   ✓ c) Diameter

   d) Circumference

7. **Your network has been attacked and you want to check the inline device that should have identified the intrusion and blocked it. Which of the following network security mechanisms will you check?**

   a) Firewall

   b) ACL

   ✓ c) IPS

   d) IDS

Activity 3-4

1. **What may be used to improve data redundancy by automatically mirroring information written on one drive to a second drive?**

   Implement RAID level 1.

2. **Which data backup method is used to copy modified files to an offsite location?**

   a) Remote journaling

   ✓ b) Electronic vaulting

   c) Incremental backup

   d) Differential backup

3. **Which of these are single points of failure?**

   ✓ a) Disks

   b) A local LAN

   ✓ c) Servers

   ✓ d) Circuits

4. **As a starting point for all backup activities, what backup method should be used?**

   a) Electronic vaulting

   b) Incremental backup

   c) Differential backup

   ✓ d) Full backup

5. A single drive has failed but recovery is not forced due to distributing parity information on all striped drives. What RAID level is in use?

    a) Level 4

    ✓ b) Level 5

    c) Level 0

    d) Level 1

Lesson 3 Follow-up

Lesson 3 Lab 1

1. Which one of the following is the correct sequence of elements in the OSI model?

    a) Physical, Network, Application, Presentation

    ✓ b) Physical, Network, Presentation, Application

    c) Network, Physical, Presentation, Application

    d) Application, Network, Physical, Presentation

2. Which OSI layer ensures that the receiver can accurately interpret the information being transmitted?

    ✓ a) Presentation

    b) Application

    c) Network

    d) Transport

3. Half-duplex communication is similar to using a:

    a) Telephone.

    ✓ b) Walkie-talkie.

    c) Super highway.

    d) Radio station.

4. A network used in a setting where multiple buildings are connected or associated together is called a:

    a) LAN.

    b) WAN.

    c) GAN.

    ✓ d) CAN.

5. Which of the following devices functions primarily at Layer 2 of the OSI model?

    a) Hub

    b) Router

    ✓ c) Switch

    d) Gateway

6. **All devices are connected to a central device that performs a traffic distribution function. In this scenario, what type of topology is in use?**

    ✓ a) Star

    b) Bus

    c) Ring

    d) Mesh

7. **How many layers are found in the TCP/IP model?**

    a) 3

    ✓ b) 4

    c) 6

    d) 7

8. **Which technology used for network access is replacing common modems with a digital transmission method provided by a telephone company?**

    ✓ a) DSL

    b) Cable modem

    c) ATM

    d) SONET

9. **The protocol used to translate IP addresses to MAC addresses is:**

    ✓ a) ARP.

    b) DNS.

    c) DHCP.

    d) APAP.

10. **A host-to-host protocol that provides reliable delivery of data is:**

    a) UDP.

    b) ICMP.

    c) TCMP.

    ✓ d) TCP.

11. **Which one of the following is not a data transfer protocol?**

    a) FTP

    b) TFTP

    ✓ c) ICMP

    d) HTTP

12. **Which of the following protocols replaces Telnet and provides higher security levels?**

    ✓ a) SSH

    b) SSL

    c) TLS

    d) STelnet

13. WAP is a protocol that deals with:

    a) Wireless access to an Ethernet network.

    b) Securing wireless networks.

    ✓ c) Wireless access to data networks using mobile phone technology.

    d) Wireless access using IPsec.

14. CHAP uses how many steps to authenticate to the dial-in service?

    a) 1

    b) 2

    ✓ c) 3

    d) 4

15. As a wireless security protocol, what does WEP stand for?

    a) Wi-Fi Encrypted Privacy

    ✓ b) Wired Equivalent Privacy

    c) Wireless Equivalency Protocol

    d) Working Encapsulation Protocol

16. Which one of the following is a network topology where each device is connected to every other device?

    ✓ a) Mesh

    b) Ring

    c) Bus

    d) Star

17. Which protocol is not used for routing on a logical network?

    ✓ a) Ethernet

    b) IPX

    c) Appletalk

    d) IP

18. What device is used to move data between dissimilar physical layer protocols at Layer 3 of the OSI model?

    a) Hub

    ✓ b) Router

    c) Switch

    d) Gateway

19. An IPv4 address has how many bits?

    a) 16

    b) 24

    ✓ c) 32

    d) 48

20. **Ethernet networks always use which type of address?**

    a) Logical

    b) IP

    c) TCP

    ✓ d) MAC

Lesson 4

Activity 4-1

1. **What benefits does information security provide?**

   It provides protection for important business resources.

   It enforces protection based on the CIA triad.

   It protects the network so that hackers cannot gain access to specific resources.

   It addresses standards set by the government laws and regulations to protect users.

2. **Which one of the following should be conducted to determine areas where an unauthorized person could access or damage resources or data?**

   ✓ a) Vulnerability assessment

   b) Risk assessment

   c) SLA

   d) Defense in depth

3. **How would you characterize the approach that defense in depth uses to keep hackers and malware out of a network?**

   Defense in depth uses a layered approach, with several rings of protection targeted against separate threat factors, to secure the network.

4. **In a typical defense in depth approach, what does the stateful inspection firewall protect networks from?**

   a) Excessive traffic

   b) Inappropriate access levels

   c) Viruses

   ✓ d) Hackers not caught by the edge router

5. **Which one or more of the following essential action items should an enterprise perform prior to engaging an outsourcing provider?**

   ✓ a) Evaluate the provider's security.

   b) Audit the provider's current security activities.

   c) Create a layered security system.

   ✓ d) Enforce security requirements for the outsourcing provider.

6. **A contract that requires 95% uptime for all network resources is an example of which of the following?**

    a) Corporate culture

    b) CBK

    c) Risk-reduction measures

    ✓ d) SLA

7. **True or False? One way in which the CISSP helps to reduce risk is by providing training to everyone in the organization on present security risks and protection methods.**

    ✓ True

    ___ False

8. **As an information security consultant, knowing a corporation's vision and mission statements would help you determine which of the following?**

    a) Corporate morale

    ✓ b) Corporate culture

    c) Corporate structure

    d) Corporate divisions

9. **What is the corresponding security impact of each technical environment change?**

d	Personal computers were attached to LANs	a.	Strong physical security was provided for large, centralized systems.
a	Mainframe computers began to use online transaction processing	b.	The use of virus scans, firewalls, and IDSs raised the cost of information security to protect organizational resources.
c	Computer terminals were replaced with PCs	c.	Computer security was decentralized to individual desktop systems.
b	Conception and evolution of the Internet	d.	Administrators became increasingly concerned with both desktop security and network security.

10. **Which organizational position includes the responsibility to safeguard the corporation's IT assets?**

    This can vary depending upon the organization, and might be assigned to a CISO, ISO, or CSO. Regardless of title, the top security position in any company includes the responsibility to safeguard the corporation's IT assets.

    On the other hand, the security office is charged with day-to-day tactical and strategic security operations to maintain future organizational security.

11. **True or False? The audit committee is responsible for SOX Act compliance.**

    ✓ True

    ___ False

12. **Which one or more of the following are recommended security governance-level activities, according to the ITGI?**

   ✓ a) Strategically align information security with business strategies.

   b) Maintain day-to-day oversight of the security infrastructure.

   ✓ c) Execute appropriate measures to manage and mitigate risks.

   ✓ d) Evaluate, monitor, and report information security governance metrics.

   ✓ e) Optimize information security investments.

13. **What is the appropriate description for each ISO role action item?**

_d_	Inform	a.	Ensure that certain laws, regulations, and policies are adhered to.
_b_	Budget	b.	Develop a plan and justify the expenditures for the organization.
_e_	Develop	c.	Ensure the user and management are prepared for information security procedures.
_c_	Train	d.	Transmit security information in the organization.
_a_	Ensure compliance	e.	Create security awareness in the corporation.

14. **What role does the organizational security model provide?**

   It is the totality of information security implementations in an organization. It separates the various security-requiring aspects of the organization into layers.

15. **What is the appropriate description for each security goal?**

_b_	Operational	a.	Long-term security goals
_a_	Strategic	b.	Short-term security goals
_c_	Tactical	c.	Medium-term security goals

16. **What types of information can be included in security goals?**

   Implementing strong network logon authentication with SSO capabilities

   Increasing security by preventing users from downloading non-trusted content

   Using certificates to provide integrity for general business email messages

   Providing integrity, non-repudiation, and confidentiality for all business email

   Enforcing the CIA triad for accounting transactions

   Enforcing security programs that limit the opportunity for fraud and collusion

Activity 4-2

1. **What benefits does the security principle known as job rotation provide?**

   Individuals within an organization can benefit from an enhanced understanding of the business and the tasks others perform. Because frequent audits can be performed as employees rotate to new positions, job rotation adds value by helping administrators discover and pinpoint fraudulent, criminal, or otherwise improper activities.

2. **True or False? SoD combat threats of fraud and collusion that otherwise might occur.**

   ✓ True

   ___ False

3. **True or False? Least privilege can be applied as an organizational security concept because users are granted the minimum permissions required for completing their designated tasks.**

   ✓ True

   ___ False

4. **From a security standpoint, what security benefit do mandatory vacations provide?**

   The corporate audit and security staffs have time to investigate and discover any discrepancies in employee activity.

   When employees understand the security focus of the mandatory vacation policy, the opportunities for fraudulent activities decreases.

5. **How is a sensitivity profile developed and what is the benefit?**

   Data owners must determine the need-to-know information for each organizational job function to create a sensitivity profile.

   The sensitivity profiles help administrators assign authorization permissions in only those areas where the profiles are deemed necessary.

6. **How can you address the major considerations of sensitivity profiling for job positions?**

   To decrease the risk of loss of sensitive information, users' authentication methods and passwords should be changed frequently.

   To ensure privileges are still intact and appropriate for the employee's current job, reviews of access capabilities should be performed frequently.

7. **Which one or more of the following should be included in general hiring practices for all positions?**

   a) Financial and/or credit history reviews

   b) Lie detector testing

   ✓ c) Criminal history checks

   ✓ d) Reference checks

   ✓ e) Work history verifications

8. **Which one or more of the following should be included in hiring practices for security-sensitive positions?**

   ✓ a) Lie detector testing

   ✓ b) Security clearances

   ✓ c) Financial and/or credit history reviews

   ✓ d) Extended background investigations

   e) Racial profiling

Lesson 4 Follow-up

Lesson 4 Lab 1

1. **Who is ultimately responsible for protecting the assets of an organization?**

   a) Data custodian

   ✓ b) Senior management

   c) IT department head

   d) Security administrator

2. **Which one of the following is part of the CIA triad?**

   a) Authentication

   b) Applicability

   ✓ c) Availability

   d) Authenticity

3. **Confidentiality is maintained if:**

   a) Unauthorized users gain unauthorized access.

   b) Important information does not leak out of the system.

   ✓ c) Access to information is given only to authorized users.

   d) Rumors about people do not spread in the company.

4. **Which one of the following is not a physical control?**

   a) A fence that deters intruders

   ✓ b) A policy detailing which physical controls to use

   c) Guard dogs roaming the property at night

   d) Lighting of doors and parking areas

5. **A pre-employment screening for a highly sensitive position should evaluate all of the following EXCEPT:**

   a) Drug use.

   b) Financial problems.

   c) Reference checks.

   ✓ d) Food preferences.

6. **A risk management team should include which of the following personnel?**

   a) Legal staff

   b) Physical plant staff

   c) Security staff

   ✓ d) Staff from throughout the organization

7. **Risk, as it applies to CISSP, is best defined as:**

    a) Taking a chance without knowledge of a predetermined outcome.

    ✓ b) The likelihood of a threat taking advantage of a vulnerability.

    c) A gamble with many chances of failure.

    d) The loss of income when someone becomes ill and has no insurance.

8. **Which is the most likely threat?**

    a) Hurricanes

    b) Tornados

    ✓ c) Disgruntled employees

    d) Water leaks in the computer room

9. **Systems are under the most threat from:**

    ✓ a) Insiders.

    b) Outsiders.

    c) Hackers.

    d) Crackers.

10. **Having multiple security schemes deployed in a hierarchical model is called:**

    a) Modular defense.

    b) Structural defense.

    ✓ c) Defense in depth.

    d) Hardened defense.

11. **Security policies represent:**

    a) Operational instructions for implementing security.

    b) Tactical instructions for implementing security.

    c) Procedures specified by senior management.

    ✓ d) High-level objectives specified by senior management.

12. **Information classification is determined by the:**

    a) Custodian.

    b) User.

    c) Coordinator.

    ✓ d) Owner.

13. **When a risk is mitigated it is:**

    a) Removed with 100% certainty.

    ✓ b) Reduced, often to an acceptable level.

    c) Estimated, but not removed.

    d) Not changed in any way.

Lesson 5

Activity 5-1

1. **What are two primary forms of classification schemes?**

   ✓ a) Commercial

   b) Private

   ✓ c) Military

   d) Confidential

2. **What is the appropriate description for each military classification scheme level?**

   d   Secret

   b   Confidential

   a   Top Secret

   c   Unclassified

   a. Information that, if disclosed to unauthorized individuals, will present the risk of grave damage to national security.

   b. Information that, if disclosed to unauthorized individuals, will present the risk of damage to national security.

   c. Information that, if disclosed to unauthorized individuals, will present no risk of damage to national security.

   d. Information that, if disclosed to unauthorized individuals, will present the risk of serious damage to national security.

3. **What is the appropriate description for each commercial classification scheme level?**

   e   Trade Secret

   c   Private

   b   Corporate Confidential

   a   Personal and Confidential

   d   Client Confidential

   a. Information of a personal nature that should be protected.

   b. Information that should not be provided to individuals outside of the enterprise.

   c. Correspondence of a private nature between two people that should be safeguarded.

   d. Client personal information that, if released, may result in the identity theft of the individual.

   e. Corporate intellectual property that, if released, will present serious damage to the company's ability to protect patents and processes.

4. **True or False? The classifier is the custodian who is charged with safeguarding previously classified information.**

   ___ True

   ✓ False

5. **Which one or more of the following are protector-specific classification tasks?**

   ✓ a) Keeping records of access to classified information

   ✓ b) Ensuring that the proper destruction procedures are followed

   ✓ c) Providing the labeling of media, as necessary

   d) Evaluating the data's risk of disclosure

   e) Being aware of the data and information that requires safeguarding

Activity 5-2

1. **True or False? There is one objective that all security policies have in common: the dissemination of standardized information to ensure that all personnel receive information necessary to fulfill their duties.**

   ✓ True

   ___ False

2. **A rigorous security implementation plan can be launched and established using a series of best practices. Which one or more of the following describe a best practice that should be used?**

   ✓ a) Promote security awareness and user responsibilities.

   ✓ b) Generate a high-level security policy stating the source of authority and responsibilities.

   ✓ c) Assess information ownership and resource controls.

   ✓ d) Determine access control and authorization.

   e) Establish dress codes.

3. **Security policies can fulfill multiple objectives for an organization. Which one or more of the following are objectives that the security policy can fulfill?**

   ✓ a) They can outline the computer system's security requirements.

   ✓ b) They can define an organization's security goals.

   ✓ c) They can inform employees about their duties and responsibilities.

   d) They can help to identify how many employees need to be hired.

4. **What is the appropriate example of each security document type?**

a	Policies	a.	Information security will ensure the protection of information by implementing security best practices.
c	Standards	b.	When travelling with laptops, users should use safety precautions to prevent laptop theft, damage, or data loss.
b	Guidelines	c.	The corporation must implement 802.1x security for all wireless networks.
d	Procedures	d.	To implement SSH on the router, enter the enable mode and then enter the appropriate commands for the router.
e	Baselines	e.	TFTP must be disabled in all servers except for those specifically used for the TFTP service.

5. **True or False? Standards are a security document type that describes a required implementation or use of tools.**

   ✓ True

   ___ False

6. **True or False? In the security policy process, the overall document environment is controlled by policies.**

   ✓ True

   ___ False

7. **What is the obligated security component responsibility of each role?**

b	CEO and Board of Directors	a.	Responsible for adhering to security goals by implementing them in their day-to-day activities
c	Security department	b.	Responsible for establishing organizational security goals and objectives
a	Employees	c.	Responsible for determining how to put the established goals into practice

8. **What is the appropriate example of each security planning effort?**

_b_	Strategic planning	a.	At a mid-size company, the server space will be running out in approximately 35 weeks. The IT team purchases the necessary equipment and hardware and plans a data move to two new servers.
_c_	Tactical planning	b.	The president of a large university is looking to hire top-quality professors, but the university currently has an inexpensive firewall in place to protect important research. To attract elite professors to the school, he decides that the university must invest more money into equipment to ensure that data is secure.
_a_	Operational and project planning	c.	Inventory records at a large school district have indicated the need for new equipment. The school district budget, however, has indicted that only one-fourth of the equipment can be purchased in each of the next four years. The IT department creates a plan to replace the oldest equipment first and continue for the next four years.

9. **Which one or more of the following are considered effective training methods that can promote security awareness?**

   ✓ a) Encourage organizational security memberships at the national or local level.

   ✓ b) Address password protection in the training.

   ✓ c) Characterize email threats for staff.

   ✓ d) Review VPN practices to protect data.

   e) Store the only copies of the security manuals in the locked server room for safe-keeping.

Lesson 5 Follow-up

Lesson 5 Lab 1

1. **Military classification includes all of the following terms EXCEPT:**

   a) Secret.

   ✓ b) Public.

   c) Confidential.

   d) Top Secret.

2. **Who is responsible for keeping records of access to classified information?**

   a) Data owner

   b) Data classifier

   ✓ c) Data custodian

   d) Data destroyer

3. **Which one of the following is an example of physical access control?**

   a) Using passwords for authentication

   b) Using permissions on files

   ✓ c) Using a cipher lock on a door

   d) Using an encryption protocol

4. **Who is responsible for the overall organizational security policy?**

   ✓ a) CEO

   b) CSO

   c) CIO

   d) COO

5. **Which document type is used to document steps taken in a process?**

   a) Policy

   ✓ b) Procedure

   c) Guideline

   d) Baseline

6. **Which document type is used to document required implementations or uses of a tool?**

   a) Policy

   b) Procedure

   ✓ c) Standard

   d) Baseline

7. **Who is responsible for implementing the security program of an organization?**

   ✓ a) Everyone

   b) Security department

   c) Senior administrators

   d) IT department

8. **Which type of planning deals with long range goals?**

   a) Tactical

   b) Organizational

   c) Operational

   ✓ d) Strategic

9. **The organization is planning to change to a new authentication process within 18 months. What type of plan would be used for this implementation?**

   ✓ a) Tactical

   b) Organizational

   c) Operational

   d) Strategic

10. **Which classification level used by the U.S. military suggests that grave damage to national security will result from an unauthorized disclosure of information?**

    ✓ a) Top Secret

    b) Secret

    c) Confidential

    d) Unclassified

11. **What type of training content would be typical for all employees to receive?**

    a) Discussions on the development of an encryption algorithm

    b) Instructions on configuring an enterprise firewall

    ✓ c) Discussions on social engineering threats

    d) Instructions on setting a clipping level for server log files

12. **A guideline is used to provide:**

    a) The minimum security required in a system or process.

    b) A required implementation practice.

    c) The steps to complete a specific task.

    ✓ d) A suggested implementation practice.

13. **Which role in an organization is responsible for determining how to implement the security policies?**

    a) Everyone

    ✓ b) Security department

    c) Senior administrators

    d) IT department

14. **Who is responsible for the proper destruction of classified media?**

    a) Individual users

    b) CFO

    ✓ c) Data custodian

    d) IT media librarian

15. **What determines the classification of data or information?**

    a) Cost to safeguard

    ✓ b) Risk of disclosure

    c) Damage to national assets

    d) The individual data owner

16. **At a minimum, how often should users receive security training?**

   a) Every week

   b) Every month

   c) Once a quarter

   ✓ d) Once a year

17. **Information access is allowed based on which one of the following principles?**

   a) SoD

   b) Need to distribute

   c) Need to analyze

   ✓ d) Need to know

18. **To avoid confusion, commercial organizations should use a classification scheme that is:**

   a) The same as the military.

   ✓ b) Specific to the organization.

   c) The standardized commercial scheme found in industry publications.

   d) Modeled after a successful company in the same industry.

19. **In an organization, what is the best reason why a security policy should be implemented if there is not one currently in place?**

   a) A policy can help the organization.

   b) A policy makes good business sense.

   c) A policy is not required.

   ✓ d) A policy is always necessary.

20. **A plan that details the penetration testing activities for the next three months is considered:**

   ✓ a) Operational.

   b) Tactical.

   c) Strategic.

   d) Organizational.

21. **Security policies are developed to protect all of the following assets except which one?**

   a) Data

   ✓ b) Employees' homes

   c) Facilities

   d) People

Lesson 6

Activity 6-1

1. **True or False? Risk analysis is the security management process for addressing any risks or economic damages that affect an organization.**

   _✓_ True

   ___ False

2. **What is the appropriate description for each risk analysis process phase?**

_b_	Asset identification	a.	This phase identifies threats and vulnerabilities so the analyst can confirm where asset protection problems exist.
_a_	Vulnerability identification	b.	This phase finds assets that require protection and determines the value of the assets.
_d_	Probability quantification	c.	This phase reduces or eliminates risk by developing countermeasures.
_c_	Countermeasures determination	d.	This phase determines the possibility that threats will exploit vulnerabilities.

3. **What is the appropriate description for each risk management principle?**

_b_	Avoidance	a.	Rather than respond to the risk, the organization may choose this principle and employ no countermeasures.
_d_	Reduction	b.	By eliminating the threat through mitigation, no risk is present. With no risk, this principle is implemented.
_c_	Transfer	c.	This principle helps to shift liability and maintain organizational profitability despite the potential exposure to unwanted security and business risks.
_a_	Acceptance	d.	This principle helps to curtail the severity of risk or lessen the probability of a loss occurring.

4. **True or False? Asset valuation is the practice of determining an asset's risk level to an organization.**

   ___ True

   _✓_ False

5. **What two essential questions does asset valuation answer?**

   a) How much did it cost to purchase the asset?

   ✓ b) What requires protection?

   ✓ c) How much loss will there be if the asset is misplaced or damaged?

   d) How will we maintain the asset?

6. **What is the appropriate description for each asset valuation method?**

c	Asset management system	a.	This method includes additional asset information that may be present, such as the cost of developing software packages.
a	Accounting system	b.	With this method, risk of loss for the assets is accepted and protected.
b	Insurance valuation	c.	This method uses an organizational system that contains a detailed record of property and similar assets.
d	Delphi method	d.	This method utilizes expert judgement to value assets, especially for those that do not have an accounting foundation.

7. **Which one or more of the following are considered natural disaster risk types?**

   ✓ a) Hurricane

   ✓ b) Flooding

      c) Theft

      d) Epidemics

   ✓ e) Wildfire

8. **To properly assess the probability and prioritization of security risks, a series of strategic process phases should be practiced and applied to your organization's information systems. In what order should the phases occur?**

   _2_ List the various, ensuing risks discovered through analysis.

   _1_ Perform risk analysis tasks on an individual basis.

   _4_ Prioritize risks by probability levels and focus on high-probability risks when building a response process.

   _3_ Determine risk probability.

9. **True or False? Qualitative risk analysis is based on numerical analysis and history.**

   __ True

   _✓_ False

10. **What is an estimate based on the historical occurrences of incidents and the likelihood of risk reoccurrence?**

    Quantitative risk analysis

11. **In computer security, what is a system weakness or safeguard deficiency that enables an attacker to violate a particular system's integrity?**

    Vulnerability

12. **In what areas are organizations typically vulnerable?**

    Physical structure: Accessibility to a room where secure information is stored can expose vulnerabilities and create a venue for sudden intrusion threats.

    Software: Worms, viruses, and Trojans are software that threaten systems. Regularly running virus scanners can help lessen or eliminate vulnerabilities.

    Network: The failure to encrypt private information as it travels across a network can heighten system vulnerability.

    Electrical: A single electrical feed that supports an entire building or enterprise can exploit an instance of vulnerability. A backup power supply is necessary to protect the availability of system data.

13. **Which one or more of the following are risk determination factors?**

    ✓ a) ARO

    ✓ b) SLE

    ✓ c) EF

    ✓ d) ALE

    　 e) SLA

14. **What criteria should be used in the selection of safeguards and why?**

    Cost effectiveness: Selecting cost-effective safeguards eliminates wasted resources.

    Risk reduction: Safeguards must be employed to reduce risk.

    Practicality: Safeguards must be practical.

Activity 6-2

1. **True or False? Ethics establish a foundation for behavioral conduct that is conducive to protecting your organizational data, environment, and infrastructure.**

    ✓ True

    ___ False

2. **When companies or governments adopt ethical codes, what benefits are generally created by doing so?**

    They no longer need to determine and manage ethical behavior on an as-needed basis.

    It helps to regulate security by minimizing risk from man-made disasters.

    It helps to create the foundation of honorable, accountable, and reliable performance from employees.

3. **True or False? Typically, information security criminals recognize that their motivations are unethical.**

    ___ True

    ✓ False

4. **Name some institutions that you have come in contact with that have commonly enforced codes of ethical standards.**

The American Medical Association (AMA) and the U.S. federal government.

Both of these organization have adopted a set of ethical standards that are enforced and typically require yearly briefings regarding requirements.

5. **What are some examples of typical ethics fallacies that information security criminals believe?**

The criminal thinks that society would benefit by the availability of the information and thus the criminal is justified to release it regardless of the information owner.

The criminal feels the computer is like a game; if it lets you do something, it must be okay.

If people are negligent enough to do foolish things, the criminal questions why he or she should be worried.

If the criminal did not break it, it must be okay to use it.

If the criminal thinks that he or she is learning from hacking in order to help society, it is unlikely a wrongful act.

6. **The IAB ethics primarily focuses on unethical activities to avoid. What are some of the actions to avoid?**

Seeking to gain unauthorized access to Internet resources

Disrupting intended Internet use

Wasting resources such as people, capacity, and computers through unprincipled actions

Destroying the integrity of computer-based information

Compromising user privacy

7. **As a prospective CISSP candidate, what are some examples of the ethics principles you will need to formally subscribe to as part of the (ISC)² Code of Ethics?**

Preamble principles of:

Ensuring the safety of the commonwealth and the responsibility and accountability to principals, (ISC)² committee members, and other CISSP professionals.

Requiring and acknowledging adherence to the utmost ethical values and standards of behavior.

Strictly observing this code to demonstrate compliance and fulfill the conditions of certification.

Canons such as:

Guarding the commonwealth, infrastructure, and society.

Behaving responsibly, justly, honestly, honorably, and legally.

Providing adept, competent, and assiduous service to principals.

Improving, enhancing, and protecting the profession.

Lesson 6 Follow-up

Lesson 6 Lab 1

1. **The process of determining the potential damage or exposure from a threat is:**

   a) Threat analysis.

   b) Impact analysis.

   ✓ c) Risk analysis.

   d) Outcome analysis.

2. **Failure to manage risks effectively can result in which one of the following?**

   a) Violation of the DAD triad

   ✓ b) Violation of the CIA triad

   c) Violation of the MAC triad

   d) Violation of the SLA triad

3. **The critical first step in risk analysis is to:**

   a) Identify the vulnerabilities.

   ✓ b) Identify the assets to protect.

   c) Identify the attackers.

   d) Identify the countermeasures.

4. **A vulnerability is:**

   ✓ a) A lack of a safeguard.

   b) A lack of a threat.

   c) A lack of a risk.

   d) A lack of an asset.

5. **Which one of the following is not a way to manage risk?**

   a) Avoidance

   b) Reduction

   c) Acceptance

   ✓ d) Substantiate

6. **Which one of the following is a way to transfer risk?**

   a) Give the asset to someone else

   b) Hire more security personnel

   ✓ c) Buy insurance for an asset

   d) Strengthen the physical security used to protect the asset

7. **Which one of the following is the least precise method used to value assets?**

    a) Asset management system

    b) Accounting system

    c) Insurance value

    ✓ d) Delphi estimates

8. **Which of these is an unintentional man-made threat?**

    ✓ a) A mistake

    b) Giving passwords to coworkers

    c) Habitually leaving classified documents on a desk, unprotected, as a normal practice

    d) Posting a password on a chat room

9. **Which of the following presents the greatest threat to security?**

    a) Hackers

    ✓ b) Employees

    c) Crackers

    d) Spam artists

10. **Which one of the following risk analysis methods is based on numerical analysis of historical incidents?**

    a) Qualitative

    b) Subjective

    ✓ c) Quantitative

    d) Objective

11. **Which risk analysis method is based on objective measures?**

    a) Qualitative

    ✓ b) Quantitative

    c) Numerical

    d) Scientific

12. **Qualitative risk analysis uses which one of the following methods?**

    ✓ a) Delphi

    b) Mind meld

    c) Book value analysis

    d) Structured walkthrough

13. **Which one of the following would not be classified as a vulnerability?**

    a) No virus scanning software

    b) Windows in the computer room

    c) Water lines over a computer room

    ✓ d) Cipher locks on the computer room door

14. **The term ARO is used to describe the:**

    a) Actual Risk Outcome.

    b) Activity Reduction Overview.

    ✓ c) Annualized Rate of Occurrence.

    d) Action Review Outline.

15. **The EF is used to:**

    a) Determine how many employees will come down with the flu.

    ✓ b) Estimate the loss of an asset as a percent should a threat occur.

    c) Account for the damage the sun can do to a CD or DVD-ROM if overexposed.

    d) Determine the cost of replacing film damaged by an X-ray machine.

16. **Which one of the following factors is not involved in calculating the ALE?**

    a) ARO

    ✓ b) AF

    c) AV

    d) EF

17. **The SLE is calculated by multiplying the:**

    a) Effective value times the actual loss.

    ✓ b) The EF times the AV.

    c) The AV times the ARO.

    d) The EF times the SLO.

18. **The ALE = $400,000. The EF = 20%. The SLE = $4,000,000. What is the AV?**

    a) $44,000,000

    b) $80,000,000

    ✓ c) $20,000,000

    d) $2,000,000

19. **The ALE = $400,000. The EF = 20%. The SLE = $4,000,000. What is the ARO?**

    ✓ a) Once every 10 years

    b) 10 times a year

    c) Once every 100 years

    d) 10 times in 10 years

20. **In determining which safeguard to use, the cost of the safeguard must be:**

    a) More than the ALE.

    b) Equal to the ALE.

    c) Less than the ALE.

    ✓ d) Equal to or less than the ALE.

21. **The IAB ethics are found in:**

    ✓ a) RFC 1087.

       b) RFC 1099.

       c) RFC 3089.

       d) RFC 1888.

22. **Which ethics statement requires users to refrain from wasting Internet resources?**

    ✓ a) IAB ethics

       b) (ISC)^2 ethics

       c) ADA ethics

       d) IEEE ethics

23. **Violating the (ISC)^2 ethics can lead to:**

       a) Money fines from the (ISC)^2.

    ✓ b) Removal of the CISSP designation.

       c) A letter of reprimand from the (ISC)^2.

       d) Criminal prosecution from the (ISC)^2.

Lesson 7

Activity 7-1

1. **What is the appropriate description for each phase of the software life cycle?**

_g_	Project initiation	a.	Concludes software use and ensures continuation of secure data
_d_	Functional design analysis and planning	b.	Prepares a detailed design of the software
_b_	System design specifications	c.	Supports software use and manages changes
_e_	Software development	d.	Determines the functions to execute during the project
_f_	Installation/implementation	e.	Coding activities to assist the design
_c_	Operational/maintenance	f.	Assesses the quality of the software using a QA group
_a_	Disposal	g.	Determines the needs for software development

2. **Which type of software is more likely to expose an organization to unexpected security vulnerabilities?**

      a) Open source software

   ✓ b) Proprietary software

3. **True or False? Security that is implemented late in the development cycle will be just as effective as security that is created early in the design phases.**

      __ True

   ✓ False

4. **Prioritize the stages in the waterfall model process.**

   _3_ Create an acceptance step at the end of each phase.

   _4_ Continue or repeat the phase, or a previous phase, if an evaluation fails.

   _2_ Estimate the phase or step time duration to determine the project length.

   _1_ Define the process phases or steps.

5. **True or False? The spiral model software development process is a repetitive process involving only risk analysis.**

   __ True

   _✓_ False

6. **Which statement describes the CMM?**

   a) A capability model that includes a detection system to monitor an organization's software development process.

   ✓ b) A process capability model that evaluates the levels of sophistication or maturity found in an organization's software development process.

   c) A process capability model that evaluates the levels of sophistication in an organization's infrastructure.

   d) An evaluation tool used to measure the readiness of an organization's software development capabilities.

7. **True or False? The CMMI is a process improvement project initiative that incorporates the different CMMs into one cohesive collection of integrated models.**

   _✓_ True

   __ False

8. **What is the appropriate description for each change control phase?**

_f_	Requesting the change	a.	Changes are put in place within scheduled parameters including date, time, by whom, and so on.
_d_	Approving the change	b.	Successful or unsuccessful changes should always be documented to management so that progress is recognized.
_c_	Documenting the change	c.	The change is recorded and scheduled in the change log.
_e_	Testing and reporting results	d.	The CCB evaluates the change request and approves the change. No change can continue until it is approved.
_a_	Implementing the change	e.	The CCB should confirm that an adequate evaluation has occurred before approving the change implementation. A backout or failure recovery plan must be in place.
_b_	Reporting the change	f.	This step requires justification that supports the potential change and a full explanation of the change.

9. **What are the appropriate key questions for each configuration management phase?**

_b_	Configuration identification	a.	What modifications have been made to the authorized configurations and what changes are pending?
_c_	Configuration change control (or change management)	b.	What configurations are authorized and should be implemented in all current, in-use systems?
_a_	Configuration status accounting	c.	What changes are being made or have been made to the authorized configurations?
_d_	Configuration verification and auditing	d.	Do the configurations in use today match the configurations found in the configuration management system? Have any unauthorized and untracked modifications been made? What are the security risks associated with the unauthorized changes?

10. **Explain the difference between compiled code and interpreted code.**

   Compiled code will be compiled one time and run many times. Interpreted code will need to be interpreted each time it is run.

11. **Explain the difference between a SLC and a SDLC.**

   The system design life cycle (SDLC) is concerned with creating the application or program. The system life cycle (SLC) extends beyond the SDLC to include operation and disposal of the application and associated data.

Activity 7-2

1. **Which of the following statements describes a data structure?**

   a) A collection of databases that store mass amounts of data.

   b) An improvised or ad hoc information method for storing information.

   ✓ c) A standardized format for storing information in a computer system so that the information can be efficiently accessed by applications.

   d) A software application with the capability to read and store mass amounts of computerized information.

2. **What is the appropriate description for each data structure?**

_d_	Primitive	a.	A collection of primitives that are inter-related.
_a_	Array	b.	An array with more than one dimension.
_c_	List	c.	A structure that contains ordered arrays.
_b_	Matrix	d.	A data element that is singular in nature and not broken down into small components when accessed.

3. **True or False? AI systems are implemented using neural networks that are meant to approximate the neural processes of the human brain.**

   ✓ True

   ___ False

4. **Which one of the following statements explains how a KBS operates?**

    ✓ a) Performs decision-making and problem solving functions through AI and access to a database of knowledge information

    b) Uses complex algorithms to mimic the human intelligence process and adapts and learns from the environment in order to make decisions

5. **What is the appropriate best practice for each software vulnerability?**

b	Buffer overflow	a.	Programmers have an obligation to ensure that information entered into fields is properly formatted; if not, it must be rejected.
d	Citizen programmers	b.	Programmers should perform length checking or bounds checking on fields within a program.
e	Covert channel	c.	Programmers and designers must defend against vulnerabilities from malicious code when designing and writing systems.
c	Malware	d.	Programmers on software development projects should be trained and experienced professionals who understand and follow acceptable procedures for application security design.
a	Malformed input	e.	Programmers and designers must avoid unsound security practices that can result in the introduction of these system exploitations into software designs.

6. **What is the appropriate best practice for each software vulnerability?**

d	Executable content and mobile code	a.	Programmers must ensure that data checks and data use occur within a minimal time interval.
c	Object reuse	b.	These development-phase access channels should be removed before system implementation.
e	Social engineering	c.	Programmers should verify that previously recorded disk space is cleared as part of a cleanup process for temporary file storage areas.
a	TOC/TOU	d.	Programmers should verify that system input does not contain unexpected information that may be executable and present a security risk.
b	Trapdoors and backdoors	e.	To protect against attacks that exploit human vulnerabilities, such as shoulder surfing, programmers should employ simple programming techniques that circumvent echoing passwords or mask password entries with characters such as asterisks (*).

7. **Which one of the following software controls is part of the operating system and enforces the RM?**

   ✓ a) Security kernel

   b) Buffer overflow security controls

   c) Cryptography

   d) Password protection

   e) Memory protection

Activity 7-3

1. **Which of the following statements describes a database system?**

   a) A mechanism that attempts to mimic or emulate the process of human intelligence by implementing algorithms that cause the system to learn about its environment and make decisions based on its learning.

   b) A standardized format for storing information in a computer system so that this information can be efficiently accessed by applications.

   c) A program that uses knowledge-based techniques to support human decision making, learning, and action.

   ✓ d) A set of related information organized within a software framework for ease of access and reporting.

2. **What is the appropriate description for each database system model?**

   d Hierarchical Database Management Model

   a. This model is implemented using pointers to other database elements so that traversing information in the database requires the use of pointers to locate subsequent entries.

   a Network Database Management Model

   b. In this model, data is accessed by gaining entry to the database component as a closed environment.

   c Relational Database Management Model

   c. This model allows a designer to create connections among the various database components.

   b Object-Oriented Database Model

   d. This model is implemented in a tree structure with internal database links to higher-level elements.

3. **What is the appropriate description for each database interface language?**

   d ODBC

   a. Allows the incorporation of documents, graphics, sound files, and other formatted information into a parent document.

   c JDBC

   b. A document description language that simplifies the presentation of database information in various formats.

   b XML

   c. A mechanism that allows Java-based programs to access databases transparently.

   a OLE DB

   d. Provides a standard API that allows programmers to access any database from any platform.

4. **What is the appropriate description for each of the database terms?**

_e_	Table	a.	A column or field in a database.
_c_	Tuple	b.	The intersection, or value, of a row and column in a database.
_a_	Attribute	c.	A row, or record, in a database.
_b_	Cell	d.	An attribute that provides a unique value in a tuple or row that uniquely identifies that row.
_d_	Key	e.	A set of rows and columns that contains related information.
_f_	Foreign key	f.	A cell value in one table that refers to a unique key in a different table.

5. **When using an RDBMS, if an entry was removed from one table but not from the others, which of the following statements describes how an invalid entry can be updated or removed correctly?**

   ✓ a) First, the RDBMS must verify the usage as a foreign key in other tables. Next, if it exists as a foreign key, then it cannot be removed until all the table references are deleted first.

   b) First, every table's attributes must be updated to include new key values. Next, the subsequent tables must be updated to match the new foreign key references.

6. **Which of the following OOP terms isolates all object processes within the object?**

   a) Object

   b) Method

   ✓ c) Modularity

   d) Encapsulation

   e) Abstraction

7. **True or False? Referential integrity ensures that data stored within a database is accurate and valid, not altered or deleted.**

   ___ True

   ✓ False

8. **What is the appropriate description for each ACID integrity term?**

_b_	Atomicity	a.	Guarantees that a transaction will maintain stability, and not be undone, once the user is notified of its completion.
_d_	Consistency	b.	A DBMS guarantees that all tasks associated with a transaction have reached completion.
_c_	Isolation	c.	Occurs when transactions and database processes cannot discern, or see, what is occurring in other, simultaneous transactions.
_a_	Durability	d.	Requires database stability before and after a transaction.

9. **Which one of the following is a pre-processed database that contains information about a specific subject from various sources, and is used for subsequent reporting and analysis?**

   a) RDBMS

   b) Data mine

   ✓ c) Data warehouse

10. **True or False? Data mining is the process of sifting through and analyzing large amounts of data to locate previously unknown or hidden information.**

    ✓ True

    ___ False

11. **What is the appropriate description for each database vulnerability?**

d	Access control bypass	a.	When a group or individual is granted established or impartial access to unauthorized information.
b	Aggregation	b.	The unauthorized release of information that is accumulated from the database.
a	Improper view restrictions	c.	When one transaction requires the use of a resource that is locked by another transaction.
e	DoS	d.	When DBAs can circumvent normal application security and gain direct access to database information.
c	Deadlocks	e.	When massive databases are scanned row by row in search of non-existent data so that the databases cannot respond to legitimate requests.

12. **What is the appropriate description for each database security mechanism?**

c	Lock controls	a.	Bounds checking, data typing, data length restrictions, and well-formed transactions are all methods used to control data corruption in the database.
b	Other DBMS access controls	b.	View-based access controls, grant and revoke access controls, and security for object-oriented databases.
e	Metadata controls	c.	Manages concurrent access to a single row in a table.
a	Data contamination controls	d.	Presents issues related to concurrency and atomicity.
d	Online transaction processing controls	e.	Information that describes specific characteristics of data, such as origin, condition, content, and/or quality.

Lesson 7 Follow-up

Lesson 7 Lab 1

1. **At which stage of the software product development process should security concerns be addressed?**

    ✓ a) During the entire product life cycle

    b) At the beginning of the process

    c) During the programming

    d) When testing begins

2. **Which one of the following statements is true about proprietary software?**

    a) Copies of the source code are normally made available to the buyers.

    b) The software is available at no cost to the user.

    ✓ c) The software source is closed and users cannot inspect the code for problems.

    d) Users cannot trust the vendors of proprietary software.

3. **A milestone is used in which one of the following software development models?**

    a) Spiral

    b) Circular

    c) Block step

    ✓ d) Waterfall

4. **Which software development model uses an iterative development process, which includes risk analysis, requirements specifications, prototyping, and testing?**

    ✓ a) Spiral

    b) Circular

    c) Block step

    d) Waterfall

5. **The concept of foreign keys is found in which one database type?**

    a) Structured

    ✓ b) Relational

    c) Hierarchical

    d) Object oriented

6. **Which one of the following is the open standard for communicating from any computer language to any database system?**

    ✓ a) ODBC

    b) JDBC

    c) XML

    d) HTTP

7. **The ACID elements of database transactions are used to protect which one database feature?**

    a) Confidentiality

    b) Availability

    ✓ c) Integrity

    d) Authentication

8. **If a database transaction is said to be durable, what is the one resulting transaction?**

    a) It will backed out if the transaction fails.

    b) It will cause a secure state in the database.

    c) It will be separated from all other transactions in the database.

    ✓ d) It will not be backed out if the user has been informed that the transaction is complete.

9. **Which statement is not true of a data warehouse?**

    a) It is a database containing information about a specific subject.

    b) The information is pre-processed.

    ✓ c) The information in the warehouse is constantly updated.

    d) A data warehouse is useful for reporting and analysis.

10. **Which one of the following techniques is used by data mining to derive useful information?**

    a) Index gleaning

    ✓ b) Aggregation

    c) Interference

    d) Scanning

11. **When transaction A is waiting for transaction B to finish, and transaction B is waiting for transaction A to finish, one state exists, which is called a:**

    a) Hidden lock condition.

    b) Process lockup.

    ✓ c) Deadlock.

    d) DoS attack.

12. **Which one of the following is used in a database to limit what data a user can see?**

    ✓ a) Views

    b) Scopes

    c) Ranges

    d) Subsets

13. **Function points are used to:**

    ✓ a) Estimate the size of a program.

    b) Detail each step in the program development cycle.

    c) Indicate the work factor in creating a manual procedure.

    d) Evaluate the levels of sophistication or maturity found in an organization's software.

14. **Metadata is:**

    a) Metropolitan population statistics used in data analysis.

    b) Large clumps of data found in a data warehouse.

    ✓ c) Data about data.

    d) Intermediate data selected prior to creating reports.

15. **A tuple is:**

    ✓ a) A row in a database.

    b) A column in a database.

    c) The intersection of a row and column in a database.

    d) The content of a cell in a database.

16. **What is a requirement of referential integrity?**

    a) A foreign key can be deleted even if it is used in another table.

    ✓ b) A foreign key cannot be deleted if it is used in another table.

    c) Keys may be created using any foreign language.

    d) Normalization rules are always followed.

17. **Normalization usually requires the:**

    ✓ a) Removal of redundant data.

    b) Use of flat files.

    c) Addition of redundant data to simplify data access.

    d) Addition of columns to tables for data recovery.

18. **The term encapsulation is most often used with which one of the following database forms?**

    a) Relational

    ✓ b) Object-oriented

    c) Hierarchical

    d) Network

19. **When an operation is first verified as allowable and then later replaced with another illegal operation, which one of the following vulnerabilities has been exploited?**

    ✓ a) TOC/TOU

    b) Race condition

    c) Malformed input

    d) Object reuse

20. **Which element of a database operating environment is ultimately responsible for overall system security?**

    a) Database

    b) Operating system

    c) Programming language

    ✓ d) Security kernel

Lesson 8

Activity 8-1

1. **A security technique that converts data from an ordinary, intelligible state known as cleartext or plaintext form into coded or ciphertext form is known as:**

    a) Cryptography.

    b) Algorithm.

    ✓ c) Encryption.

    d) Cryptosystem.

2. **True or False? Without the correct key, the receiver can decrypt the ciphertext if the algorithm is known.**

    ___ True

    ✓ False

3. **Place the universal cryptography process in order.**

    _4_ Transport or store the ciphertext until needed.

    _3_ Encrypt the plaintext into ciphertext.

    _1_ Start with the plaintext.

    _2_ Select an encryption method and key.

    _5_ Decrypt the ciphertext using a key to display the original plaintext.

4. **True or False? A work factor is the study of cryptosystems with the intent of breaking them.**

    ___ True

    ✓ False

5. **Which era in the cipher evolution allowed the implementation of a cryptographic process to be performed with little or no user knowledge?**

    ✓ a) Software

    b) Mechanical

    c) Early

    d) Late

6. **What are the characteristics of the ideal cipher that Claude Shannon described in terms of usability and secrecy?**

   Usability—A cipher must provide an environment where keys and algorithms are simple and easy to implement. Errors should not propagate and the ciphertext should not be longer than the plaintext.

   Secrecy—Assuming that the enemy knows the system, the secrecy of the key is vital to the protection of the information.

7. **During processing, where does substitution occur?**

   a) Within the key

   b) Within the password

   c) Within the plaintext

   ✓ d) Within the cipher algorithm

8. **Which one of the following occurs during the transposition process?**

   a) Cryptographic output is replaced to hide the original information.

   ✓ b) Cryptographic output is rearranged to hide the original information.

   c) Cryptographic output is encrypted using a cipher algorithm.

   d) Cryptographic output is decrypted using a cipher algorithm.

9. **What is the appropriate description for each alternative cipher method?**

_b_	Steganography	a.	An embedded image that identifies the source of the image for copyright protection and for other uses.
_a_	Watermark	b.	A picture that hides information by replacing the low-order bits of each byte in the picture with elements from the hidden information.
_d_	Code book	c.	A tool that contains a very long, non-repeating key that is the same length as the plaintext.
_c_	One-time pad	d.	Used in a series to represent common words or phrases that might be used in communication.

Activity 8-2

1. **What are some characteristics of symmetric encryption?**

   It is a two-way encryption scheme in which encryption and decryption are both performed by the same secret key.

   The key can be configured in software or coded in hardware.

   The key must be securely transmitted between the two parties prior to encrypted communications.

   Symmetric encryption is relatively fast, but is vulnerable if the key is lost or compromised.

2. **True or False? A stream cipher is usually more secure, but it is also slower than block encryption.**

    ___ True

    ✓ False

3. **Which one of these is used to reduce the likelihood that identical ciphertext will be created?**

    a) One-time pad

    b) Symmetric encryption

    ✓ c) Initialization vector

    d) Two-way encryption scheme

4. **What is the appropriate description for each symmetric encryption algorithm?**

b	DES	a.	A freely available 64-bit block cipher algorithm that uses a variable key length.
c	AES	b.	A block algorithm that uses a 64-bit block and a 64-bit key.
a	Blowfish	c.	A block cipher that uses 128-bit blocks and keys of 128, 192, and 256 bits in length.
e	CAST-128	d.	A block cipher first proposed in 1991 and used in Open PGP.
d	IDEA	e.	A symmetric encryption algorithm with a 128-bit key.

5. **To accomplish transportation, what must be used when considering the implementation of symmetric encryption algorithms?**

    Secure procedures to protect the secrecy of the keys.

6. **What is the appropriate description for each phase of the DES standard process?**

b	Expansion	a.	Thirty-two 4-bit blocks are arranged based on a predefined scrambling process.
d	Key mixing	b.	Each 64-bit block is split into two 32-bit half-blocks.
c	Substitution	c.	After the key-mixing process, these are performed to mask the original data values.
a	Permutation	d.	Each 48-bit half-block is XORed with one of the subkeys.

7. **What is the appropriate description for each block cipher mode?**

c	ECB	a.	The IV is encrypted with the key and then chained to the next block's encryption step.
e	CBC	b.	The IV is first encrypted using the key and then XORed with the plaintext to create the ciphertext.
b	CFB	c.	This breaks the plaintext down into 64-bit blocks and then encrypts each block separately.
a	OFB	d.	This uses a counter to provide the IV.
d	CTR	e.	64-bit plaintext blocks are XORed with a 64-bit IV and then encrypted using the key.

8. **What is the appropriate description for each key management factor?**

a	Key control measures	a.	Determining who has access to keys and how they are assigned.
e	Key recovery	b.	The process of altering keys to systems on a periodic basis.
f	Key storage	c.	Creating random keys for better data protection.
c	Key generation	d.	The process of splitting a key into multiple parts and then storing each part at a different location.
d	Key escrow	e.	Salvaging lost keys.
b	Key change	f.	A secure repository for key assignment records.

Activity 8-3

1. **True or False? Asymmetric encryption is a two-way encryption scheme that uses two different keys and are based on the use of a one-way function with a trapdoor.**

   ✓ True

   __ False

2. **Which statement is true about an asymmetric private encryption key?**

   a) It contains fewer bits than the public key.

   ✓ b) It is kept secret by one party during two-way encryption.

   c) A specific application is used to generate only private keys.

   d) A specific application is used to generate only public keys.

3. **How can public-key encryption support secrecy? How can it support integrity?**

   It supports secrecy because only the private key holder can decrypt data encrypted with a freely available public key. It supports integrity because recipients can use a public key to decrypt data encrypted by the sender's private key, and this can be used to verify that the content of a message has not been altered in transit or transmitted by another party.

4. **What is the appropriate description for each asymmetric encryption algorithm?**

<table>
<tr><td><u>b</u></td><td>RSA</td><td>a.</td><td>A method of public-key encryption that requires shorter keys than other public-key algorithms.</td></tr>
<tr><td><u>c</u></td><td>Elgamal</td><td>b.</td><td>Has a variable key length and block size and is based on factoring the product of two large prime numbers.</td></tr>
<tr><td><u>a</u></td><td>ECC</td><td>c.</td><td>A public-key algorithm based on functions using discrete logarithms.</td></tr>
</table>

5. **True or False? A digital certificate validates the certificate holder's identity and is also a way to distribute the holder's private key.**

    __ True

    ✓ False

6. **The PKI consists of which one or more of the following components?**

    ✓ a) Software

    b) Network protocols

    ✓ c) CAs

    ✓ d) Certificates

7. **Which one of these PKI components is responsible for verifying users' identities and approving or denying requests for digital certificates?**

    a) Certificate repository database

    b) Certificate management system

    c) Certification authorization system

    ✓ d) RA

8. **Which one or more of the following is included in the PKI process?**

    ✓ a) Procedures for revoking certificates when they expire

    b) Procedures for creating network user accounts

    ✓ c) Procedures for revoking certificates when the security of the private key is in doubt

    d) Procedures for key escrow

Activity 8-4

1. **After one-way hashing encryption transforms cleartext into ciphertext, what is the result?**

    The ciphertext is never decrypted.

    This is called a hash. The hash has a fixed length regardless of the length of the cleartext.

2. **What are some other names for a hash?**

    Hash value

    Message digest

3. **True or False? A message hash is always combined with a secret key that is sent with the message.**

    __ True

    ✓ False

4. **Which one of these digest/hashing algorithms includes four updated algorithms?**

    a) HAVAL

    ✓ b) SHA

    c) MD5

5. **Compare and contrast the use of a MAC to the use of a message digest.**

    Both methods provide for integrity of a message. However, the MAC uses secret-key cryptography rather than a hashing algorithm to create the ciphertext and only encrypts a block of the data.

Activity 8-5

1. **What can Pretty Good Privacy (PGP) be defined as?**

    A publicly available email security method that uses a variation of public-key cryptography to encrypt email.

2. **What can Secure Multipurpose Internet Mail Extensions (S/MIME) be defined as?**

    A security protocol that uses encryption and digital signing to protect email and email attachments from attackers who might intercept and manipulate the contents of the message or of the attachments.

3. **Which one of the following is an Internet security device that is attached to each end of a transmission line to encrypt and decrypt data?**

    ✓ a) Link encryption

    b) IPsec

    c) HTTPS

    d) WPA

4. **Match each wireless access protocol with its appropriate description.**

_b_	WEP	a.	Uses the RC4 algorithm and the TKIP algorithm
_a_	WPA	b.	Uses RC4 for encryption
_c_	WPA2	c.	Uses the AES algorithm

Activity 8-6

1. **What is the appropriate description for each cryptographic attack?**

_b_	Ciphertext-only	a.	Once knowledge of a common message format is obtained, the attacker can use a limited amount of information to figure out the encryption key using a copy of the plaintext and ciphertext.
_a_	Known plaintext	b.	Once the key for one sample encrypted message is determined, the attacker can decrypt the other messages using samples of messages encrypted with the same algorithm.
_d_	Chosen plaintext	c.	Once the key is manipulated, the attacker can decode a message and uncover the entire key working with part of the ciphertext.
_c_	Chosen ciphertext	d.	Once the key is manipulated, the attacker can decode a message and uncover the entire key working with part of the plaintext.

2. **Which one of these encryption-based attacks exploits weakness in the mathematical algorithms used to encrypt passwords?**

   a) Factoring attack

   b) Dictionary attack

   ✓ c) Birthday attack

   d) Frequency analysis

3. **What is a good example of how frequency analysis is conducted?**

   Using a substitution algorithm to break encryption by comparing character usage in an encrypted document against known statistics about the frequency with which characters appear in typical samples of a particular linguistic alphabet.

4. **True or False? Reverse engineering is a cryptographic process of analyzing and determining the structure, function, and operation of a cryptosystem.**

   ✓ True

   ___ False

5. **What type of security risk do temporary files present?**

   a) The files exploit the probability of different plaintext inputs producing the same encrypted output.

   b) The files contain biased random numbers that could be used during statistical analysis to decrypt files.

   ✓ c) The files contain remnants of the encryption or decryption process.

Lesson 8 Follow-up

Lesson 8 Lab 1

1. **The original message found before encryption and after decryption is called the:**

    a) Ciphertext.

    ✓ b) Plaintext.

    c) Cipherstream.

    d) Originstream.

2. **An algorithm that results in a large change in the encrypted data from a small change in the original message exhibits which one of the following?**

    a) Tsunami effect

    b) Hurricane effect

    c) Land slide effect

    ✓ d) Avalanche effect

3. **If it is possible to prove the identity of the sender of a message, which one of the following principles is in effect?**

    a) Origination identity principle

    ✓ b) Non-repudiation

    c) Hashed message control

    d) Strong identification

4. **When a public key is used to encrypt data and a private key is used to decrypt it, the data in transit is assured:**

    a) Confidentiality only.

    b) Availability.

    ✓ c) Integrity and confidentiality.

    d) Integrity only.

5. **Symmetric-key cryptography uses which of the following key types?**

    ✓ a) Secret

    b) Public

    c) Private

    d) Confidential

6. **The work factor is:**

    a) The amount of time needed to encrypt a file.

    b) The amount of time needed to decrypt a file.

    c) The amount of time needed to scrub a hard drive.

    ✓ d) The amount of time needed to break a cryptosystem.

7. **What is the effective key length used with 3DES?**

   a) 64 bits

   b) 40 bits

   c) 112 bits

   ✓ d) 168 bits

8. **Which one of the following is the most recently adopted symmetric algorithm?**

   a) IDEA

   ✓ b) AES

   c) 3DES

   d) CAST-128

9. **Public-key encryption was developed by:**

   ✓ a) Diffie and Hellman.

   b) Merkle and Adams.

   c) Tavares and Rivest.

   d) Rivest and Merkle.

10. **What item allows an encryption algorithm to be successfully reused?**

    a) Algorithm

    b) Users

    ✓ c) Key

    d) Computer system

11. **Which computer logical function is the basis of most cryptosystem algorithms?**

    ✓ a) XORed

    b) And

    c) Not

    d) Exclusive nor

12. **Which one of the following is not a hashing algorithm?**

    a) MD5

    b) SHA

    c) HAVAL

    ✓ d) RC4

13. **Which one of the following encryption algorithms is not used to protect Wi-Fi networks?**

    a) WEP

    ✓ b) WAP

    c) WPA

    d) WPA2

14. **IPsec uses which of the following processes to exchange keys?**

 ✓ a) IKE

   b) PKI

   c) SA

   d) BRP

15. **The process using all possible values of a key to attempt to break a cryptosystem is called:**

 ✓ a) Brute force.

   b) Atomic attack.

   c) Superscan.

   d) Key dictionary attack.

16. **A process used to break simple substitution ciphers by studying the uses of various letters in a language is called:**

   a) Letter analysis.

   b) Vocabulary distribution.

   c) Selective letter analysis.

 ✓ d) Frequency analysis.

17. **Which is true about random number generators used in encryption and decryption?**

   a) They are always 100% random in their output of numbers.

   b) They always rely on clock pulses, which are random on most computers.

   c) They can be checked against a second generator using the same processes.

 ✓ d) They are not truly random and can present weaknesses in the algorithms used.

18. **Who proposed the ideal cipher?**

 ✓ a) Claude Shannon

   b) Shannon Clarke

   c) Ron Rivest

   d) Desmond Lucipher

Lesson 9

Activity 9-1

1. **Which one of the following physical protection areas includes network hardware and wiring along with the areas in which they reside?**

   a) Personnel

   b) Physical plant

 ✓ c) Data network

   d) Computer facilities

2. **The computer facility's physical protection area includes which of the following?**

    a) Protection from electronic and physical attacks from authorized or unauthorized personnel

    ✓ b) Server rooms and data centers

    c) Routers, switches, firewalls, cabling, and wireless access points

    d) Lighting, doors, windows, fencing, and plumbing

3. **Give some examples of internal and external man-made threats.**

    The release of company information by an employee is an internal threat.

    A power failure at the local utility company is an external threat.

4. **Which one of the following is generally considered to be the first layer of defense in a layered protection scheme?**

    a) Standard access

    b) Secured area access

    c) Facility access

    ✓ d) Perimeter access

5. **Why is lighting considered a physical barrier?**

    Lights illuminate large areas such as perimeters of buildings or fences.

    Glare lighting can cause disorientation for intruders.

    Lights can help guards and others identify areas where intrusions occur.

6. **In secure areas, which of the following physical access barriers should meet the same fire protection standards as walls?**

    ✓ a) Doors

    b) Fencing

    c) Locks

    d) Windows

7. **Which one or more of the following are examples of a biometric entry system?**

    ✓ a) Hand geometry sensors

    ✓ b) Iris scanners

    c) Motion detectors

    ✓ d) Fingerprint sensors

8. **Which one of the following facility control devices is a physical entry portal with two doors on either end of a secure chamber?**

    a) IDS

    ✓ b) Man traps

    c) Card entry systems

    d) Alarms and responses

9. **Why might you choose a keyed over a keyless lock?**

   A key lock might be appropriate for a private office where only a single individual and, per-haps, maintenance and security staff need access. Only a few keys need to be distributed and the employee is assured privacy because few have access.

   A keyless lock might be appropriate for a general entry door, so the combination can be issued to all employees and changed as needed without having to control key distribution.

10. **For which of the following layered protection areas would a fence typically be used?**

    a) Standard access

    b) Secured area access

    c) Facility access

    ✓ d) Perimeter access

Activity 9-2

1. **Which of the following facility control system components can help identify unau-thorized access attempts?**

   a) Access verification

   b) Activity logging

   c) Entry restriction

   ✓ d) Intrusion detection

2. **Maintaining identification and authentication information for authorized individuals is a part of which of the following facility control system components?**

   ✓ a) Entry restriction

   b) Intrusion detection

   c) Activity logging

   d) Surveillance

3. **In a layered protection strategy, while protecting a facility's perimeter, which of the following does the PIDS sense?**

   a) Unauthorized access to the facility

   ✓ b) Changes in the environment

   c) Keypad inaccuracy

   d) Theft

4. **What is the appropriate description for each PIDS type?**

_g_	Motion sensor	a.	Emits a calculable electrical field in which changes are measured.
_d_	Pressure-sensitive sensor	b.	Measures vibrations caused by breaking glass, collisions with solid objects, or footsteps.
_e_	Heat detector	c.	Measures changes in a magnetic field.
_a_	Proximity detector	d.	Detects pressure when weight is directly applied to the device.
_b_	Vibration detector	e.	Measures temperature increases emitted from a heat source such as a human, fire, or animal.
_c_	Magnetic detector	f.	Detects a change in the light level in a designated area, specifically a windowless room or area.
_f_	Photometric detector	g.	Uses movement to detect a perimeter approach or presence inside a controlled area.

5. **Surveillance can occur through which one or more of the following?**

    ✓ a) Audio recording devices

    b) Trip and glare lighting

    ✓ c) Visual human detection

    ✓ d) Visual recording devices

6. **True or False? Physical access logs are maintained by access control systems and by security guards.**

    ✓ True

    ___ False

7. **A smoke detector in an unattended warehouse sends an alarm directly to the local municipal fire department. This is an example of which one of the following?**

    a) Local activation/local response

    b) Remote activation/local response

    ✓ c) Remote activation/remote response

    d) Bells and sirens

Activity 9-3

1. **What are the levels of protection you can employ to create a restricted work area?**

    Restricting access to those with clearance; adding locks; keeping an entry or exit log; strengthening the area with physical hardening of walls, doors, and floors; restricting device use; instituting surveillance.

2. **Which one of these media risks necessitates special protection such as locked storage and media labeling?**

    a) Accidental erasure of secure information

    ✓ b) The highly portable nature of most media types

    c) The possible overwrite of secure information

    d) Unauthorized viewing of secure information

3. **What is the definition of the two-man rule?**

   a) Requiring the presence of two people to move media from one location to the next

   b) Requiring that once media is moved, two people must authorize the new location of the media

   ✓ c) Requiring the presence of two people to monitor behavior when criteria are met

   d) Requiring that once media is created, two people must make copies of it for security reasons

4. **True or False? Once an authorized individual has been granted access to a secure location or to secure information, security is no longer needed.**

   __ True

   ✓ False

5. **What is the primary goal of physical security outlined by the (ISC)²?**

   a) Facility safety

   b) Perimeter safety

   c) Information safety

   ✓ d) Personnel safety

6. **True or False? The intrusion response policy states who is required to make a notification and how the notification should be made in the event of forced physical entry into any corporate facility.**

   __ True

   ✓ False

7. **A calling tree is an example of which one of the following emergency response procedures?**

   a) Accounting for employees

   ✓ b) General employee notification

   c) Key staff and organization notification

   d) Training, drills, and exercises

Activity 9-4

1. **Which one of the following is an often overlooked component of layered defense for facilities?**

   a) The number of employees in the facility

   b) The time of day that the facility is accessed

   ✓ c) The facility layout and design

   d) The location of the facility

2. **Which one of the following should be in place to maintain the security system and allow for the controlled shutdown of vital computer assets?**

   a) Positive ventilation

   ✓ b) Backup power supplies and generators

   c) Water and sewer lines

   d) Additional computer systems

3. **True or False? The air pressure inside computer and server rooms should be lower than the external air pressure.**

   ___ True

   ✓ False

4. **What is the appropriate description for each power problem?**

_b_	Blackout	a.	A short-term, high-voltage power malfunction.
_c_	Brownout	b.	A complete loss of power.
_d_	Sag	c.	A long-term, low-voltage power failure.
_a_	Spike	d.	A momentary low-voltage power failure.
_f_	Surge	e.	A surge or spike that is caused when a device is started that uses a great amount of current.
_e_	In-rush	f.	A long-term, high-voltage power malfunction.

5. **Which one of the following power protection systems is a device that provides instant power to connected circuits when the main source of power becomes unavailable?**

   ✓ a) UPS

   b) Generator

   c) Surge/spike protector

   d) Power line monitor

6. **Environmental controls are an important part of ensuring the reliability of which one or more of the following?**

   a) Ventilation systems

   ✓ b) Computer resources

   ✓ c) Network resources

   d) Utility systems

7. **What is the first rule in fire protection?**

   ✓ a) Fire prevention

   b) Fire detection

   c) Fire suppression

   d) Fire evacuation

8. **Which one or more of the following are fire detection systems?**

    a) Fire extinguishers

    ✓ b) Flame detectors

    ✓ c) Heat sensors

    ✓ d) Smoke detectors

9. **True or False? Fire extinguishers are universal and can be used to put out all types of fires.**

    __ True

    ✓ False

10. **Which of the following was designed to extinguish fires in computer facilities?**

    a) Hand-held fire extinguishers

    b) Water

    ✓ c) FM-200

    d) Sand

11. **Which one of the following water-based extinguishers is not used in computer facilities due to high water output?**

    a) Wet pipe

    b) Dry pipe

    c) Preaction

    ✓ d) Deluge

Lesson 9 Follow-up

Lesson 9 Lab 1

1. **Physical threats to security come from all of the following areas EXCEPT:**

    a) Internal activities.

    b) External activities.

    ✓ c) Computer-generated activities.

    d) Natural disasters.

2. **Which one of the following is not typically used in a layered protection scheme for physical threats?**

    a) Perimeter access controls

    b) Facility access controls

    ✓ c) Logical (computer) access controls

    d) Secured area access controls

3. **A fence that is three to four feet high is used to:**

   a) Deter determined attackers.

   b) Keep most people out because it is hard to climb.

   ✓ c) Delimit the property line and keep out casual trespassers.

   d) Provide the most effective boundary control.

4. **When using lighting to deter or identify intruders the usual illumination is:**

   ✓ a) Two foot candles of illumination at eight feet high.

   b) Eight foot candles of illumination at 20 feet high.

   c) A flash system to blind the intruder and freeze him/her in place.

   d) Room-level lighting.

5. **A door securing an area must have the same fire protection capability as:**

   ✓ a) The walls of the secured area.

   b) The other doors in the building, regardless of where they are located.

   c) The closest external door.

   d) The windows of the secured area.

6. **The security of a manual lock is enforced by all of the following EXCEPT:**

   a) The security of the key.

   ✓ b) The lights used around the lock location.

   c) The strength of the lock components.

   d) The key distribution policies and processes.

7. **Which one of the following physical safeguards is most effective in identifying a threat?**

   a) Guard dog

   b) Physical IDS

   ✓ c) Human guard

   d) CCTV

8. **If it is necessary to determine if a person has crossed a barrier, but it is not practical to use lights, which system might be most effective in a large area?**

   a) CCTV

   ✓ b) Pressure sensitive sensors

   c) Human guard

   d) Motion sensors

9. **Which one of the following is useful in determining who entered a given area of the facility?**

   a) CCTV

   ✓ b) Card entry systems

   c) Manual locks

   d) IDSs

10. **What is the principal goal for any physical security system?**

    ✓ a) Safeguard human life

    b) Safeguard corporate property

    c) Safeguard information

    d) Safeguard computer systems

11. **In a computer facility, at what levels should HVAC systems maintain humidity?**

    a) 40% to 80% relative humidity

    b) 40% to 45% relative humidity

    c) 20% to 40% relative humidity

    ✓ d) 40% to 60% relative humidity

12. **Automatic fire detection systems use all of the following methods EXCEPT:**

    a) Rate of temperature rise.

    b) Temperature level.

    c) Presence of smoke.

    ✓ d) Human determination.

13. **A type B fire extinguisher is used to put out which one of the following types of fires?**

    a) Paper

    ✓ b) Liquids and fuels

    c) Electrical

    d) Kitchen

14. **Halon has been outlawed as a fire-extinguishing gas. Which of the following chemicals is a preferred replacement?**

    a) Kryptonite

    b) H2O

    c) Chlorofluorocarbon

    ✓ d) FM-200

15. **A fire control system that does not charge the system with water until a fire is detected is called a:**

    a) Wet pipe system.

    b) Damp pipe system.

    c) No-water system.

    ✓ d) Dry pipe system.

16. **Which one of the following systems is not used in a computer area because of the amount of water discharged?**

    a) Wet pipe

    b) Dry pipe

    c) No-water

    ✓ d) Deluge

17. **Which one of the following is a momentary high-voltage power problem?**

    ✓ a) Spike

    b) Sag

    c) Brownout

    d) Surge

18. **What method might be a traditional approach that is still useful in developing and employing an employee notification system?**

    a) Emails

    b) Instant messages

    ✓ c) Calling trees

    d) Emergency networks

19. **In looking at building design, secure areas of a building should be located:**

    a) Near an exit for easy egress in an emergency.

    b) Close to external walls next to the street.

    ✓ c) In the center of the building with reinforced walls and ceiling.

    d) Close to the restroom facilities for convenience.

20. **When granting access to a physical area, which one of the following is not a determining factor?**

    a) Need to know

    b) Least privilege

    c) Two-man rule

    ✓ d) Access control cost

Lesson 10

Activity 10-1

1. **OPSEC deals with which of the following issue types?**

    ✓ a) Near-term

    b) Breaches in progress

    c) Mid-term

    d) Long-term

2. **What is the core purpose of OPSEC?**

   To deny adversaries critical information about a business through a structured process.

3. **What is the appropriate description for each operations security action item?**

_d_	Identifying critical information	a.	Identifying vulnerabilities through a business planner examination, pinpointing viable OPSEC measures for each.
_c_	Analyzing threats	b.	Employing selected measures after integrating a risk assessment into OPSEC plans for future business functions and activities.
_e_	Analyzing vulnerabilities	c.	Recognizing potential adversaries through research and analysis of adversarial intelligence, organizational counterintelligence, and open source information.
_a_	Assessing risk	d.	Determining whether data is vital to an adversary, which makes that information critical.
_b_	Applying suitable OPSEC measures	e.	Identifying and comparing probable indicators against an adversary's intelligence-gathering capacity.

4. **Which one or more of the following are operations security roles involved in detailing and enforcing permissions and access capabilities?**

   ✓ a) System administrator

   ✓ b) Security administrator

   ✓ c) User

      d) Password manager

5. **Which one of the following operations security protection areas assigns users to groups that have specific characteristics?**

      a) Special privileges

      b) Password and password management

   ✓ c) Account characteristics

      d) Security clearance

6. **Which one or more of the following describes a security profile?**

   ✓ a) A description of security-relevant information for protected system elements.

      b) A system-generated report that lists security information for each system on a network.

   ✓ c) A repository for items such as user name and user-specific password strength requirements.

      d) A description listing all the hardware and software used within an organization.

7. **Which of the following best practices describes a system property in which a single non-functioning component does not cause a complete system failure?**

   a) Misuse prevention

   b) Backup and restore

   c) Record retention

   ✓ d) Fault tolerance

8. **Which of the following best practices involves deterring unauthorized individuals from accessing classified materials as the first step?**

   a) Material destruction

   ✓ b) Material safeguarding

   c) Material reuse

   d) Sensitive media handling

9. **A corporate security policy is an example of which one of the following operations security control categories?**

   a) Detective

   ✓ b) Directive

   c) Deterrent

   d) Compensating

10. **True or False? Enforcing user IDs and passwords used to authenticate authorized users is an example of a corrective security control category.**

    ___ True

    ✓ False

11. **What is the appropriate description for each security control method?**

b	SoD	a.	Manages individual information access based on job scope and job function requirements.
a	Need to know	b.	Monitors task implementation based on the specific responsibilities of authorized personnel.
d	Least privilege	c.	Enforces a minimum of one week of time off per year, allowing management ample time to audit employee activities.
e	Job rotation	d.	Limits individuals' capabilities to the lowest level specifically needed by them to perform their jobs.
c	Mandatory vacations	e.	Creates a foundation for cross-training that increases employee availability in the organization.

12. **What is the appropriate description for each additional security control method?**

b	Antivirus management	a.	Tracks hardware and software changes to ensure they are properly authorized and implemented, and that they follow procedural specifications.
d	Audit	b.	Monitors and updates malware prevention signatures and software.
c	Closed shop	c.	Allows only authorized users access to system information.
a	Change control	d.	Identifies problem areas by reviewing user and system activities.

Activity 10-2

1. **Which one or more of the following events does security auditing focus on?**

   ✓ a) System-level

   ✓ b) Application-level

   ✓ c) User-level

   d) Organizational-level

2. **True or False? Security audit event log entries contain information such as the identification of the event, the time of the event, and the identification of the individual or process causing the event.**

   ✓ True

   __ False

3. **Security monitoring uses which one or more of the following to track operational events for unusual or unauthorized activity?**

   ✓ a) Penetration testing

   ✓ b) Intrusion detection

   c) Violation prevention

   ✓ d) Violation processing

4. **What is the purpose of violation analysis?**

   To identify intrusion attempts by tracking anomalies in user behavior.

5. **Which one of the following violation factors addresses the likelihood and level of consequences for a security violation?**

   ✓ a) Severity

   b) Source

   c) Frequency

   d) Response

Activity 10-3

1. **What is the appropriate description for each OPSEC threat?**

_d_	Disclosure	a.	Continually disrupting system operations, disabling the availability of critical data.
_b_	Destruction	b.	Compromising availability of data because it is no longer accessible to authorized parties.
_a_	Interruption of service	c.	Exploiting information integrity by altering or damaging electronic data.
_c_	Corruption and modification	d.	Exposing private business information without authorization.

2. **What is the appropriate description for each additional OPSEC threat?**

_c_	Theft	a.	Individuals who detect and exploit system flaws to acquire or prohibit unauthorized system access and password data.
_d_	Espionage	b.	Using unauthorized software to penetrate access rights and privacy and to damage data confidentiality, integrity, and availability.
_a_	Hackers and crackers	c.	Confiscating computer equipment and assets that target confidentiality and availability.
_b_	Malicious code	d.	Confiscating private information through physical or electronic means, affecting confidentiality, integrity, and availability.

3. **True or False? Security violations may result in criminal prosecution, regardless of their severity.**

   _✓_ True

   ___ False

4. **Which one or more of the following activities are included in logical violations?**

   ✓ a) Cracking passwords using brute force

   b) Disconnecting electrical or communications services

   ✓ c) Obtaining access information though a social engineering attack

   d) Stealing equipment

5. **Why is assessing training and awareness an appropriate response to a security violation?**

   Users must be more aware and responsible for recognizing potential physical threats, such as social engineering attacks and unauthorized individuals on facility premises.

Lesson 10 Follow-up

Lesson 10 Lab 1

1. **Operations security deals with which type of need?**

   a) Strategic

   b) Tactical

   c) Mid-term

   ✓ d) Day to day

2. **Who determines which users can access which data?**

   a) Security administrator

   b) IT administrator

   ✓ c) Data owner

   d) CEO

3. **Which of these is a risk associated with changing passwords infrequently?**

   a) They are often written down.

   b) They are targets for social engineering.

   ✓ c) They may be guessed or broken by brute force.

   d) They increase physical vulnerabilities.

4. **A user has been granted special privileges to modify data due to a programming error. Which one or more of the following should be performed to safeguard data in the system during this time?**

   a) Remove any security controls protecting the date to make it easier to modify.

   b) Remove access control shortly after the modification is complete.

   ✓ c) Remove the special privileges immediately after the modification has been made.

   d) Disable auditing so as to not interfere with the ability to modify the program.

5. **What is a security profile?**

   ✓ a) A description of the security-relevant information about each user or protected element in the system.

   b) The description of the security kernel in the system architecture design document.

   c) The collection of permissions for each user that is stored in the system access control log.

   d) A written description of the policy for granting access to resources.

6. **Fault tolerance is implemented by using what?**

   ✓ a) Redundant hardware

   b) Employee briefings on personality quirks

   c) Extra security guards and CCTV to protect the facility

   d) Reset buttons and switches on computer consoles and HVAC systems

7. **A directive operations security control might be found in which one of the following documents?**

✓ a) Security policy

b) Guideline

c) Procedure

d) Baseline

8. **A facility that only allows authorized users is called:**

a) An impenetrable facility.

✓ b) A closed shop.

c) An open shop.

d) A secure bastion.

9. **In a security context, what are mandatory vacations used for?**

a) To reward good employees

b) To ensure that all employees get a chance for some time off throughout the year

✓ c) To allow auditing of employee activities

d) To reduce payouts at employee termination

10. **A system that is used to track user and program activity is called:**

a) A system tracker.

b) An event monitor.

c) An activity log.

✓ d) An audit log.

11. **What security level should the audit logs have?**

a) Modification ability for anyone

b) Violation alarm notice

c) Restricted access for any company personnel

✓ d) Encryption to protect the contents

12. **Evaluating an audit log to locate conditions that might indicate a security issue due to repeated mistakes is called what?**

✓ a) Violation analysis

b) Log review

c) Error determination

d) Activity review

13. **A response to a repeated error found in an audit log should be measured and determined by which of these?**

a) The person committing the error.

✓ b) The security risk associated with the error.

c) The lack of training of the user committing the error.

d) The cost of a severe response to the situation.

14. **Theft of information targets which of these CIA areas?**

    a) Confidentiality and integrity

    b) Integrity and availability

    ✓ c) Confidentiality and availability

    d) Confidentiality only

15. **What is one of the best ways to ensure the operational security of the organization?**

    a) Lock systems down so no security errors will occur.

    b) Provide frequent, ongoing security training to personnel.

    ✓ c) Conduct vulnerability testing to locate shortcomings.

    d) Hire an outside contractor to control security.

16. **With trusted recovery, the system is ensured to:**

    a) Restore backups automatically, without assistance.

    ✓ b) Recover from a failure to be restored to a secure state.

    c) Recheck the TCB for normal operation.

    d) Support recovery from small problems.

17. **Which of the following typically dictates how often audit log reviews are conducted?**

    a) Laws

    ✓ b) Corporate policy

    c) Financial information

    d) Regulations

18. **SoD would allow which of these pairs to work together in completing each others' tasks?**

    a) Audit and administration

    b) Security and users

    c) Programmers and software testers

    ✓ d) None of these pairs should work together

19. **A hacker has been found trying to obtain data from a swap file area on a disk drive. What is this type of activity known as?**

    a) Object pilfering

    b) Subject extraction

    c) Dumpster diving

    ✓ d) Object reuse

20. **Which of the following require constant follow-up to ensure the latest versions are available and used?**

    a) Operating system complete releases

    ✓ b) Virus signature files

    c) Password encryption algorithms

    d) Corporate security policies

Lesson 11

Activity 11-1

1. **There is a BCP in effect at your corporation. As the security administrator, you are responsible for ensuring that this policy coincides with the organization's everyday needs. To accomplish this, you plan to review and test the BCP:**

    a) Once every five years.

    b) At least monthly.

    c) Only when business operations change.

    ✓ d) At least annually.

2. **Place the BCP development phases in order from first to last.**

    1 Initiate the plan creation process and set goals.

    3 Determine how to prevent the events.

    2 Determine the impact of various events to the business.

    6 Provide updates to the solutions and plans.

    5 Check to see if the solutions actually work.

    4 Determine what to do if the events cannot be prevented.

3. **Your organization is located in an area where there is a threat of hurricanes. As a member of the BCP team, you need to determine what effect there would be if a hurricane halted business activities at your corporation. What BCP phase is this an example of?**

    a) Critical business processes

    ✓ b) BIA

    c) MTD

    d) RPO

4. **Your organization is located in a major shipping port at the edge of large lake. Therefore, the building is susceptible to damage in the event of flooding, a cargo spill, or a maritime collision. As the security administrator, you need to conduct an investigation to identify the areas of the building with the highest level of risk associated with these threats, then calculate the cost of providing additional protection in case of this type of emergency. Which one of these BCP concepts does this represent?**

    a) Critical business processes

    b) MTD

    ✓ c) Vulnerability assessment

    d) Recovery point objectives

5. **You work for a major urban newspaper. Brainstorm a list of critical and non-critical business processes for your organization.**

   Critical: Printing the paper, taking advertising orders, billing subscribers and advertisers, purchasing newsprint, and communicating with wire services.

   Non-critical: Stocking the employee lunchroom and purchasing routine office supplies.

6. **You work for a local chain of auto repair shops. You are responsible both for the design and the budgeting for your company's BCP. Will you recommend a near-zero RTO/RPO? Why or why not?**

   No, because this type of business does not need to maintain operations and customer response 24x7, and the cost of a near-zero RTO/RPO solution might be greater than the losses associated with a temporary suspension of operations.

Activity 11-2

1. **You work for a large multi-national corporation. As the Chief Security Officer, you have been asked to chair the BCP advisory team for the company headquarters. Who might you invite to join the team?**

   Senior vice presidents or directors from various business units; key business partners or suppliers; the IT director; the corporate counsel or other legal representative; representatives from the company's other business locations.

2. **The advisory committee has met for its monthly meeting and you have left the meeting with a beta-level draft of the BCP. You have been charged with evaluating the BCP prior to implementation. What are some examples of items that you will be evaluating?**

   Plan coverage adequacy for all of the areas in the business.

   Threat identification and vulnerability analysis.

   The response prioritization according to business needs.

   Testing the plan and providing training.

   Methods of communication.

   Staffing for the BCP team and time allocation.

   The frequency and methods for plan updates.

3. **You and your colleague have just performed a walkthrough of the plan that would be put in effect in the event of damages to your portside building from a maritime collision within the port area. The two of you think that you need to perform more rigorous tests to ensure the effectiveness of the BCP. What are some other testing methods you might want to recommend?**

   Parallel testing

   Simulations

   Full interruption testing

4. **High water conditions in the harbor have caused shore flooding and made it impossible for your employees to report to work. Civil authorities have notified you first because you are on record as the primary emergency contact for your company. What actions should you take?**

    Use the communications systems specified in the BCP to notify all stakeholders, including the affected employees. Consult the BCP to follow the required steps that need to be taken in the event of a disaster that makes operations at the primary site impossible, and implement the plans to begin continuity operations. Once operations have begun, assess the situation to see if normal operations will resume without further intervention, or if the Disaster Recovery Plan must be activated.

Activity 11-3

1. **Your company has implemented a BCP and charged your team with responsibility for the DRP for your organization. What are some examples of items that you will need to include in your organization's DRP?**

    A list of individuals responsible for recovery.

    An inventory of hardware and software.

    A series of steps to take in the event of a disaster to respond and rebuild damaged systems.

2. **During the DRP development, you took the list of critical business processes that were itemized for your company's BCP and ranked them in order of business need. Which disaster recovery factor is this an example of?**

    Prioritization

3. **You have met with the BCP/DCP team and have discussed several backup strategies that will be utilized in the event of a disaster. The advisory committee has decided that, in an effort to protect company data, you will be transferring backup volumes to an offsite location. In the event of an emergency, a copy of this saved data will be prepared and sent to the remote site so that it can be restored. Which backup strategy is this an example of?**

    Electronic vaulting

4. **Your company's main trunk phone line goes down in an electrical storm. Customers cannot call and place orders. What priority level would you assign this?**

    ✓ a) Short-term

    b) Mid-term

    c) Long-term

    d) Not required

5. **How might you deal with the loss of the phone line?**

    Make failover arrangements with the local phone company to cut you over to a backup circuit as soon as possible.

    If you must leave the building, move order-entry employees to a phone bank set up at a hot or warm site.

6. **The storm damaged pavement in the employee parking lot. There is still adequate parking, but some employees may have a longer walk to the building until the area is re-paved. How would you prioritize this issue?**

   a) Short-term

   b) Mid-term

   ✓ c) Long-term

   d) Not required

7. **How would you deal with the parking lot issue?**

   Block off the area and schedule re-paving when other business operations have returned to normal and funds can be obtained.

Activity 11-4

1. **After a flood at your business, you need someone to respond immediately to ensure everyone's safety and get the business operating at your remote site. What team will you send in?**

   The recovery team.

2. **In addition to alerting the team, what other actions should you take to respond to this disaster?**

   Alert other stakeholders. Monitor the recovery team to ensure that the team is able to begin emergency operations. Once operations are underway, look into assessing the damage and your ability to return to your main facility.

3. **The business is operating again. Now you need someone to assess the water damage to carpeting and floors, what it will cost to replace them, and to oversee the restoration. What team will you send in?**

   The salvage team.

4. **The DRP process has been evaluated. The advisory committee has decided that, to complete the validation of the DRP, an offsite test will be conducted, including evaluations of software, data, and personnel. At this warm site, operations will proceed as if a disaster has occurred, and will test the DRP and pinpoint areas needing improvement. Which disaster recovery testing method is this an example of?**

   Offsite restoration.

5. **What disaster recovery evaluation method could you implement to fully validate that the DRP will enable you to sustain operations in the event of a real disaster?**

   A mirrored site cutover.

Lesson 11 Follow-up

Lesson 11 Lab 1

1. **What is the purpose of a BCP?**

    a) To take care of one-time disasters.

    ✓ b) To ensure the business continues after a disruption or crisis.

    c) To identify key players in the business.

    d) To keep key business documents available when needed.

2. **Which of these is the most important aspect to consider for ensuring BCP success?**

    ✓ a) Senior management is involved and supports BCP creation.

    b) All aspects of the organization are studied carefully.

    c) The impact for all types of interruptions is understood.

    d) Physical security is continued.

3. **Which of these is a top consideration for a BCP?**

    ✓ a) Safety of personnel

    b) Safety of hardware

    c) Safety of software and information

    d) Safety of the facility

4. **Who should the BIA team include?**

    a) Senior management only

    b) Security management team

    c) IT management team

    ✓ d) Individuals from all parts of the organization

5. **What is MTD?**

    ✓ a) The longest period of time that the business can suspend functioning without the business failing.

    b) The longest time a server can fail without needing to be rebooted.

    c) The tolerance the users show when a system fails.

    d) The time a server takes to restore a failed backup.

6. **The RPO is often related to which one of the following?**

    a) The last restore of the system.

    ✓ b) The last backup of the system.

    c) The point at which the system fails.

    d) The point at which the system is recovered.

7. If the RTO extends beyond the MTD, what is likely to happen?

    a) The users become more upset.

    b) The customers are unhappy with the business.

    ✓ c) The business is likely to fail.

    d) The cost of doing business expands exponentially.

8. If the RPO and RTO are nearly zero, what financial impact might be felt?

    ✓ a) Near-zero RPOs and RTOs are very expensive to support.

    b) Near-zero RPOs and RTOs are cheap because downtime is minimal.

    c) Near-zero RPOs and RTOs are revenue neutral and have no financial impact.

    d) Near-zero RPOs and RTOs are moderately expensive to support.

9. Which of these is a critical business process?

    ✓ a) A process that if it were to sustain a loss or damage, it could lead to business failure

    b) A process that takes too much money from other processes

    c) An essential security function

    d) A process that is related to every other function in the business

10. Which of these is the most important factor for a BCP coordinator to have?

    a) Enough funds

    b) Enough contact with other employees

    c) A thorough knowledge of all parts of the business

    ✓ d) A high level of support from top management

11. Which one of the following is not a typical item that the BCP team must incorporate?

    a) Determine threats and vulnerabilities

    b) Prioritize recovery efforts

    c) Document BCP plans

    ✓ d) Restore operations

12. Which of these is a BCP testing method that verifies system functioning at an alternate site without disrupting business operations?

    a) Reviewing BCP contents

    b) Walkthroughs

    ✓ c) Parallel testing

    d) Full interruption testing

13. Which of these is a BCP review that involves desk checking?

    a) Simulation

    ✓ b) Checklist

    c) Walkthrough

    d) Full interruption

14. **How often should a BCP be reviewed and revised?**

    a) Once a year only

    ✓ b) With major changes to business operations

    c) Twice a year

    d) When senior management decides

15. **When the BCP fails to mitigate risks and a disaster occurs, which plan is implemented?**

    a) BCP

    b) ARP

    c) DCP

    ✓ d) DRP

16. **Why is a mirrored site the best when recovery time is considered?**

    ✓ a) A mirrored site is a complete copy of the original and has a very short recovery time should a disaster occur.

    b) A mirrored site is inexpensive since it uses an exact mirror located at the original site.

    c) A mirrored site has little benefit because of the cost and distance to move equipment and people.

    d) A mirrored site is easy to set up and maintain.

17. **An incremental backup strategy is one that requires a full backup followed by which of these?**

    a) Periodic backups that do not reset the archive bit

    ✓ b) Periodic backups that reset the archive bit

    c) Periodic backups of files selected by the backup operator

    d) Occasional backups performed as necessary based on administrator decisions

18. **The objective of the DRP team is to begin operating within the time limit of which of these?**

    a) RPO

    b) RTO

    ✓ c) MTD

    d) MDT

Lesson 12

Activity 12-1

1. **In the case of common law, if a prior decision does not adhere to a certain case, a judge can create which type of new law?**

    a) Procedure

    ✓ b) Precedent

    c) Tort

    d) Codification

2. **Which one of the following types of law is passed by federal, state, and local legislatures?**

    a) Administrative law

    b) Common law

    c) Intellectual property law

    ✓ d) Statutory law

3. **Which one of the following types of laws defines what constitutes legal harm and creates means for damage recovery from intentional malicious acts or accidents?**

    a) Administrative law

    b) Codification

    ✓ c) Tort law

    d) Criminal law

4. **How many types of statutory offenses are known in the U.S. legal system? What are some prosecution and penalty characteristics of these offenses?**

    Criminal—Acts that a society has specifically prohibited by law. For example, a hacker may be prosecuted by state or federal authorities for breaking into a computer system. The penalty could be either a fine, prison, or both. Guilt is determined by a high standard, such as "beyond a reasonable doubt."

    Civil—Wrongs done between private parties such as individuals or corporations. A lawsuit is filed by the damaged party, and then the damage needs to be proven in court. The penalties include court cost, legal fees, and fines. Guilt is determined by a lower standard than in criminal law, such as by "preponderance of the evidence."

5. **Which branch of the U.S. government is responsible for developing appropriate regulations and guidelines, within the law, for businesses to adhere to?**

    ✓ a) Executive branch

    b) Legislative branch

    c) Judicial branch

6. **What is the appropriate description for each intellectual property law?**

f	Patent	a.	Legal protection of creator's materials that are usually issued in copies for purchase.
e	Trademark	b.	Legal protection of artistic work that lasts for 70 years past the death of the creator.
b	Copyright	c.	Legal protection or secrecy of an individual's information maintained by a legal principle.
d	Trade secret	d.	Legal protection of an item that, if lost, would severely damage the business and must be properly secured and protected.
a	Licensing	e.	Legal protection of a phrase or design used to identity a product that lasts for 10 years but can be renewed using an affidavit.
c	Privacy	f.	Legal protection of an invention that lasts for 20 years.

7. What is the appropriate description for each information privacy law?

d	Privacy Act of 1974	a.	Protects the privacy of educational information held in any federally funded institution of higher learning.
a	FERPA	b.	Protects the privacy of any health insurance information that can identify a patient, including medical records or payment history.
c	ECPA	c.	Protects the privacy of employee activities during the use of electronic communications devices unless employees are notified in advance that monitoring will be taking place.
b	HIPAA	d.	Protects the privacy of individual information held by the U.S. government.

8. What is the appropriate description for each additional information privacy law?

c	GLBA	a.	The requirement of large corporations to keep long-term records of email, voicemail, and instant messaging to control how the corporations report about and audit themselves.
b	COPPA	b.	Protects the privacy of children online, requiring parent consent for any information collected from children or provided to children over the Internet.
d	USA PATRIOT Act	c.	Protects the privacy of an individual's information held by financial institutions or tax preparation companies.
a	SOX Act	d.	Allows the government to take additional measures, such as wiretaps and the control of financial information, to combat terrorism.

9. **Which one of the following computer crime laws is in effect to fulfill training needs and plan developments for information and systems security?**

    a) CFAA

    ✓ b) CSA

    c) NIIPA

    d) FISMA

10. **Which one of the following computer crime laws particularly targets Internet infra-structure security?**

    a) CFAA

    b) CSA

    ✓ c) NIIPA

    d) FISMA

11. **True or False? Understanding and interpreting compliance laws is the responsibility of the security professional in an organization.**

    ___ True

    ✓ False

12. **Which one or more of the following are terms for the general expectation of company behavior while performing normal business functions?**

    a) Liability

    b) Compliance

    ✓ c) Due care

    ✓ d) Due diligence

13. **What are some examples of tasks that internal and external audit departments perform?**

    Internal audit departments—Review processes, logs, and transactions to ensure compliance. Verify that organizations comply with federal, state, and local laws and regulations.

    External audit departments—Validate and verify compliance and provide additional oversight to an organization.

Activity 12-2

1. **What are some examples of typical computer crimes?**

    Unauthorized access to a computer or network

    Distributing illegal information via a computer network

    Stealing classified information stored on a computer

    Social engineering attacks that involve illegal activity

2. **What is the appropriate description for each computer criminal incident response process?**

_e_	Response capability	a.	Determination of events and assessment by an incident response team.
_a_	Incident response and handling	b.	Response to a computer crime-related situation based on criticality.
_b_	Triage	c.	Securing the scene of the incident as to not damage evidence.
_d_	Investigative	d.	Identification, examination, and inspection of a problem by either an internal response team or local law enforcement.
_c_	Containment	e.	Formation of an incident response or computer crime team by an organization.

3. **What is the appropriate description for each additional computer criminal incident response process?**

_c_	Analysis and tracking	a.	Replacing damaged components or systems to aid in the preservation of crime evidence.
_d_	Recovery	b.	Informing management of the incident and suggesting the next best course of action to reduce the possibility of future events from occurring.
_a_	Repair	c.	Examination of facts and evidence by forensic analysts.
_b_	Debriefing and feedback	d.	The restoration of backup files, reprocessing transactions, and auditing the system to return the system to operating condition.

4. **True or False? Collecting evidence about cybercrimes requires different and special training methods.**

   ✓ True

   __ False

5. **What is the appropriate description for each evidence type?**

_d_	Best	a.	A copy of an original document that is not as admissible in court as is best evidence.
_a_	Secondary	b.	Permanent evidence that cannot be disputed.
_e_	Direct	c.	Classified into either the expert or non-expert types.
_b_	Conclusive	d.	Required to be admissible in a court of law.
_c_	Opinion	e.	Received from the testimony of an individual that witnessed the crime.

6. **What is the appropriate description for each additional evidence type?**

_c_	Corroborative	a.	Presented by someone who was not in direct observation of a crime.
_d_	Circumstantial	b.	Used to explain events that took place during the crime.
_a_	Hearsay	c.	Gathered from multiple sources that support other types of evidence in a court of law.
_b_	Demonstrative	d.	Gathered from multiple sources to infer a conclusion in a court of law.

7. What are the phases of the chain of evidence?

The record of evidence history from collection, to presentation in court, to return or disposal.

8. What are five common rules of evidence?

Reliable

Preserved

Relevant

Properly identified

Legally permissible

9. True or False? An organization never has the right to collect evidence within the perimeter of their buildings, due to having the same level of restriction as law enforcement.

____ True

✓ False

10. What are some of the ways that forensic experts can obtain computer system-specific evidence?

Analyze software.

Obtain forensic copies of disk drives.

Analyze disk drives for hidden information.

Analyze network traffic.

Shut down systems.

Lesson 12 Follow-up

Lesson 12 Lab 1

1. **In a criminal investigation, what is considered evidence?**

   ✓ a) Computer disks

   b) Computer hardware

   c) Program source files

   d) Program code

2. **Computer-generated evidence is considered to be:**

   a) Direct.

   b) Demonstrative.

   ✓ c) Hearsay.

   d) Differential.

3. **Which one of the following should not be included in an evidence record?**

   a) Who collected it

   b) Where it was collected

   c) When it was collected

   ✓ d) The replacement cost of the evidence

4. **In what circumstances can copies of documents not be used as evidence?**

   a) If the original was destroyed

   b) If the original cannot be subpoenaed

   c) If the original has been damaged

   ✓ d) If the copy was seized illegally

5. **When can audit logs be used as evidence?**

   ✓ a) If they have been periodically reviewed as part of their collection process

   b) If they have not been subject to a clipping level

   c) If the logs have been written to media, disallowing modifications

   d) If the lawyers certify their correctness

6. **It is best for a forensic analysis to be performed by whom?**

   a) Local security analysts

   ✓ b) Trained professional forensic analysts

   c) Local police departments

   d) Local college professors

7. **Which amendment of the U.S. Constitution prohibits illegal search and seizure?**

    ✓ a) 4th Amendment

    b) 2nd Amendment

    c) 9th Amendment

    d) 22nd Amendment

8. **Which law prohibits the monitoring or interception of electronic communications without notice to employees or those who will be monitored?**

    ✓ a) ECPA

    b) Network Interception, Monitoring and Data Act

    c) Privacy Act of 1974

    d) Home Secrecy Act

9. **In a criminal investigation, what is enticement used for?**

    a) To trap a person who is not intending to perform a criminal act

    ✓ b) To coax a criminal into performing a criminal act that they are intending to do

    c) To trick a person into stealing computer hardware left laying on a table

    d) To prevent a criminal from performing a criminal act

10. **Which one or more of the following locations can be used to hide evidence on a disk drive?**

    ✓ a) Slack space

    b) Disk driver

    c) Disk controller

    d) File Allocation Table

11. **Which of the following are considered external auditors?**

    a) Employees of the company being audited who work in the external audit department.

    b) Employees of the company being audited who do not work in the internal audit department.

    ✓ c) A group that verifies compliance with laws, regulations, and policies but are not employees of the audited company.

    d) Accounting experts who also know about security issues.

12. **The penalty for violating civil law consists of which of the following?**

    a) A jail term.

    ✓ b) A cash fine.

    c) A cash fine and jail term.

    d) A jail term, court costs, and lawyer fees.

13. **The evidence standard of "beyond a reasonable doubt" is used to determine guilt in which type of case?**

    a) Civil case

    b) Administrative law case

    c) Statutory case

    ✓ d) Criminal case

14. **A patent is a legal protection of what?**

    a) A written work of an author.

    ✓ b) An invention.

    c) A mark identifying a product.

    d) A trade secret.

15. **A trademark is protected for how many years in the United States?**

    a) 5 years

    b) 20 years

    ✓ c) 10 years

    d) 40 years

16. **Which act protects the privacy of health-related information?**

    a) ECPA

    b) SOX Act

    c) GLBA

    ✓ d) HIPAA

17. **What does the Computer Fraud and Abuse Act of 1984 protect?**

    ✓ a) Federal government systems

    b) State systems

    c) Personal computer systems

    d) Commercial computer systems

18. **Which law replaced the Computer Security Act?**

    ✓ a) FISMA

    b) NIIPA

    c) FERPA

    d) COPPA

19. **Which one of the following is not usually considered a computer crime?**

    a) Phishing

    b) Hacking

    c) Cracking

    ✓ d) Identity theft

20. Who protects intellectual property in an international setting?

✓ a) WIPO

   b) IPPO

   c) POPI

   d) KIPSW

Glossary

2DES

(Double DES) The same symmetric encryption algorithm as DES with the exception that the encryption process is repeated twice in an attempt to strengthen the output.

3DES

(Triple DES) A symmetric encryption algorithm that uses the DES algorithm but employs three keys to encrypt the same information in three processes.

802.11i

A wireless access protocol that is implemented with the AES encryption algorithm. Also known as WPA2.

abstraction

As an OOP term, this is when classes are generalized to the highest, most appropriate level needed to use them.

acceptance

A risk management principle that retains losses when they occur and employs no countermeasures.

access control matrix

A technical access control consisting of a tabular display of access rights.

access control

The process of allowing only authorized users, programs, or other computer systems such as networks to observe, modify, or otherwise take possession of the resources of a computer system.

accounting system

An asset valuation method that references existing asset costs and quantifies potential risk based on logged expenses.

accreditation

The Designated Approving Authority's acceptance of system security risks.

ACID integrity

(atomicity, consistency, isolation, and durability) Database integrity that concentrates on four essential areas of integrity assurance.

ACL

(access control list) A list of permissions that is associated with each object, which specifies the subjects that can access the object and the subjects' level of access. It is used on routers and switches to filter protocols on interfaces, either inbound or outbound.

addressing path

The third and last physical computer bus pathway that transfers information between a CPU and an I/O device.

administrative access controls

A broad area of security including policies and procedures, personnel security, monitoring, user and password management, and permission management.

administrative law

The laws set by regulatory agencies. Also known as regulatory law.

Advisory Committee-BCP team

A group of individuals from varying backgrounds within the community who collectively assemble to create the BCP and assist in plan maintenance.

AES

(Advanced Encryption Standard) A symmetric block cipher that has been approved by the U.S. government for encrypting Secret and Top Secret information.

aggregation

A data mining technique used to summarize information found in the data repository. The summarization can be implemented for different reasons.

Agile software development

This model uses incremental and iterative rounds of development using cross-functional teams. It encourages short, iterative sessions over long life-cycle development.

AI

(artificial intelligence) A mechanism that attempts to mimic or emulate the process of human intelligence by implementing algorithms that cause the system to learn about its environment and make decisions based on its learning.

ALE

(Annualized Loss Expectancy) An equation factor used to determine risk by estimating the expected loss from each identified threat on an annual basis.

algorithm

In encryption, the rule, system, or mechanism used to encrypt data.

appliance

A specialized networking, single-purpose device with functionality limited to provide support for a single task.

Application layer

A TCP/IP model layer that is similar in function to the Session, Presentation, and Application layers of the OSI model. At this layer, application programs begin sending information, and end at the destination device or application.

Application layer

An OSI model layer (Layer 7) that provides services and utilities that enable application programs to send information into the communications network.

application state

A CPU mode that can execute only non-privileged instructions, protecting the system from unauthorized activities by user programs.

ARO

(Annualized Rate of Occurrence) An equation percentage factor that determines the likelihood of events and the estimated number of times an identified incident or threat will occur within a year. Also known as Annual Rate of Occurrence.

ARP

(Address Resolution Protocol) A protocol used in the TCP/IP model to determine the MAC address for a known IP address.

array

A data structure that houses collections of primitives that are interrelated.

assembly language

A low-level programming code. The code is processed by an assembler utility to create machine code.

asset management system

An asset valuation method that provides an asset value based on accounting principles, detailed records of corporate property, and similar assets.

asset valuation

A method of determining how much an asset is worth to an organization.

asymmetric encryption

A two-way encryption scheme that uses paired private and public keys.

asynchronous messaging

A data services function where the sender and receiver are not directly and simultaneously interacting, and some delay is included in the communication process. Email is an asynchronous messaging protocol.

asynchronous token system

The user is sent a small amount of text or a number. When the user enters it into a device, the device will create a separate code that the user then combines with his password to authenticate to the system.

ATM

(Asynchronous Transfer Mode) A protocol used to move all types of data at high speeds in a fiber-based network.

atomicity

The first component of ACID integrity that ensures the completion of all tasks associated with a particular transaction.

attribute

A column, or field, in a database.

audit committee

A structural faction of an organization that is responsible for ensuring legal adherence and regulation compliance.

audit log

In information security, an electronic record of operating system, application, and security information. Also known as an audit file.

AV

(Asset Value) An equation factor used to determine impact by containing the value of the asset prior to a damage-causing event.

availability

The fundamental principle of ensuring that systems operate continuously and that authorized persons can access data that they need.

avalanche effect

A process found in a cipher that causes a very small change in the plaintext to produce a very large change in the ciphertext.

avoidance

A risk management principle that eliminates threats through mitigation, thereby significantly reducing risk.

backdoor attack

A software attack where the attacker creates a software mechanism to gain access to a system and its resources. This can involve software or a bogus user account.

backdoor

A mechanism for gaining access to a computer that bypasses or subverts the normal method of authentication.

baseline

A security document that specifies the minimum security required in a system or process.

bastion host

A server that provides a very special function with everything else stripped away. It is traditionally hardened to withstand attack.

BCP

(Business Continuity Plan) A policy that defines how normal day-to-day business will be maintained in the event of a business disruption or crisis.

best practices

Commonly accepted activities related to business operations.

BIA

(business impact analysis) A BCP phase that identifies present organizational risks and determines the impact to ongoing, business-critical operations if risks are actualized.

Biba Model

An integrity model that uses integrity levels to depict the trust level of the information.

birthday attack

A type of cryptographic attack that exploits weaknesses in the mathematical algorithms used to encrypt passwords, to take advantage of the probability of different password inputs producing the same encrypted output.

blackout

A power failure in which all power is lost.

blind testing

A type of penetration test where the target organization is not aware of testing activities.

block cipher

A type of symmetric encryption that encrypts data a block at a time, often in 64-bit or 128-bit blocks. It is usually more secure, but is also slower, than stream ciphers.

Blowfish

A freely available 64-bit block cipher algorithm that uses a variable key length.

BLP Model

(Bell-LaPadula) A confidentiality model that limits the access to classified objects to those subjects with an equal or higher clearance.

bollard

An obstacle designed to stop a vehicle.

botnet

A group of computers or an entire network of computers that is taken over by malware without the knowledge of the network's owner.

Brewer-Nash Model

A security model that relates to the control of the conflict of interest in a computer system.

brownout

A long-term, low-voltage power failure during which lights go dim for an extended period of time.

brute force

A type of password attack where an attacker uses an application to exhaustively try every possible alphanumeric combination to try to crack encrypted passwords and circumvent the authentication system.

buffer overflow

A TCB vulnerability that moves too much information into a program memory area.

buffer overflow

An attack against the buffers that are written into applications and hardware devices.

bus topology

A network topology in which network nodes are arranged in a linear format.

CA

(certificate authority) A server that issues certificates and the associated public/private key pairs.

cable modem

A specialized interface device used in a cable television infrastructure to provide high-speed Internet access to homes and small businesses.

cache memory

A category of RAM used to expedite access to security instructions that require processing.

CAN

(campus area network) A network that covers an area equivalent to an academic or enterprise campus.

cardinality

In databases, the types of relationships that are available.

CASE

(Computer-Aided Software Engineering) The adoption of tools and techniques to help with large-scale software projects.

CAST-128

A symmetric encryption algorithm with a 128-bit key, named for its developers, Carlisle Adams and Stafford Tavares.

CBC

(Cipher Block Chaining) A block cipher mode wherein 64-bit plaintext blocks are XORed with a 64-bit IV and then encrypted using the key.

CCTV

(closed-circuit television) A visual recording device that uses video cameras to transmit images to monitors and video recorders. It is placed in strategic locations in an organization to record movement or actions of employees.

cell suppression

Intentionally hiding cells containing highly confidential information. The cells may be suppressed for everyone or they might be suppressed based on the ID of the user accessing the data.

cell

The intersection, or value, of a row and column in a database.

centralized access control

The process of administering access controls at a centralized site.

CER

(crossover error rate) Where FRR and FAR biometric errors intersect on a graph; the biometric measurement with the lowest CER provides the best protection.

certificate management system

A system that provides the software tools to perform the day-to-day functions of the PKI.

certificate repository

A database containing digital certificates.

certification

A risk evaluation of information system security.

CFAA

(Computer Fraud and Abuse Act) Legislation passed in 1984 to protect government systems from illegal access or from exceeding access permissions. Amended in 1994, 1996, and 2001 to extend coverage to new types of attacks.

CFB

(Cipher FeedBack) A block cipher mode wherein the IV is first encrypted using the key and then XORed with the plaintext to create the ciphertext.

chain of evidence

The record of evidence history from collection, to presentation in court, to disposal.

chaining

A method for strengthening block ciphers in which the results of one cipher step alters the encryption process for the subsequent step.

change control

A formal process of tracking hardware and software changes to ensure they are properly authorized and implemented and follow procedural specifications.

CHAP

(Challenge-Handshake Authentication Protocol) An encrypted remote-access authentication method that enables connections from any authentication method requested by the server, except for PAP unencrypted authentication.

CIA triad

(confidentiality, integrity, and availability) The same as the information security triad. Also called triple.

cipher

The specific software or other technology that uses an algorithm to encrypt, decrypt, or hash information.

ciphertext

The coded, encrypted form of data.

CIRT

(computer incident response team) A team comprised of individuals from IT, HR, legal, and others trained to respond appropriately to security events.

civil law

The legal category that governs a wrong committed against a business or individual resulting in damage or loss to that business or individual.

Clark-Wilson Model

An integrity model that relates trust to the integrity of the processes surrounding the data.

class
As an OOP term, this defines the general characteristics of a type of object, including attributes, fields, and operations.

classification
A labeling scheme that measures the risk of information loss or modification.

cleanroom model
The idea that in software development, it is easier and cheaper to eliminate defects before code is written, rather than trying to remove them afterwards.

cleartext
The original form of a message. Also referred to as plaintext.

clipping level
In security auditing, a logging technique that sets a limit on the number of log records created for a given incident.

closed shop
A security control method in which only authorized users are allowed access to system information.

CMDB
(configuration management database) A software tool that serves as a repository for configuration management information.

CMM
(Capability Maturity Model) An evaluation model that indicates the level of sophistication or maturity found in an organization's software development process.

CMMI
(Capability Maturity Model Integration) A process improvement project initiative that incorporates the different CMMs into one cohesive collection of integrated models.

COBIT
(Control Objectives for Information and related Technologies) A security framework for security governance best practices developed by the ISACA.

code book
An alternative cipher. A book or booklet that contains a series of codes that are used to represent common words or phrases that might be used in communication.

codification
Laws, rules, and regulations that are documented and grouped by subject.

cohesion
The level of independence of software modules of the same application. A highly cohesive module is highly independent from other modules.

cold site
A predetermined alternate location where a network can be rebuilt after a disaster.

collision
When a hash function generates identical output from different input.

COM
(Component Object Model) A Microsoft technology used to create reusable software components that can be linked together to create applications. The links may be between one or more applications running on the same machine.

Common Criteria
A security standard where security targets can be submitted by consumers and describe system protection expectations. It was developed to replace TCSEC and ITSEC and published by the ISO/IEC.

common law
A set of unwritten but well-understood and normally accepted principles of justice.

compartmentalization
Complements least privilege and need to know by separating and isolating subjects that work on different projects.

compensating access control
A control that is implemented when the system cannot provide protection required by policy.

compensating controls

In OPSEC, controls that mitigate the lack of another control.

compiled languages

Program languages where source code is run through a compiler.

compiler

A program that transforms the source of code of a higher level language to object code that is understood by the device or operating system.

compliance

The awareness of and adherence to relevant laws and regulations that are set forth by and apply to a particular corporation, public agency, or organizational entity.

computer bus

The set of physical connections between devices that are attached to a computer's motherboard.

computer crime

A criminal act that involves the use of a computer as the source or target, instead of an individual.

confidentiality

The fundamental principle of keeping information and communications private and protecting them from unauthorized access.

configuration management

The process used to track hardware and software components in an enterprise to ensure that existing configurations match implementation standards.

confusion

An encryption technique used to create a complex cipher by mixing up the key values.

consistency

The second component of ACID integrity that requires database stability before and after a transaction.

constrained interfaces access control

A non-discretionary access control technique that limits access.

contact card

Smart cards that has small metal contacts and must be used with its corresponding reader.

contactless card

A smart card that uses radio waves and must be used in close proximity to a reader.

content dependent access control

A non-discretionary access control technique that limits a subject's access to objects by examining object data to see if the subject has access rights.

context dependant access control

A non-discretionary access control technique where the context of the request is determined before processing.

COPPA

(Children's Online Privacy Protection Act) Legislation passed in 1998 to protect the online privacy of children. Includes the right to opt out of any information sent by a provider, to limit the amount and type of information collected from children, and to require parental consent for any information provided to children.

copyright

Intellectual property law that protects original material created by an author or a musician.

CORBA

(Common Object Request Broker Architecture) An open, vendor-neutral object broker framework that provides functionality similar to DCOM.

corrective access control

A control that responds to the security violation to reduce or completely eliminate the impact.

corrective controls

In OPSEC, controls such as file backup restorations that remedy problems caused by security setbacks.

coupling

The degree and complexity of interaction among modules in an application.

covert channel

An unauthorized communications path wherein unexpected data flows are detected by the Information Flow Model.

covert storage

A TCB vulnerability where a file saved by one process should be unavailable to another process, but the second process may be able to learn information just by seeing that a file exists.

covert timing

A TCB vulnerability where the watching process is able to monitor the traffic or CPU utilization and make determinations based on this information.

CPU

(Central Processing Unit) The computer component that executes security instructions that allow a computer system to operate successfully.

CRC

(Cyclical Redundancy Check) A function used by Ethernet to detect transmission errors in the Data Link layer of the OSI model.

criminal law

The legal category that governs individual conduct violating government laws enacted for public or societal protection.

critical business process

An activity that, if not recovered, can lead to business loss or failure.

CRL

(Certificate Revocation List) A list of the serial numbers of revoked or otherwise invalid certificates that is maintained by a CA and made available to CA users.

cryptanalysis

The study of cryptosytems with the intent of breaking them.

cryptography

The analysis and practice of information concealment for the purpose of securing sensitive data transmissions.

cryptology

The study of both cryptography and cryptanalysis.

cryptosystem

The general term used or the hardware and/or software used to implement a cryptographic process.

CSA

(Computer Security Act) Legislation passed in 1987 to protect computer systems and fulfill training needs and plan developments for information and systems security. Replaced by FISMA in 2002.

CTR

(Counter) A block cipher mode where a counter provides the IV.

DAC

(discretionary access control) A means of restricting access to objects based on the identity of the subjects and/or groups to which they belong.

data access service

A function that mediates the access of data over a network.

data backup

Copies of data captured at a point in time and stored in a secure area as a precautionary safeguard in case of a disaster.

data exchange service

A protocol that allows individuals to access information on a central server and, in some cases, transfer that information to the individuals' local computers.

Data Link layer

An OSI model layer (Layer 2) that organizes bits into frames. Most Data Link layer protocols define the structure of a frame.

data mining

The practice of analyzing large amounts of data to locate previously unknown or hidden information.

data network topology

The physical and logical arrangement of nodes in a network.

data network

A collection of hardware and software that allows the exchange of information between sending and receiving application processes.

data path

The first of three physical computer bus pathways that transfers information between a CPU and an I/O device.

data remanence

An electronic property where faulty information is left on media during the file erasure and deletion process.

data services

The functions that are provided and the applications that are accessible by connecting devices to a network.

data structure

A standardized format for storing information in a computer system so that this information can be efficiently accessed.

data warehouse

A pre-processed database that contains information about a specific subject from various sources, and is used for subsequent reporting and analysis.

database integrity

An assurance that data stored within a database is accurate and valid and not unknowingly altered or deleted. Also known as ACID integrity.

database system

A set of related information organized within a software framework for ease of access and reporting.

database

A data structure in which the data environment uses primitives, arrays, lists, and matrices to store and present data to applications.

DCOM

(Distributed Component Object Model) An extension of COM that allows for components to be located throughout the network. It is also Microsoft technology.

DDoS

(distributed denial of service) A software attack that uses multiple source machines to perpetrate a logical DoS against a chosen victim.

deadlock

A database vulnerability wherein two or more competing processes are waiting for the other to release a particular resource.

decentralized access control

The process of administering access control elements that are found in distributed locations throughout the enterprise.

decipher

The same as decryption.

decryption

A security technique that transforms encrypted data into a readable form, revealing the content.

defense in depth

A risk concept that uses a layered approach to mitigate security threats at multiple levels within the networks and systems. Also known as layered defense.

Delphi method

A systematic and interactive communication technique that involves iteratively questioning a panel of independent experts to obtain asset value forecasts.

deluge

A water-based extinguishing system wherein high output sprinklers in wet or dry pipe systems saturate the affected area.

demonstrative evidence

Evidence that is used to demonstrate or explain events, such as the use of a model to explain how a computer crime was committed.

DES

(Data Encryption Standard) A symmetric block algorithm that uses a 64-bit block and a 64-bit key.

detective access control

A control that identifies attempts to access an entity without proper authorization.

detective controls

In OPSEC, controls such as an IDS that discover the location of unauthorized access infiltration or unauthorized access attempts in a system.

deterrent access control

A control that discourages individuals from violating security policies.

deterrent controls

In OPSEC, controls that encourage compliance with security guidelines and practices.

DHCP

(Dynamic Host Configuration Protocol) A protocol used to assign IP addresses to devices in an IP network.

Diameter

An authentication protocol that allows for a variety of connection types, such as wireless.

dictionary attack

A type of cryptographic attack that automates password guessing by comparing encrypted passwords against a predetermined list of possible password values.

differential backup

A method that copies all modifications since the last full backup to the backup media.

Diffie-Hellman

A cryptographic protocol that provides for secure key exchange.

diffusion

An encryption technique used to create a complex cipher by mixing up the plaintext.

digital certificate

An electronic document that associates credentials with a public key.

digital signature

An encrypted hash value that is appended to a message to identify the sender and the message.

direct evidence

Evidence received from the testimony of an individual who observed the crime or activity. Evidence that clearly indicates that the crime was committed and proves the case on its own merits.

directive access control

A control that provides direction to employees and can often take the form of policies and guidelines.

directive controls

In OPSEC, controls such as corporate security policies that provide guidance.

distributed system architecture

A network architecture that is used for systems in which a number of computers are networked together and share application processes and data.

DMZ

(demilitarized zone) See screened subnet.

DNS

(Domain Name Service) A protocol used to resolve or translate device and domain names into IP addresses using a central repository.

DoS

(denial of service) Any attack that will render a service, server, or system unavailable. DoS can happen at the physical layer and/or the logical layer.

drivers

Software modules that interface between the operating system and the I/O devices.

DRP

(Disaster Recovery Plan) A policy that defines how people and resources will be protected in the case of a natural or man-made disaster, and how the organization will recover from the disaster.

dry pipe

A water-based extinguishing system wherein the pipes are not filled with water until a fire is detected. Sprinkler heads can be individually activated or activated by a system.

DS

(directory service) A data services technology used to provide information about users and resources in a computer network.

DSL

(Digital Subscriber Line) An Internet access protocol that uses telephone lines and digital signaling at high frequencies to attach users to the telephone company-supplied ISPs.

dual-homed firewall

Hardware that has two network interfaces. It establishes the perimeter between the trusted and untrusted network.

due diligence

Establishes the generally recognized expectations of behavior that companies or entities in a given industry must adhere to when performing normal business functions.

dumpster diving

A human-based attack where the goal is to reclaim important information by inspecting the contents of trash containers.

duplexing

Writing data to a disk using multiple drive controllers and multiple disks. It provides very high reliability, a higher cost, and slightly longer write times than striping.

durability

The fourth component of ACID integrity that ensures transaction stability upon notification to the user of transaction completion.

EAP

(Extensible Authentication Protocol) An authentication protocol that enables systems to use hardware-based identifiers, such as fingerprint scanners or smart card readers, for authentication.

ECB

(Electronic Code Book) A block cipher mode that breaks the plaintext down into 64-bit blocks and then encrypts each block separately.

ECC

(elliptic curve cryptography) A public-key, asymmetric encryption algorithm that is based on developments in discrete logs and requires short keys.

ECPA

(Electronic Communications Privacy Act) Legislation passed in 1986 to protect the privacy of educational information held in any federally funded institution of higher learning.

EF

(Exposure Factor) An equation factor used to determine impact by estimating the damage or loss caused by one event.

EJB

(Enterprise JavaBean) A tool from Sun Microsystems that allows for distributed multi-tier application in Java.

electronic vaulting

A data backup method used to copy modified files to an offsite location.

Elgamal

A public-key, asymmetric encryption algorithm developed by Taher Elgamal.

emanation

A software attack where protected information is leaked through the natural process of electrons passing through a wire or over the radio.

encapsulation

As an OOP term, this is when the functional details of a class are concealed or masked from the calling objects.

encipher

The same as encrypt.

encryption
A security technique that converts data from its ordinary, intelligible state, or plaintext form, into coded, or ciphertext form so that only authorized parties with the necessary decryption information can decode and read the data.

enticement
The practice of attracting criminals to repeat a particular illegal act as a means to catch them.

entity integrity
This requires that each tuple in a database has a unique primary key that is not null, thereby assuring uniqueness

entity
A term of reference that identifies multiple things in security access control, such as a user or computer program.

entrapment
The practice of capturing an individual at a crime scene who did not have criminal intentions to perform an illegal act.

Ethernet
A LAN and CAN protocol that supports communication between devices at the Physical and Data Link layers of the OSI model.

ethics
Pertaining to an organization, refers to the principles of acceptable and proper conduct as well as the organization's moral value system.

expert system
An extended AI and KBS system that provides problem-solving assistance. Equipped with a knowledge base of information about a specific subject area such as a medical diagnosis.

facility control system
A set of support information services that combine with physical security protection processes to protect and limit access to facilities.

factoring attack
A type of cryptographic attack that attempts to determine the prime numbers used in asymmetric encryption as a means to break cryptosystems.

Fair Cryptosystems
In cryptography, an escrow method that allows a key to be split into "N" parts that re-create the original key.

FAR
(false acceptance rate) A biometric error where an unauthorized individual is given access.

fault tolerance
A system property in which a single component fault does not cause a complete system failure. Often enabled through redundancy.

FERPA
(Family Educational Rights and Privacy Act) Protects the privacy of educational information held in any federally funded institution of higher learning. Passed in the same session of Congress as the Privacy Act of 1974.

firewall
A software program or hardware device that protects networks from unauthorized data by blocking unsolicited traffic.

firmware
Small chips designed to hold a small set of instructions to assist devices.

FISMA
(Federal Information Security Management Act) Legislation passed in 2002 to remedy the evolutionary nature of information systems security in the federal government.

flat file
An early storage mechanism for computer data.

foreign key
In databases, a cell value in one table that refers to a unique key in a different table, thus enabling the creation of relations between tables.

frequency analysis

A method for breaking encryption when simple substitution algorithms are used. It is based on the fact that certain letters will statistically appear more often than others.

FRR

(false rejection rate) A biometric error where an authorized individual is denied access

full backup

A method that backs up all selected files. It is used as a starting point for all backup activities that copies all information to the backup media.

full disclosure

This involves releasing information regarding security flaws immediately and publicly.

full-duplex

A Session-layer communication mode that allows for simultaneous, two-way data transmission.

function point

A unit of measurement used to size software applications and convey the quantity of business functionality that an information system offers its users.

generator

A power protection device that creates its own electricity through the use of motors.

GLBA

(Gramm-Leach-Bliley Act) Legislation passed in 1999 to protect the privacy of an individual's financial information that is held by financial institutions and others such as tax preparation companies.

governance

Pertaining to an organization, refers to the organization's methods of exercising authority or control as well as its system of management.

Graham-Denning Model

A security model that deals with the creation and deletion of objects and subjects, as well as the reading, granting, deleting, and transferring of access rights.

guessing

A human-based attack where the goal is to guess a password or PIN through brute force means or by using deduction.

guideline

A security document that recommends or suggests a specific action, implementation, or use of tools as a best practice for meeting the policy standard.

half-duplex

A Session-layer communication mode where data transmission occurs in both directions, but is restricted to one direction at a time.

Harrison-Ruzzo-Ullman Model

A security model used for changing access rights and creating and deleting subjects or objects.

hash value

The same as hash.

hash

The value that results from hashing encryption. The same as hash value and message digest.

hashing

One-way encryption that transforms cleartext into ciphertext that is never decrypted.

HAVAL

A modified MD5 hash algorithm that produces 128-bit, 160-bit, 192-bit, 224-bit, and 256-bit hash values.

hearsay evidence

Evidence that is presented by an individual who was not a direct observer but who heard, or received word, about the event from others. Computer records are considered hearsay because they cannot directly testify.

heat detector

A perimeter IDS that is installed to measure temperature increases emitted from a heat source such as a human, fire, or animal.

HIDS

(host-based intrusion detection system) Software that is installed on a host computer to monitor and detect host and network traffic anomalies and report the anomalies to the network administrator.

Hierarchical Database Management Model

A database system model that is implemented in a tree-like structure with relationships that are created with a parent-child view.

HIPAA

(Health Insurance Portability and Accountability Act) Legislation passed in 1996 to protect people with health insurance when they transferred from one company to another. Modified in 2003 to add a privacy component that protects a class of information called the Protected Health Information (PHI).

HIPS

(host-based intrusion prevention system) An application that is installed on the host and is designed to monitor host and network activity that affects that host to block suspicious network and system traffic in real time and report findings to the network administrator.

HMAC

(hash message authentication code) An authentication code algorithm that creates a hash of a file that is then encrypted for transmission.

Host-to-Host layer

A TCP/IP model layer that is similar in function to the Transport layer of the OSI model. This layer's protocols support application-to-application information transfer using port numbers to identify applications.

hot site

A fully configured alternate network that can be online quickly after a disaster. Also known as a mirror site.

HTTPS

(Hypertext Transfer Protocol Secure) A secure version of HTTP that supports web commerce by providing a secure connection between the web browser and server. It is a combination of HTTP and SSL/TLS. The SSL/TLS component will provide encryption and identification to the HTTP protocol, thereby providing secure communications between the connecting devices.

HVAC system

(heating, ventilation, and air conditioning) A physical system that controls the environment inside a building.

hybrid access control

The process of administering access controls in centralized and decentralized domains.

I/O

(input/output) Devices that provide input to and output from a computer system. Secondary storage is a form of I/O device.

ICMP

(Internet Control Message Protocol) A protocol used by operating systems and network devices to send error messages or relay messages back to devices that are available.

IDEA

(International Data Encryption Algorithm) A block cipher first proposed in 1991 that is used in Open PGP.

IDS

(intrusion detection system) A hardware or software solution that identifies and addresses potential attacks on a computer (or host) or a network.

IGMP

(Internet Group Management Protocol) A protocol used with IP multicasting to indicate when a device is joining a multicast-enabled application data stream.

IKE

(Internet Key Exchange) Used by IPsec to create a master key, which in turn is used to generate bulk encryption keys for encrypting data.

IM

(instant messaging) A synchronous messaging protocol where participants in the communication process are online and send and receive messages to and from each other at the same time.

IMAP

(Internet Message Access Protocol) An email retrieval protocol that allows a user to view the mail on the server and retrieve the mail from a host of their choosing.

in-rush

A surge or spike that is caused when a device is started that uses a great amount of current.

incremental backup

A method that clears the archive bit and reduces backup time and media by only copying files and databases that have been modified since the last full backup.

inference

A data mining technique used to review data trends and formulate predictions about the subject matter.

Information Flow Model

A security model that controls the direction of data flow among the various security levels when allowed.

information privacy law

Law protecting the information of private individuals from malicious disclosure or unintentional misuse.

information security triad

The three principles of security control and management: confidentiality, integrity, and availability. Also called the CIA triad or triple.

infrared device

A motion sensor that emits a beam of infrared light that is sensed by the receiver. Has a limited distance of operation.

instruction path

The second of three physical computer bus pathways that transfers information between a CPU and an I/O device.

insurance valuation

An asset valuation method that relies on insurers to accept the risk of loss for the assets they insure and to perform an analysis of the risk associated with the policies they issue.

integrity

In asymmetric encryption, it is supported when the sender encrypts using the sender's private key and the receiver decrypts with the sender's public key.

integrity

The fundamental principle of ensuring that electronic data is accurate and free of error or unauthorized modification.

intellectual property law

Law that protects the rights of ownership of ideas, trademarks, patents, and copyrights, including the owners' right to transfer intellectual property and receive compensation for the transfer.

interpreted languages

Program languages that are not put through a compiler, but rather use an interpreter that translates the code line by line into machine code each time the application is run.

IP

(Internet Protocol) A protocol used to move information between nodes on an IP network.

IPS

(intrusion prevention system) A computer security monitoring device that tracks and blocks suspicious and malicious activities to prevent damage to a system or network.

IPsec

(Internet Protocol security) A set of open, non-proprietary standards that you can use to secure data as it travels across the network or the Internet through data authentication, hashing, and encryption.

ISO 27002

This document is the current international standard for information systems security.

ISO/IEC 27001

A formal standard that is concerned with the standardization of a company's Information Security Management System (ISMS).

isolation

The third component of ACID integrity wherein transactions and database processes cannot discern the progress of other, simultaneous transactions.

ITIL

(Information Technology Infrastructure Library) An IT management structure developed by the United Kingdom's OGC that includes concepts and techniques for conducting development, infrastructure, and operations management.

ITSEC

(Information Technology Security Evaluation Criteria) A security standard developed in Europe that evaluates systems based on targets provided by the customer, against the vendors.

IV

(initialization vector) A string of bits that is used with the cipher and the key to produce a unique result when the same key is used to encrypt the same cleartext.

JDBC

(Java Database Connectivity) A database interface language that allows Java-based programs to access databases transparently.

job rotation

A security principle that encourages organizations to build a highly qualified staff by exposing employees to different job areas.

KBS

(knowledge-based system) A program that uses knowledge-based techniques to support human decision making, learning, and action.

Kerberos

A single sign-on (SSO) method where the user enters access credentials that are then passed to the Authentication Server (AS), which contains the allowed access credentials.

kernel mode

See supervisor state

key clustering

An encryption anomaly in which two different keys generate the same ciphertext from the same plaintext.

key escrow

In cryptography, the process of splitting a key into two parts and storing each part with a different escrow agency.

key generation

A process of generating a public and private key pair using a specific application.

key

In cryptography, a specific piece of information that is used with an algorithm to perform encryption and decryption.

key

In databases, an attribute that provides a unique value in a tuple or row that uniquely identifies that row.

keyspace

Key size; the total number of keys available from a key of a given size. A 32-bit key allows for over four billion possible keys.

L2TP

(Layer 2 Tunneling Protocol) A protocol that combines PPTP and L2F to provide for authentication but not for confidentiality. L2TP allows for the use of additional protocols like IPsec to provide encryption and confidentiality.

LAN

(local area network) A self-contained network that spans a small area, such as a single building, floor, or room.

Lattice Model

A security model used to implement mandatory access controls where data is classified or labeled and users are cleared for access.

layered protection
In computer architecture, the process of building security into various hardware, firmware, and software components. In physical security, a mechanism that begins from the perimeter, or outermost boundary of a facility, and continues inward through the building grounds, entry points, and interior. Also known as layered defense or defense in depth.

least privilege
A security principle that ensures employees and other system users have only the minimum set of rights, permissions, and privileges that they need to accomplish their jobs.

liability
A legal responsibility for any damage caused by one individual or company to another.

licensing
Intellectual property law that protects materials in use by an individual or organization other than the creator.

link encryption
An Internet security device that is attached to each end of a transmission line to encrypt and decrypt data.

list
A data structure that contains ordered arrays.

MAC address
(Media Access Control) A unique, hardware-level address assigned to network access devices by its manufacturer.

MAC
(mandatory access control) A means of restricting access to objects based on the sensitivity of the information contained in the objects and the formal authorization of subjects to access information of such sensitivity.

MAC
(message authentication code) An authentication code algorithm that uses a shared secret key to encrypt a file, taking the last block of encrypted data and sending it as an authentication code with the unencrypted file.

machine code
See machine language.

machine language
The lowest level of code, down to the zeros and ones that a CPU executes.

magnetic detector
A perimeter IDS that is installed to measure changes in a magnetic field. Reacts to conductors like keys or coins.

maintenance hook
Application and hardware developers create these shortcuts during development. If these are not removed before the product ships, they may be lead to exploits.

malicious code attack
A type of software attack where an attacker inserts malicious software into a user's system to disrupt or disable the operating system or an application. A malicious code attack can also make an operating system or an application take action to disrupt or disable other systems on the same network or on a remote network.

malicious software
Unauthorized software that can cause system failures or malfunctions or other ill effects.

malware
Malicious code, such as viruses, Trojans, or worms.

man trap
A facility control device that is a physical entry portal with two doors on either end of a secure chamber.

man-in-the-middle attack
A network attack that occurs when an attacker interposes a device between two legitimate hosts to gain access to their data transmissions. The intruder device responds actively to the two legitimate hosts as if it were the intended source or destination.

MAN
(metropolitan area network) A network that covers an area equivalent to a city or other municipality.

matrix

A data structure that includes an array with more than one dimension.

MD2

(Message Digest 2) An early hash algorithm developed as part of the MD series that is optimized for 8-bit computers and produces a 128-bit hash value. Predecessor to MD4 and MD5.

MD4

(Message Digest 4) A hash algorithm developed as part of the MD series that is optimized for 32-bit computers and produces a 128-bit hash value. Predecessor to MD5.

MD5

(Message Digest 5) This hash algorithm, based on RFC 1321, produces a 128-bit hash value and is used in IPsec policies for data authentication. It provides a considerable amount of security over MD4.

MDC

(modification detection code) The same as MIC.

mesh topology

A network topology in which each node has a direct, point-to-point connection to every other node.

message digest

A specific application of hashing used to create cryptographic data that verifies the contents of a message that has not been altered. It is either keyed or non-keyed.

message hash

The same as message digest.

metadata

Information that describes specific data characteristics.

method

As an OOP term that describes an object's abilities.

MIC

(message integrity code) An authentication code that does not imply the use of a secret key and therefore must be transmitted in encrypted form to ensure message integrity.

microwave system

A motion sensor that emits a narrow beam of low-intensity radio signals that are sensed by the receiver. Used in coverage areas that are too large for infrared device detection.

MIME

(Multipurpose Internet Mail Extension) An internal labeling process used to define email attachment types.

mirror

Data is written simultaneously to two drives thereby protecting the data should either drive fail. It still relies on a single drive controller which allows a single point of failure. It provides high availability but slightly longer write times than striping.

mitigation

A risk management principle that curtails the severity of risk or lessens the probability of a loss occurrence.

mobile code

Executable software that is obtained from remote systems and installed on a local system sometimes without the recipient's knowledge, consent, or doing.

modularity

As an OOP term, this is when all object processes within the object are isolated.

motion sensor

A perimeter IDS that uses movement to detect an approach or presence inside a controlled area.

MPLS

(Multiprotocol Label Switching) Aggregate different types of traffic onto a MPLS cloud. MPLS uses labels rather than addresses to move data efficiently through the network.

MTD

(maximum tolerable downtime) The longest period of time a business can be inoperable without causing the business to cease.

multifactor authentication

A system wherein more than one type of authentication is used in accessing a system or facility. Also called two-factor authentication.

multiprocessing

A multiple processor technique that permits multitasking across numerous processors to reach optimal system performance.

multiprogramming

Allows for the simultaneous execution of more than one program.

multistate

A processor technique where different execution modes can be run.

multitasking

A single processor technique that allows more than one program to appear to be running at one time.

multithreading

A single processor technique that allows the parallel execution of multiple threads on a computer system.

NAS

(Network Attached Storage) Dedicated devices that are connected to a network to provide data file storage and sharing functions.

NAT

(Network Address Translation) A simple form of Internet connection and security that conceals internal addressing schemes from the public Internet.

need to know

A security principle based on an individual's need to access classified data resources to perform a given task or job function.

Network Access layer

A TCP/IP model layer that covers the physical networking requirements of generating frames on a cable, fiber, or wireless network.

Network Database Management Model

A type of hierarchical database system model that is implemented using pointers to other database elements.

Network layer

An OSI model layer (Layer 3) that uses logical networking addresses to represent network interfaces.

network scanning

A type of penetration test that uses a port scanner to identify devices attached to the target network and to enumerate the applications hosted on the devices.

network session

A logical communications connection between two hosts, or nodes.

Networking layer

A TCP/IP model layer that creates logical networks using IP network addresses.

NIDS

(network intrusion detection system) A passive hardware system that uses sensors to monitor traffic on a specific segment of the network.

NIIPA

(National Information Infrastructure Protection Act) Legislation passed in 1996 to target new computer security threats. Created legal remedies for hacking, stealing trade secrets, and damaging systems and information.

NIPS

(network intrusion prevention system) An inline prevention control security device that monitors suspicious network and system traffic and reacts in real time to block it.

Non-Interference Model

A security model that limits the interference between elements at different security levels.

non-repudiation

The security goal of ensuring that the party that sent a transmission or created data remains associated with that data. In asymmetric encryption, it is supported when the sender's public key is used to decrypt the message.

normalization

A database design technique that reduces redundant information and duplication between tables to ensure that each table contains only the minimal number of rows and columns required to store information and retrieve it meaningfully.

NTP

(Network Time Protocol) A network-based information service that allows network components to synchronize their clocks with a central clock source.

object reuse

As a software attack, the act of reclaiming classified or sensitive information from media that has been erased.

Object-Oriented Database Model

A database system model that uses object-oriented programming techniques with database technology.

object

As an OOP term, this is a specific instance and implementation of a class. It inherits the class' attributes and defines specific values for each attribute.

object

The security entity being accessed.

ODBC

(Open Database Connectivity) A database language that provides a standard application program interface (API) that allows programmers to access any database from any platform.

OFB

(Output FeedBack) A block cipher mode wherein the IV is encrypted with the key and then chained to the next block's encryption step.

offshoring

Outsourcing in another country.

OLE DB

(Object Linking and Embedding Database) A database language that allows the linking and embedding of documents, graphics, sound files, and other formatted information into a parent document.

OLTP

(online transaction processing) A database security mechanism that presents issues related to concurrency and atomicity.

OOD

(Object Oriented Databases) The object oriented programming approach has been extended into database design with OOD.

OOP

(Object Oriented Programming) Program languages that create reusable objects that combine methods and data.

open source software

Software that is provided to a buyer with a complete copy of the source code.

operational and project planning

A planning effort that deals with the near term, from the present to 12 months out.

OPSEC

(operations security) A process of denying adversaries information about business capabilities and plans by identifying, controlling, and protecting indicators associated with sensitive business activities.

ORBs

(Object Request Brokers) These tools are used to locate objects and can act as middleware for connecting programs.

organizational security model

The totality of information security implementations in an organization.

OSI model

(Open System Interconnection) A reference model for how data is exchanged between any two points in a telecommunications network.

OTP

(one-time pad) An alternative cipher containing a very long, non-repeating key that is the same length as the plaintext. The key is used one time only and then destroyed.

outsourcing

Using a chosen partner organization for business processes previously done internally.

P-box

(permutation box) A component of symmetric-key algorithms that is used to arrange S-boxes by scrambling them.

packet filtering firewall

A firewall where decisions are made on packets as they pass through.

PAN

(personal area network) A very small network that might include a small office/home office (SOHO) network or a Bluetooth connection between a mobile phone and a headset.

PAP

(Password Authentication Protocol) A remote access authentication method that sends client IDs and passwords as plaintext.

parity

An error detection method in which the number of ones within a transmitted data word is compared with those received. If the count matches, the data is assumed to be valid.

partial disclosure

This involves sharing information regarding security flaws with hardware and software vendors before the general public.

PAT

(Port Address Translation) A type of NAT that uses port numbers, as a means of providing uniqueness, to allow hundreds of internal users to be serviced by a single, exterior IP address.

patent

A legal protection provided to unique inventions. Protects the item's creator from competition for a given period of time.

PDU

(Protocol Data Unit) A unit of data as it appears at each layer of the OSI model.

peer-to-peer services

A data services application that does not use the typical client/server model for implementation; all participants in the application are considered equals.

PEM

(Privacy-Enhanced Mail) A standard that provides for secure exchange of email over the Internet and applies various cryptographic techniques to allow for confidentiality, sender authentication, and message integrity.

penetration testing

The controlled use of attack methods to test the security of a system or facility.

perturbation

The intentional addition of spurious data into database fields with the intention of defeating inference attacks.

PGP

(Pretty Good Privacy) A method of securing emails created to prevent attackers from intercepting and manipulating email and attachments by encrypting and digitally signing the contents of the email using public-key cryptography.

phishing

A type of email-based social engineering attack in which the attacker sends email from a spoofed source to try to elicit private information from the victim.

photometric detector

A perimeter IDS that is installed to detect a change in light level in a designated area, specifically a windowless room or area. Sounds an alarm if its emitted beam does not hit a receiver.

physical access controls
These controls are used to limit an individual's physical access to protected information or facilities, such as locks, doors, fences, and perimeter defenses.

Physical layer
An OSI model layer (Layer 1) that transmits bits of data across a physical medium.

physical security
The implementation and practice of various control mechanisms that are intended to restrict physical access to facilities.

PKI
(public key infrastructure) A cryptographic system that is composed of a CA, certificates, software, services, and other cryptographic components, for the purpose of enabling authenticity and validation of data and/or entities. For example, PKI can be used to secure transactions over the Internet.

plaintext
The original, unencrypted form of data. Also referred to as cleartext.

policy
A high-level security document that states management intentions.

polyinstantiation
As an OOP term, this is when a single class is instantiated into multiple independent instances.

polymorphism
As an OOP term, this occurs when classes are treated as equivalents and are referenced identically.

POP
(Post Office Protocol) An email retrieval protocol that generally pulls the mail from the server to whatever the device the user is currently utilizing.

portable site
A mobile site, such as a van or trailer, that can be operated anywhere should a disaster occur. It houses computer hardware, networking capabilities, and communications equipment to restore and maintain business operations.

power line monitor
A power protection device that is used to evaluate the source of electrical power.

PPP
(Point-to-Point Protocol) A remote access protocol used to support dial-up services and automatic configuration.

PPTP
(Point-to-Point Tunneling Protocol) An early remote access protocol used to implement VPNs.

preaction
A water-based, dry pipe extinguishing system that has special sprinkler heads that are heat sensitive. Water is discharged after the system is activated and the nozzles are activated.

precedent
A new or changed law, never before established, that is created by a judge to specifically pertain to a particular issue or case.

Presentation layer
An OSI model layer (Layer 6) that translates data so that the receiver can properly interpret the transmitted information.

pressure-sensitive sensor
A perimeter IDS that is used to detect pressure when weight, such as a human or animal body, is applied to the device.

preventative access control
A control that stops a subject's unauthorized access to an object.

preventative controls
In OPSEC, controls such as user IDs and passwords that prevent unauthorized access or data modification.

primary storage

A common term used for memory based on its immediate availability as an information storage location.

primitive

A data structure in which data elements are singular in nature and are not broken down into small components when accessed.

Privacy Act of 1974

Protects the privacy of individual information held by the U.S. government. Mandated in response to the abuse of privacy during the Nixon administration.

privacy

A legal principle that maintains the secrecy or protection of an individual's information.

private key

The component of asymmetric encryption that is kept secret by one party during two-way encryption.

procedural languages

Program languages that use routines, subroutines, methods, and functions.

procedure

A security document that describes implementation practices and the steps taken to complete an activity.

program coordinator

The individual responsible for implementing and controlling an organization's BCP.

proprietary software

Software that is developed by organizations that do not disclose the source code.

protocol analyzer

A surveillance tool used to intercept and record computer network traffic. Also known as a sniffer.

prototyping model

A model that provides early prototypes for users to see and test. This early feedback from users can then be used to develop better products more quickly.

proximity detector

A perimeter IDS that is installed to emit a measurable electrical field while in use. Also called a capacitance detector.

proxy firewall

A firewall that acts as an intermediary server or gateway that will terminate a connection and then re-initiate it if the traffic is warranted.

prudent man rule

Another name for the prudent person rule.

prudent person rule

A common law standard or principle that suggests that adequate protection is the protection that a prudent person would use in normal circumstances.

public key

The component of asymmetric encryption that can be accessed by anyone.

public-key cryptography

The same as public-key and asymmetric encryption.

qualitative risk analysis

A best-guess estimate of risk occurrence that is not based on numerical analysis or history.

quantitative risk analysis

An estimate based on the historical occurrences of incidents and the likelihood of risk reoccurrence.

RA

(registration authority) An authority in a network that processes requests for digital certificates from users.

race condition

A TCB vulnerability that occurs when two processes try to access and modify information at the same time.

RADIUS

(Remote Authentication Dial-in User Service) An authentication protocol used to authenticate and authorize dial-in users.

RAID

(Redundant Array of Independent Disks) A storage technology used to provide better disk performance or data redundancy depending on the implemented RAID type. Also called Redundant Array of Inexpensive Disks.

RAIT

(Redundant Array of Independent Tapes) A storage technology used to provide better tape performance or data redundancy.

RAM

(Random Access Memory) A type of computer data storage that uses short-term memory to store program instructions and data for immediate use.

RAS

(Remote Access Service) A data service that provides access to a computer system or network from a separate location, often for administrative reasons.

RBAC

(role-based access control) A non-discretionary access control technique that is implemented when a subject's access to objects is based on the job performed by the subject.

RC algorithms

(Rivest Cipher) A series of variable key-length symmetric encryption algorithms developed by Ronald Rivest.

RDBMS

(Relational Database Management System) A collection of multiple tables that are related to one another through the use of the foreign key concept.

recovery access control

A control that returns the system to an operational state after a failure to protect the CIA triad.

recovery controls

In OPSEC, controls such as trusted recovery that assist in correcting security problems by returning the system to a secure state.

recovery team

A group of designated individuals who implement recovery procedures and control the recovery operations in the event of an internal or external disruption to critical business processes.

redundancy

Using more than one resource to maintain availability.

referential integrity

A database that ensures the proper maintenance of all table values that are referenced by the foreign keys in other tables.

Relational Database Management Model

A database system model that allows a designer to create relationships among the various database components.

remote journaling

A data backup method wherein real-time copies of database transactions are stored in journals at a remote location. Journals can be replayed to transfer a database back to normal conditions.

replay attack

A type of cryptographic attack that can be used to bypass the encryption protecting passwords while in transit.

reverse engineering

A cryptographic process of analyzing and determining the structure, function, and operation of a cryptosystem.

ring topology

A network topology in which all network nodes are connected in a continuous circle.

risk analysis

The security management process for addressing any risk or economic damages that affect an organization.

risk

The likelihood of a threat exposing a vulnerability.

RM

(reference monitor) A component of some types of access control systems that determines if the subject can access the object.

RNG

(random number generator) A device that is used to create keys and to perform cryptographic functions.

ROM

(Read-Only Memory) A type of computer data storage that uses long-term memory to store program information and configuration information used during the initiation process of a computer.

router redundancy

A technique for employing multiple routers in teams to limit the risk of routing failure should a router malfunction.

router

A networking device used to connect multiple networks that employ the same protocol.

routing

A Network layer function that allows the devices in one network to send information to and receive information from other logical network devices.

RPC

(remote procedure call) A data services process used to cause the execution of a module, subroutine, or procedure at a remote location.

RPO

(Recovery Point Objective) The point in time, relative to a disaster, where the data recovery process begins.

RSA

(Rivest Shamir Adleman) The first successful asymmetric algorithm to be designed for public-key encryption. It is named for its designers, Rivest, Shamir, and Adleman.

RTO

(Recovery Time Objective) The length of time within which normal business operations and activities must be restored following a disturbance.

rule-based access control

A non-discretionary access control technique that is based on a set of operational rules or restrictions.

S-box

(substitution box) A component of symmetric-key algorithms that is used to camouflage plaintext-to-ciphertext relationships.

S-HTTP

(Secure Hypertext Transfer Protocol) A security protocol that is an alternate form of protecting HTTP data.

S/MIME

(Secure/MIME) An extension of MIME that prevents attackers from intercepting and manipulating email and attachments by encrypting and digitally signing the contents of the email using public-key cryptography.

sag

A momentary low-voltage power failure.

salvage team

A group of designated individuals who restore the primary site to its normal operating environment.

SAN

(Storage Area Network) A specialized physical network that is made up of dedicated storage devices that perform block-level operations.

sashimi software development model

A modification of the waterfall model where there is an intentional overlap between phases.

screened subnet

A subnet between two firewalls. Also known as a DMZ.

screening host

A router that protects the internal network with an ACL.

SCRUM

An Agile software development methodology that employs iterative and incremental development by using the timeboxed approach and emphasizing the importance of teamwork.

secondary storage

A means of storage that keeps information for long periods of time and in great volumes.

secret-key cryptography

The same as shared-key and symmetric encryption.

security auditing

The practice of recording security-relevant events in an audit file for future analysis.

security kernel

Implements the RM in an operating system.

security monitoring

The practice of monitoring operations controls to identify abnormal computer activity.

security perimeter

An imaginary line that surrounds the TCB and separates the trusted and untrusted parts of a computer system.

security profile

A description of the security-relevant information about each user or protected element in a system.

security violation

A breach of security regulations or policies that may or may not result in a system compromise.

segment

A small unit of information created by the Transport layer of the OSI model to control information flow to the layers above.

SEM

(security event management) The collection and analysis of security event logs from a wide variety of devices.

sensitivity profile

A security document that details the information an individual needs to know to effectively perform a specific job role.

SESAME

(Secure European System for Applications in a Multi-vendor Environment) A single sign-on (SSO) method created in Europe.

Session layer

An OSI model layer (Layer 5) that establishes the startup, continuation, and termination of a network session. The Session layer supports full-duplex, half-duplex, and simplex data transmission.

SHA

(Secure Hash Algorithm) This hash algorithm is modeled after MD5 and is considered the stronger of the two because it produces a 160-bit hash value. There is also SHA-256, SHA-384, and SHA-512, with the numbers representing the block size.

shared-key encryption

The same as symmetric encryption.

shoulder surfing

A human-based attack where the goal is to look over the shoulder of an individual as he or she enters password information or a PIN number.

side channel attack

A type of cryptographic attack that targets the cryptosystem by gathering information about the physical characteristics of the encryption and then exploiting them.

simplex

A Session-layer communication mode where the transmission of data occurs in only one direction.

single point of failure

Any device, circuit, or process that causes the unavailability of data upon failure.

SLA

(service level agreement) A business document that is used to define a pre-agreed level of performance for an activity or contracted service.

SLE

(Single Loss Expectancy) The estimated impact of an event.

SLIP

(Serial Line Internet Protocol) A simple remote access communications protocol that encapsulates IP datagrams carried over dial-up networks.

smart card

A credit card-sized device that contains a chip that can provide storage and intelligence to the authentication process as "something you have."

SMTP

(Simple Message Transport Protocol) A protocol used for email delivery.

sniffer

A software attack that uses special monitoring software to gain access to private communications on the network wire or across a wireless network. This type of attack is used either to steal the content of the communications itself or to gain information that will help the attacker later gain access to the network and resources. Also called eavesdropping.

social engineering

A human-based attack where the goal is to obtain sensitive data, including user names and passwords, from network users through deception and trickery.

SoD

(separation of duties) A division of tasks between different people to complete a business process or work function.

SONET

(Synchronous Optical Networking) A fiber optic-based network that is used to move data at higher speeds than a traditional Ethernet.

source code

Higher-level programming language that is generally human readable.

SOX Act

(Sarbanes-Oxley) Legislation passed in 2002 to help control how corporations report about and audit themselves. Also referred to as Sarbox.

spam

An attack that causes network over-utilization by filling networks with unwanted email messages.

spike

A short-term, high-voltage power malfunction.

spiral software development model

A method of developing software iteratively through risk analysis, requirements specification, prototyping, and testing or implementation.

spoofing

A human-based or software-based attack where the goal is to pretend to be someone else for the purpose of identity concealment. Spoofing can occur in IP addresses, MAC addresses, and email.

spyware

Code that is secretly installed on a user's computer to gather data about the user and relay it to a third party.

SSH

(Secure Shell) An administrative services protocol that replaces Telnet and provides a secure, encrypted environment for command line access to devices for configuration purposes.

SSL

(Secure Sockets Layer) A security protocol used to provide confidentiality services to the IP protocol suite for information transfer.

SSO

(single sign-on) A method of access control wherein a single user ID and password will allow a user to access all of his or her applications.

standard

A security document that describes a required implementation or use of tools.

star topology

A network topology that uses a central connectivity device with separate point-to-point connections to each node.

State Machine Model
A security model that monitors the system as it moves from one state to another.

stateful inspection firewall
A firewall that determines the state of the packets as they pass through.

statutes
Laws enacted by the legislative branch of a government.

statutory law
Written law comprised of statutes passed by federal, state, and local legislatures defining day-to-day laws and how bodies of government function.

steganography
An alternative cipher process that hides information by enclosing it in other files such as a graphic, movie, or sound file.

strategic planning
A long-range planning effort that reviews required security activities, focusing on major changes or improvements in the security posture of an organization.

stream cipher
A relatively fast type of symmetric encryption that encrypts data one bit at a time.

striping
A disk-performance-enhancement feature in which data is spread across multiple drives to improve read and write access speeds.

structured development model
A model based on structured programming concepts that require a careful combination of sequencing, selection, and iteration to achieve a desired result.

subject
The entity requesting security access.

substitution
A technique that replaces parts of a message or cryptographic output to hide the original information.

supervisor state
A CPU mode that can execute any security instructions that are available.

surge
A long-term, high-voltage power malfunction.

surge/spike protector
A power protection device that provides power protection circuits that can reduce or eliminate the impact of surges and spikes.

surveillance system
A physical security mechanism that monitors designated internal and external areas of a facility for unusual behavior or a potential intruder.

switch
An interconnecting network device used to forward frames to the correct port based on MAC addresses. A switch can work with pairs of ports, connecting two segments as needed.

symmetric encryption
A two-way encryption scheme in which encryption and decryption are both performed by the same secret key.

SYN flood attack
A type of DoS attack in which the attacker sends multiple SYN messages initializing TCP connections with a target host.

synchronous messaging
Real-time communication between two or more people. IM is a synchronous messaging protocol.

synchronous token system
The time or counter on the user's device will need to be synchronized with the authentication server as it expects a particular code to be entered.

table
A set of rows and columns in a database that contains related information.

TACACS
(Terminal Access Controller Access Control System) An authentication protocol that accepts login requests and authenticates the access credentials of the user.

tactical planning
A mid-term planning effort that is in-between operational and strategic in duration.

tailgating
A physical threat whereby an individual closely follows someone else into a secure environment with the intent of avoiding authentication by the control system.

targeted testing
A type of penetration test where the target organization is informed of the test.

TCB
(Trusted Computing Base) The hardware, firmware, and software components of a computer system that implement the security policy of a system.

TCP
(Transmission Control Protocol) A connection-oriented transport protocol used in the TCP/IP model.

TCP/IP model
(Transmission Control Protocol/Internet Protocol) A model that represents a collection of communications protocols used to govern data exchange on the Internet.

TCSEC
(Trusted Computer System Evaluation Criteria) The first attempt at a system security evaluation process implemented by the U.S. Department of Defense.

technical access controls
These controls are implemented in the computing environment, often in operating systems, application programs, database frameworks, firewalls, routers, switches, and wireless access points.

theft
A human-based attack where the goal is to blatantly steal information and resources.

threading
A computing technique that enables a program to split itself into two or more concurrently running tasks.

threat
An agent that will expose a vulnerability and cause harm.

time-based access control
A non-discretionary access control technique that limits when an individual can access the system.

TKIP
(Temporal Key Integrity Protocol) A security protocol created as an improvement to the number of and usage of keys. It is an algorithm that secures wireless computer networks by changing the keys on packets for each packet exchange

TLS
(Transport Layer Security) A security protocol that is an updated version of SSL, with mutual authentication as an added service.

TOC/TOU
(time of check/time of use) Uses a weakness in the TCB where access is granted at one point in time and used much later on.

TOGAF
(The Open Group Architecture Framework) An open framework that provides common terms and methods that can be followed to create a secure organization.

tort law
The legal category that identifies what constitutes a legal harm and creates the means for recovering damages in the case of intentional malicious acts or accidents.

trade secret
An item that requires protection that the loss of which will severely damage the business.

trademark
A design or phrase used to identify products or services.

transfer

A risk management principle that reallocates risk acceptance to another party, such as an insurance company, by means of a contract.

Transport layer

An OSI model layer (Layer 4) that ensures reliable data transmission by breaking up big data blocks into segments that can be sent more efficiently on the network. The Transport layer also implements flow control to preserve information from buffer overflows or other network problems.

transport mode

An IPsec mode that protects the information in a payload of an IP datagram.

transposition

The process of rearranging parts of a message or cryptographic output to hide the original information.

trapdoor attack

A software attack where a hidden entry point into a program or operating system bypasses the normal identification and authentication processes.

triage

In computer crime, an incident response approach where a criminal act or event is intercepted and responded to based on its criticality and degree of risk. Typically known as a medical term that indicates the priority of patient treatment.

Trojan horse

Unauthorized software that masquerades as legitimate software. Also known as a Trojan program.

trusted recovery

A protection mechanism used in data recovery that ensures the security of a computer system that crashes or fails by recovering security-relevant elements in a trusted or secure state.

tunnel mode

An IPsec mode that allows the encryption of the original IP datagram and the entire payload.

tuple

A row, or record, in a database.

two-man rule

A media protection technique that requires the presence of two individuals at all times to monitor behavior when certain criteria are met.

Type 1 error

See FRR.

Type II error

See FAR.

UDP

(User Datagram Protocol) A connectionless transport protocol, used in TCP/IP as an alternative to TCP, that supports process identification using port numbers and error detection.

untrusted recovery

A data recovery level wherein a recovery process is performed that does not ensure that the result is a secure and trusted environment.

UPS

(Uninterruptible Power Supply) A device that continues to provide power to connected circuits when the main source of power becomes unavailable.

USA PATRIOT Act

(Uniting and Strengthening America by Providing Appropriate Tools Required to Intercept and Obstruct Terrorism) Legislation passed in 2001, following 9/11, that increased the governmental ability to wiretap and control financial transactions used to fund terrorism.

user state

A CPU mode that can execute only non-privileged instructions. Implements the same function as the application state.

vibration detector

A perimeter IDS that is installed to measure vibrations caused by breaking glass, collisions with solid objects, or footsteps.

view

A user portal into a database.

violation analysis

A security monitoring technique that tracks anomalies in user activity. Also called violation processing or violation tracking.

virtual memory

A category of storage that emulates physical memory by using random access disks to temporarily store information needed by the operating system and application programs.

virus

A malware or malicious program that attaches itself to another program.

VoIP

(Voice over IP) A data services protocol that implements the transmission of voice over the Internet Protocol.

VPN

(Virtual Private Network) Creates a protected pathway secured with various means and used to move enterprise information between corporate locations using the Internet instead of private corporate resources.

vulnerability assessment

A BIA process that focuses on financial and operational loss impact and locates threat exploitation indicators in an organization.

vulnerability scanning

A type of penetration test that exploits known weaknesses in operating systems and applications that were identified through reconnaissance and enumeration.

vulnerability

Any weakness in a system or process that could lead to harm.

WAN

(wide area network) A network used to connect physically distributed networks over long, geographical distances.

WAP

(Wireless Access Protocol) A protocol associated with the implementation of mobile phone and PDA applications that access the Internet.

war dialing

A type of penetration test that uses a modem and software to dial a range of phone numbers to locate computer systems, PBX devices, and HVAC systems.

war driving

A type of penetration test that locates and attempts to penetrate wireless systems.

warm site

A location that is dormant or performs non-critical functions under normal conditions, but can be rapidly converted to a key operations site if needed.

waterfall software development model

A method of designing and creating software that has defined phases that flow from one to the next, as water flows from one level of a waterfall to another.

watermark

An alternative cipher. An embedded mark or image that identifies the source of the image for copyright protection and other uses.

WEP

(Wired Equivalent Privacy) Provides 64-bit, 128-bit, and 256-bit encryption using the RC4 algorithm for wireless communication.

wet pipe

A water-based extinguishing system wherein the pipes store water at all times. When a given temperature is reached, the system discharges the water.

work factor

The amount of time needed to break a cryptosystem.

worm

A malware program that does not require the support of a target program in the way a virus does.

WPA

(Wi-Fi Protected Access) A security standard that provides additional encryption capabilities for wireless transmissions.

WPA2

A wireless access protocol that is implemented with the AES encryption algorithm. Also known as 802.11i.

XML

(eXtensible Markup Language) A document description language that simplifies the presentation of database information in various formats.

Zachman

A security framework designed to get the different groups working on a project to communicate with each other; it is commonly associated with the who, what, when, how, where, and why of information security.

Index

authentication, authorization, and accounting
   See: AAA
authorization, 8, 147
automatic access control, 274
automatic recovery, 64
AV, 164
availability, 2, 305
  and cryptography, 223
avalanche effect, 222
avoidance
  and risk, 160
awareness program objectives, 152

B

backdoor attack, 34, 62, 197
background check
  for information security, 136
background investigation
  for information security, 136
backup strategy, 352
backup tape, 9
bandwidth limiter, 84
baseline, 148, 150
  hiring procedures, 136
bastion host, 104
BCP, 147, 330, 332
  contents, 344
  development phases, 332
  framework, 332
BCP team
    See: Advisory Committee-BCP team
behavioral IDS, 103
Bell-LaPadula Model
    See: BLP Model
best evidence, 380
best practices, 372
best-guess estimate, 164
BIA, 333, 335
  organizational goals, 334
  process, 334
Biba Model, 56
  impact, 58
biometric device, 25, 147
  acceptance, 26
  entry system, 274
  errors, 27
  types, 25
birthday attack, 261

bit patterns
  predefined, 227
  substitute, 227
black box, 182
  testing, 40
black screen of death, 63
blackout, 293
blind testing, 41
block cipher, 232, 234, 236
  modes, 238
Blowfish, 234, 236
BLP Model, 56
blue screen of death, 63
Board of Directors, 125, 150
bollard, 271
botnet, 34
bounds checking, 197
Brewer-Nash Model, 56
bridge device, 79
British Standard
    See: BS
brownout, 293
brute force, 34, 37, 234, 306, 324
BS, 70
BS 17799, 70
BS 7799, 70
buffer overflow, 34, 62, 197, 198
built-in bounds, 203
bus topology, 87
business continuity
  and the ISO, 127
Business Continuity Plan
    See: BCP
business continuity process, 346
business impact analysis
    See: BIA
business plan
  evaluation, 345
  maintenance, 346
  testing, 345

C

C&A, 72
CA, 245
cable modem, 90
cabled media, 88
cache memory, 50

expert system, 196

Exposure Factor
   See: EF

Extended Binary Coded Decimal Information
   Code
   See: EBCDIC

Extensible Authentication Protocol
   See: EAP

external
  audit, 372
  physical threat, 269

extranet, 104

F

facial recognition, 25, 150

facility
  access, 271
  control device, 274
  control system, 278
  design, 292
  protection categories, 292

factoring attack, 261

Failure/Fault Resistant Disk System
   See: FRDS

Fair Cryptosystem, 238

fair hiring regulations, 136

false acceptance rate
   See: FAR

false rejection rate
   See: FRR

Family Educational Rights and Privacy Act
   See: FERPA

FAR, 27

fault tolerance, 308

FE-13, 298

feasibility, 180

Federal Information Security Management Act
   See: FISMA

federal sentencing guidelines, 370

Feistel process, 234

fencing, 271

FERPA, 368

FHSS, 98

fiber optics, 86

File Transfer Protocol
   See: FTP

file transmission, 251

filtering algorithm, 84

financial history review
  for information security, 136

financial impact, 158

fingerprint scanner, 25, 99, 274

fire
  code, 271
  detection methods, 296
  policy, 288
  prevention methods, 296
  protection level, 271

fire extinguisher
  hand-held, 296
  water-based, 297

firewall, 84, 103, 117
  types, 104

firmware
  error, 63

FISMA, 370

flat file, 195

flood impact, 334

FM-200, 298

FOIA, 15

For Official Use Only
   See: FOUO

foreign key, 205, 207

forensic analyst, 378

foundation document, 372

FOUO, 15

Fraggle attack, 101

frame relay, 86

fraud
  and SoD, 134
  limiting of, 117

FRDS, 109

free information
  and ethics fallacies, 171

Freedom of Information Act
   See: FOIA

frequency analysis, 262

frequency-hopping spread spectrum
   See: FHSS

FRR, 27

FTP, 91

full backup, 110, 352

full interruption testing, 345

full-duplex, 79

function point, 187

behavioral, 103

categories, 39

modes, 38

perimeter, 279

IEEE, 98

IETF, 29

IGMP, 83

IKE, 258

in IPsec, 258

IMAP, 83

implementing the change phase, 188

in-rush, 293

incident response team, 378

incomplete parameter check/enforcement, 198

incremental backup, 110, 352, 353

index, 203

Inergen, 298

inference, 196, 211

information

concealment, 220

disclosure prevention, 151

distribution, 144

ownership, 147

privacy law, 368

protection, 151

service, 91

Information Flow Model, 198

information security

and cryptography, 223

and laws and regulations, 116

criminals, 171

database access, 205

governance, 125

importance of, 116

reporting options, 124

strategic alignment, 126

threats, 117

Information Security Officer

See: ISO

information security triad

See: CIA triad

information systems

security standards, 70

Information Systems Audit and Control Association

See: ISACA

Information Technology Security Evaluation Criteria

See: ITSEC

informative security policy, 148

infrared device, 279

Initial maturity, 188

initialization vector

See: IV

input/output devices

See: I/O devices

installation/implementation phase, 180

Institute of Electrical and Electronics Engineers

See: IEEE

instruction path, 50

instructor-led training, 151

insurance

department, 124

valuation, 161

integrity, 2, 244

and cryptography, 223

intellectual property, 147

exposure, 121

international protection, 368

law, 367

internal audit, 371

department, 124

internal physical threat, 269

International Data Encryption Algorithm

See: IDEA

International Electrotechnical Commission

See: IEC

International Information Systems Security Certification Consortium

See: (ISC)²

International Organization for Standardization

See: ISO

Internet Architecture Board

See: IAB

Internet Control Message Protocol

See: ICMP

Internet Engineering Task Force

See: IETF

Internet Group Management Protocol

See: IGMP

Internet Key Exchange

See: IKE

Internet Message Access Protocol

See: IMAP

Internet Protocol
> *See:* IP

Internet Protocol security
> *See:* IPsec

Internet Security Association and Key Management Protocol
> *See:* ISAKMP

Internet Service Provider
> *See:* ISP

interpreted languages, 178
interruption of service, 323
intrusion detection, 278
intrusion detection system
> *See:* IDS

intrusion prevention system
> *See:* IPS

intrusion protection, 319
intrusion response policy, 288
IP, 79, 83
> spoofing, 34

IPS, 9, 38, 103, 119
IPsec, 97, 98, 257
> and encryption, 259
> and IKE, 258
> process, 258

iris scanner, 25, 274
ISACA, 46
ISAKMP, 258
ISC2
> *See:* (ISC)²

ISO, 70, 79, 123
> IEC 27002, 70
> responsibilities, 126
> roles, 127

ISO/IEC 27001, 46
isolation, 210
ISP, 90
IT department, 123, 124
IT Governance Institute
> *See:* ITGI

IT Infrastructure Library
> *See:* ITIL

ITGI, 126
ITIL, 46, 189
ITSEC, 70
IV, 234, 258

J

Java Database Connectivity
> *See:* JDC

JDBC, 204
job position sensitivity profiling, 135
job rotation, 7, 133, 312

K

KBS, 196
Kerberos, 29
kernel mode
> *See:* supervisor state

key, 203, 205, 222
> clustering, 222
> escrow, 238
> generation, 243
> generation process, 263
> management in cryptography, 238
> private, 243
> public, 243

key lock, 273
key management
> and job rotation, 133

key staff, 289
keyless lock, 273
keyspace, 222
keystream, 232
knowledge-based system
> *See:* KBS

known-plaintext attack, 262

L

L2TP, 98
labeled access, 15
labeling scheme
> *See:* classification

LAN, 83, 86, 90, 98, 117
Lattice Model, 56
law violations
> surveillance, 383

Layer 2 Tunneling Protocol
> *See:* L2TP

layered defense, 50
layered protection, 50, 270
> and physical security, 270
> areas, 271

LCP, 98
least privilege, 5, 11, 134, 211, 306, 312

message authentication code
   See: MAC
message digest, 250
  and digital signature, 253
  encryption algorithm, 251
Message Digest 2
   See: MD2
Message Digest 4
   See: MD4
Message Digest 5
   See: MD5
message hash
   See: message digest
message integrity code
   See: MIC
messaging services, 91
metadata, 212
method, 208
metropolitan area network
   See: MAN
MIC, 252, 258
microwave system, 279
mid-term priority, 351
milestone, 183
military classification, 142
MIME, 256
mirror, 108
mirror site, 353
mirrored
  backup, 352
  site, 351
  site cutover, 358
mirroring, 109
mission statement, 122
  and security, 123
misuse prevention, 308
mitigation, 336
mobile code, 34, 197
mobile device locks, 274
modem, 97
modification, 323
modification detection code
   See: MDC
modularity, 208
motion sensor, 279
MPLS, 90
MTD, 337, 338
multifactor authentication, 28

multilevel security mode, 64
multiprocessing, 55
Multiprotocol Label Switching
   See: MPLS
Multipurpose Internet Mail Extension
   See: MIME
multistate, 54
multitasking, 54
multithreading, 54

N

NAS, 105, 109
National Fire Protection Association
   See: NFPA
National Information Infrastructure Protection Act
   See: NIIPA
National Institute for Science and Technology
   See: NIST
National Institute of Standards and Technology
   See: NIST
national security, 142
National Security Agency
  NSA, 372
natural
  disasters, 162
  emergency policy, 288
  hazards, 333
  physical threat, 269
NDA, 64, 143
nearline, 308
need to know, 6, 11, 135, 144, 211, 287, 306, 312
  no, 135
network
  architecture components, 84
  attacks, 101, 121
  data services, 91
  IDS, 39
  neural, 195
  scanning, 41
  security, 102, 103
  session, 79
  transmission methodologies, 90
  vulnerability, 162
Network Access layer, 82
Network Access Server
   See: NAS
Network Attached Storage
   See: NAS

protocol-based IDS, 39

prototyping, 184

  model, 186

proximity card, 23

proximity detector, 279

proxy firewalls, 104

prudent person rule, 365, 371, 372, 378

PSTN, 90

public key, 243

  cryptography, 242, 256

  encryption, 242

public key infrastructure

   See: PKI

Public Switched Telephone Network

   See: PSTN

Purple Book, 68

Q

QA, 180

QoS, 83

qualitative risk analysis, 164

quality assurance

   See: QA

quality of service

   See: QoS

quantitative risk analysis, 164

Quantitatively Managed maturity, 188

query language, 203

R

RA, 246

race condition, 62

radio frequency identification

   See: RFID

RADIUS, 31, 105, 150, 258

RAID, 108, 308

  levels, 109

Rainbow Series, 68, 70

  Orange Book, 68

  Purple Book, 68

  Red Book, 68

RAIT, 109

RAM, 50

Random Access Memory

   See: RAM

random number generator

   See: RNG

RARP, 83

RAS, 91

RATS, 197

RBAC, 16

RC, 234, 236

RC4, 258

RDBMS, 205

  key usage, 205

reactive system IDS, 39

read property, 56

Read-Only Memory

  ROM, 50

reasonable man rule

   See: prudent person rule

rebuilding, 351

reconnaissance, 40

records

  management, 344

  retention, 308

recovery, 378

  access control, 9

  controls, 311

  team, 357

  with limited errors, 64

  without errors, 64

recovery levels

   See: data recovery

Recovery Point Objective

   See: RPO

Recovery Time Objective

   See: RTO

Red Book, 68

reduction

  and risk, 160

redundancy, 308

Redundant Array of Independent Disks

   See: RAID

Redundant Array of Independent Tapes

   See: RAIT

Redundant Array of Independent/Inexpensive

  Disks

   See: RAID

reference check

  for information security, 136

reference monitor, 4, 50, 198

referential integrity, 209

registration authority

   See: RA

regulatory compliance, 147

spyware, 34, 197
SQL injection attack, 211
SSH, 91, 257
SSL, 102, 257
SSO, 29, 105, 117
  methods, 29
staff workers, 123
standard, 148, 150
standards vs. guidelines, 149
star
  property, 56
  topology, 87
State Machine, 56
State Machine Model, 56
stateful inspection firewall, 104, 119
statutes, 366
statutory law, 366
statutory offense
  types, 366
steganography, 227
Storage Area Network
  See: SAN
strategic alignment, 126
strategic security goals, 116
stream cipher, 232, 234
striping, 108
structure vulnerability, 162
structured development model, 185
subject, 4
substantial proof, 378
substitution, 227, 232
substitution box
  See: S-box
supervisor state, 50, 198
surge, 293
  protector, 294
surveillance
  law violations, 383
  system, 280
  system types, 281
  techniques, 382
switch, 79, 84
switched network, 86
symmetric encryption, 231, 261
  and reverse engineering, 263
symmetric encryption algorithm, 234, 243
  issues, 235
  overview, 236

values, 236
SYN flood attack, 101
synchronized clocks, 234
synchronous messaging, 91
Synchronous Optical Networking
  See: SONET
system break-in, 317
system design specifications phase, 180
system development life cycle
  See: SDLC
system life cycle
  See: SLC
system security
  characteristics, 308
system vulnerability, 162
system weakness
  See: vulnerability
system-high security mode, 64
system-level audit log, 318
systems responsibilities, 147

T

T1 and T3, 90
table, 205
TACACS, 31, 105
TACACS+, 105
tactical planning, 150
tactical security goals, 116
tagged, 79
tailgating, 278
taking candy from a baby
  and ethics fallacies, 171
tape backup, 352
targeted testing, 41
Targets of Evaluation
  See: TOE
TCB, 48, 68
  compromise, 63
  hardware protection, 52
  software protection, 54
  vulnerabilities, 62
TCP, 79, 83, 101
TCP SYN flood, 101
TCP/IP, 79
  model, 82
  protocols, 83
TCSEC, 68
  divisions and classes, 69

085199 SPB rev 1.0
ISBN-13 978-1-4246-1975-7
ISBN-10 1-4246-1975-0

90000

9 781424 619757